Practically Over
The Anglo-Boer War 1899-1902
in context

Robin Smith

TSL Publications

Published in Great Britain in 2022
By TSL Publications, Rickmansworth

Copyright © 2022 Robin Smith

ISBN: 978-1-915660-04-6

The right of Robin Smith to be identified as the authors of this work has been asserted by the authors in accordance with the UK Copyright, Designs and Patents Act 1988.

All rights reserved. No part of this publication may be reproduced, stored in a retrieval system or transmitted, in any form or by any means without the prior written permission of the publisher, nor be otherwise circulated in any form of binding or cover other than that in which it is published and without a similar condition being imposed on the subsequent buyer.

Acknowledgements

How do I recognise the willing help and assistance I have had from so many fellow devotees of our South African history over decades?

There are literally hundreds of people whom I have come into contact with on battle sites and in meetings and social gatherings at various times who have helped me in some way or other. The list below is just some of them – If your name has been omitted, my apologies, but you are really not forgotten.

Quite a few of the places that I have written about were visited in company with two brothers, David and Peter Scholtz. David has put together a considerable record of the grave sites of British officers who lie buried in our soil and Peter is developing a photographic record. Together we have visited a myriad of places in the old provinces, and Boer republics, of the Transvaal and Orange Free State.

David and Peter it was who constantly badgered me to put my journal articles together into some readable form and this book is the result.

Sandy Buchanan's group, the Buchanan's Mounted Infantry, Sandy, Ron Schreuder, Roger Fritz, who sadly is no longer with us, is a triumvirate with whom I have covered a lot of ground. Marion Moir is a fully-fledged member too.

Paul Naish, who we call "the Major" – ex B.S.A.P and the South African Army – is the consummate tour guide and organiser and through him I have become acquainted with a number of Australians who seem to be just as interested in "our" war as we are – or even more so. I think of Dennis Weatherall, Nigel Webster, Tony Stimson, John Sweetman and Miles Farmer, all of whom have graced us with their presence, a couple of them on multiple occasions.

Steve Watt, the doyen of war grave experts, has taken me to a number of obscure sites where clashes occurred more than 120 years ago now (and I have taken him to some places where he had not previously left footprints). His book *In Memoriam*, besides listing more than 20,000 deaths of imperial soldiers, is much more than just a list of names. My casualty lists are always compiled from *In Memoriam*.

Bloemfontein Boer history experts Arnold van Dyk and Johan Loock have guided me to a number of places in the Free State – and to some other places that do not appear in this book.

Susanne Blendulf who has edited the *Military History Journal* of the South African Military History Society has edited many of the articles that make up this book for publication in the Journal. And now she has edited all of them (and a few extras) again to make up this book.

I could go on and on but thank you everyone.

Finally, may I make a dedication? This is for you Ken Gillings, wherever you are!

Contents

What this book is all about.

Each of the parts of the book is an account of a particular action during the Anglo Boer war of 1899-1902. Both English and Afrikaans sources, both primary and secondary, have been used to write the narrative but each and every one of the battle sites of the clashes that are reported here have been physically visited by the author, in some cases a number of times.

Many of the maps and diagrams have been drawn by hand, but from sources such as the modern survey maps and also from the Imperial maps of 1900 which bear the signature of Colonel G.F.R. "Frank" Henderson.

Many of the photographs are my own but those of others are acknowledged. Only pictures from public domain sources have been used.

Political aspects have been largely avoided as there are many aspects of the war that are sensitive for some of South Africa's population groups. Even so I cannot expect everyone to agree with my conclusions. There are at least two sides to every question – and often many more.

	Page
The Anglo Boer war of 1899 – 1902.	7
After Ladysmith was relieved – On Buller's advance into northern Natal, the Boers were able to ambush a British Colonial unit patrol on the road to Vryheid: 20 May 1900.	11
Into the Transvaal and the first casualty to a soldier from Canada. Unwary horsemen who ignored warnings that farms flying a white flag should be approached with caution.	18
Mafeking – many books describe the long siege from October 1899 to May 1900, Tim Jeal's *Baden-Powell* being about the best. This is more about the relief and the I.L.H.'s part in it.	25
After Mafeking had been relieved the western Transvaal seemed to be completely subdued, but after a Boer reverse at Diamond Hill, outside Pretoria, in mid-June, General de la Rey and Commandant Manie Lemmer were sent to revive the flagging spirits.	29
The First de Wet hunt ended at Crocodile Drift, north of the Magaliesberg and near the present-day town of Brits. De Wet looked like he was trapped but somehow he managed to find a route over the mountain barrier and return to the Free State. The war went on.	38
At a *krygsraad* (council of war) at Kroonstad in April 1900 the decision was made to split the Boer army into smaller, more nimble units. British columns with ox wagon transport were too slow but soon better tactics were evolved to counter the wily Boers. At Doornkraal, south of Bothaville, de Wet and Free State President Marthinus Steyn had a narrow escape.	49
By the end of 1900, guerrilla warfare was raging in the Transvaal, the Free State and the northern Cape Colony. Ben Viljoen conducted the last set-piece battle at Rhenosterkop in November 1900.	66
Australians and New Zealanders were now present in considerable numbers, were competent riders and used to living in the bush. That's not to say they were more than a match for their adversaries, as reverses at Brakpan Farm and Wilmansrust were to show.	76

Peace negotiations 1901: Botha met with Kitchener at Middelburg in February and then Transvaal and Free States leaders met at the Waterval *krygsraad* in June 1901. They resolved to continue the war and take the fight into Natal and Cape Colony. 91

Many Boers became Hensoppers or Joiners, those who refused to fight and those who took the money that the British offered to join them. Here is a tragic story of two young men who became Joiners through economic necessity. 98

Botha and Smuts led the raids into the two British colonies. Botha was driven back into the Transvaal Highveld but Smuts crossed the Orange River into the Cape, evaded numerous pursuing British columns, and was still at large eight months later when the war ended. 105

Still looking for Smuts, a column composed of Australian and New Zealand soldiers clashed with a small Boer contingent at Mokari Drift on the Caledon River. Four Queenslanders were killed and Commandant Louis Wessels and his men lived to fight another day. 114

On Botha's return to the Transvaal he gave orders for his Commandants to concentrate all their forces against Colonel G.E. Benson, alone on the Highveld. The battle of Bakenlaagte was the result. 122

With thousands of fresh troops, the British put the commandos in the eastern Transvaal Highveld under severe pressure by the end of 1901. One ambush of the Queenslanders who formed the advance guard of Colonel Plumer's column took place at Onverwacht at the beginning of January 1902. 133

In January 1902, a night attack on a column of men of the Royal Sussex Regiment caused the death of Lieutenant-Colonel Louis du Moulin at Abram's Kraal, the site now under the waters of the Kalkfontein Dam. 142

A young doctor of the Royal Army Medical Corps was awarded the Victoria Cross at Syferfontein, near Standerton, for his treatment of wounded while under heavy fire. Remarkable in itself, this man, Arthur Martin-Leake earned another such medal in the Great War in 1914, the first to double V.C. ever. 152

In January 1902 President Steyn became desperately ill with food poisoning and was unable to ride. De Wet took his president on a desperate journey to the western Transvaal to consult de la Rey's Russian doctor. They had first to break through a line of blockhouses at Langverwacht, south of Vrede, which resulted in the combat deaths of a number of young New Zealand soldiers. 165

De la Rey in the western Transvaal now became the priority as the war drew to a close. Columns closed in on his men but the capture of the wounded Lord Methuen at Tweebosch showed that the fighting was not yet over. 173

Three Boers who were accused of actions "contrary to the usages of war" were court-marshalled after the war's end, Salmon van As and two others. Van As was executed by firing squad but the other two escaped conviction. 190

The village of Val saw a number of actions in its vicinity and a number of train derailments by Boer commandos. In April 1902 General Louis Botha came to Val to take a special train to the peace negotiations in Klerksdorp. 200

Index 208

Practically Over

The Anglo Boer War

The Anglo Boer War of 1899-1902 was a war that was to some extent thrust upon an unwilling British Government. The British Army in the colonies of the Cape and Natal was not prepared for war. They were poorly placed to resist armed incursions into the Cape and Natal, British self-governing colonies, after being presented with an ultimatum by the Kruger government of the Zuid-Afrikaansche Republiek[1] which the British continued to call the Transvaal. An 1897 mutual assistance pact obliged the Republic of the Orange Free State, which had no dispute with Britain, to support their northern neighbour.

The British forces in the two colonies were inadequate to stem the Boer advances. Sir Alfred Milner the British High Commissioner and Governor of the Cape promised his Natal counterpart, Sir Walter Hely-Hutchinson, that Natal would be defended by the whole might of the Empire. It took some time to assemble the whole might however. British soldiers came from Britain, India, Malta, Crete and other Empire outposts while the Dominions, Canada, Australia and New Zealand lent a hand too. But it was several months before they arrived in South Africa. South African Colonists from the Cape and Natal and *uitlanders* from Johannesburg enlisted in considerable numbers as well.

It needed some time to organise and equip the necessary Army Corps, so that the Boers were able to occupy northern Natal and raid further south. They penetrated a short distance into the Cape Colony at Colesberg and further east at Stormberg. A further drive southwards was held up by their forces settling into besieging Mafeking, Kimberley and Ladysmith. It was unlikely that Boer citizen forces could bear the inevitable casualties that would have resulted from all-out assaults, so that all three towns easily held out until the reliefs arrived.

Once war was declared there was no going back. The two bearded patriarchs, Kruger and British Prime Minister Lord Salisbury, both knew that this was a struggle about regional paramountcy. Salisbury would have "preferred a peaceful outcome but if sweeping away the shame of Majuba took a war – then so be it." In a letter that Salisbury sent to Secretary for War, Lord Lansdowne on 30 August 1899, wrote, "I see before us the necessity for considerable military effort – and all for people whom we despise and for territory which will bring no profit and no power to England."[2]

It was not about gold and diamonds. It was about the fact that Britain could not countenance a situation whereby the southern part of Africa was in the hands of a hostile power. A political climb-down, as happened in 1881 after the first bout of hostilities with the Boers, was not going to happen this time. The Boer republics were not of sufficient importance to warrant any of the other Great Powers going to war on their behalf. It was firmly believed that the Cape Afrikaners would heed a call to arms from the two republics. Quite a number of them did, risking execution for treason if captured, but not nearly enough to tip the balance in favour of the Boer Republicans.

Once reinforcements were in place the conventional war was quickly over, but not before the British suffered tactical defeats at Magersfontein, Stormberg and Colenso. These setbacks did not affect the ultimate outcome, the Boers were driven out of the Cape and Natal and the three besieged towns were relieved. With the capture of the capitals of the two republics, Bloemfontein and Pretoria, the surrender of the Boers was anticipated. Field-Marshall Lord Roberts, Commander-in-Chief, decided that the war was practically over, and said as much in a speech in Durban at a private dinner,[3] after handing over command to General Lord Kitchener in November 1900. Further operations would be a police action – only some mopping up was needed. His departure for England was delayed by the illness of his daughter but he was back home in England in good time for Christmas.

But it was not just mopping up that was needed. Kruger was not much good as a motivator for his demoralised Transvalers by now. He was old and ill, practically a fugitive in the eastern Transvaal, and about to accept the offer of passage to Holland aboard a Royal Dutch Navy cruiser, the *Gelderland*. But the President of the Orange Free State, Marthinus Steyn, arrived in Nelspruit and made a number of inspirational speeches to what commandos were still in the field. He followed the march of those Transvaalers to Pietersburg where the flag of the ZAR was still flying and the government officials were all still at their posts. Steyn

---

[1] The full text of the ZAR ultimatum is given below. It was to have been much shorter but the Orange Free State President, M.T. Steyn insisted on more preamble to the four demands. An original copy can be found in No 53 in C9530 of the British Parliamentary Papers.

[2] Quoted in Roberts *Salisbury Victorian Titan* p732. Note that the "people whom we despise" are the *uitlanders*, the Boer term for foreigners, mostly British, who were resident in the Transvaal, not the Boers!

[3] From the diary of Lieutenant-Colonel Sir Henry Rawlinson, National Army Museum, London 5201/33.

addressed a large crowd in the village of Nylstroom and Louis Botha did likewise. Afterwards there was a *krygsraad* attended by all the Boer officers and plans were made to go forward.[1]

Many of the older politician generals were still around but, perhaps fortunately, the Commandant-General Piet Joubert had died in March probably from internal injuries incurred in a fall from his horse during the Natal campaign in November 1899. Louis Botha, only just 37 was appointed in his place and Ben Viljoen, only 30 years old, had been a general for some months. In the Orange Free State (now annexed by Britain and renamed the Orange River Colony) Christiaan de Wet was Chief Commandant, in place of Marthinus Prinsloo who had surrendered to British General Archibald Hunter with 4,000 men in the Brandwater Basin in July 1900.

De Wet was 45, a little older than his Transvaal counterpart, but a ferocious fighter and energetic organiser who was determined to fight to the bitter end. After the disasters to the Free Staters at Paardeberg and the Brandwater Basin the remaining Boer fighters were hardly less demoralised than their counterparts from the Transvaal. De Wet and Steyn set to work to change this. They appointed many younger men as Commandants and rounded up those who had signed an oath of allegiance offered by the British and persuaded them to re-join the commandos. De Wet and Steyn were largely responsible for the Boer revival at the end of 1900.[2]

The Boers now resorted to raiding the British lines of communication and attacking supply columns, tactics that de Wet had been advocating and actively pursuing for some time. For the first time they were exploiting their major advantage over the British Army – their superior mobility. While the British never managed to match the Boers in this respect, General Lord Kitchener understood very quickly that a whole new strategy needed to be evolved. Ponderous British infantry columns with transport, artillery, medical personnel and engineers were quite unable to catch and trap the fleet-footed Boer commandos.

Many more horsemen were needed and many more horses. Horses were brought to South Africa from the U.S.A., Argentina and Hungary as there just were not enough in Britain to meet the demand. Horsemen came from Australia, New Zealand and Canada with their horses. There were South African Colonial mounted regiments as well as Yeomanry and the British mounted their infantry. The mounted infantry concept whereby these units used horses only to improve their mobility was not entirely successful as infantrymen often knew little about the care and feeding of horses when on campaign. The mortality and wastage of horses was, at times, alarming.

Part of the strategy was aimed at protection of the railways. A series of blockhouses, envisaged as small forts, were built to protect bridges and causeways. They were built with locally-available materials, usually stone, and cost nearly £1,000 each. To erect such structures all along the railway lines was beyond the resources even of Britain, so a cheaper model was developed. Made of two concentric circular corrugated-iron pieces which were filled with earth or shingle, they were proof against rifle bullets and were home to a small garrison. By 1902 these little forts, which cost a mere £16 each, had been erected all along the railway lines. Lines that went cross-country were intended to hamper the movement of the Boer commandos. More than 8,000 had been erected by the war's end in May 1902.[3]

With each blockhouse within sight of the blockhouses on each side and connected with a barbed wire entanglement, the country was thus divided into smaller sections. Drives were organised whereby soldiers were spread out in a line that stretched across from one blockhouse line to another. Moving forward day by day it was rather like a game drive, the Boers being driven ahead and captured when they reached the apex of the lines. This was the theory, in practice it did not quite work that way as the Boers were able to break through the lines. Nevertheless, the lines made movement cross country by the Boer commandos much more difficult.[4]

Another arm of the strategy was to deny supplies of any kind to the commandos. This necessitated the removal of people from their farms and the confiscation and sometimes destruction of all livestock. Refugee camps had been established as early as June 1900 when the British first crossed the Vaal River and found some hundreds of homeless people who had been driven from their farms by the fighting. Once the Boers began their hit-an-run strategy there were many people on farms who were totally unprotected from marauders of all sorts.

Camps were established in numbers of locations usually alongside a railway line. The inhabitants were not prevented from leaving and in some cases were even gainfully employed in nearby towns. A measles epidemic, the disease at that time unknown in South Africa and untreatable, caused terrible mortality among those least able to resist it, the children and some of the older people. This handed the Boers a propaganda weapon that has been fully-exploited by Afrikaner Nationalists for many years after the war.

Much of the fighting in the last eighteen months of the war was by Australian, New Zealand and Canadian soldiers augmented by Yeomanry volunteers from England. The British regular mounted infantry was also heavily involved while many of the infantry units were deployed in guarding the lines of communication. Drives in the Free State along the lines of the blockhouses were never able to capture De Wet or Steyn, but the strategy was successful in that the Boer commandos were gradually starved of supplies and especially ammunition.

Peace came with an offer from the Government of the Netherlands to mediate between the two sides. This was totally unacceptable to the British Government but some of the correspondence was sent without comment to Kitchener who forwarded it, again without comment, to Botha and Steyn. The Boers indicated that they would be prepared to meet with the British authorities to discuss terms for the cessation of hostilities. The Boer leaders met first in

---

[1] Viljoen *My Reminiscences of the Anglo-Boer War* pp146-150.
[2] de Wet *Three Years' War* pp132-156 Chapters XVIII and XIX tell of this time.
[3] The blockhouse system is described in Volume V of the *Times History* pp396-412.
[4] Christiaan De Wet in *Three Years War* is forthright that the blockhouses were "all money thrown away! And worse than thrown away!" on pp271-73.

Klerksdorp and then thirty delegates from each of the Boer republics wrangled among themselves at Vereeniging. The discussions were protracted and heated at times but finally the leaders were authorised to travel to Pretoria to meet with Kitchener and Milner. The British presented terms which required only a "Yes" or a "No" and they were signed by both parties just in time to meet the deadline of midnight on 31 May 1902.

This Peace of Vereeniging was signed at Melrose House in Pretoria, the terms being substantially those offered to Commandant-General Louis Botha at a meeting with Kitchener in Middelburg more than a year previously. It took a heart-to-heart talk between Botha and Kitchener in the passage outside the meeting room to persuade the Boer generals to sign the document. After a forthcoming general election in Britain, a government more sympathetic to granting self-government to the two former Boer republics, as they now were, might well come to power, explained Kitchener.

Sure enough this happened a few years later when the Liberals swept to power and Sir Henry Campbell-Bannerman became Prime Minister. Self-government was indeed granted and Afrikaner political parties came to power in the Transvaal and the Orange River Colony in 1906. The Orange River Colony became the Orange Free State once more. In 1908 investigations began in order to establish the feasibility of combining the five southern African political entities (the Protectorates of Basutoland (Lesotho), Bechuanaland (Botswana) and Swaziland were not to be included). In 1910 the Union of South Africa came into being comprising the four provinces of the Cape of Good Hope, Natal, the Orange Free State and the Transvaal. Rhodesia declined to join.

South Africa was now a sovereign state, a dominion of the British Empire. There was a Governor-General, the King's representative, but he had little, if any, political power and could act in an advisory role only. This did not entirely satisfy certain sections of the population who nurtured Afrikaner Nationalism and an anti-British policy which finally resulted in South Africa quitting the British Commonwealth in 1961. Portraying the Anglo Boer war in terms that made the British Empire into an evil and unfeeling ogre bent on destroying the Afrikaner nation was a cornerstone of the Nationalist doctrine.

In fact, the tenacity of the Boers and their sheer dogged refusal to accept defeat was greatly admired in Britain. Botha, de la Rey and de Wet were feted when they visited England in 1903. With a fraction of the resources of their opponents they had held the British Army at bay for nearly two years of guerrilla warfare, until finally forced to yield.

ULTIMATUM REJECTED

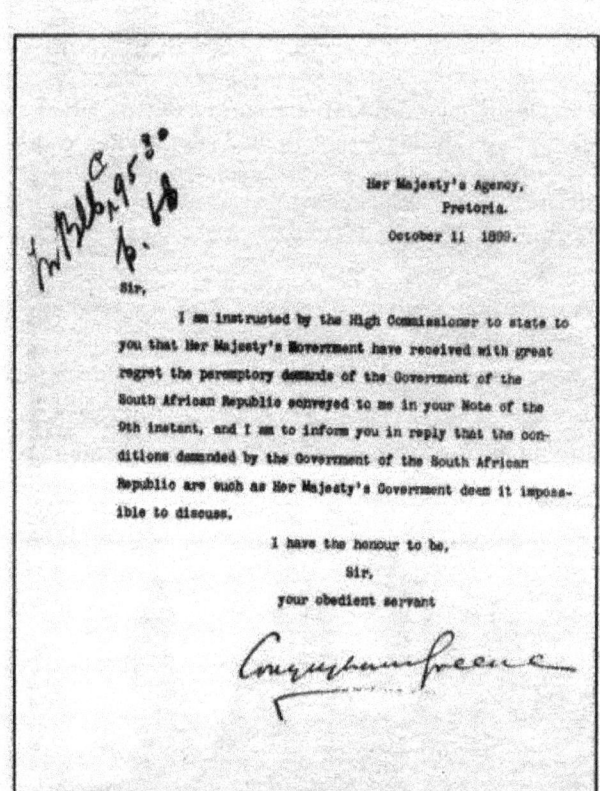

Document handed by Greene to the Transvaal government

Our correspondent in Pretoria was shown the brief note that the agent of the British government in Pretoria, Sir William Conyngham Greene, handed over personally to President Kruger at four o'clock on the afternoon of 11 October. It was addressed to the State Secretary and read as follows:

'I am instructed by the High Commissioner to state to you that Her Majesty's Government have received with great regret the peremptory demands of the Government of the South African Republic conveyed to me in your Note of the 9th instant, and I am to inform you in reply that the conditions demanded by the Government of the South African Republic are such as Her Majesty's Government deem it impossible to discuss.'

After handing over the note, Greene requested his passport and immediately left the Republic.

The Ultimatum

SIR, - The Government of the South African Republic feels itself compelled to refer the Government of the Her Majesty the Queen of Great Britain and Ireland once more to the Convention of London, 1884, concluded between this Republic and the United Kingdom, and which in its 14th Article secures certain specified rights to the whole population of this Republic, namely, that:-

> "All persons other than natives conforming themselves to the laws of the South African Republic: (a) will have full liberties, with their families, to enter, travel, or reside in any portion of the South African Republic. (b) They will be entitled to hire or possess houses, manufactories, warehouses, shops or premises. (c) They may carry on their commerce, either in person or by any agents who they may think fit to employ. (d) They will not be obliged, in respect of their persons or property, or in respect of their commerce or industry. To pay any taxes, whether general or local, other than hose which are or may be imposed by the citizens of the said Republic."

This Government wishes further to observe that the above are the only rights which Her Majesty's Government have reserved in the above Convention with regard to the Outlander population of this Republic, and that the violation only of these rights could give that Government the right to diplomatic representation or intervention, while, moreover, the regulation of all other questions affecting the position of the rights of the Outlander population under the above-mentioned Convention is handed over to the Government and the representatives of the people fo the South African Republic. . . This Government has also, by the formulation fo the now exiting franchise and the resolution with regard to representation, constantly held these friendly discussions before it eyes.

On the part of Her Majesty's Government, however, the friendly nature of these discussions assumed a more and more threatening tone, and the minds of the people in this Republic and in the whole of South Africa have been excited, and a position of extreme tension has been created, while her Majesty's Government could no longer agree to the legislation respecting franchise and the resolution respecting representation in this Republic, and, finally by your note of September 25th last, broke off all friendly correspondence on the subject and intimated that they must now proceed to formulate their own proposals for a final settlement. . . Even while friendly correspondence was still going on, an increase of troops on a large scale was introduced by Her Majesty's Government and stationed in the neighbourhood of the borders of the Republic.

Having regard to the occurrence in the history of this Republic, which it is unnecessary here to call to mind, the Government felt obliged to regard this military force in the neighbourhood of it borders as a threat against the independence of the South African Republic, since it was aware of no circumstances which could justify the presence of such a military force in South Africa and in the neighbourhood of its borders. In answer to an enquiry with respect thereto, addressed to His Excellency the High Commissioner, this Government received, to its great astonishment, in answer a veiled insinuation from the side of the Republic an attack was being made on Her Majesty's Colonies, and at the same time a mysterious reference to possibilities whereby it was strengthened in its suspicion that the independence of this Republic was being threatened. As a defensive measure it was, therefore, obliged to send a portion of the burghers of this Republic in order to offer the requisite resistance to similar possibilities.

Her Majesty's unlawful intervention in the internal affairs of this Republic, in conflict with the Convention fo London, 1884, caused by the extraordinary strengthening of troops in the neighbourhood of the borders of this Republic, has thus caused an intolerable condition of things to arise, whereto this Government feels itself obliged, and in the interest not only of this Republic but also of all South Africa, to make and end as soon as possible, and feels itself called upon and obliged to press earnestly and with emphasis for an immediate termination of this state of things, and to request Her Majesty's Government to give it the assurance:-

> (a) That all points of mutual differences shall be regulated by the friendly course of arbitration, or by whatever amicable way may be agreed upon by this Government with Her majesty's Government.

> (b) That the troops on the borders of this Republic shall be immediately withdrawn.

> (c) That all reinforcements of troops which have arrived in South Africa since 1st June, 1899, shall be removed from South Africa within a reasonable time to be agreed upon with this Government and with the mutual assurance and guarantee on the part of this Government that no attack upon or hostilities against any portion of the possessions of the British Government shall be made by the Republic during further negotiations within the period of time to be subsequently agree upon between the Governments, and this Government will, on compliance therewith, be prepared to withdraw the armed burghers of this Republic from the borders.

> (d) That Her Majesty's troops which are now on the high seas shall not be landed in any portion of South Africa.

The Government must press for an immediate and affirmative answer to these four question, and earnestly requests Her Majesty's Government to return such an answer before or upon Wednesday, October 11th, 1899, not later than five o'clock p.m. And desires further that in the event – unexpectedly – of no satisfactory answer being received by it within that interval it will, with great regret, be compelled to regard the action of Her Majesty's Government as a formal declaration of war, and will not hold itself responsible for the consequences thereof; and in the event of any further movements with troops taking place within the above-mentioned time in the nearer direction of our borders this Government will be compelled to regard that also as a formal declaration of war.

I have, etc

October 8th 1899   F.W. REITZ, State Secretary

Once Ladysmith was relieved

General Sir Redvers Buller's Natal Field Force needed time to reorganise after his men entered Ladysmith in the first few days of March 1900. The railway line needed repairs so that supplies could be brought up to the town to feed Lieutenant-General Sir George White's defenders and the civilian residents. Sick and wounded from Intombi Hospital, between the lines in "no man's land" during the siege, were sent to hospitals down the line at Mooi River, Howick, Pietermaritzburg and Durban. The garrison members needed time to regain their health. Re-supply of clothing, food and ammunition was going to take time. And besides, the two forces, Buller's Natal Field Force and Lieutenant-General Sir George White's Ladysmith garrison needed to be reorganized and integrated.

Field-Marshal Lord Roberts had relieved Kimberley on 15 February, after a daring charge by Major-General John French's mounted men. He then cornered General Piet Cronjé's several thousand burghers at Paardeberg who surrendered on 27 February. Bloemfontein was occupied on 12 March. A serious outbreak of enteric (typhoid fever) was caused by contaminated water. The Boers had cut the main water supply source at Sanna's Post and now the only source of fresh water was from boreholes. Bloemfontein, like Johannesburg, is some distance from a major river. Roberts did the only thing he could do – call a halt there to build up supplies and take measures to ensure that the epidemic abated.

With Kimberley and now Ladysmith no longer besieged, there remained the problem of Mafeking, surrounded and virtually cut off from help. The important town was nearly 400kms north of Kimberley with Vryburg, occupied by the Boers, straddling the road. Boer commandos could intercept any force advancing to the relief. Roberts determined to come to the rescue of the small garrison and its commander, Colonel Robert Baden-Powell. The troops he needed were drawn from Buller's force around Ladysmith – Major-General Geoffrey Barton's Fusilier Brigade and the Imperial Light Horse, Colonials mostly from Johannesburg but including a number of Australians. Major-General Archibald Hunter, until then White's deputy commander in Ladysmith, was sent to take command.

Piet Joubert's Boer forces had withdrawn to the next range of hills to the north, the Biggarsberg and the British had moved out of the unhealthy environs of Ladysmith. Louis Botha was effectively in command, Commandant-General Joubert still recovering from a fall from his horse and far from well. The British camped as far away from Ladysmith as Elandslaagte, scene of Major-General John French's significant victory five months previously.[1] A number of clashes took place between patrols and pickets but Lord Roberts had ordered Buller to remain on the defensive while the advance through the Orange Free State was stalled in Bloemfontein. Once he was ready to advance then Buller was given orders to advance in concert.

Buller's tactics were to out-flank the Boer lines along the Biggarsberg and his first thrust was up the Uithoek Pass into the village of Helpmekaar. The advance continued along the high ground and Dundee was recaptured on 15 May. On 20 May occurred an ambush of Bethune's Mounted Infantry at Scheeper's Nek outside Vryheid. This minor setback for Buller's force and operation was a nasty setback for Bethune's unit which had acquitted itself well up until then, attached to Lord Dundonald's Composite Regiment[2]. Lieutenant-Colonel E.C. Bethune's small force were flank guards for Buller's main operation and their setback is described in the next section.

Bethune's Mounted Infantry ambushed at Scheeper's Nek

20 May 1900

Travelling to Vryheid along the R33 highway from Dundee, there is an enclosure in a field on the left of the road. Within this fenced area is a monument to those men of Bethune's Mounted Infantry killed in a Boer ambush on 20 May 1900. The action took place a short distance away on the old wagon road. The site contains two mass graves and a pyramid-shaped cairn, the original monument, as well as a much more elaborate structure erected a short while after the end of the war in 1902. A solid brass name plaque, engraved with the names of the casualties and the badge of the regiment, is on the west-facing side. Two crossed flags, a Union Jack and a regimental colour,[3] flank the regimental crest with the motto "Pro rege, pro lege, conamur" ("For right, for law, we strive").

The original brass plaque on the monument, containing the names of those killed in action and one who died of his wounds, had come loose. The Commonwealth War Graves Commission accordingly removed it to their store for safekeeping. This plaque is a magnificent piece of work and contains the names of those killed in the action (bar yet another who died of wounds) and who lie buried on either side of the pyramid cairn. A new black granite replica of the plaque has been made and fitted. Being made of polished granite, it is unlikely to suffer damage or theft. The original brass plaque will be donated to the Talana Museum in Dundee where it will be on permanent display.

---

[1] French, who, as Field Marshall, was General Officer Commanding of the British Expeditionary Force in France, in the First World War wrote sixteen years later on the anniversary of the battle: "It was the first battle that I commanded – it seemed like yesterday." Holmes *The Little Field Marshall* p14.

[2] Brigadier-General Lord Dundonald came to South Africa at his own expense and was given command of the mounted troops in Natal by Buller. He arrived in Mooi River just as Piet Joubert's raid into Natal was approaching the town on 23 November 1899. Dundonald *My Army Life* p94.

[3] The labels on the regimental colour might at first glance be taken for battle honours, as would be attached to the regimental colour of a regular regiment. They are in fact merely the names on the clasps that would have been attached to the medal ribbons of Queen's and Kings Boer War medals awarded to members of BMI.

Bethune's Mounted Infantry was one of a number of irregular mounted units raised in the Colony of Natal when war was declared in October 1899. Major E.C. Bethune of the 16th Lancers, an officer in South Africa on special service, undertook to raise the regiment of 500 mounted men. He was given command and promoted Lieutenant Colonel. In Natal they formed part of the Composite Brigade of Mounted Infantry with the Natal Carbineers, a squadron of the Imperial Light Horse and Thorneycroft's Mounted Infantry, another irregular regiment. They were present with General Redvers Buller's army in the campaign to lift the siege of Ladysmith.

Major General Lord Dundonald, commanding officer of the brigade, was favourably impressed with Bethune and his men, and said of them that "Colonel Bethune, with Bethune's Mounted Infantry, now did the scouting, and well and rapidly was his work done."[1] This when Dundonald took his brigade around Thabanyama, west of Spionkop, in an attempt to outflank the Boer defences on 18 January 1900. On 11 February Bethune's M.I. were sent to Greytown. They formed part of a small force including the local Greytown volunteer regiment, the Umvoti Mounted Rifles and the Natal Artillery. Command of this force was given to Lieutenant Colonel Bethune. They were to watch the Boers near the Zululand border and thus missed the fighting that resulted in the relief of Ladysmith.[2]

Once Buller's army started its march towards the Transvaal border, Bethune's M.I. advanced from Greytown northwards towards Helpmekaar. Buller's plan was to outflank the Boers and advance along the Biggarsberg from Helpmekaar towards Newcastle and Laing's Nek. By 11 May Buller had crossed the Waschbank River and bivouacked at Vermaak's Kraal. On the following day the attack up the Uithoek Pass towards the small village of Helpmekaar was made by Dundonald's mounted men. The Natal Volunteers took the hills to the west of the pass while Thorneycroft's M.I. went straight up the pass. They were somewhat surprised to find Bethune and his men already at the top having come in from the west in the early morning.[3]

The main body of the Boers retired northwards but a small number under Christiaan Botha moved back eastwards towards their homes around Vryheid. Still watching Buller's right flank, Bethune's detached command was sent eastwards to Nqutu. No Boers were found there but the magistracy was re-established. The opportunity was taken to assemble the Zulu *indunas* from around the area and to thank them for "the restraint that they had exercised and for the patient attitude they had maintained during the many months that the Boers had occupied their country."[4]

Bethune's orders were to march to Newcastle but intelligence was gained from local Africans near Blood River who "reported that we might find a few Boers, forty or fifty perhaps, just outside Vryheid..."[5] B.M.I.'s intelligence officer, Lieutenant L.W. Lanham, resident for many years in the Transvaal, was leading the scouts. Bethune's orders were for Captain William Goff and 'E' squadron to advance cautiously to Vryheid, keeping well to the rear of the scouts and giving them ample time to reconnoiter. Goff, a promising young officer of the 3rd Dragoon Guards, had only recently joined the B.M.I. His own regiment only arrived in South Africa in February 1901 but he was one of a number of British regular officers who were sent to South Africa on special service.[6]

The scouts were given their orders and left Blood River at 3 p.m. followed by Goff leading 'E' squadron and followed by Captain Ford and 'D' squadron at ten minute intervals. De la Warr, accompanying Colonel Bethune, described how "we had to ride hard to keep up with the leading squadrons."[7] Goff and his men were "nearing a hollow, when six Boers came forward, firing a few shots at them and then retiring." This was a decoy and the British spurred forwards over the rise and into a trap.

The road curved around a little hollow a short distance from where it breasted a rise between two pieces of high ground – Scheeper's Nek. To the right of the road was a rocky outcrop behind which the main Boer force was sited. At farmhouses at either end of the hollow were more Boers. Goff's men were assailed from three sides and not a single man escaped unscathed. De la Warr gives the casualty count as "thirty killed, twenty-eight wounded and thirteen prisoners."[8] Ford's "D" squadron attempted a rescue but were driven back by heavy fire. As it was becoming dark, Bethune judged that it was prudent to withdraw and return to Nqutu. There is no record of even a single casualty on the Boer side although Ford's squadron opened fire and landed "a few well-directed shots among the enemy" with two Hotchkiss guns.[9]

The dead were buried by the Boers in a field a short distance from where the fight took place, the ground being softer than the rocky ground along the road. The wounded who were their prisoners were taken into Vryheid and "well cared for" while Bethune sent Archdeacon Johnson from St Augustine's Mission, near Rorke's Drift, to read the burial service over the graves.[10]

The B.M.I. retired back to Nqutu and made their way the following day to Newcastle. When Vryheid was occupied on 19[t] September the B.M.I. were involved in turning the strong Boer position. For the rest of the war the regiment was occupied in patrolling the south of the Transvaal and the Utrecht area. In one his dispatches Buller had this to say about Colonel Bethune: "Raised this regiment and commanded it most efficiently throughout the campaign."[11]

Postscript

In May 2013 the new granite plaque was affixed to the Scheeper's Nek monument. It is exactly the same size and

---

[1] Dundonald *My Army Life* p117.
[2] Stirling *The Colonials in South Africa* pp63-4.
[3] Williams *The Times History of the War in South Africa* Vol IV pp171-72. Dundonald *My Army Life* p157.
[4] De la Warr *Some reminiscences of the war in South Africa* p115.
[5] De la Warr *Some reminiscences of the war in South Africa* p116.
[6] Hall *The Hall Handbook of the Anglo Boer War* p72.
[7] De la Warr *Some reminiscences of the war in South Africa* p117.
[8] The casualty list gives considerably more than this
[9] De la Warr *Some reminiscences of the war in South Africa* p119.
[10] De la Warr *Some reminiscences of the war in South Africa* p120. De la Warr does not say when this was but likely several days after the battle.
[11] Stirling *The Colonials in South Africa* pp65.

design as the original brass plaque that it replaced except that the names on the regimental flag were too small to be reproduced.

An additional monument has been erected within the enclosure to the three Hamilton brothers, all fatalities of the Anglo Boer war. Ernest was killed in action at Scheeper's Nek, probably unaware that his brother Kenneth had died of enteric (typhoid fever) four days previously in Bloemfontein. A third brother, Alastair, was struck by lightning and killed in December 1902 near Machadodorp in the eastern Transvaal (now Mpumalanga). The monument is an exact replica of the gravestone to Kenneth Hamilton, now badly damaged, that stands in the President Street military cemetery in Bloemfontein.[1]

References

1. John Stirling *The Colonials in South Africa 1899-1902* William Blackwood & Sons, Edinburgh & London 1907 (reprint by J.B. Hayward & Son, Polstead, Suffolk).
2. The Earl de la Warr *Some reminiscences of the war in South Africa* Hurst and Blackett, Limited, 13, Greta Marlborough Street, London 1900.
3. Basil Williams (editor) *The Times History of the War in South Africa* Vol IV Sampson Low, Marston and Company, Ltd, London 1906.
4. Hedley Chilvers (editor) *The Times History of the War in South Africa* Vol V Sampson Low, Marston and Company, Ltd, London 1907.
5. Maurice, Major General Sir Frederick *History of the war in South Africa* Vol 4. Hurst and Blackett Limited, London 1910.
6. Mildred G. Dooner *The Last Post* J.B. Hayward & Son, Polstead, Suffolk 1980 (reprint of edition of 1903).
7. H.W. Wlson *With the Flag to Pretoria II* London 1903.
8. Steve Watt *In Memoriam* University of Natal Press, Pietermaritzburg 2000.
9. The Earl of Dundonald *My Army Life* Edward Arnold & Co, London 1926.
10. Darrell Hall *The Hall Handbook of the Anglo Boer War* University of Natal Press, Pietermaritzburg 1999.
11. Gert & Erika van der Westhuizen *Guide to the Anglo Boer War in the Eastern Transvaal* Gert & Erika van der Westhuizen, Volksrust 2000.

[1] Watt *In Memoriam* notes that the three Hamiltons were brothers. Gert & Erika van der Westhuizen *Guide to the Anglo Boer War in the Eastern Transvaal* has a picture of the grave of Alan Hamilton with an inscription that incorrectly proclaims it to be the mass grave of the three brothers.

Scheeper's Nek 2013: The new monument to the three Hamilton brothers.

Casualty list

All from "E" Squadron, Bethune's Mounted Infantry.

Killed in Action on 20 May 1900:

Captain	W.E.D.	Goff
Lieutenant	L.W.	Lanham
Lieutenant	D.F.	McLachlan
S Sgt Major	E.S.	Hadler
Sergeant	F.W.	Moon
Corporal	W.A.	Benson
Corporal	E.H.	Roberts
Trooper	J.S.	Beyers
Trooper	H.S.	Billing
Trooper	E.	Coleman
Trooper	H.	de Lorme
Trooper	W.	Garfield
Trooper	M.C.	Gillies
Trooper	E.	Hamilton
Trooper	C.B.	Hammond
Trooper	S.	Ingham
Trooper	R.S.O.	Ingle
Trooper	W.F.	Johnstone
Trooper	J.	Lang
Trooper	G.	Paige
Trooper	P.J.H.	Rudderforth
Trooper	D.	Seaton
Trooper	A.	Stanley
Trooper	T.	Stansby
Trooper	B.D.	Stone
Trooper	H.	Thompson
Trooper	R.H.	Tuckwell
Trooper	E.	Udell
Trooper	S.	Watson

Died of wounds: (both buried in the town cemetery, Vryheid):

| Sgt Farrier | J. | Cock | (Died 28 May 1900) |
| Trooper | L.A. | Cowie | (Died 6 June 1900)* |

* Cowie's name appears on the plaque on the monument at Scheeper's Nek.

Wounded:
A further 45 men listed as wounded.

Scheeper's Nek: The original name plaque in place in 1995. David Rattray, with the *Times History* under his arm, looks at the newly-painted monument. The pyramid cairn with Staff Sergeant Major Edgar Schmitt Hadler's separate grave. Hadler's headstone.

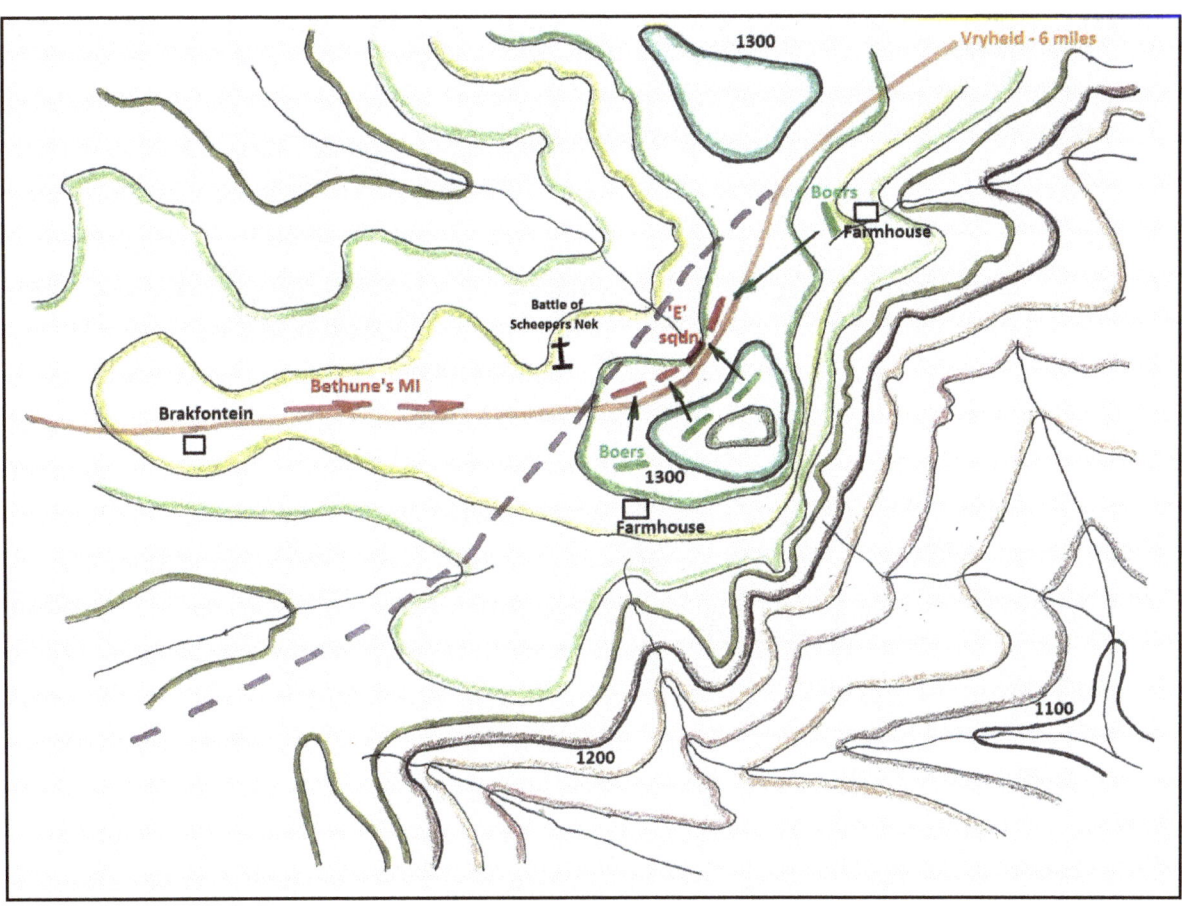

The battle: The BMI were advancing towards Vryheid. "E" squadron, under Captain W. Goff advanced at the gallop and were assailed by Boers sited on the high ground to their right.

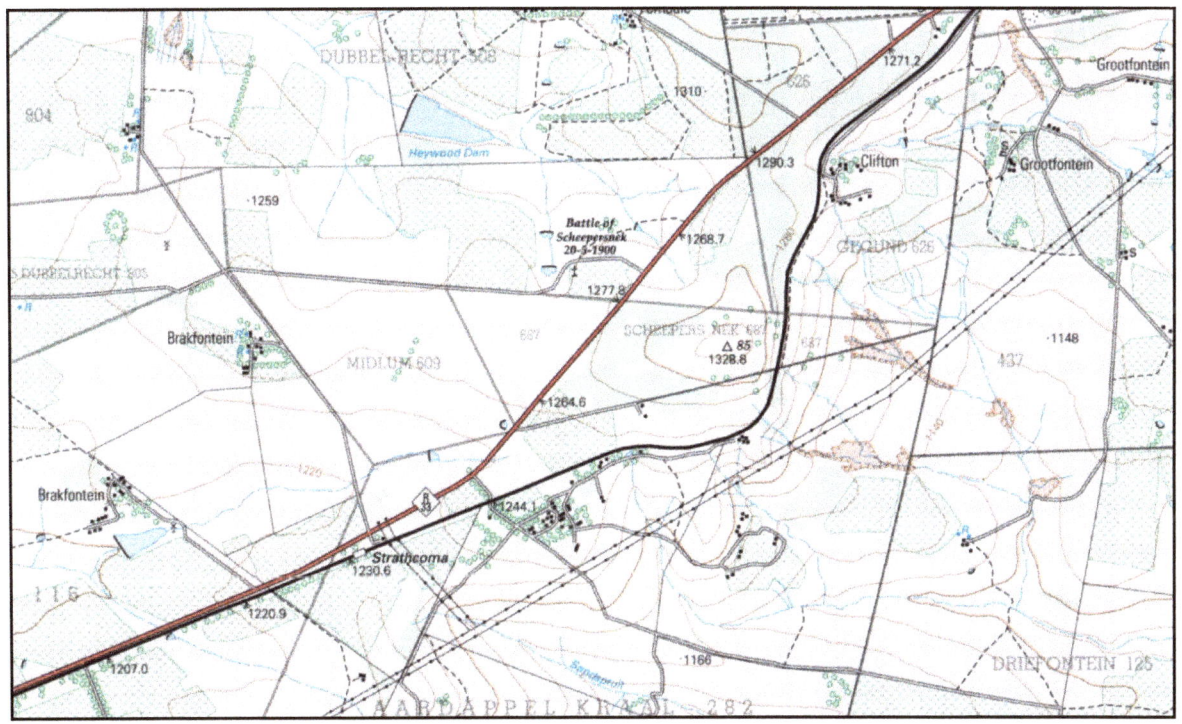

Section of 1:50 000 survey map 2730DC.

Scheeper's Nek 1995: The old wagon road in a view looking to the west. This is the precise spot where 'E' squadron were ambushed and shot down by Boer rifle fire from the rocky outcrop out of sight to the left of the picture. This area has now been planted with timber and there are no visible traces of the old road.

Scheeper's Nek 1995: The rocky outcrop which overlooks the old road.

Scheeper's Nek 1995: Some items picked up on the battle site. A piece of a whisky bottle, pottery shards, a complete 303 cartridge and a soda water cartridge.

Scheeper's Nek 2013: Fitting the new granite plaque. Drilling the holes for the rawlbolts.

Into the Transvaal

Newcastle was practically undefended by the Boers who had determined to make a stand at Laing's Nek, the border of the Transvaal and the scene of their great victory in the First Boer War twenty years previously. The railway goes through a tunnel here and the mouth of the tunnel was blown up. Several trucks laden with dynamite in the middle of the tunnel failed to explode. Rather than attack this difficult position frontally, Buller refused battle at Laing's Nek sending just a few units there to provide a diversion while the main force turned to the west and climbed up Botha's Pass into the Orange Free State, incurring very few casualties on the way. There was still the obstacle of Alleman's Nek to be overcome but Volksrust was occupied on 13 June.[1]

Northern Natal had been cleared of Boer forces as Louis Botha's men retreated northwards. The objective now was to join hands with Lord Roberts's men occupying Pretoria and about to be engaged at Diamond Hill to the east of the city. The British occupied Standerton on 22 June, by which time Johannesburg and Pretoria were in British hands. But there was a problem of logistics.

An army needs food, clothing, ammunition and water daily for its operation and at this time Lord Roberts's men were dependent on the single railway line from the Cape ports. Besides being extremely difficult to protect against damage from Boer guerrilla action, trains travelling from Cape Town to Johannesburg and Pretoria had to follow a somewhat circuitous route. The main line from Cape Town to the north was to the west through Kimberley and Mafeking to Rhodesia. There was no direct connection, as there is today, from Kimberley or Mafeking to Johannesburg. Supplies were mostly sent from Port Elizabeth and some from East London as these lines ran through Colesberg to Bloemfontein and to the Transvaal.

It was vitally important to open the line from Natal to Johannesburg. This route was shorter and more direct but in early June the line from Standerton to Heidelberg was still in Boer hands. Lieutenant-General Francis Clery was given the job of securing this piece of vital infrastructure. Major-General A. Fitzroy Hart occupied Heidelberg on 25 June and Clery's men progressed rapidly meeting only sporadic resistance from local Boer commandos. The rail line needed to be repaired as they advanced and Clery and Hart linked up on 4 July, leaving garrisons at each station. The stretch of railway line from Volksrust to Elandsfontein, the junction outside Germiston where the Natal and Cape lines joined, now became the focus of considerable sabotage activity on the part of the Boer commandos.[2]

It is said that more than 60 trains were derailed on this stretch of line from June 1900 until the end of the war in May 1902. Boer *modus operandi* was to bury a dynamite charge next to the rail with a detonator. To fire the detonator, a rifle without the barrel would be buried in such a way that the train running over it would operate the trigger and fire a bullet into the detonator. A Martini-Henry minus stock and barrel was the easiest to arrange.[3] Most of this activity ceased once the line was secured with blockhouses every 900 metres, and linked with barbed wire, by the middle of 1901. Thereafter derailments were rare with a line of barbed wire on both sides of the line. Tin cans attached to the strands would rattle and send the alarm to the blockhouse garrison should anyone approach. Rifles clamped in position would fire along the wire so approaching at night was fraught with hazard. Crossing the line was not impossible but a very dangerous undertaking.

The Boers used dynamite from the date monopoly dynamite factory but sometimes also stock stolen from coal and gold mines. Usually the charge was only just enough to derail the locomotive, damaging it only very slightly. This stretch was operated all through the war by the Natal Government Railway (N.G.R.). The Railway Pioneer Regiment or the railway personnel, would jack the locomotive and some of the wagons back onto the line and quickly repair any damage to the line or culverts. Damage to locomotives and rolling stock could be made good in repair facilities in a number of cities in British hands. By mid-1900 the Boer supplies of explosives were not abundant and it was seldom that a large enough charge was set to damage the locomotive beyond repair.

Once Buller crossed into the South African Republic, which the British called the Transvaal, the volunteer soldiers of Natal were required to return to the Colony as their government did not permit its soldiers to go into action outside their borders. The Colony of Natal had had no argument with the Boer republics and even though their territory had been violated by both, they forbore to retaliate further than by defending their own borders. The Natal regiments, Natal Carbineers, Natal Mounted Rifles, Border Mounted Rifles and Umvoti Mounted Rifles returned to their home bases and Buller's Natal Field Force was reinforced with a number of British regiments that had recently arrived in Durban.

Among these reinforcements was a Canadian unit, Lord Strathcona's Horse. They were policemen from the North West Territory Police from western Canada, big men with distinctive uniforms commanded by the legendary Colonel Sam Steele. This tough experienced leader insisted that they take an active role rather than just guarding outposts and railway lines. They certainly did just that and on 1 July they lost Trooper Angus Jenkins, killed in an ambush near the hamlet of Val. A few days later, 5 July, another Strathcona, Sergeant Arthur Richardson, was awarded the Victoria Cross in an action to the north of Standerton. Very few units made their presence felt so quickly and they were constantly in action as scouts for the whole of the year that they were in South Africa.

---

[1] Details of the operation to clear Northern Natal can be found in Maurice *History of the War in South Africa* Chapter X pp249-85. See also *The British advance and the Boer retreat through Natal* by Ken Gillings SA Military History Journal October 1999.

[2] See Maurice *History of the War in South Africa* Chapter XIX pp457-68 for an account of events on the Johanneburg-Durban line, June-November 1900.

[3] See *An improvised explosive device* by Lieutenant-Colonel I.P. Mills in the South African Military History Journal June 2010 for details of how this was achieved.

Lieutenant-General Clery's men advanced through Greylingstad with its hill overlooking what was then just a tiny village with a railway station. On the commanding hill above the village a small fort was established, the ideal place to site a heliograph station to transfer messages back and forth. In time this fort grew to be an extensive fortification, the remains of which are still existent.

The next village along the line was McHattysburg, named after a local farmer. A few years later this cumbersome name was changed to Balfour after the Right Honourable Arthur Balfour who was then the British Prime Minister, having succeeded his uncle, Lord Salisbury. Only when he was 72 years of age in 1922 was he ennobled as the Earl of Balfour. Thus he entered the House of Lords to become an elder statesman and adviser to King George V. He was always remembered by the Boers for his attempts to prevent the outbreak of war in South Africa in 1899 by toning down the demands that were being pressed on President Kruger by Chamberlain and Milner.[1]

The Heidelberg commando under Commandants Buys, Hendricks and Spryt were active in the area until the end of the war. There is a famous picture of their officers assembled at Kraal station to hear Louis Botha explain to them the terms of the Peace of Vereeniging on 4 June 1902. The Heidelbergers were certainly responsible for many of the train derailments along the line until the line of blockhouses put a stop to this activity. One event that certainly happened, but perhaps not the way it was described by Jack van den Heever in his little book, *On Commando with Commandant Buys*, is commemorated with a plaque on a farm near Val.

The incidents with the Canadians and Jack van den Heever's train derailment are detailed in the next section.

Trooper Angus Jenkins, the first casualty of Lord Strathcona's Horse

Canada Day, 1 July 1900

Without any question Trooper Angus Jenkins was shot and killed on 1 July 1900 on the farm Witnek, near the village of Val about 30kms west of Standerton. He was buried on the farm and his grave was marked in some way. The LSH (Lord Strathcona's Horse) bivouacked that night on Witnek. With this first fatal casualty, in the way of soldiers, they mourned the passing of Jenkins, but it was a momentous day, their first day in action. Only four days later one of their Sergeants was awarded the Victoria Cross after a clash with a few Boers north of Standerton. That made even bigger headlines back in Canada.

Canada had been the last of the Empire's Dominions to send troops to the war with the Boer Republics. The Canadian Prime Minister was Sir Wilfred Laurier, a member of the French-Canadian community who were opposed to any Canadian participation in the war. However, Laurier soon realized that it was politically impossible for him to oppose those in favour of raising a Canadian contingent. The first contingent arrived in Cape Town on 29 November and were immediately sent off to join the British forces outside Kimberley. A second contingent arrived early in February 1900. Canadians had locally made uniforms of khaki canvas rather than the British drill.[2]

Lord Strathcona's Horse was an élite regiment composed of men from the north western provinces of Canada, Saskatchewan, Manitoba, Alberta and British Columbia. On 31 December 1899, clearly concerned about the implications of the bad news concerning "Black week",[3] the wealthy Canadian High Commissioner, Lord Strathcona, offered to raise a military unit of mounted riflemen at his own expense. He cabled his proposal to Prime Minister Wilfred Laurier, who readily agreed, but subject to the approval of the British War Office and the Canadian Militia Department. This was readily given and in March 1900 this homogeneous corps, being composed entirely of men from one region, left Canada on its way to South Africa. These contingents were required by the Canadian Militia Department to be commanded by their own officers. This was accepted by the British army, the only proviso being that General Buller as Commander-in-Chief would "retain a free hand to deal with the Brigade as he likes".[4]

Strathcona was a remarkable man, nearing 80 years of age in 1900, who had investments in the Hudson Bay Company as well as railroads, insurance and banking. He at first did not want his name to be associated with the project. However, it was announced in the Canadian press shortly after his "munificent offer" was accepted by the British War Office and the Canadian Militia Department. Strathcona wanted four hundred (later raised to five hundred) mounted men, all from the Canadian North-West, "proficient and experienced rough riders and rangers, unmarried, expert marksmen and at home in the saddle." Strathcona also insisted that all officer appointments must be approved by him personally. Unlike the previous contingents, Lord Strathcona's Horse possessed the status of a temporary unit of the British army.[5]

Strathcona had no reason to regret the appointment of Colonel Sam B. Steele to command Strathcona's Horse. Steele was 50 years of age in 1899 and had been a soldier or policemen from the age of 16. He was "an energetic, shrewd, tough, but diplomatic manager of men...with no regard for the stupidities of barrack square drill."[6] Many of the other officers were police inspectors from the North-West Mounted Police given the rank of Major or Captain. Horses were all from the Canadian North-West but many were lost on the voyage to Cape Town, so many in fact that someone unkindly christened the regiment Strathcona's Foot.[7] With remounts, they were sent to Natal to join General Buller's

---

[1] See, for example, Smith *The Origins of the South African War* p269: "Balfour was uneasy about the direction the direction which was being taken under the powerful influence of Milner..." concerning the situation that was developing in May 1899.

[2] Miller *Painting the Map Red* p52.
[3] "Black week" was the week when the British army suffered defeats at the hands of the irregular forces of the Boers at Stormberg, Magersfontein and Colenso on 10, 11 and 15 December 1899 respectively.
[4] Miller *Painting the Map Red* p50.
[5] Miller *Painting the Map Red* p289.
[6] Miller *Painting the Map Red* p291.
[7] Miller *Painting the Map Red* p305.

Natal Field Force. They made a serious impression on Frank Crozier, a Trooper in Thorneycroft's Mounted Infantry, who described them as "strange men in Stetson hats, big fellows all with brown boots and slightly different uniforms..."[1]

After the relief of Ladysmith, General Redvers Buller's Natal army moved forward early in May. They entered the Transvaal after battles at Botha's Pass on 6 and 7 June and Allemansnek on 11th. The advance guard entered Volksrust on the 12th, by the 22nd Standerton was occupied.[2] Strathcona's Horse joined the 3rd Mounted Brigade under Brigadier General the Earl of Dundonald during June. In effect Strathcona's Horse replaced the Natal Volunteers whose government did not permit them to operate outside the borders of the Colony. Colonel Steele insisted that his men were scouts, "doing any important work that experienced horsemen and good shots can do".[3] Steele insisted that they be engaged in scouting, outpost and patrolling work and not assigned to garrison duty.

On 1 July[4] Strathcona's Horse furnished a detachment, "A" and "B" Squadrons, to scout and do reconnaissance on the right flank of Lieutenant General Sir Francis Clery's 2nd Division. Clery had camped at Val (a station between Greylingstad and Standerton) the previous night and reached Greylingstad that day. Dundonald wrote that "the work of cavalry in this difficult country was arduous in the extreme; without the excitement of a general action there were daily losses."[5]

As regards what happened to the patrol that day, the Strathcona regimental diary is one of the prime sources. Troopers George Bowers and Robert Rooke also kept detailed diaries. There is also the account of C. England Cowan in *The Natal Mercury* of 26 July 1900. Miller's *Painting the Map Red* also describes the incident, quoting Colonel Steele's papers, evidently a letter or report to Lord Strathcona of 20 July 1900.

The regimental diary states that the weather was fine and that they marched at 7:30 a.m., "crossing the spruit at Smith's Store". This must have been the Waterval River. England Cowan says that "the column had stopped for a rest and a hasty lunch at noon when it was interrupted by two scouts coming in at the gallop."[6] Lieutenants Tobin and Kirkpatrick led their men towards a farmhouse that was flying a white flag, signifying that the farm was supposedly safe to approach. This would seem to have been Witnek. The men had been warned to be cautious about approaching the white flag. Boer patrols, perhaps unbeknown to the farm owners, made use of kraals and outbuildings for concealment.[7]

The Boers were concealed in an orchard and waiting for the Canadians to get close. One of Kirkpatrick's men, Trooper Angus Jenkins, was killed in the volley of fire and Sergeant Herbert Nichol's horse was shot and killed. A war correspondent wrote, "The Canadians charged the orchard and the Boers scattered."[8] The Strathcona diary puts it like this: "The troops under Tobin and Kirkpatrick (both Lieutenants) came under a fire directed from a rocky kopje and farm flying a white flag, on the right front. They retired a short distance under cover and the reserve moved up in support. In the meantime "A" battery Royal Horse Artillery shelled the position and the enemy retired." "Other patrols had similar, though less costly encounters that day. "A" Squadron's second-in-command, Captain Donald Howard and Jonathan Hobson walked into a party of Boers they mistook for Canadians and were both captured."[9] They had run into a patrol of General Ben Viljoen's force that was shadowing the British advance along the railway to Greylingstad. That night, according to Trooper Bowers, "there was some sharp firing on our left flank but no one was hurt."[10] Another version says that: "The Boers were pursued. "B" and "E" Companies T.M.I. finally caught up with them and a running fight went on for some distance until the Boers scattered."[11]

Dundonald had spoken to his men before they entered the Transvaal: "You have seen the devastation by the Boers in Natal. Don't go in for revenge. Respect the property of the Boers and pay for everything that you want." A week after they entered the Transvaal one of his men was killed on a farm though on it was flying a white flag – Trooper Angus Jenkins. Dundonald described it as murder "mostly by strangers to the locality and not by the farmer." Jenkins had been a "cowpuncher" according to his attestation papers before joining Lord Strathcona's Horse and was just 20 years of age.[12]

There are several accounts concerning the burial of Trooper Angus Jenkins. The Strathcona Regimental diary says that they "Bivouacked that night at Vitnek Farm near Wachout Spruit. Buried Jenkins in the garden of the farm. Lord Dundonald and Staff attended the funeral. They always do the right thing." Lieutenant-Colonel Sam Steele is not mentioned as attending the funeral but it almost inconceivable that he did not. Bowers' diary says, "Buried Jenkins in garden here" after writing that, "After firing had ceased we again moved forward and made camp at Washout Spruit about 4 miles further on."[13] Trooper Robert Rorke's account says, "We buried Jenkins under a tree in the garden of a farm at Waterval, not far from Val Station, where we camped that night."[14]

In the Garden of Remembrance in Standerton are a number of the red granite headstones made in Canada,

---

[1] Crozier *Angels on Horseback* p231.
[2] Maurice *History of the war in South Africa* Vol 3 pp281-284 gives details of these operations. See also Drooglever *Thorneycroft's "Unbuttoned"* pp172-76.
[3] Letter from Steele to Strathcona, 2 May 1900 quoted in Miller *Painting the Map Red* p312.
[4] 1 July was Dominion Day in Canada, commemorating the anniversary of the formation of Canada as a Dominion, joining Nova Scotia, New Brunswick and the Canada province (Ontario and Quebec) in 1867.
[5] Dundonald *My Army Life* p165.
[6] C. England Cowan in *The Natal Mercury* of 26 July 1900.
[7] Miller *Painting the Map Red* p313.

[8] C. England Cowan in *The Natal Mercury* of 26 July 1900.
[9] Miller *Painting the Map Red* p313.
[10] Trooper Bowers' diary entry for 1 July.
[11] Drooglever *Thorneycroft's "Unbuttoned"* p178.
[12] Dundonald *My Army Life* p165.
[13] "Vitnek" is how it is spelt in the Canadian diaries which is how the Afrikaans word "Witnek" (White Neck) is pronounced. The "Washout Spruit" is the "Oudehout" (Dutch) nowadays marked on survey maps.
[14] "Boer War Reminiscences of Trooper Robert Percy Rorke" p16.

shipped to South Africa and erected in this and many other places where Canadian soldiers lie buried. Trooper Angus Jenkins is so remembered in Standerton. Numbers of other casualties, including some Canadians, were buried in a small graveyard at Waterval and removed to Standerton in the 1960's re-interment program. However, the records of the National Monuments Council do not show Jenkins as having been one of them.[1] A letter from Angus Jenkins's father William dated 1902, just before the cessation of hostilities, is the result of a letter from the government asking if he has any objection to the erection of a monument on his son's grave.

What does seem very likely is that Jenkins's remains were moved at that time and reinterred in the graveyard at Waterval and subsequently reinterred once again to Standerton. As he was the very first casualty of Lord Strathcona's Horse, as well as the fact that the funeral was attended by a number of senior officers, the grave would have been very well marked. Although Jenkins's name does not appear on the War Graves Commission granite column in Standerton, it does appear on a Canadian monument in Bloemfontein giving a number of names of Canadian soldiers who have no known grave. We may never know the exact truth of the matter.

Lord Strathcona asked the Canadian Militia Department to recruit an additional fifty men and one lieutenant with horses and equipment to serve as reinforcements. Lieutenant Agar Adamson[2] was placed in charge of getting the recruits to South Africa and they reached Cape Town on 3 June. They joined the Natal Field Force on 2 July. Together with the South African Light Horse Regiment, whose reputation as men with scant respect for Boer property was well-known, they marched to Standerton. The rest of Lord Strathcona's Horse had moved on and was now at Vlakfontein, just south of Heidelberg. They only rejoined the rest of the regiment on 23 July at Zuikerbosch Spruit, near Heidelberg.[3]

The Canadians shared the outpost and picket duties with the S.A.L.H. and were in action on 5 July for the first time. As the advance guard of the S.A.L.H. in a movement to the north of Standerton they encountered small bodies of Boers who disappeared over the nearest ridge as the Light Horsemen approached. Adamson devised a plan: "The Canadians were to go forward in extended order, draw the Boers' fire, then withdraw while the Light Horse divided and took up positions on the flanks."[4]

Unfortunately the Boers had a similar plan and it was the Canadians who found themselves surrounded. Three of Adamson's men were wounded and Trooper Alex McArthur, wounded in the arm and hip and without a horse, was rescued by Sergeant Arthur Richardson. Richardson rode back on a wounded horse and under heavy fire to effect the rescue and was awarded the Victoria Cross for his gallantry. The clash took place north of Standerton along the Wolvespruit, in an area now largely under the water of the Grootdraai Dam.

Richardson was the first Canadian to win the award of the Victoria Cross and his fellow Canadians presented him with an award of £3,000 as a token of their esteem.[5]

Born in Southport, Lancashire, England he emigrated to Canada at the age of 20 in 1892. He worked as a rancher before joining the North-West Mounted Police. As a corporal he was recruited to join Lord Strathcona's Horse, but was not one of their initial choices, travelling to South Africa in the party of reinforcements, as related. Richardson was discharged in March 1901 with the rest of the men who were returned to Canada. He rejoined the N.-W.M.P. and rose to the rank of Sergeant-Major. He was for a time Town Constable of Indian Head, Saskatchewan.

However, in 1907 poor health forced him to purchase his discharge and, eventually, to settle in Liverpool, England, where he became a recluse. During this period, another man named Arthur Richardson, a corporal in The Gordon Highlanders, began passing himself off as the winner of the Victoria Cross. He succeeded so well that, when he died, he was buried with military honours. Ironically, the real Arthur Richardson, VC was discovered marching in the funeral cortège of his imposter. He died in Liverpool on 15 December 1932.[6]

References

1. George A. Bowers *The Diary of 446 Trooper George Alexander Bowers "C" Squadron #4 Troop Lord Stratcona's Corps, South Africa June 16th 1900 to March 2nd 1901* (unpublished).
2. Hedley Chilvers (editor) *The Times History of the War in South Africa* Vol V Sampson Low, Marston and Company, Ltd, London 1907.
3. F.P. Crozier *Angels on Horseback* Jonathan Cape, London 1932.
4. Mildred G. Dooner *The Last Post* J.B. Hayward & Son, Polstead, Suffolk 1980 (reprint of edition of 1903).
5. Robin Drooglever *Thorneycroft's "Unbuttoned" The story of Throneycroft's Mounted Infantry in the Boer War 1899 – 1902* Robin Drooglever, Melbourne, Australia 2011.
6. Lieutenant General the Earl of Dundonald *My Army Life* Edward Arnold & Co, London 1926.
7. Major General Sir Frederick Maurice *History of the War in South Africa* Vol 3 Hurst & Blackett Limited, London 1908.

---

[1] Watt *In Memoriam* p218 lists #509 Pte Jenkins, A, Lord Strathcona's Horse KIA (killed in action) Waterval Stn nr, Witnek 01-07-1900 Standerton (now interred in) U10 (Unknown, 1=name on main monument, 0= the Canada headstone) \Val\Witnek (originally buried at Witnek, re-interred at Val Station), B squadron.
[2] Adamson is noted for having been very critical of Colonel Steele, Commanding Officer of Strathcona's Horse. See Miller *Painting the Map Red* p303.
[3] Miller *Painting the Map Red* p319.
[4] Miller *Painting the Map Red* p318.

[5] Uys *Victoria Crosses of the Anglo-Boer War* p58. It would seem likely that the amount of the award was considerably less than this, a very substantial amount of money in 1900. One year's wages for an L.S.H. trooper would have been about £90.
[6] This paragraph from the National Defence and Canadian Forces internet site.

8. Carman Miller *Painting the Map Red: Canada and the South African War 1899–1902* Canadian War Museum, Ottawa Ontario & University of Natal Press, Pietermaritzburg 1993.

9. Robert Percy Rooke *Boer War Reminiscences of Trooper Robert Percy Rooke* (unpublished).

10. John Stirling *The Colonials in South Africa 1899-1902* William Blackwood & Sons, Edinburgh & London 1907 (reprint by J.B. Hayward & Son, Polstead, Suffolk.

11. Ian Uys *Victoria Crosses of the Anglo-Boer War* Fortress Financial Group, Knysna 2000.

12. Steve Watt *In Memoriam Roll of Honour Imperial Forces* University of Natal Press, Pietermaritzburg 2000.

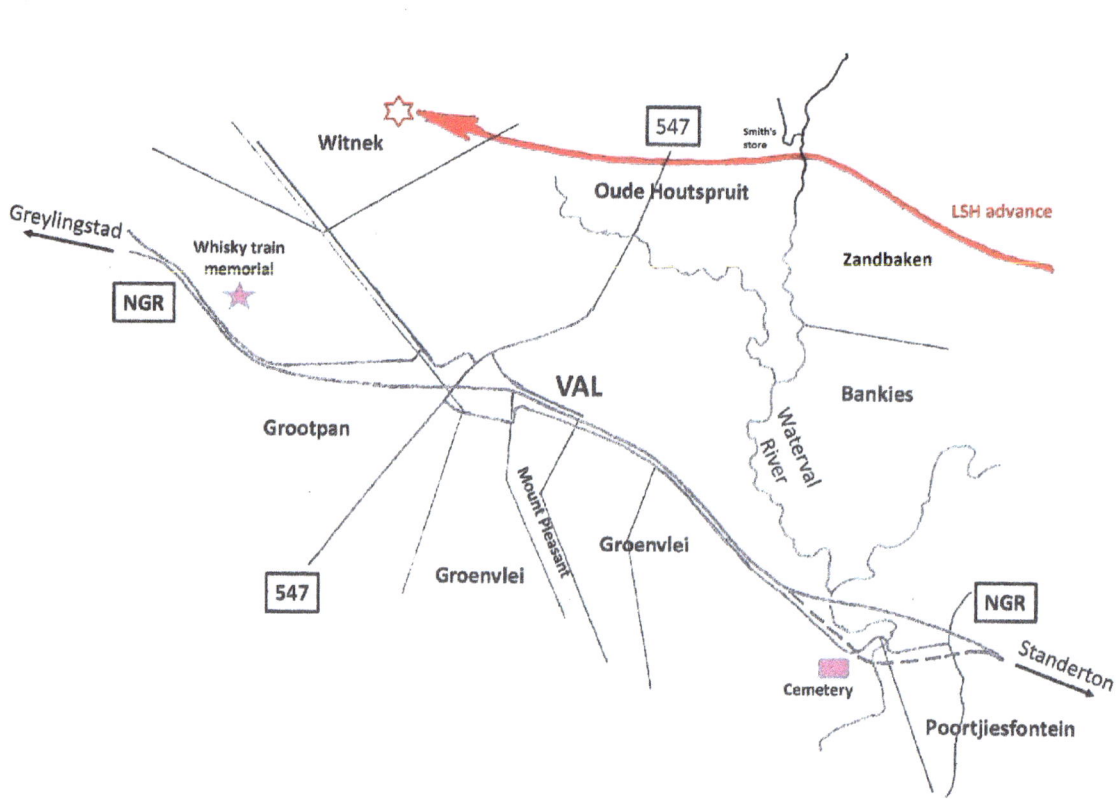

Val: The Canadian patrol crossed the Waterval River near Smith's store. This was landmark on the old wagon road from Standerton to Heidelberg and Pretoria. The plan of the Waterval cemetery, below, was discovered in the Archive in Pretoria and shows the cemetery itself with the names of the farms and the railway line as it was then – it has subsequently been rerouted and straightened. The pumping engine is shown, as are the water tanks, the foundations of which still exist. The names of those who died in the vicinity of Val, the last in July 1900, do not include Jenkins who was buried in the orchard at Witnek farm.

The diagram on the next page is the original survey drawing showing the location of Waterval cemetery. This is where the military graves in the area were consolidated before they were exhumed and re-interred in the Garden of Remembrance in Standerton cemetery.

Waterval Cemetery.

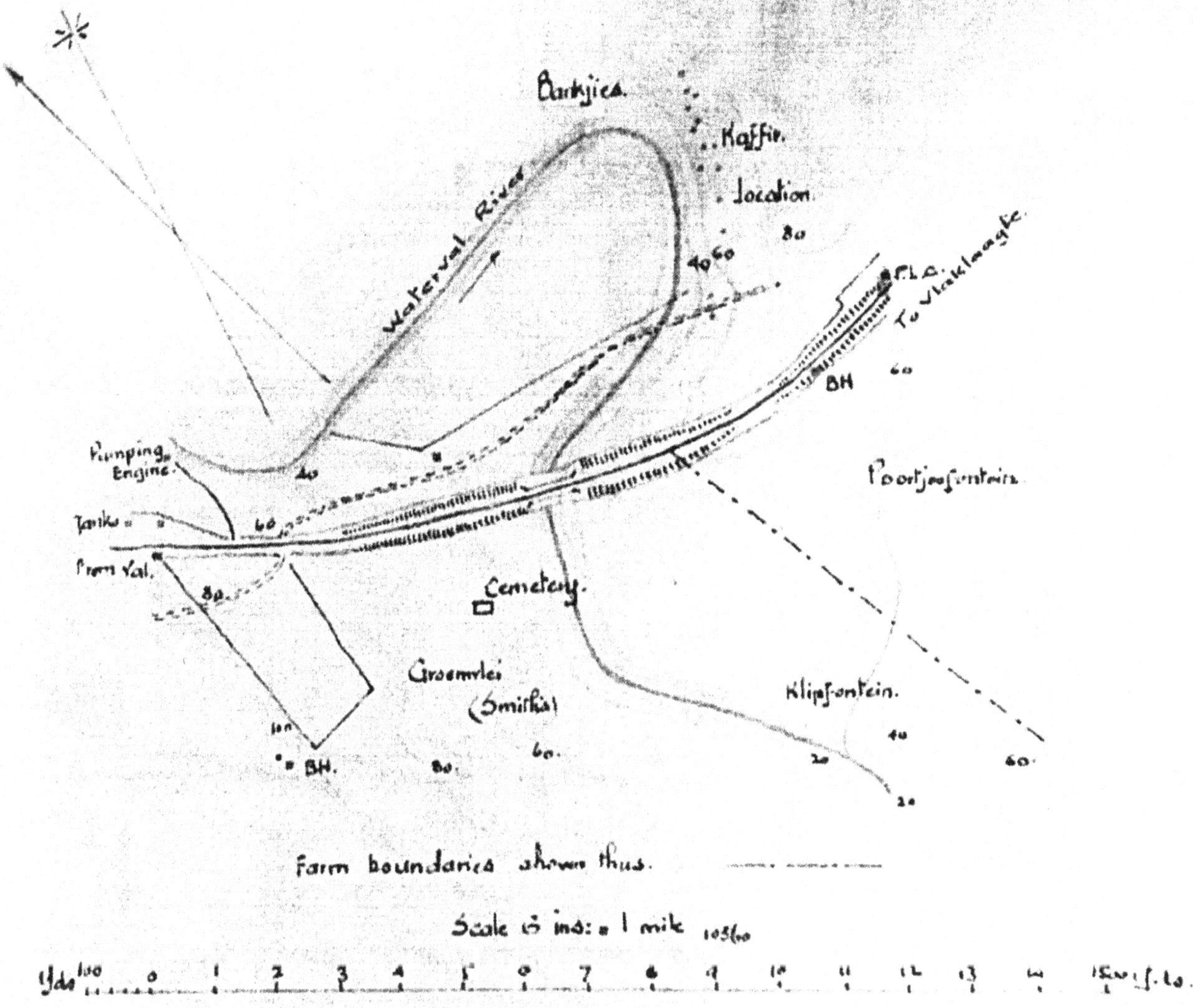

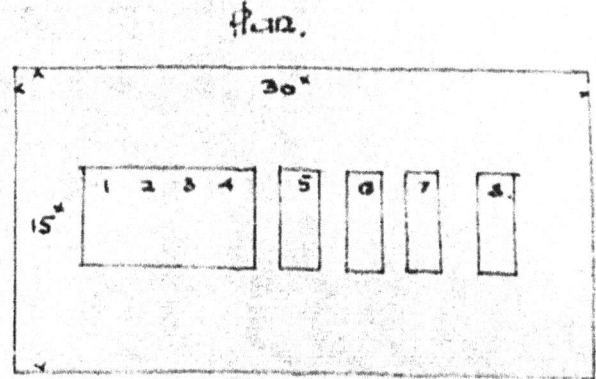

Farm boundaries shown thus. _____

Scale 6 ins: = 1 mile 105/60

Plan.

No: 1 Sergt. R. Jones   E. Cy. T.M.I.   Killed 6th Sept. 1900.   Stone cross over grave.
  2.   " W.C. Corbett E. Cy. T.M.I.   do.   do.
  3.   Tpr. H. Kannemeyer E. Cy. T.M.I.   do.   do.
  4.   " A. Oddy. E. Cy. T.M.I.   do.   do.
  5.   " A. Barden E. Cy. T.M.I.   do.   do.
  6.   Sergt. E.C. Parker C. Squadron Strathcona's Horse. Killed July 30th 1900. Wood cross.
  7.   Corpl. D.H. Lee   C   "   "   "   "   "   "   "
  8.   Sergt. J. Reid. S.A.L.H. Killed July 10th 1900. Stone Headstone.

Lord Strathcona's Horse: Trooper Angus Jenkins, Segeant Arthur Richardson and Trooper Jenkins's memorial headston in the Standerton Garden of Remembrance. The official headstone has omitted the name of the regiment but this has been corrected with an additional plaque.

Mafeking[1] – lifting the siege

Field-Marshal Lord Roberts' strategy was to capture the capitals of the Boer Republics as well as many of their principal towns. With these in British hands the Boers, he concluded, would be obliged to surrender or, at least, come to some arrangement to cease hostilities.

Boer strategy was clearly based on the false premise that, just as in 1880 after Majuba, the lack of political will to continue the struggle would cause the British to abandon the campaign. Hence, instead of a thrust for the coast, Joubert and Cronjé, the two senior Boer generals, settled down to besiege three important towns in British territory, Ladysmith, Kimberley and Mafeking. None of the three ever looked like being overwhelmed. Their elderly politician leadership could not countenance the inevitable heavy casualties that would have been the inevitable result of storming the towns' defence lines.

Relief of the three besieged towns would allow Roberts to take the initiative. By the end of February 1900 Boer forces had been driven away from Ladysmith and Kimberley but Mafeking was still surrounded. Access to the town from the south was not possible, the road from Kimberley vulnerable to incursions from Transvaal Boer commandos. The road and railway line from Kimberley ran close to the border of the Transvaal and what was then British Bechuanaland, annexed to the Cape in 1895. Boer command of the road was problematical to any relieving force and there was damage to the rail line.

About the only way into Mafeking was to land a force in Beira and transport them through Portuguese territory to Marandellas in Rhodesia. Thence to Bulawayo and the railway that led to Mafeking and further south. Much of the infrastructure was inadequate for rapid movement of large

---
[1] Mahikeng, formerly and still commonly known as Mafikeng and historically Mafeking in English, is the capital city of the North-West Province of South Africa.

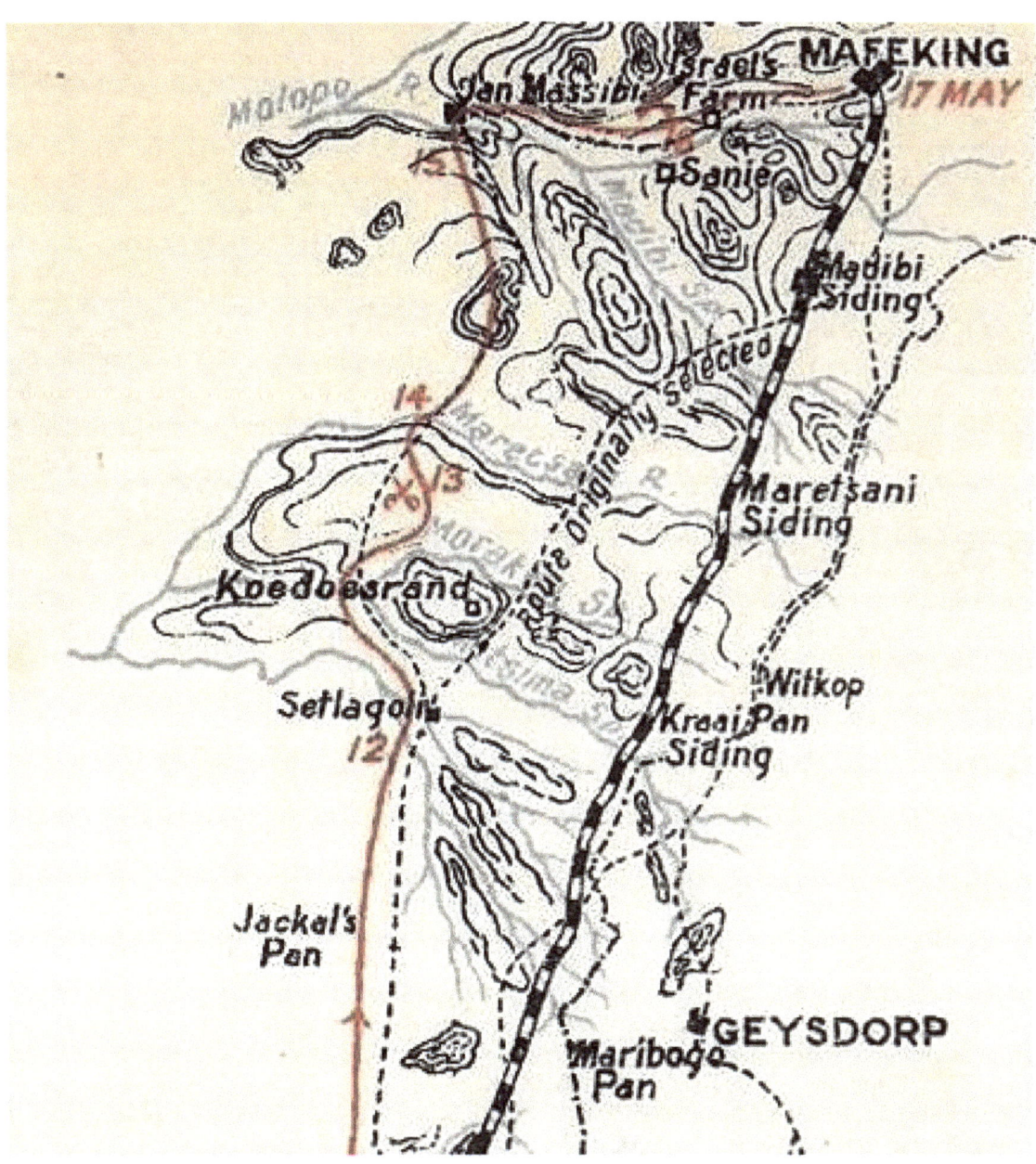

Colonel Bryan Mahon's approach to Mafeking – 12 to 17 May 1900.

numbers of troops, the only railway from Beira to Umtali was a narrow gauge line with very limited capacity. From Marandellas, closer to Bulawayo than Salisbury, the capital of the British South Africa Company's territory of Rhodesia, the only means of transport was by stage coach. It was May 1900 before significant numbers of Australian, New Zealand, Canadian and Yeomanry troops had reached Plumer on the outskirts of Mafeking.

Colonel Herbert Plumer, with a small force of Southern Rhodesian Volunteers and some British South Africa Company Police advanced southwards harried by Boers all along the line. From the south came a relief column composed of troops sent around from Ladysmith, the Imperial Light Horse and some infantry from the Fusilier Brigade, together with squadrons of Kimberley Mounted Regiment, no doubt pleased to be re-united with their horses. Colonel Bryan Mahon's column was all mounted, the infantry riding on mule wagons and they made rapid progress.

Plumer and Mahon combined, rode into Mafeking on 17 May 1900 and the siege was over. Colonel Robert Baden-Powell for seven months had inspired his small force to maintain an energetic defence. He was later to head what is now the largest non-political social organisation in the world, the Boy Scouts. Substantially outnumbered, he had kept his tiny garrison motivated and activated to resist constant sniping and at least one major attack for a period of seven months. No wonder there was great rejoicing around the British Empire when news of Mafeking's relief was announced.[1]

The I.L.H. Monument at Maritzani

(How Lance-Corporal Clifford Hill lost and found his comrade – the late Trooper Charles Gardner, both "reported missing" after the action of 14 May, on his way to the Relief of Mafeking – an extract from "The Story of the Imperial Light Horse" by G.F. Gibson.)

Prior to the Relief of Mafeking, a permanent squadron of scouts were appointed to act as such during the entire trip; Lance-Corporal Clifford Hill and Trooper C. Gardner were two of those special scouts.

Instructions to the scouts were that they were, if possible to avoid engaging the enemy and that the objective of the Column was the Relief of Mafeking. Night and day, with brief halts for rest, the force pushed on; at night the route of the column could easily be followed by a listening scout; there was the intermittent raucous call of the korhaan or lesser bustard which, when disturbed, rise screaming from the ground, and the deep rumbling of the four guns and that of the wagons could be heard some distance away.

On nearing Koodoos Rand, at midday on the 13th, the column had halted for a while, and "C" Squadron Scouts, just in from a spell of duty, were busy with brushwood, preparing their billies for tea, horses standing by. Hill, coming from an interview with the squadron officer, gave an order: "Put out the fires, get mounted," mounted his horse "Billy" (No. 54, a Basuto pony, allotted to him at Pietermaritzburg, where the regiment was formed) and rode off into the bush and found a spot where a more extended view was to be had. A quick survey revealed that a Boer force was closing in from the right with a view to getting positions ahead of the British column. He reported back to the squadrons, and the scouts began extending at intervals of from one to two hundred yards according to the density of the bush. The Column was now on the move and the scouts kept well out on the right at the same time taking care to keep in touch. Hill took up a position on the extreme right and about 50 yards on his left rode Gardner. About a mile or more on the left and somewhat in the rear was the main column. Just in front of the scouts and somewhat to the right, lay a bit of slightly higher ground with fairly extensive growth; this ran for some distance parallel with the line of march; suddenly, charging out of this in wild alarm, came seven hartebeest, with their characteristic loping bounce when going at full speed; they passed between Hill and Gardner, and "Billy," cocking his ears and straining at the bit, tried his level best to join in the chase. "No, gallant little horse, not yet."

Some movement was observed and it was now evident that the enemy were in ambush all along the ridge and that the scouts were well within range of their rifles. A message to that effect was sent back and the scouts remained halted and behaved as though they were ignorant of the proximity of the enemy. Back came a message "Push on." Forward trotted the scouts, and they had barely gone another 100 yards when the sudden crack of Mausers broke the stillness of that apparently peaceful afternoon.

Hill, lying low on "Billy's" neck, gave him his head and made for the squadron at full speed; all went well for some fifty yards when horse and man went crashing down; Hill found himself on his back with "Billy" across his legs. He lay there for some time and gradually the tumult and firing grew less; apparently the action was moving more left and away from the spot where the enemy were first encountered. All round Hill could hear the movement of horses and the voices of men, and then close by a voice in Dutch spoke, "Die een lê hier en die ander daar!" (One lies here and the other there!) A party of the enemy had come up and Hill was in their hands. "He is not dead," said one as he picked up the rifle which had shot from its bucket in the fall and lay close by in the grass. Hill remembered, as he fell, instinctively flinging the field glasses which he had held in his hands, into a patch of nearby shrubbery. As the men somewhat roughly began dragging at his bandolier and haversack, Hill said in Dutch: "No, not dead, not even wounded; and what sort of darned people are you that you handle a man in this way; can't you pull the horse off one first?" "Excuse!" was the reply as they rolled the horse off and a thought struck one of them: "Jy is ook een Afrikander?" (You are also an Afrikander?) "Yes!" was the reply, "English, not Dutch." "It was my shot that brought you down," said one. I could have killed you, maar ek het jammer gekrij (but I took pity on you) and shot the horse instead." The horse had been shot just behind the off shoulder and the bullet, passing through the heart had come out at the point of the near shoulder; the man speaking was evidently a noted big game hunter and apparently the crack shot of that group; was it pity or hunter's instinct behind that shot? "Thanks and good luck

---

[1] See *Baden-Powell* by Tim Jeal for a detailed account of the long siege of the town.

to you!" responded Hill. As the men were busily getting the saddle and bridle off, one turned angrily to Hill. "What have you done with your field glasses? I saw them in your hand when you were looking at us a little way back; where are they now?" "Don't know!" was the reply; "I certainly had verkijkers; they must have dropped while I was racing away." A little way off another group was busy over something in the grass, while another Boer was catching Gardner's horse which had remained near his master; Hill turned to the men near him; "I am going to see how it is with my comrade," he said, and walked off; no one hindered him. The Boers were turning my gallant comrade over, freeing him of his belt and belongings. "Is he dead?" asked Hill, "Yes!" said one, "quite dead. He has been shot through the heart. See for yourself." Heavy firing was still taking place somewhere to the left front, and a Boer officer rode up, giving orders to the men to hurry up and get ahead, at the same time he ordered two of them to take the prisoner back to their wagon; where those field glasses were ever found is not known, and soon that spot was left to Gardner and the dead horse, and there they remained for many months undisturbed. As the two men with their prisoner were retiring from the scene of action. a thought struck Hill: "See here, you two fellows, I have a few shillings on me, they will be of no use to me as a prisoner and will probably be taken from me at your camp, you have treated me well; if you want them you are welcome to them and nothing will be said about it." "Yes, thank you, we can do with them," and the cash promptly changed hands. Soon after, the halting place of the Boer Commando was reached, and presently it became apparent to Hill, from snatches of conversation he overheard and from the demeanour of the men, that the British column had succeeded in beating off the attack, and several dead and wounded Boers were brought in

It was now getting late when Hill was interviewed by a man who spoke very good English, and was said to be Adjutant to Commandant Liebenberg.

A. I want to ask you a few questions. Who are the I.L.H. and what do you think your column is trying to do?

H. Imperial Light Horse, we were at Elandslaagte and through the siege of Ladysmith, and have come round especially to join this column. We intend to relieve Mafeking.

A. You are late, we have already taken Mafeking.

H. You will not keep it for long, if that is so.

A. What is your particular work and what is the force?

H. I am an N.C.O in charge of squadron scouts, and I have not much chance of judging the numbers of our column as the scouts work ahead, on the flanks, and have very little to do with the column itself.

A. In other words you are a spy?

H. Nonsense, you know well enough the difference between a spy and a scout. I work with my squadron and always wear uniform.

A. Have you ever been in this part before? Do you know the country around here?

H. Never been here in my life.

A. What do you reckon the strength of your force is?

H. At a rough guess, something like two thousand.

A. Nonsense. We have positive information that you are only nine hundred strong.

H. Nonsense. If you know anything of our column you must know the units it is composed of; ourselves, the I.L.H., we consist of six squadrons, A, B, C, D, E, F. Each squadron numbers 130 men; then there are the Kimberley Horse, I do not know their strength, then the C.M.R., and Cape Police, and, as you seem to know all about us, there is the battalion of Infantry. Also guns, maxims and pom-poms.

A. Infantry! No Infantry could possibly keep up at the pace you are going.

H. They are not on foot, they ride on mule wagons.

A. You really think your column will get to Mafeking?

H. I don't think so. I *know* they will get to Mafeking; they are picked troops and you will not stop them.

Dismissed by the Adjutant, Hill saw a Cape cart in which sat a man, evidently a Britisher, and this was put in charge of the Guard. The man had been in charge of the equipment and outfit of one of the War Correspondents with the Relief Column; he had lagged behind and had been bagged.

It is an ill wind that blows nobody any good, and he provided Hill and the Guard with a good meal from his supplies and a blanket or two; the nights being extra-ordinarily cold. At dusk the Boer Column got under way. The prisoners were put in a wagon under guard.

Two Transvaal Police drove off with them in a Cape cart en route for Potchefstroom and Pretoria. One of the Police, named Rod, spoke English well, and as he had been in Johannesburg and struck on the names of one or two mutual acquaintances, they soon were on the best of terms. At Lichtenburg they stopped at the hotel, and Hill seized the opportunity of scribbling his name in the visitor's book. Later on, when the I.L.H. were passing through, one of them, by chance, looked through this book, and it was the first intimation they had as to the identity of the I.L.H. prisoner with the Boers (Both Hill and Gardner had been posted "missing"). They had ascertained from Boer information that one of the missing men was alive and a prisoner, but nothing more except "Hy was 'n parmantige kêrel!" ("He was a pugnacious kind of man"), and this did not help much as it did not describe either of the missing men.

On arrival at Potchefstroom the guards began to assume a distinctly military air and, for the first time, Hill, who had been treated more like an honoured guest than a prisoner, was put into a cell for the night. Next day, the journey was resumed by train and, after passing through Johannesburg, Pretoria was reached. For a few weeks Hill remained there a prisoner of war in a small enclosure, where the ground had more than a fair share of grey backed insects. He was then removed to the big camp at Waterfall and remained there about two weeks, when the entry of Lord Roberts' forces from the south brought about his release.

Hill now learned that his column, under Colonel Mahon, had successfully joined up with Colonel Plumer, and that the combined force had entered and relieved Mafeking without much difficulty, also that the information given him by the Boer Adjutant was not devoid of truth, as a few days before the relief, the Boers had attacked and actually captured one or two forts in Mafeking which they held for some time before they were themselves forced to surrender to the garrison.

At the first opportunity, Hill re-joined his Regiment in the Transvaal, and took part in the operations around Rustenburg and Warmbaths, and then on to Barberton and the mountainous country in that area.

Months had passed since the Relief of Mafeking, and reorganisation was taking place in the I.L.H. Many of the men were required for their work on the gold mines and others were returning to their normal occupations elsewhere. When Hill reported to the Orderly Room for his passport papers, one of the officers, probably the Adjutant, on duty referred to the affair at Koodoos Rand and remarked to Hill: "I see you are bound for the Cape and are detraining at Grahamstown. Gardner came from the Eastern Province; it is a sad thing for his people to realise that his body was never found." Hill let his mind wander back to that distant afternoon and place; he seemed once more to see the stampeding hartebeest, he felt "Billy" strain at the bit, he heard the outburst of rifle fire, felt the rush of the horse as he was given his head, saw the knots of Boers standing round the fallen horse and man; the whole scene was plainly before him; "If I can get near Kraaipan on the railway and find Koodoos Rand, and if any trace of the bodies remain, I will find the spots where they fell," he remarked. The matter was soon arranged, and armed with official letters and a passport, he started off by rail through the Transvaal and Free State, and up again through Kimberley, past Vryburg, and eventually reported to the military post nearest to the scene of the late engagement. The O.C. Post seemed to think the whole thing rather a wild goose chase, and that Hill would probably run into a party of Boers known to be hanging around that vicinity, when the Post would be minus a horse; however, Hill got mounted and pushed off the same afternoon on a rough track into the back country and made for a farmhouse where the owner and his wife were still in residence, as he had been informed at the Post that he could probably get some first-hand information as to direction, etc.

At Wright's farmhouse he was informed that no Boers had been around for some time, and so decided to spend the night there, and the owner said he would accompany him in the morning to the actual scene of the fight, but held out very little hope of success as the neighbourhood had been searched thoroughly. It was soon apparent to Hill that the scene of the heaviest engagement was not near the spot he wanted, and after riding through the bush for about two miles, he began to sense that the country seemed familiar; yes, surely that bit of rising ground was the line held by the Boers, and if so he must be very near to the object of his search; he would ride on a line along which he estimated he was galloping that day and had scarcely covered fifty yards when, lying in the grass, all in a heap, he came on the skeleton of a horse with hoofs intact; on the near fore-hoof, clearly visible were the letters I.L.H., No. 54.; he had found the remains of his horse "Billy", and not far away he found the complete skeleton of his dear old comrade, Gardner, in exactly the same spot. The remains were reverently taken to the farmhouse where Hill again stayed the night, and next day he returned to a somewhat anxious but much astonished Post Commandant, and handed over all that was left of his comrade for proper burial. A granite monument now marks the spot near Kraaipan.

The Western Transvaal after the Relief of Mafeking

With Mafeking relieved and the railway line north and south from there now reasonably secure, attention was given to pacifying the western Transvaal and establishing a supply route from Mafeking to Johannesburg and Pretoria. Lieutenant-Colonel Herbert Plumer occupied Zeerust but he was soon sent off to Pretoria to command a mounted column. For a while Zeerust was governed by British Prime Minister Lord Salisbury's son, Lord Edward Cecil, now released from his enforced stay in Mafeking.

While there was some skirmishing in the area and a few casualties were suffered, a number of them buried in Zeerust, by and large the western Transvaal burghers had returned to their homes and farms. Among the casualties was Captain Samuel Hübbe, commander of the 3rd South Australians – before the war he had been a notable explorer of the Australian outback. Baden-Powell, now promoted Major-General, advanced to Rustenburg and then moved further east to Pretoria once the Transvaal capital was occupied. He was given command of mounted troops who swept north of the city but the Boers at this time were dispirited and in no mood to continue the war.

Things were soon to change. After the Boer reverse at Diamond Hill, Commandant-General Louis Botha instructed General Koos de la Rey to leave the main army and take his commandos to the west. De la Rey himself attacked a British outpost guarding a pass over the Magaliesberg at Silikaat's Nek and overwhelmed them on 7 July. The Magaliesberg range of mountains stretches west from Pretoria and for much of its length can only be crossed at places where there is a pass (or *poort* in Afrikaans). These gaps in the mountain barrier became important in the actions which were to continue in the west from now until the close of the war, nearly two years later.

De la Rey sent Commandant Hermanus Lemmer with a small commando, mostly of Rustenburg men, to recapture that town which was defended only by Major Hanbury-Tracy with a small garrison of Australians and some policemen. Lemmer found it difficult to recruit men for his commando, the prosperous Rustenburg burghers were unwilling to leave their comfortable homes and farms. Lemmer tried to capture the British strongpoint, the Landdrost's office, and failed. He then led his men further west over the Magato Nek, another of the gaps in the Magaliesberg, establishing a base on the farm Woodstock. There his commando attacked supply convoys making their way from Zeerust via Elands River (today's town of Swartruggens) to Rustenburg.

At Elands River the British had established a base around the water supply and wagons were halted there until the road to Rustenburg had been cleared. This is what a force of 300 Australians in Rustenburg was ordered to do by Baden-Powell who had returned to take command of what was now becoming a serious problem as de la Rey and his much larger force had arrived in the area. De la Rey's force was growing as he was able to persuade many of the burghers to dig up their buried rifles and rejoin their commandos.

The supply route was never established as the 300 Australians came to grief when attacked by Lemmer's small commando at Koster River on the farm Wysfontein. Shortly after this the British base at Elands River was besieged by de la Rey and his men. The siege took a fortnight and the need to relieve them was another headache for Lord Roberts.

Maritzani: The I.L.H. obelisk and the inscription which can be seen along the #18 main road just south of the Kalgold mine.

Koster River or Wysfontein

22/23 July 1900

> He's a tracker and trooper branch and root
> And he'll want a bit of beating
> When he grants the Boers a meeting
> And he'll show 'em how to ride and shoot.[1]

As many as 20,000 Australians fought in the Anglo Boer war of 1899-1902. When the population of Australia was little more than 3,500,000, a total of 16,175 volunteers were accepted to fight in South Africa. The services of as many again were turned down. Unsuccessful applicants in considerable numbers made their way to the Cape and Natal to join the ranks of the colonial forces. All the volunteer regiments from the Cape Colony and Natal had large numbers of Australians in their ranks. This was due to the influx of Australians who in pre-war days lived and worked in South Africa. Public opinion supported the policy of the various colonial governments to show loyalty to Britain, their mother country. The first contingents offered were little more than a token effort. Most Australians thought that the 1,200 men who sailed into the Indian Ocean in the first convoy on their way to the Cape would have little direct military effect.[2]

British reverses at Colenso, Magersfontein and Stormberg in December 1899 "stirred the Australian and New Zealand colonies to a fresh pitch of patriotic fervour."[3] Second contingents were raised, like the first, from the militia army regiments of the various colonial governments. The Imperial Government was now expressing a preference for mounted men rather than infantry. However, an idea was mooted in Sydney for a force of 500 Bushmen, sponsored by public subscription, to be sent to the war. "It supported the widespread belief that...stockmen and drovers, with a background and training...similar to the Boers themselves" could well match the Boers in the irregular warfare that was being waged.[4]

Impressive sums were soon raised from all sections of the community and there was "a rush to enlist despite warnings that only genuine bushmen need apply". Their abilities were tested and the average age of the Bushmen was higher than that of the earlier contingents reflecting the selection of only experienced rural men. In 11 weeks 1,400 men around Australia were enlisted, drilled and equipped in what were Citizens' Bushmen units, one squadron each from South and Western Australia, two each in Victoria and Queensland, four in New South Wales and half a squadron from Tasmania. Only those from New South Wales used the designation "Citizen Bushmen".[5]

There were very few suitable officers, almost no Australian had lived in the bush and also commanded soldiers in wartime. The New South Wales commandant, Major-General George French, chose Lieutenant-Colonel Henry Airey to command their contingent, an artilleryman nearly 60 years of age but with service in India and Burma. From Western Australia Major Harry Vialls was appointed, 40 years of age and with service in India and Afghanistan. The South Australian commander was Samuel Hübbe who had once commanded a militia unit. However, he had been crossing the dry centre of Australia for the last thirty years, finding routes and clearing land.[6] About 1,100 men embarked at the various Australian ports, the transports with the Citizens' Bushmen arrived in Cape Town early in April. After spending the better part of a month in the cramped conditions of the troop ships, they did not disembark in Cape Town but were sent on to Beira in Portuguese East Africa.

On 17 May 1900 the Boer siege of Mafeking (today Mahekeng) was relieved by British forces coming from Rhodesia and a column from Kimberley to the south. The column from the south, under the command of Colonel Bryon Mahon, consisted mostly of horsemen, the Imperial Light Horse and the Kimberley Mounted Corps. Infantry, only 100 of them divided evenly between fusilier regiments from England, Scotland, Ireland and Wales, rode on the 60 mule wagons comprising the transport. "M" Battery of the Royal Horse Artillery made up the balance of a powerful, mobile flying column, altogether about 1100 men.[7]

From the north came Colonel H.C.O. Plumer with a column hastily put together from the meagre forces in Rhodesia,[8] less than 500 men. They were mostly policemen of the B.S.A.P. and soldiers of the Rhodesia Regiment together with some untrained Southern Rhodesian Volunteers. They had tried to relieve the beleaguered town before Mahon's column had arrived but were driven back by the Boers.[9] On 14 May some welcome reinforcements arrived from Bulawayo in the form of 100 men of the 3rd Queensland Mounted Rifles escorting four guns of "C" Battery of the Royal Canadian Artillery.[10] Three days later, the combined columns drove away the Boer besiegers and the longest siege of the war was at an end. After the town was relieved, numbers of Australian Bushmen units arrived down the railway from Rhodesia.

There had been a threatened Boer invasion of Rhodesia in the early months of the war. However, Plumer's

---

[1] Rhyme from contemporary newspaper in Umtali (now Mutare)
[2] Details of all those who served in the Anglo Boer War in contingents from the various states are detailed in Murray *Official Records of the Australian Military Contingents to the War in South Africa.*
[3] Wallace *The Australians at the Boer War* p231.
[4] Wallace *The Australians at the Boer War* p232.
[5] On the day that most of the Citizen Bushmen were embarking, the Colonial Secretary, Joseph Chamberlain, telegraphed to the Premier of New South Wales asking for a further 2,000 men of the same class as the Bushmen. They were required for general service in South Africa and the British Government undertook to bear all the costs of raising and sending the force. These were the Imperial Bushmen Contingents, better trained and disciplined than the Citizen's Bushmen units and raised in all six colonies. Wilcox *Australia's Boer War* p38.
[6] Wilcox *Australia's Boer War* p36.
[7] *The Times History* Vol IV p216.
[8] Today Zimbabwe – in this context it makes no sense to write "Zimbabwe".
[9] Wilson *With the Flag to Pretoria II* p593.
[10] Miller *Painting the Map Red* pp 181-84.

operations in the Tuli Block had resulted in the Boer commandos being withdrawn.[1] Plumer moved down with what forces could be spared from Rhodesia and was tasked with an attempt to relieve Mafeking. The Australian Bushmen Contingents and a Canadian artillery battery were intended to be reinforcements for Plumer. At that time, with Kimberley still besieged, the only way for them to get to Mafeking was through Rhodesia and along the railway line which ran down the eastern side of Bechuanaland.

The voyage to Beira went well and by 11 April four ships carrying the Australian volunteers were anchored off the port. The British Government had negotiated with the Portuguese to use the port to enable men and materials to be sent across their territory into Rhodesia. Beira, at that time was a fairly new town with buildings mostly constructed of corrugated iron. The Portuguese administration welcomed the men with a reception, and a garden party for the officers and a ball that night.[2] There were twelve hotels and bars in Beira, the scene of frequent rollicking impromptu concerts.

Major-General Sir Frederick Carrington arrived from England at the same time to take command of the Rhodesian Field Force. He was a soldier with great experience in southern Africa, from the wars in the Transkei, the Anglo-Zulu War of 1879 and Warren's expedition to Bechuanaland in 1884-85. In 1893 and 1896 he had command of the forces in Rhodesia during the troubles with the Matabele.

From Beira to Rhodesia was a railway of sorts, one section having a gauge of 2ft 6ins, served by only six locomotives. It took some considerable time before all the Bushmen were transported the 350 miles to Marandellas in Rhodesia. The climate of the Portuguese coastal strip was unhealthy for men and horses and there were heavy losses from malaria and horse sickness. The Canadians and their four guns were a priority and so they together with the 3rd Queensland Mounted Infantry[3] and the New South Wales Citizen Bushmen and their officers were the first to reach the Marandellas rail terminus on 20 April.[4]

The journey of the Canadian artillery battery, accompanied by 100 dismounted troopers of the 3rd Queenslanders under the command of Major C.W. Kellie was continued to Bulawayo by stagecoach drawn by mules. The next leg to Mafeking was by rail with a great sendoff from Bulawayo – "the whole town turned out to see us off, and we were escorted to the train by the Police band."[5] They were in Ootsie, north of Mafeking, as far as the train would go, on Friday 11 May, and marched the final 80 miles to Plumer's camp. Advancing with Plumer and Mahon the Queenslanders and Canadians then took part in the operations leading to the relief of Mafeking on 17 May.[6]

Once Mafeking was relieved, Colonel Plumer led a composite Colonial force to Zeerust, about 30 miles inside the Transvaal border. The town surrendered without a fight and various Bushmen units kept arriving from Bulawayo, the New South Wales Citizen unit narrowly missing the entry into Mafeking with the relief force. Colonel Robert Baden-Powell marched into the Transvaal and by 14 June was in Rustenburg. Pretoria fell to Lord Roberts on 5 June and a week later the Boers were driven away from the east of Pretoria after the battle of Diamond Hill.

In the western Transvaal all seemed quiet and peaceful. The Bushmen swept through the country east of Zeerust and with the fall of Pretoria the burghers seemed to be more than willing to lay down their arms. Captain J.F. Thomas, a small-town lawyer from Tenterden in New South Wales and later the defendant of Breaker Morant, said that: "For the most part they seem to be heartily glad that the war is drawing to a close and that they are back on their farms again. But I fear that nothing like the proper number of Mauser rifles are handed in. There are Martini-Henris, Westley-Richards and other out-of-date weapons, even old flint-locks, but the much-prized Mausers are far scarcer than they should be."[7]

Lord Roberts now believed the west to be thoroughly pacified and ordered Baden-Powell to make a sweep north of Pretoria along the railway line. The only British presence in Rustenburg was the B.S.A. Police under Lieutenant-Colonel C.O. Hore and a few New South Wales Bushmen. The presence of so few troops was interpreted by the citizens of Rustenburg as a sign of the direct interposition of the Almighty in response to their prayers. In the Dutch Reformed Church the text of the service was: "Wait patiently for the Lord, who will shortly drive out your enemies from amongst you."[8]

With the area pacified it seemed that a supply route could be established from the railway at Mafeking via Zeerust and the drifts over the Elands River to Rustenburg. At the drift over the Elands River there was just a store in 1900, the small town of Swartruggens came much later. On high rising ground to the east a fortified depot was established with a good commanding position of the surrounding country.

There was a Boer *krygsraad* at Balmoral after the reverse at Diamond Hill and Botha instructed General Hermanus Lemmer to head back to Rustenburg and persuade the burghers in the districts of Lichtenburg, Marico and Rustenburg to leave their farms and return to the commandos. On his way there, Lemmer fell in with the small remnant of 130 Rustenburgers under Commandant Caspar du Plessis. On 3 July Baden-Powell, now at the British base of Rietfontein northwest of Krugersdorp, ordered the New South Wales Bushmen to retire to Zeerust. The Union Jack still flew from the Landdrost's office as the column with 40 wagons left Rustenburg in a severe thunderstorm on 5 July.[9] Only 60 policemen were left under the command of Major A.H.C. Hanbury-Tracy which Lemmer immediately saw as an opportunity to recapture the town.

---

[1] Burrell *Plumer's Men*
[2] According to Australian Nursing Sister Isobel Ivey. Wallace *The Australians at the Boer War* p237.
[3] "Although designated as Mounted Infantry, the 3rd Queensland were recruited as, and referred to, as Bushmen." Harvey *Letters from the Veldt* p47.
[4] Harvey *Letters from the Veldt* p50.
[5] Harvey *Letters from the Veldt* p52.
[6] Harvey *Letters from the Veldt* p53.
[7] Quoted in Wallace *The Circumstances Surrounding the Siege of Elands River Post* p10.
[8] Quoted in Wallace *The Circumstances Surrounding the Siege of Elands River Post* p13.
[9] Wallace *The Circumstances Surrounding the Siege of Elands River Post* p17.

Lemmer had had some difficulty with those Rustenburgers who had signed the oath of neutrality with the British and were sitting on their farms. He was unsuccessful in his attempts to recruit more men from those who had already decided to surrender.[1] On 7 July Lemmer nevertheless called on Hanbury-Tracy to surrender even though he had but a small group of men under his command. The New South Wales Bushmen were nearing Zeerust when the call came for them to render assistance back in Rustenburg. They arrived back there in time to drive the Boers away with Commandant du Plessis being killed and five Boer prisoners being taken, all of whom had British protection passes in their pockets. Major Weston-Jarvis of the Rhodesia Regiment said, "I hope to goodness that they will shoot the lot…it would stop the nonsense once and for all."[2]

As a result of this attack, Baden-Powell arrived back in Rustenburg with a force of 1,500 men. General Koos de la Rey, whom Commandant General Louis Botha had put in command of the western Transvaal, followed Lemmer westwards. He had only a small number of men with him but together with Commandant P.F. Coetzee's 300 men they overwhelmed the British defenders of Zilikaat's Nek on 11 July. A squadron of the Scots Grays and eighty-four men of the Lincolnshire Regiment surrendered.[3] The Boer victory, "although not very important in itself",[4] had the effect of convincing large numbers of Boers that, having sinned by signing the British oath of allegiance, their "only true repentance was to violate that sinful oath"[5] and go back on commando. Within weeks there were commandos forming all over the western Transvaal.[6]

Lemmer's men now occupied Olifants Nek after his abortive attempt to occupy Rustenburg. He was driven away by a column under Lieutenant-General Lord Methuen assisted by Baden-Powell coming from Rustenburg on 21 July. Lemmer himself moved to the west and laagered on the farm Woodstock. There he was engaged in what he had been sent to the western Transvaal to do – encourage the burghers in the district to rejoin their commandos. Some of his men were sent to occupy positions which commanded the road from Rustenburg to Zeerust. At Elands River a number of supply convoys now were unable to proceed any further. This was the main supply route to Rustenburg and stocks were low. The Boers had cut the telegraph line and the smoky atmosphere from grass fires made heliograph communication very difficult.

Two Rhodesian Regiment cyclists had made their way unmolested from Elands River to Rustenburg at about this time. The decision was therefore taken to send 150 loaded wagons along that road on 17 July. The Elands River garrison had an anxious wait to hear whether the convoy had arrived safely and it is a mystery why there was no interference from the Boers.[7] On 20 July two men, Troopers MacDonald and Albert Gould set out at midnight with despatches for Baden-Powell. The bicycles were camouflaged so that nothing bright would glint in the bright moonlight. At Koster River the Boers had lit fires in a big laager off the road on the far side of the drift. The two cyclists paddled across the river and continued on, only to be forced off the road by another group of Boers. They passed through Magato Nek, occupied by fellow Bushmen, and arrived in Rustenburg in time for breakfast.[8]

Now that the two cyclists had located the Boer laager, Baden-Powell issued orders for a force of Bushmen to clear the road from Elands River. Supplies and a garrison had been building up there, unable to continue along the road to Rustenburg. Three hundred men of the Australian Bushmen contingents were sent back along the road to clear Lemmer's men away.[9] The Bushmen had seen little action up to now.[10]

They set off in the dark in the evening of 21 July, somewhat sullen that they were missing their sleep and covered the eight miles from Mogato Nek in about four hours. Colonel Henry Airey was in command with Lieutenant-Colonel Holdsworth, a 7th Hussars officer on special service in Rhodesia, as his second-in-command. They were required to bring in a convoy from Elands River when once they had dealt with the Boers. The advance guard, some distance in front of the rest of the column, was fired on as they came over a small rise and approached a stream called the Rooipoeier Spruit.

It was just about midnight, the troops were dismounted and told to maintain their extended formation until daylight. A big Western Australian with a tremendous yawn, voted: "Fighting a damn nuisance…at this hour of night!"[11] Once it was light a detour was decided upon. The column moved off the road to their right. There was more apprehension that the Boers would evade a clash than any serious concern that they were in any danger. They crossed the Rooipoeier Spruit a little downstream past its confluence with the Koster River, turning once again, this time to their left, which meant crossing the Koster River. Just before they crossed what was little more than a trickle at that time of year, they picked up another road leading back to the main road from Rustenburg. The occupants of a large Boer farmhouse at the crossing watched them as they passed by.

---

[1] Smuts *Memoirs of the Boer War* p93 says that "All through the war the Rustenburgers had been somewhat refractory material."
[2] Wallace *The Circumstances Surrounding the Siege of Elands River Post* p19.
[3] Maurice *History of the War in South Africa* Vol 3 p240.
[4] Smuts *Memoirs of the Boer War* p92.
[5] Smuts *Memoirs of the Boer War* p86.
[6] One source says that soon "No less than 7,000 were in the field" but gives no source. Wallace *The Circumstances Surrounding the Siege of Elands River Post* p14.
[7] Wallace *The Circumstances Surrounding the Siege of Elands River Post* p29 suggests that "the timing…of the uncontested passage coincided with some difference of opinion among the commandants."
[8] The account of the two cyclists is told in A.S. Hickman *Rhodesia Served the Queen* and is quoted in Wallace *The Circumstances Surrounding the Siege of Elands River Post* p31. Baden-Powell issued a Special General Order commending the "gallant conduct of Troopers McDonald and Gould…"
[9] The force consisted of 300 men from New South Wales, Queensland, Victoria and Western Australia.
[10] Wilcox *Australia's Boer War* p109: "Four squadrons strong, no regular officer in command, no regular troops to slow them down – here was the Bushmen chance to teach the Boers how to ride and shoot."
[11] From the account of Bert Toy, war correspondent with the Western Australians, quoted in Chamberlain and Drooglever *The War with Johnny Boer* p280.

Turning towards the west along the main road they now entered a small valley. The road led to another crossing of the Koster River and rising ground on the other side. To their left was a scrub-covered koppie, to the right the ground sloped down to the river. Not far from the river was an abandoned farmhouse. The advance guard spotted a considerable number of Boers on their left but Airey told them to push on towards Elands River. Trooper Gould and his Raleigh were pointing out the location of the Boer laager. Airey was with the advance guard but he now led the New South Wales squadron to the right away from the main road. A message to Captain Richard Echlin ordered him and his Queenslanders to keep to the main road. They had passed the koppie on their left when the Boers, hidden in the scrub opened fire. Only one man was hit and one horse. The Australians quickly dismounted and formed a line to the left of the road.

There was no cover at all except for the long grass. The Bushmen could only lie flat and the first man hit was a Queenslander, Bugler Herbert Keogh. When they heard firing on their right flank and left rear they "showed uneasiness", but Echlin and his officers thought they could hold out until darkness would give them a chance to escape. Some, unable to move, fell asleep and one even made the wry comment, "I wonder if the bastards will stop for dinner?"[1] Trooper Gould jumped into a donga but then decided to ride on and managed to get half a mile along the road to Elands River. Then he ran into some Boers, threw his bicycle into the bush and crawled back to his fellows in the river bed.

The horse holders led the horses away to the north, five to a man, but it was the horses which were a prime target for the Boers' sharpshooting. They were taken down to the river where there seemed to be at least some cover. Most of them were killed during the morning as some Boers appeared on the north side of the river. Numbers of horses stampeded and ended up with the Boers. Some of the horse holders attempted to pacify the unmanageable horses and several managed to mount and ride away, some ending at Elands River and some taken prisoner by the Boers. According to Lieutenant Charles Brand, 3rd Queensland: "…in ten minutes only fifteen horses were alive out of the 250…"[2] Trooper William Cowley, 3rd Western Australian Bushmen: "The whole place was covered with dead and dying horses…"[3]

The Boers were invisible and their Mausers had smokeless ammunition. The Australians at first tried to fire a few volleys but these had no effect. With nothing to fire at, for some hours they lay flat in the grass, any movement provoking a shower of bullets. Captain Echlin found a small ditch and managed to get some of the wounded to shelter. Colonel Airey took shelter in the abandoned farmhouse which was a makeshift hospital and numbers of Queenslanders and New South Wales men also used the ruined mud walls as cover. Some of the Boers advanced to a hedge on the eastern side so that fire was coming from three sides. With ammunition running short, a young bugler, Arthur Forbes, ran out from the farmhouse and ransacked the saddle wallets on a number of dead horses.[4]

At some time during the morning a young girl by the name of Emily Back arrived at the farmhouse looking for medical assistance. She had attended to the wounds of a Victorian who had been injured in the stampede of the horses. The soldier had made it to the farm Woodstock where Emily was a teacher at their school. Seeing the other wounded around the farmhouse and further afield she rendered assistance to a number of these, all the time under heavy fire.[5] There is mention too of a Miss McDonald but it seems that she remained at Woodstock with the wounded man.

The Boers had first put the Australians under fire at about 8 a.m. and as the time went by there were shouts for Airey to give orders. No orders came and Major Harry Vialls of the Western Australians at the end of the line and now the closest to the Boer position on the koppie, decided to take the initiative. It was about 2 p.m. "Get together what men you can and we'll charge the hill!" he told his officers. The charge was made by a series of short rushes and the Boer trenches were overrun. At about the same time, reinforcements from Rustenburg came into sight under the command of Captain Charles FitzClarence whose Protectorate Regiment fired a number of volleys at the Boers now retreating to the south.[6]

Colonel Airey sent several notes by orderly to Major Vialls. Apparently these notes suggested a surrender as Airey and Holdsworth had decided that, with all their horses killed and ammunition running short, their force would be unable to hold out until dark. They had no white flag and so they improvised one with five white handkerchiefs knotted together. It was fortunate that the Boers did not catch sight of this symbol of surrender and take advantage. Vialls received three messages from Airey telling him that they were to surrender, the third message being "a peremptory intimation that orders must be obeyed" whereupon Vialls marched down the slope and confronted Airey to inform him that his men had captured the main Boer position.[7]

Lieutenant-Colonel Lushington who led the relief force, arrived a half hour before sundown. He was loath to remain any longer than necessary. Wounded horses were despatched by revolvers under the fire of a few determined Boer snipers. Lushington did not pursue Lemmer's Boers fleeing southwards. Dark was approaching and he was required to shepherd the survivors back to Rustenburg. Thus orders were given to undertake the march back to Magato's Nek and Rustenburg. Only about thirty were mounted. Not all the horses had been killed – the Boers claimed to have

---

[1] Quoted in Wilcox Australia's Boer War p110.
[2] Harvey Letters from the Veldt p64.
[3] Quoted in Coetzee Emily Back and the action at Koster River p4, a letter dated 29 July 1900 written from Magato's Nek.
[4] Harvey Letters from the Veldt p67. Forbes was awarded the D.C.M. The citizens of Brisbane presented him with a silver bugle and a purse of sovereigns.
[5] Smuts Memoirs of the Boer War p96 says that the Boers "would not fire on a woman."
[6] Smuts Memoirs of the Boer War p95, no admirer of Baden-Powell, says that in his response to urgent calls for reinforcements, Baden-Powell sent "small driblets which each in turn suffered the fate of the force they were sent to relieve." Doubtful, there is no record of such small actions.
[7] Report by Bert Toy quoted in Chamberlain and Drooglever The War with Johnny Boer pp289/90.

captured as many as 100 but that still left 170 dead horses on the field. It must have been a trying march, eight miles to Magato Nek and another four into Rustenburg. Echlin said that "the last four miles told, the poor chaps were rolling and staggering like drunken men. They did not trouble about supper and slept the sleep of the just until daylight."[1]

The body of Captain Claude Robertson of the New South Wales Citizen Bushmen was taken to Rustenburg and buried in the old cemetery. True to tradition, the rankers were buried near the ruined farmhouse to be reinterred in Rustenburg in 1905. The human casualties were comparatively light in relation to the losses among the horses. The Boers' objective was clearly to eliminate their enemies' mobility for now they were surely trapped. However, Lemmer did not have enough men to risk an assault on the Bushmen lying prone and virtually invisible in the long grass.[2] A young Boer, Lodewyk Botha, who had been wounded and ended up being captured, told his captors that "there were about 1,000 Boers" and they had the Bushmen surrounded. The Boers thought that there was a trap being prepared for them because the Bushmen were keeping so still.[3]

The battlefield today is easily identified at the Moedwil School along the N4, west of Magato's Nek. A monument to Emily Back has been erected within the school grounds to recognize what Jan Smuts called "one of the bravest deeds of the war."[4] Baden-Powell recognized her contribution and wrote to the Chief of Staff in Pretoria asking him to "bring to the notice of the Field-Marshall Commander-in-Chief the gallant conduct of Miss Back during the engagement at Koster River on 22 July 1900." This letter never reached its destination as it was intercepted by the Boers. However, Smuts said that: "This recommendation I felt happy in saving from the wreck of his (Baden-Powell's) intercepted correspondence and in subsequently presenting to the girl..."[5] The original letter is now a part of the collection of Mr A.C. Houston, her grandson.

On the crest of the koppie occupied by part of the Boer force is another small monument which has sadly been vandalized. It is a short climb to get to the top but there is today a great deal more bush in the area and the landmarks are no longer visible or easily identified.

Two weeks later the camp at Elands River was attacked, surrounded and besieged by De la Rey and a much larger commando than Lemmer had at Koster River. Defended by 505 Australians and Rhodesian Colonials they held out for twelve days in horrendous conditions and their heroic defense has rightly overshadowed the clash at Koster River.

---

[1] From the official account of the battle by Captain Richard Echlin quoted in Chamberlain and Drooglever *The War with Johnny Boer* pp293. Smuts *Memoirs of the Boer War* p96 says that the Australians "arrived hatless, breathless and with bleeding feet."
[2] Smuts *Memoirs of the Boer War* p95.
[3] Letter from Private A.M. Davies quoted in Chamberlain and Drooglever *The War with Johnny Boer* pp292. It is unlikely that Lemmer's force amounted to much more than 100.

[4] Smuts *Memoirs of the Boer War* p96.
[5] Smuts Memoirs of the Boer War p96.

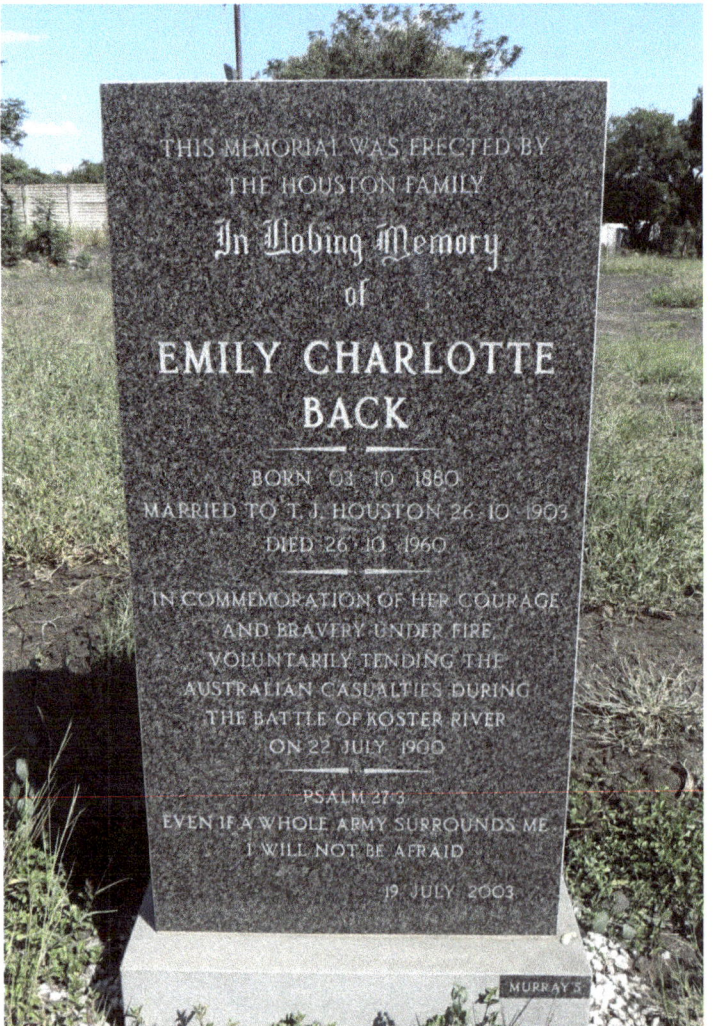

The monument to Emily Back in the grounds of the Koster River School.
(Peter Scholtz photo)

Casualty List
BRITISH
Killed

	Name	Unit	Status	Date
	Captain Claude William Robertson	NSWCB	KIA	22.07.00
	Lieutenant John Leask	3QMI	DOW	28.08.00
404	Sergeant David Hamilton Pruden	3VB	KIA	22.07.00
395	Sergeant Herbert John Goodman	3VB	KIA	22.07.00
320	Trooper Robert Cameron	NSWCB	KIA	22.07.00
418	Trooper Samuel Joseph Oliver	3VB	KIA	22.07.00
488	Trooper Henry Oliver Walford	3VB	KIA	22.07.00
518	Trooper Norman Campbell	NSWACB	DOW	
432	Lance-Corporal James McLure	3VB	DOW	26.07.00
440	Trooper John Irwin McCartney	3VB	DOW	31.07.00

Severely Wounded

	Name	Unit
	Surgeon-Captain Frederick John Ingoldsby	3WAB
287	Corporal James Blair	3QMI
540	Lance-Corporal John James William Errol Peters	3VB
191	Trooper George Matthew Jorgenson	3QMI
476	Trooper William Harris	3VB
6	Trooper William Oliver Jones	3WAB
20	Trooper Jeremiah Scott	3WAB

Slightly Wounded

	Name	Unit
	Lieutenant John Davies	3WAB
	Lieutenant Arthur Eckford	NSWCB
	Lieutenant Richard Henry Walsh	3QMI
76	Private George Augustus	3WAB
141	Lieutenant Felix Bernard Theodore Koch	3QMI
284	Trooper George Richard Forrest	3QMI
193	Bugler Herbert William Keogh	3QMI
182	Trooper Thomas Walters	3QMI
174	Trooper James Delore	NSWCB
431	Trooper John Kennedy	3VB
455	Trooper William Woods Anderson	3VB
381	Trooper Lilford Thomas Butler	3VB
383	Trooper Sydney Benjamin Brooker	3VB
400	Trooper J. McCastle	3VB
500	Private William Henry Bastian	3VB
15	Private Edmund Cox	3WAB
52	Private Joseph Leeson	3WAB

Taken Prisoner

439	Trooper A. Hayes	NSWCB
255	Trooper A. Wise	NSWCB
223	Trooper G. Woodley	NSWCB
64	Trooper J.W. Hewitt	NSWCB
528	Trooper C. Gardiner	NSWCB
384	Trooper S. Rowley	NSWCB
17	Trumpeter A.H. McKoy	NSWCB

Missing

| 561 | Trumpeter Harry Haycroft | 3VB |
| 85 | Trooper Charles Allen Lyons | 3WAB |

BOERS
Killed

P.W. Venter; C. Malan; J. (Fanie) Viljoen; Spencer R. Drake; D.S. du Toit; S.F. Malan.
The names of the following appear on the monument at Koster River:
P.W. Venter; C. Malan; J. Viljoen; Spencer R. Drake.

Wounded
4 men.

Prisoner
Lodewyk Botha   Son of Commandant J.D.L. Botha.

References

1. L.S. Amery *The Times History of the War in South Africa 1899-1902* Vol IV London 1906.
2. Robert S. Burrell *Plumer's Men: The Rhodesia Regiment and the Northwest Frontier and the Second South African War 1899-1902* Just Done Productions Publishing Durban 2009.
3. Edited by Max Chamberlain and Robin Drooglever *The War with Johnny Boer – Australians in the Boer War 1899-1902* Australian Military History Publications 2003.
4. P.C. Coetzee *Emily Back and the action at Koster River / Rooipoeier Spruit: A Tribute to a Brave Woman* Pretoria July 2003.
5. Len Harvey *Letters from the Veldt: An account of the involvement of Volunteers from Queensland at the war in South Africa (Boer War) 1899-1902* Maryborough Family Heritage Institute and the Maryborough Sub-Branch Returned Services League of Australia, Maryborough, Queensland. 1994.
6. Maj-Gen F.W. Maurice *History of the War in South Africa* Vol 3 Hurst and Blackett *Emily Back and the action at Koster River* Limited, London 1907 (reprint by The Naval & Military Press Limited)
7. Carman Miller *Painting the Map Red: Canada and the South African War*. Canadian War Museum, Ottawa and University of Natal Press, Pietermaritzburg 1993.
8. Compiled and edited for the Department of Defense by Lt-Col P.L. Murray *Official Records of the Australian Military Contingents to the War in South Africa*, reprint by The Naval & Military Press Ltd, Sussex 2007.
9. Major A.W.A. Pollock *With Seven Generals in the Boer War – A personal narrative.* Skeffington & Sons, London 1900.
10. Geoffrey Powell *Plumer: The Soldiers' General* Leo Cooper, Barnsley 1990 (reprint Pen & Sword 2004).
11. Captain S.E. St Leger *Mounted Infantry at War* Adam & Charles Black, Soho Square, London (reprint Galago Publishing, Alberton 1986).
12. Raymond Sibbold *The War Correspondents: The Boer War* Jonathan Ball, Johannesburg 1993.
13. Jan Smuts (Edited by S.B. Spies & Gail Natrass) *Memoirs of the Boer War* Jonathan Ball, Johannesburg 1994.
14. R.L. Wallace *The Australians at the Boer War* The Australian War Memorial and the Australian Government Publishing Service, Canberra 1976.
15. R.L. Wallace *The Circumstances Surrounding the Siege of Elands River Post* Robert L. Wallace Wollstonecraft N.S.W. 1992.
16. Craig Wilcox *Australia's Boer War* Oxford University Press (in association with the Wallace Australian War Memorial) 2002.
17. H.W. Wilson *After Pretoria: The Guerrilla War I* Harmsworth Brothers, Limited London 1902.
18. Lionel Wulfsohn *Rustenburg at War: The story of Rustenburg and its citizens in the First and Second Anglo-Boer Wars* Rustenburg 1992.

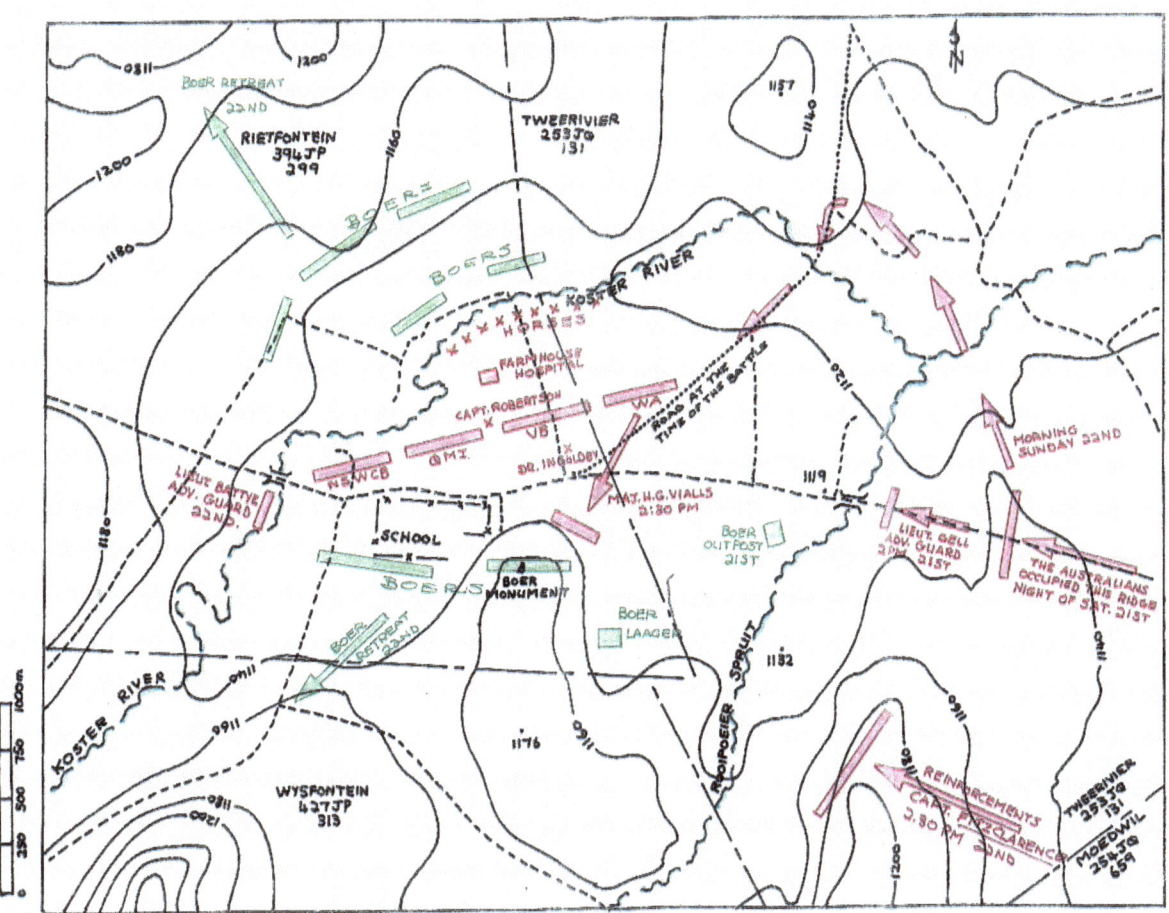

Map from P.C. Coetzee *Emily Back and the action at Koster River*

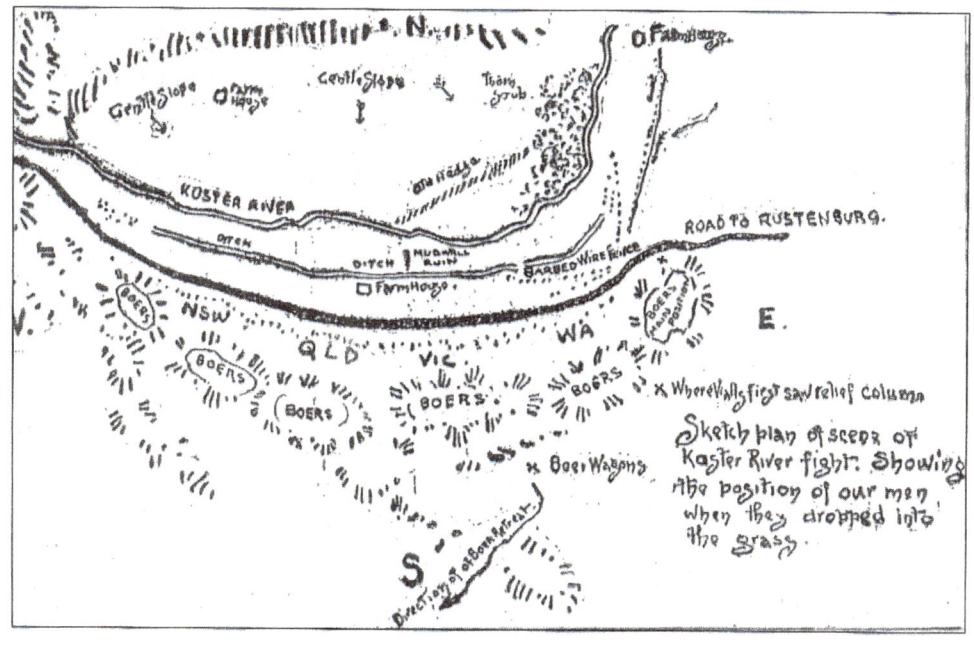

KOSTER RIVER (JULY 1900)

Map from Chamberlain and Drooglever *The War with Johnny Boer*

The First de Wet Hunt

With Pretoria occupied, Lord Roberts now attended to the remnants of the Boer armies of the Z.A.R. and the O.F.S. Large numbers of Transvaal commandos were clustered along the ridges to the east of Pretoria and the battle of Diamond Hill was fought on 14 and 15 June 1900. Roberts, with thousands of soldiers dispersed to guard the vital railway lines from Durban and the Cape, outflanked the Boer from the south and sent his cavalry under Major-General John French to Kameelfontein at the northern end of the line of ridges. The Boers were driven away to the east and there was skirmishing throughout July east of the Transvaal capital. Roberts awaited Buller's advance through the eastern Transvaal before moving east himself in force.

The Boers unwisely decided to defend a line at Bergendal along the edge of the escarpment just east of the town of Belfast. They were no match for the large force that the British brought against them. From now on the war became for the British army a struggle with irregular bands of Boers who descended on railway lines, small outposts and any weak point that offered some prospect of success, however minor. A coordinated strategy between the two Boer republics never really evolved and, beyond an abortive invasion of Natal by a commando led by Louis Botha and a more successful foray into the Cape by Jan Smuts, there was only a determination by the Boer leaders to continue the conflict to the bitter end.

In the advance northwards from Bloemfontein the Orange Free State commandos, those who were still in the field after Paardeberg, had made their way into the Brandwater Basin. This was an area south of Bethlehem and west of Fouriesburg which is surrounded by mountains and hills on all sides but where there was ample grazing and water was plentiful. The main British force had by-passed that area although there were garrisons in Kroonstad and Lindley.

General Christiaan de Wet was now Chief Commandant of the Orange Free State. In April, east of Bloemfontein at Sanna's Post, he had cut off the British from their water supply and captured a large number of their supply wagons. Continuing south he enjoyed another significant success at Mostert's Hoek outside Reddersburg where a strong contingent of Royal Irish Rifles surrendered after being surrounded and bombarded, trapped on a rocky outcrop. The vulnerable single railway line, Roberts's only supply line for Bloemfontein, should surely have been his next objective. But de Wet turned east instead, following his heart rather than his head. The garrison of the town of Wepener, on the border with Basutoland, was comprised principally of men of the colonial regiments, the Cape Mounted Rifles and the Kaffrarian Rifles. De Wet considered these men to be fighting against their own people, the Boers.

These Colonials had moved across the river from the town to a position overlooking the Jammersberg Drift. All De Wet's attempts to take the position were in vain. Boer burghers, essentially civilian volunteers, could not sustain the high casualties that an all-out assault would have entailed, just as happened at Ladysmith, Kimberley and Mafeking. Guerrilla fighters do not attack (or defend) fixed positions, surprise is their principal weapon. After a number of days of surrounding the Jammersberg position, the advance of a relief force, Major-General Brabant's Colonial Division from East London, caused the Boers to make off to the north.

There was action around Lindley but British forces pushed the Boers back into Bethlehem which was soon evacuated. De Wet and his men then joined the other Free State commandos clustered together in the Brandwater Basin where confusion reigned. Although General Christiaan de Wet was Chief Commandant of the Orange Free State, the Boer system required that a *krygsraad* (council-of-war) be convened. A decision for further action had to be approved in such a meeting with all officers present. Should the British block the several passes that were the only escape routes then the Boers would have little alternative but to surrender. De Wet was not content to sit idly by while this happened and he took his men and their transport out of the Brandwater Basin through Slabbert's Nek to the west which had not yet been blocked by the advancing British columns. With him were 2,000 men and 400 wagons and carts so that he and his followers covered quite a stretch of road. For the British, searching for him. The decision was whether this mighty host was headed west or north, and north seemed the least likely direction for him to be heading.

The remaining Boers (Commandant J.H. Olivier and his men had escaped via Naauwpoort Nek) were unable to decide who was to take over command in the absence of the Chief Commandant. The British were now attacking and would soon break through. The thrusting Major-General Archibald Hunter had taken command and it was a time of crisis for the Boers as Marthinus Prinsloo and the Reverend Paul Roux argued. A message was sent to Hunter asking for an armistice until such time they had elected a leader. Hunter naturally refused such a bizarre request and Prinsloo, hastily elected leader, decided therefore that surrender was their only possible course of action. The surrender took place near the modern town of Clarens and perhaps as many as 4,000 burghers laid down their arms. The British made a bonfire of the rifles and ammunition and there remains a bare patch on the hillside to this day where the grass will not grow.

De Wet was by now far away and it was several days before Colonel Robert Broadwood's scouts eventually caught sight of their quarry. On 20 July Christiaan and his younger brother Piet parted company when Piet expressed his doubts as to the ability of the Boers to continue the struggle. Piet surrendered at Kroonstad and eventually took up arms against his own people as leader of the National Scouts. The Boers split into two or even three lines to reduce the length of the column and managed to keep ahead of their pursuers. They made for the rugged area of the northwest Free State, west of the town of Vredefort, and holed up on the farm Rhenosterpoort.

There seemed to be no escape as British columns converged on his hiding place but somehow de Wet found a hole in the cordon, crossed the Vaal River at Schoeman's Drift and managed to find his way out to the north and into the Transvaal. Pursued by Major-General Lord Methuen's column, de Wet managed to evade his pursuers and cross the Magaliesberg. The Orange Free State President, Marthinus Steyn, headed off with a small commando to consult with President Kruger. In a most remarkable exploit, de Wet managed once again to evade his pursuers and cross the Magaliesberg at a place where only baboons crossed and return to Rhenosterpoort.

Crocodile Drift – The End of the First de Wet Hunt

19 August 1900

In the casualty lists and two of the references quoted below are the names of two New Zealand soldiers killed at Crocodile Drift on 19 August 1900. The casualties were Lieutenant H.H. Bradburne and Trooper L. Perham, both killed, and Trooper J.J. Hersley wounded, of the 3rd New Zealand Mounted Rifles.[1] They were members of the New Zealand 3rd Contingent sent to South Africa, and had arrived in East London on 26 March 1900.[2]

They joined the Colonial Division under Major-General E.Y. Brabant and participated in the relief of Wepener in April. After some actions in the southern Orange Free State they took part in the advance on Johannesburg and Pretoria and fought at Diamond Hill, east of Pretoria in June. They were employed in patrolling around Pretoria until in August they were attached to a column under the command of Lieutenant-General Ian Hamilton.

Hamilton was given a column of no less than 7,600 cavalry, mounted infantry, infantry and artillery with orders to contact Major-General Robert Baden-Powell and evacuate his force from Rustenburg.[3] The fortifications at Olifants Nek, occupied by Colonel Robert Kekewich, were also to be destroyed and abandoned. A garrison was to be left at Commando Nek so as to hold that passage through the Magaliesberg. The column marched along the south of the Magaliesberg with Brigadier-General Brian Mahon's mounted troops to the north of that range. Mahon's force was somewhat obstructed and Hamilton decided to cross to the northern side. He made the crossing at Zilikaat's Nek which was held by a Boer commando under Commandant Hansie Coetzee but probably not more than 300 or 400 strong.[4]

After marching along the road on the north of the Magaliesberg, Hamilton was returning to Pretoria. He had arrived at Wolhuter's Kop and camped on the farm Bokfontein on 6 August. Colonel Robert Baden-Powell's troops had evacuated Rustenburg and joined Hamilton as did Colonel R.G. Kekewich a day later. He was ordered to abandon and demolish the defences at Olifants Nek. The Magaliesberg is impenetrable and can only be crossed at a few places. Silikaat's Nek and Commando Nek were now both strongly held but Olifant's Nek and Magato's Nek were unoccupied.

Late on the night of 8 August news was received that Christiaan de Wet's Boer force, made up of Free Staters and a few Transvaalers from Potchefstroom, was moving northwards from the Vaal River. De Wet had broken through the cordon of British columns that surrounded his bivouac at Rhenosterpoort. He crossed the Vaal River at Schoeman's Drift on Monday 6 August, evading a number of columns chasing and trying to intercept the Boer convoy as it made its way northwards.[5] There were no British troops between Commando Nek and Mafeking (except for the besieged garrison at Elands River). De Wet's force was the only large Boer force operating in the Free State and to destroy or disperse it and capture its famous leader was of the highest priority.

That night Hamilton, at Bokfontein, received a message from Lord Roberts. Roberts was concerned that De Wet was moving so rapidly that he feared the British columns chasing him would not be able to overtake him. Roberts had very little reliable information as to De Wet's whereabouts, knowing only that he was heading north. Hamilton moved his force, as ordered, over Commando Nek to Grootplaats where he was advised not to move further in case De Wet turned eastwards in an attempt to join Louis Botha's Transvaalers. De Wet crossed the Krugersdorp-Potchefstroom railway line between Frederickstad and Welverdiend on 10 August and veered to the southwest in order to join up with General Piet Liebenberg's commando of western Transvaalers. It was clear therefore that Hamilton's force must move to the west but it also allowed Methuen to close the gap.[6]

Major-General Lord Kitchener, who had been sent to the Free State by Roberts at the end of July to take charge of the pursuit, was following behind with four more columns.[7] These were the columns of Hart, Broadwood, Little and Ridley.[8] There were now some 18,000 British troops north of the Vaal River.[9]

---

[1] Only officers are shown in Dooner *The Last Post* which lists on p36 Lieutenant H.H. Bradburn. Bradburn and Perham are listed in *The South African War Casualty Roll* both shown as killed in action.
[2] Hall *New Zealanders in South Africa* p35. New Zealand was the first of the Dominions to offer troops for the war against the Boer Republics of the Transvaal (the *Zuid-Afrikaansche Republiek*) and the Orange Free State to be soon followed by the six Australian colonies and then Canada.
[3] Hamilton's force was made up of Brigadier-General B.T. Mahon's mounted forces and Brigadier-General G.G. Cunningham's infantry brigade with three batteries of artillery. Maurice *History of the War in South Africa* Vol 3 p336.
[4] On 11 July a British force, five companies of the Lincolnshire Regiment, a squadron of the Scots Greys and guns of 'O' Battery

R.H.A. had surrendered to a Boer commando. See Maurice *The History of the War in South Africa* Vol 3 pp238-40. Coetzee, then Field Cornet, fired the first shot of the war when he fired on the armoured train at Kraaipan on 11 October 1899.
[5] This is the so-called First de Wet Hunt, which is well-described in Williams *The Times History of the War in South Africa* Vol IV pp414-428, Maurice *History of the War in South Africa* Vol 3 pp335-356. Pretorius *The Great Escape of the Boer Pimpernel* pp111-209 has the most detailed account.
[6] Maurice *The History of the War in South Africa* Vol 3 p330.
[7] Kitchener at that time held the rank of Major-General, thus Lieutenant-General Lord Methuen was his senior.
[8] Maurice *The History of the War in South Africa* Vol 3 p425. See sketch map by Methuen in Miller *Lord Methuen and the British Army* p203.

It was now clear that De Wet was not making for Commando Nek – but he could be breaking to the west to join De la Rey. Lord Methuen, heading the pursuit actually had De Wet's column in sight at times but was delayed by the Boer artillery and by a false report that the Boers were holding a strong defensive position just ahead.[1] De Wet gained a few hours and the pursuit was further delayed by a faulty report from the British intelligence officer at Krugersdorp. He reported wrongly to Pretoria that De Wet had tried to cross the railway line at Welverdiend but had been attacked by Major-General Smith-Dorrien's 19th Brigade. Methuen now had a fix on De Wet's position and, leaving behind his infantry, advanced with his mounted troops, 600 Imperial Yeomanry and a further 600 men of the Colonial Division.[2]

On Sunday 12 August Methuen's 78th Battery R.H.A., who were following hard on the Yeomanry's heels, opened fire on the rearguard at Modderfontein and recaptured a 15-pounder gun which turned out to be the same gun lost by Major-General Gatacre at Stormberg during Black Week in December 1899. The Yeomanry pressed the Boers very hard and their bombardment of the rear of the convoy caused a number of British prisoners to be released, including four Lieutenants who had been captured on 21 July when Danie Theron captured a train at Serfontein Siding on the Bloemfontein-Pretoria railway line. The prisoners had much information of military importance to impart to Methuen, that the Boers numbered about 4,000 and that they had plenty of Mauser ammunition but were short of artillery shells. Both sides' animals and men were totally exhausted and Methuen called a halt for the night on the farm Doornplaats.[3]

The Boers however continued on, reaching the farm Leliefontein later that night.[4] By sunrise on Monday 13 August the rearguard was at Middelfontein while De Wet and the vanguard had veered to the west as if making for Magato's Nek, further north than Olifants Nek, camping for the night on the farm Roodewal on the Selons River. That same day Methuen reached Leliefontein and followed De Wet's tracks, unaware that he had split from the rearguard. Methuen bivouacked for the night at Rietfontein on the south side of the Witwatersberg.

On 11 August Hamilton was advised by Roberts to move to Hekpoort but his unwieldy column made it only to Bultfontein while Mahon's mounted men were a little further along at Hartebeestfontein. The Magaliesberg west of Commando Nek as well as Rustenburg and Potchefstroom were no longer in British hands. Roberts's advice to Hamilton was false, as we have seen, and Hamilton failed to appreciate that De Wet was in fact making a bee-line for Olifants Nek, now vacated by the British. Hamilton chose to ride along the south side of the Witwatersberg allowing him a better view of the country around rather than close up to the Magaliesberg. Convinced by Roberts's obsolete information, he thought that by taking this route his column would head off De Wet's force somewhere near Tafelkop.

On the morning of 14 August Hamilton's column was approaching Zandfontein, 40kms from the Nek, but De Wet at that time had left his camp on the Selons River and reunited with his rearguard at the foot of the Magaliesberg. Methuen's scouts had a brush with De Wet's rearguard at Buffelshoek in the early morning.[5] As far as Methuen knew, Olifant's Nek and Rustenburg were strongly held by British troops. He had also been advised that Hamilton was on his way there. De Wet was now being driven towards Olifants Nek where he would surely be surrounded and captured. But by the afternoon De Wet and his commandos, wagons, carts and oxen were over Olifants Nek and safely outspanned on President Paul Kruger's farm Waterkloof.[6]

Reports that De Wet "had crossed the mountains by Olifants Nek but these were absurd – we (the British) held the Nek." Unfortunately it was true and "poor Methuen was quite overcome."[7] The men were exhausted, 16 horses had to be destroyed and supplies were low so that pursuit was out of the question. Hamilton with Mahons' mounted men recaptured the pass on 17 August after an exchange of fire with some Boer commandos. Methuen attacked Magato's Pass on 15 August, driving away General Piet Liebenberg's men who then rejoined De Wet now free to move north of the Magaliesberg.

De Wet decided that Waterkloof was not likely to be a safe haven for much longer. The Boers moved to the east, keeping well clear of the Magaliesberg and headed towards Zoutpansdrift, camping at Krokodil Drift, the site of the present town of Brits. While encamped there, the decision was made that President Steyn should be escorted through the bushveld so as meet with President Paul Kruger, then said to be running the Z.A.R. government from a railway carriage in Machadodorp on the Pretoria-Delagoa Bay railway.[8] The Free Staters were concerned that the recent setbacks to the Transvaalers had caused them to become dispirited and Steyn's counsel was needed to keep them fighting. He was accompanied by some of the Free Staters and a few men of the Pretoria commando including Dietlof van Warmelo who had been scouting along the Magaliesberg. They were driven out of Rustenburg by the arrival of Methuen's column on 15 August.[9]

Most of De Wet's men were sent north to the bushveld where they could rest and allow their horses to recover some strength.[10] The first De Wet hunt was not yet over as he now found that he was trapped north of the Magaliesberg. De Wet retained with him General Philip Botha and Commandant Michiel Prinsloo with 200 men. Captain Scheepers and his scouts were retained and together with his staff they numbered altogether 246 men.[11] Looking for a way to cross

---

[9] Maurice *The History of the War in South Africa* Vol 3 p422.
[1] Pretorius *The Great Escape of the Boer Pimpernel* p145.
[2] Maurice *History of the War in South Africa* Vol 3 p351.
[3] Pretorius *The Great Escape of the Boer Pimpernel* p164.
[4] Pretorius *The Great Escape of the Boer Pimpernel* p173.

[5] Miller *Lord Methuen and the British Army* pp206-7. See also Howland *The Chase of De Wet* pp171-81.
[6] Pretorius *The Great Escape of the Boer Pimpernel* p185.
[7] Miller *Lord Methuen and the British Army* pp207. Quote by Methuen's Chief of Staff, H.E. Belfield.
[8] De Wet *Three Years' War* p146 says that President Steyn left the Krokodil Drift laager on 14 August but it must have been about two days later, the 16th.
[9] Van Warmelo *On Commando* p52 does not give a date.
[10] De Wet *Three Years' War* p144 and Pretorius *The Great Escape of the Boer Pimpernel* p191 uses the De Wet reference, has more detail but does not indicate the source.
[11] De Wet *Three Years' War* p147.

the Magaliesberg so as to head back to the Free State they first tried Silikaat's Nek which De Wet clearly thought was still held by General de la Rey's men after their capture of the pass on 11 July. Hamilton had recaptured the Nek on 6 August, as related, and left a strong garrison in place.

De Wet camped near Wolhuter's Kop on 17 August and next tried Commando Nek, the next feasible crossing place, which was strongly held.[1] It was at Commando Nek that De Wet sent a message to the British commander of the occupying force claiming that he had 2,000 men and eight guns, demanding the surrender of the post. Baden-Powell well understood the ruse and Lieutenant-Colonel C. Barter, in command of the King's Own Yorkshire Light Infantry, professed not to understand its meaning. He replied asking whether he was required to surrender to De Wet or whether De Wet was to surrender to him.[2] The message was repeated the following morning, 18 August, but by that time De Wet had left and was heading westwards. The Boers came across two British scouts, one of whom was captured, who told him that a British force was camped at Bokfontein near Wolhuter's Kop.[3] The Boers headed north and camped on the east bank of the Crocodile River at Rooikoppies.

Boer scouts had now discerned Hamilton's advance from Zilikaat's Nek. On 19 August Colonel Mahon's mounted men from Bokfontein met the Boers strongly entrenched at Rooikoppies. Together with De Wet's men who were to cross the Magaliesberg and return to the Free State were Commandant Steenekamp's men. Steenekamp was to lead the main Boer body north to the bushveld. Mahon's men were engaged all day at Rooikoppies but the Boer force was in a strong position and, although Colonel T.D. Pilcher of Ridley's 3rd Mounted Infantry Brigade, crossed the river in an attempt to outflank them, the British were forced to fall back on their camp at Bokfontein, this being the skirmish mentioned in the opening paragraph of this account. The casualty list shows two fatal casualties, Lieutenant H.H. Bradburne, died of wounds on 22 August and Trooper L. Perham killed in action on 19 August. Both were members of the 3rd New Zealand Mounted Rifles and these two casualties were described in the official history as a "trifling loss".[4]

Hamilton's mounted men were a short distance away and Mahon had been joined by the mounted brigade of Colonel C.P. Ridley. Another force accompanying a supply column for Hamilton under the command of Major E.B. Urmston was on the way from Zilikaat's Nek. Surrounded on all sides, De Wet now desperately needed to find a way over the Magaliesberg which all had thought to be impenetrable in this area. British troops could be seen emerging from the camp at Wolhuter's Kop, no doubt informed of De Wet's whereabouts by the escaped scout. De Wet was concerned that the British had fresh horses and "this was a moment when a man has to keep his presence of mind. I decided on climbing the Magalies Mountains, without a path or road." At this point there is a small kloof which leads quite a distance into the mountain and presumably De Wet thought that at least they might be able to hide and evade their pursuers.[5]

The Boers happened on an African hut and De Wet enquired of the occupant whether it was possible to cross the mountain here. The reply was that men cannot but baboons often do. De Wet thereupon decided to cross where the baboons did and led his men up a small ravine which hid them for a while. As they got higher they came into sight of the British at Wolhuter's Kop but they were out of range even of the artillery. It was a very steep and rough track that they were using. They had to dismount and lead their horses over smooth granite slabs. It was an exhausting climb and De Wet said that "never before had I been as tired as I was now." The descent was a little less precipitate but still difficult but by the evening they arrived at a Boer farm. They crossed the railway line near Bank station, met up with Danie Theron and his scouts, and on 21 August they were back at Rhenosterpoort, his bivouac for two weeks earlier in the month.[6]

The first De Wet hunt was now over. De Wet started to reassemble the Free State commandos. His successful escape persuaded many Boers to tear up the oath of allegiance that they had signed, dig up their buried Mausers, mount their horses and rally to De Wet's call. The war would go forward again!

---

[1] There are a limited number of places where there are gaps in the Magaliesberg range. It was never possible to cross at Hartebeestpoort, the site of the present-day dam, which was extremely rugged.

[2] Maurice *History of the War in South Africa* Vol 3 p361. Van Warmelo *On Commando* p51.

[3] De Wet *Three Years' War* p147.

[4] Maurice *History of the War in South Africa* Vol 3 p362. See also Stirling *The Colonials in South Africa 1899-1902* p347. Hall *New Zealanders in South Africa 1899-1902* p37.

[5] De Wet *Three Years' War* p148.

[6] Several dates are given in various sources for this exploit of De Wet but 19 August seems to be the most likely. De Wet himself says 18 August and Pretorius quotes references that point to 21 August.

References

1. General Christiaan de Wet *Three Years' War* Archibald Constable and Company, London 1902 (reprint by Galago Publishing, Alberton 1986).
2. Mildred Dooner *The Last Post* J.B. Hayward & Son, Polstead, Suffolk (reprint of 1904 edition).
3. D.O.W. Hall *New Zealanders in South Africa 1899-1902* War History Branch, Department of Internal Affairs, Wellington 1949 (reprint by The Naval & Military Ltd).
4. *J.&B. Hayward & Son The South African War Casualty Roll – The "South African Field Force" 11th Oct. 1899 – June 1902.*
5. Frederick Hoppin Howland *The Chase of De Wet* Preston and Rounds Company, USA, 1901.
6. Huw M. Jones & Meurig G.M. Jones *A Gazeteer of the Second Anglo-Boer War 1899-1902* The Military Press, Milton Keynes 1999.
7. Major-General Sir Frederick Maurice *The Times History of the War in South Africa* Vol 3 Hurst and Blackett Limited, London 1908.
8. Stephen M. Miller *Lord Methuen and the British Army: Failure and Redemption in South Africa* Frank Cass, London, Portland OR 1999.
9. FransJohan Pretorius *The Great Escape of the Boer Pimpernel – Christiaan de Wet* University of Natal Press, Pietermaritzburg 2001.
10. Dietlof van Warmelo *On Commando* A.D. Donker/Publisher, Johannesburg 1977.
11. John Stirling *The Colonials in South Africa 1899-1902* William Blackwood & Sons, Edinburgh and London 1907 (reprint by J.B. Hayward & Son).
12. Dietlof van Warmelo *On Commando* A.D. Donker Publishers, Johannesburg 1977.
13. Steve Watt *In Memoriam* University of KwaZulu Natal Press, Pietermaritzburg 1999.
14. Basil Williams *The Times History of the War in South Africa* Vol IV Sampson Low, Marston & Company Ltd, London 1906.

Casualties
(Crocodile Drift 19 August 1900)

678	Trooper L. Perham	Killed	3rd NZMR
	Lieutenant H.H. Bradburn	Killed	3rd NZMR
647	Trooper J.J. Hersley	Wounded	2nd NZMR

Stirling *The Colonials in South Africa* p347 also says that Captain A. Hutson was wounded at Crocodile Drift but *The South African War Casualty Roll* shows him as wounded at a place "not stated" on 1 August.

Watt *In Memoriam* shows Bradburne died of wounds on 22 August 1900.

"Bradburne" is spelled thus in Hall *New Zealanders in South Africa* and Watt *In Memoriam*. "Bradburn" in all other references.

(The two New Zealanders were originally buried at Bokfontein, the exact burial site now lost, reinterred later in the war at Rietfontein, near the present-day Hartebeespoort Dam, where their names appear on the South African War Graves Commission granite column.)

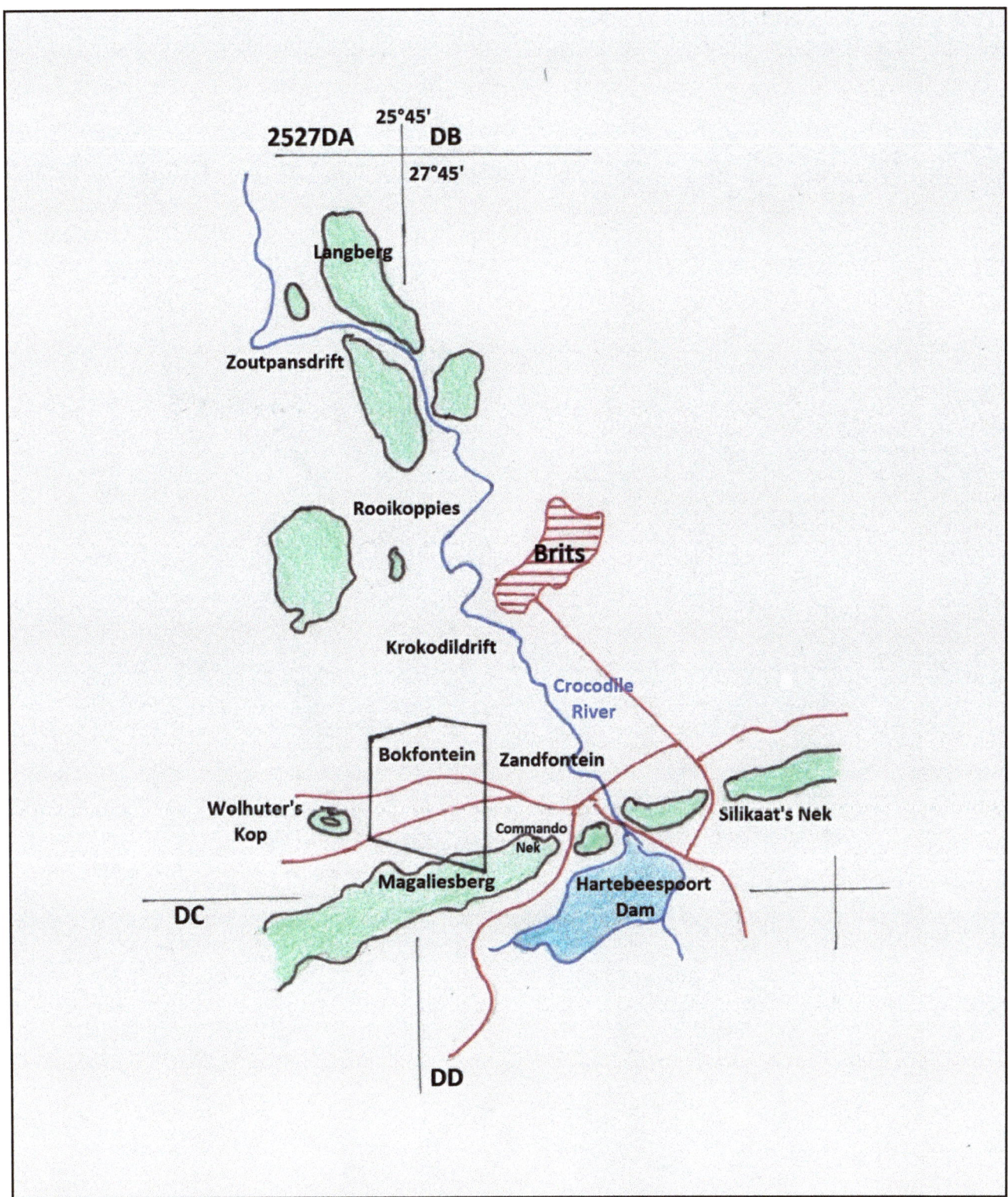

Sketch map of the area around Bokfontein based on the 150k survey maps, numbers given. Hartebeespoort (Afrikaans spelling) was always virtually impassable due to the huge boulders virtually closing off the gap in the Magaliesberg.

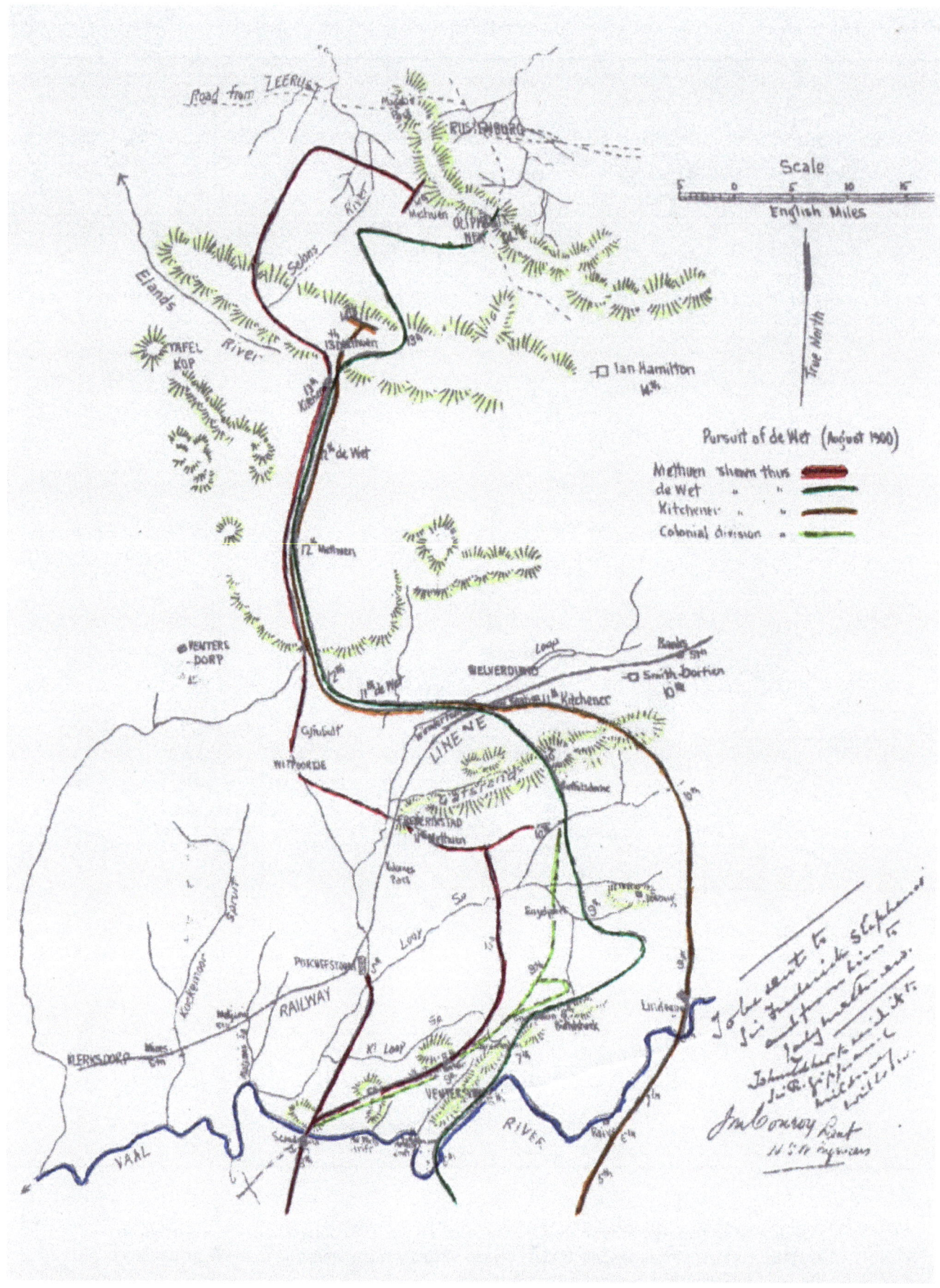

Sketch map by Lord Methuen of his part in the First De Wet Hunt.

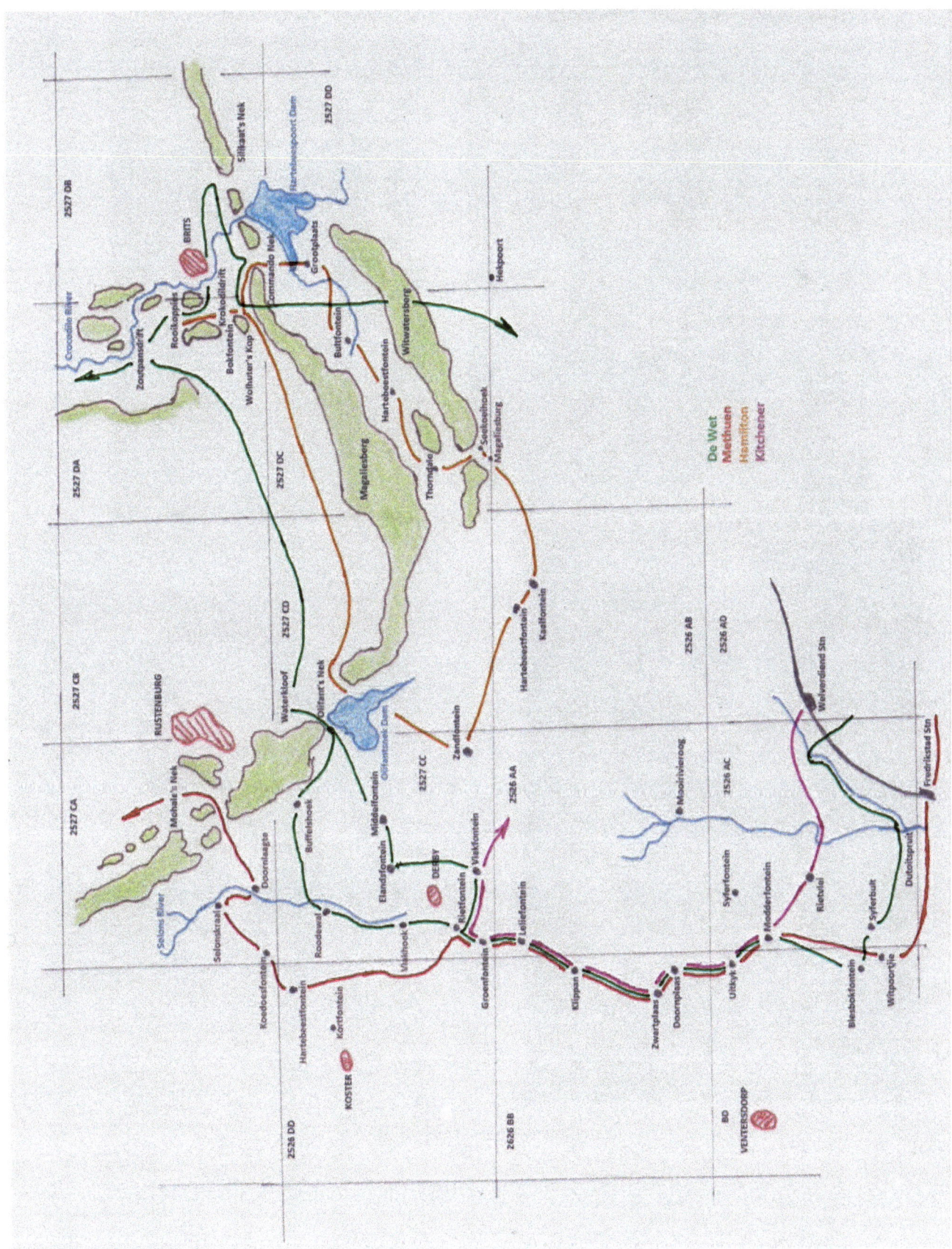

Sketch map based on the 1:50k survey maps of the area showing the last part of the First De Wet hunt. North is to the top as per the written script (to the left as the sketch is placed on the page).

Methuen, Hamilton, Mahon, de Wet.

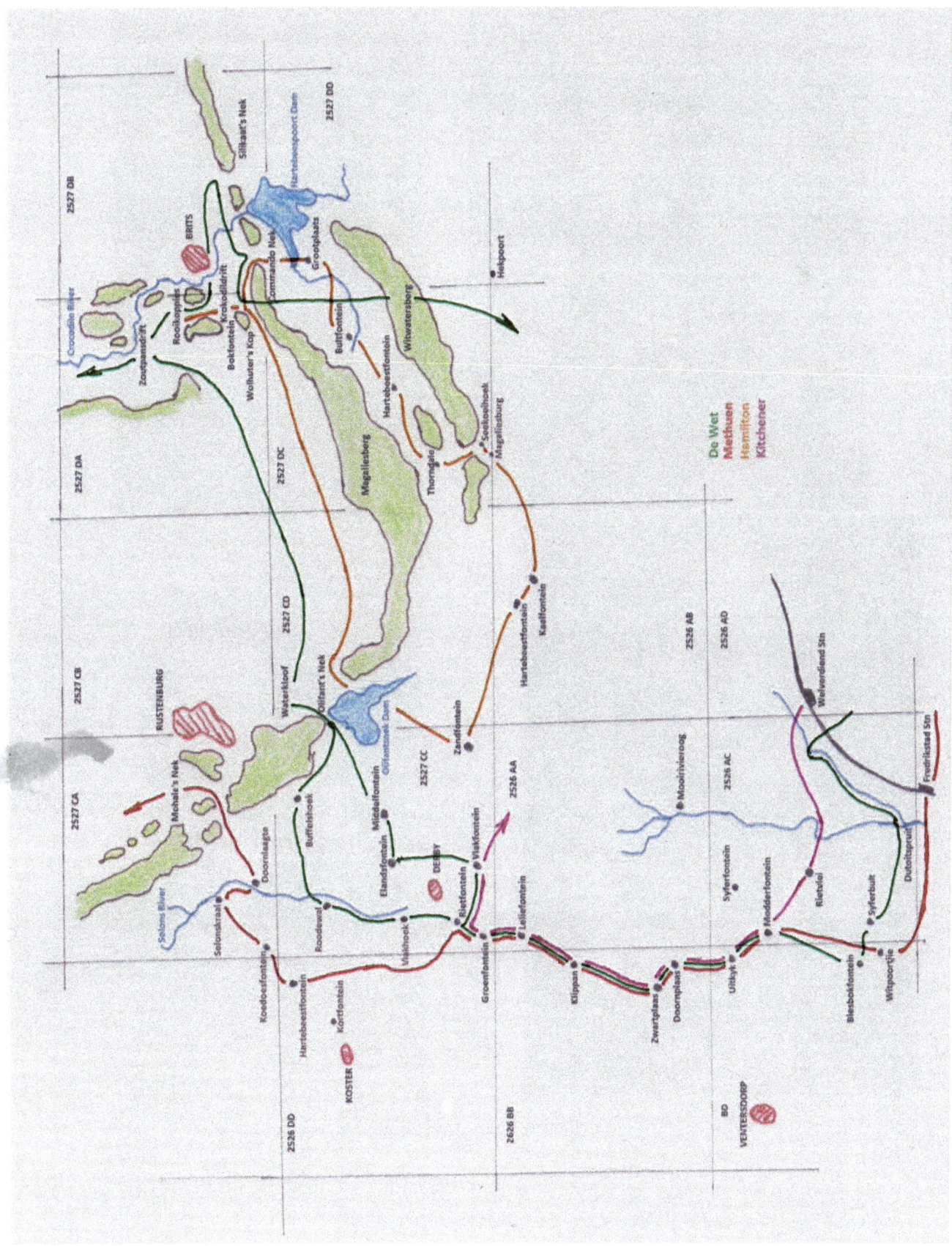

Sketch map based on the 1:50k survey maps of the area showing the last part of the First De Wet hunt. North is to the top as per the written script (to the left as the sketch is placed on the page).

Methuen, Hamilton, Mahon, de Wet.

The 78th R.H.A.'s attack on De Wet's rearguard between Syferbult and Modderfontein.

De Wet's escape route over the Magaliesberg:

View to the south over the Hekpoort Valley. (below)

View to the north, Wolhuter's Kop to the left of centre (picture at the foot of page 46)

De Wet's escape route over the Magaliesberg: The stone cairn at the top of the pass and one of the areas of smooth granite that caused such difficulty to the horsemen.

The Boer Decision to Split into Smaller Units

At the Boer *krygsraad* in Kroonstad in April 1900, the younger Boer generals and commandants had advocated splitting their forces into smaller units. Even at this early stage they realized that their citizen soldiers were unable to prevent Roberts's and Buller's armies from carrying all before them. The older Boer commanders, many of them prominent politicians, could not countenance abandoning their towns and cities without a fight.

The Boers preferred to be called "burghers" – Dutch for citizens – rather than soldiers. They lacked the organization and discipline of regular armies, the heavy armament and logistic equipment. Every man in the field needs food, water and ammunition on a daily basis although even regular armies are hard put to manage this at times. The burghers had largely to fend for themselves in the field. That they were able to do this made them into formidable guerrilla fighters.

At Doornkop, to the west of Johannesburg, the Boers determined to make a stand but were unable to even delay the British advance. Pretoria was abandoned to their enemy without a fight. On the long ridge to the east, Diamond Hill, Louis Botha and Koos de la Rey attempted to hold their ground on 14 and 15 June. Roberts brushed them away and continued his advance eastwards. It was late in August when the Boers made a final stand on the edge of the escarpment near the town of Belfast. The two armies of Buller and Roberts were now combined. Bergendal was the scene of a last desperate effort to hold onto at least some territory. President Kruger, having left Pretoria in some haste, even leaving his wife, was in his luxurious private rail carriage parked in the station at Machadodorp. This was now too close to the British army poised for a descent into the *lowveld* region.[1]

Nineteen-year-old Queen Wilhelmina of the Netherlands, was appalled at the actions of the British in waging war against two small Boer republics. She offered Kruger the services of a Dutch Navy cruiser, the HNLMS *Gelderland*, to take him in safety to Holland. Kruger's train moved on to Nelspruit, then little more than a halt on the line to Lourenco Marques in Portuguese East Africa.[2] He met with President Marthinus Steyn of the Orange Free State while he was there. However he was suffering from an eye disease and due to take ship for Holland.

Steyn attempted to motivate the Transvaal burghers to continue the fight but those burghers still in the field were forced to make their way through the bushveld to Pietersburg[3] by the further advance of Buller's army. Major-General Reginald Pole-Carew and his Guards Brigade reached Komatipoort on 24 September. A number of Boers, unable or unwilling to make the *trek* through the fever-ridden low country, crossed the border into Portuguese territory, were interned and some even ended up in Portugal.

Now only those Boers who were determined to see things through were left in the field.

The Clash with Christiaan de Wet at Doornkraal, near Bothaville

6 November 1900

As the year 1900 was drawing to a close, the Boers were badly demoralized after a string of military defeats. Christiaan de Wet had managed to escape capture in the Brandwater Basin where most of the Free State army surrendered to Lieutenant-General Archibald Hunter. De Wet, with the Orange Free State President, Marthinus Steyn, made his way over Slabbert's Nek on 15 July. Pursued by British columns he made his way to Rhenosterpoort, near Vredefort, holed up there for nearly two weeks, and then once more evaded the columns surrounding him. Crossing the Vaal River at Schoemansdrift, he made his way over the Magaliesberg and into the bushveld to the north.[4]

De Wet ordered his men to make their own way back to the Free State. He himself took 246 men and managed to cross the Magaliesberg at a place to the west of Commando Nek.[5] President Steyn and an escort circled around to the north of Pretoria making for Machadodorp and a meeting with Transvaal President Paul Kruger, then living in a railway carriage in the station. By the time Steyn arrived, Kruger had retreated to Nelspruit and was making ready to leave to board the cruiser *Gelderland* sent to fetch him by the 18-year old Dutch Queen Wilhelmina.[6]

Kruger's meeting with President Marthinus Steyn affirmed their joint resolve to fight on. Kruger was not in good health, ageing and suffering with his eyes, hence the decision that he should leave for Europe.[7] The Transvaal commandos had almost all dispersed. Steyn visited those that remained, "arousing anew their enthusiasm for the cause with some stirring speeches."[8] Generals Louis Botha and Ben Viljoen and State Secretary Francis Reitz were as determined as ever to fight for their independence and led their men through the bushveld, now the Kruger National

---

[1] The *lowveld* is the eastern region of Mpumalanga and Limpopo provinces, lower altitude than the central plateau which is the *highveld*.
[2] Lourenco Marques now Maputo.
[3] Now Polokwane.
[4] See FransJohan Pretorius *The Boer Pimpernel*. This incident is referred to as the First De Wet Hunt and is described in Amery *The Times History of the War in South Africa Vol IV* as well as Maurice *The War in South Africa*
[5] Surrounded by British columns, de Wet had to cross the Magaliesberg where there was no path or road. A black herder told him that only baboons could cross here but de Wet declared that "where a baboon can cross, we can cross." De Wet *Three Years' War* p148.
[6] Wilhelmina had a stern dislike of the United Kingdom partly as a result of the annexation of the republics of Transvaal and the Orange Free State.
[7] See de Villiers *Healers, Helpers and Hospitals* p166 for Kruger's eye disease.
[8] Amery *The Times History of the War in South Africa Vol IV* p474.

Park, to Pietersburg (now Polokwane). The Transvaal Government was still functioning there and the Vierkleur, the flag of the Zuid Afrikaansche Republiek, still flew over the government buildings. Steyn followed and made fiery patriotic speeches at gatherings in a number of towns, that in Nylstroom (now Modimolle), drawing a sizable crowd.[1]

Steyn needed to return to the Free State but first wanted to meet with General Koos de la Rey at Ventersdorp and ordered De Wet to attend as well. First, though, it is necessary to describe De Wet's movements on his return to the Free State and Rhenosterpoort. De Wet had little trouble making his way across the Krugersdorp-Potchefstroom railway line, thence to Van Vuurenskloof, across the Vaal, and back to Rhenosterpoort on 22 August. Here he was joined by the commandos of Vrede and Harrismith, as well as Generals Piet Fourie, C.C. Froneman and Judge Barrie Hertzog. The next month was occupied in reorganizing the Free Sate commandos.

By the beginning of October there were considerable numbers of Boers back on commando in spite of their having taken the oath of allegiance that Lord Roberts had offered after the fall of Bloemfontein. It was at this time that de Wet went to Potchefstroom which was as yet unoccupied by the British. The Boers were busily engaged in refurbishing rifles taken from the pile of surrendered weapons which was burned by the British on their way through to Pretoria in May 1900. De Wet had his photo taken with the 200th repaired weapon.[2]

In mid-October De Wet responded to a request from General P.J. Liebenberg to join forces and attack the column of General Geoffrey Barton, encamped at Frederikstad Station. Frederikstad, said De Wet, "was a miserable affair altogether",[3] and on 25 October De Wet and his men headed for Van Vuuren's Kloof on the north bank of the Vaal River, the hills which form the rim of the Vredefort Dome.[4] They needed to cross the river but many of the drifts were guarded. While the battle at Frederikstad was taking place, Lord Roberts issued orders to Major-General Charles Knox to assemble a relief force. Knox was then, 21 October, at Heilbron, moving to Witkopjes on the 23rd to combine with Lieutenant-Colonel Henry de Lisle's column with the Colonial Division under Colonel John Maxwell. On the 25th, Colonel Philip le Gallais arrived from Bothaville to join the force at Reitzburg.[5]

No longer needed to relieve Major General Geoffrey Barton at Frederikstad, Knox's objective was now to find de Wet's force and deal with it. His force was all mounted and with four guns of "U" Battery Royal Horse Artillery.[6] This meant that they almost matched the mobility of their Boer adversaries, in contrast to "the ponderous columns of infantry"[7] which had been fruitlessly chasing their elusive foe. Nevertheless it had taken some time to concentrate at Reitzburg, still at least a few days march from Frederikstad, twelve miles (eighteen kilometres) north of Potchefstroom.

Leaving Le Gallais at Tygerfontein so as to block de Wet's possible escape route over the Vaal River at Schoeman's Drift, Knox occupied Potchefstroom on 26 October. There he learnt that De Wet was indeed not far away. His information was that De Wet was headed to Lindeque's Drift. The Boers, who had found their way barred by Le Gallais at Tygerfontein, had been forced to double back, and continue upstream looking for a crossing place. Le Gallais was ordered to cross the Vaal at Venterskroon and work towards Vredefort with a view to intercepting the Boers if they attempted to cross the Vaal.[8]

On 26 October the Boers spent the day travelling upstream and sometime after midday they reached Rensburg Drift. This was not really a recognized crossing place but a place where the Vaal splits up into a number of streams and small islands. In the early morning of 27 October they crossed and off-saddled. In spite of their chief's strictures that wagons and carts should not accompany the commandos, they had some horse-drawn carts with them but in addition they had artillery, three 75mm Krupps, two captured British guns and two machine guns. It would have taken some time to get all the guns and transport across.[9]

On the same day, the men of de Lisle's column set off in pursuit of the Boers. At 8 a.m. they came upon the site of the Boer laager of the previous night, "with the fires hardly yet cold" according to Lieutenant Livingstone-Learmonth of the 1st New South Wales Mounted Rifles.[10] This must have been some distance away from the Vaal River and in the Van Vuuren's Kloof hills. Learmonth describes how they passed over open rolling country before the road "closed in to a high narrow valley which led for ten or twelve miles to the Vaal." Here they were held up for a short while by a few Boers at a small koppie who opened fire. This was an area of thick thorn bush and, in scattering to return fire, the Australians discovered an abandoned 12-pounder Krupp gun, minus the breech-block of course – clearly they were close to overtaking the Boers.[11]

Learmonth says that they reached the Vaal at about 4 p.m. and sighted the whole Boer army which had just crossed the drift. The advanced scouts of the 1NSWMR passed the word for the main body to come up at a gallop. A pom-pom under Captain Stirling and two guns of "R" Battery R.H.A. under Captain Lamont opened fire and "the Boers numbering about a thousand, scampered off in every

---

[1] Viljoen *My reminiscences of the Anglo Boer War* pp146-150. Chapter XXIV is an interesting account of this period when he describes the Transvaal Boers as "dispirited and demoralized".
[2] De Wet *Three Years' War* p153 gives the full story of this enterprise. See also the famous picture of de Wet holding the 200th refurbished rifle.
[3] de Wet *Three Years' War* p167.
[4] The Vaal River flows through a spectacular series of hills in this area, formed when a giant meteorite collided with the earth about 2 billion years ago. See Truswell, J.F. (1977). *The Geological Evolution of South Africa*".
[5] Childers *The Times History of the War in South Africa*, Vol V p13.
[6] Knox's force consisted of the Colonial Division (600), de Lisle's column (Australians) and le Gallais's (5,7,8th MI, IY, R.H.A, Australians)
[7] Childers *The Times History of the War in South Africa*, Vol V p13.
[8] Childers *The Times History of the War in South Africa*, Vol V p14.
[9] De Wet *Three Years' War* p168.
[10] Chamberlain and Drooglever *The War with Johnny Boer* p346. Letter from Lieutenant Livingstone-Learmonth of the 1st New South Wales Mounted Rifles.
[11] Lord Roberts subsequently "had much pleasure in acceding to the request of the New South Wales Mounted Rifles" to take their captured guns back to Australia and hoping that they would capture many others.

direction". Colonel Henry de Lisle passed the word that "the drift must be crossed at all hazards"[1] and soon "we had two streams of men crossing the Vaal and the enemy in frantic retreat in front of them."[2] The Boers seemed to be making for Witkopjes (Wittekoppies) but were seen to turn east, making off in the direction of Parys.

Le Gallais, coming up from Vredefort was also in pursuit, this being the reason for the Boers retiring to the east rather than south towards Vredefort. From Schoemans Drift, Le Gallais had moved north along the right bank of the Vaal River but was able to cross at Venterskroon where there are the remnants of a disused drift. This brought his column in contact with the Boers retiring from Rensburg Drift. Just at sunset Le Gallais's pom-pom put a shell into a Boer wagon which was carrying ammunition. There was a huge flash as it exploded. There they found the "mangled remains of a couple of Boers, half a head and trunk here. A leg there and so on."[3] The *Times History* says that De Wet lost two guns, eight wagons and 24 killed, wounded and captured, one of whom was Lieutenant Wessels of Theron's Scouts. Lieutenant Learmonth says, "It was better than a good fox hunt. They (the Boers) were fairly on the run, every man for himself and the devil take the hindmost – wagons were dotted about and pack mules cast off every here and there. By now it was absolutely dark and the rain came down in torrents."[4]

When darkness fell, the Boers altered direction, made off to the south west, and the British completely lost the scent, partly because the rain may have erased some of the tracks. Knox and his men camped at Groote Eiland for the night, without wagons, blankets and food, all the transport only making it across the river late on the 28th, although sufficient supplies had arrived to give the men breakfast that morning. Also, Knox did not order an immediate pursuit which certainly helped his quarry to get clean away.

De Wet in his book *Three Years' War* has quite a different account, telling of how they were attacked by the British "just as we had partaken about noon of a late breakfast."[5] The Boers headed southwest and spent that night "at Bronkhorstfontein near the Wikopjes".[6] The night of 28 October they were at Winkelsdrift, on the Rhenoster River. There de Wet received a message that President Steyn was returning from his visit to President Kruger and wished to meet with him. De Wet left the commandos under the command of Commandant C.C. Froneman with instructions to "go in the direction of Bothaville" and went with a small escort to Ventersdorp in the Transvaal to meet with Steyn. Although the British were not to know, Steyn and De Wet had decided that an attempt was to be made to invade the Cape Colony. De Wet's meeting with Steyn was on 31 October and by 5 November he and the President were back with the commandos near Bothaville.[7]

After the clash at Rensburg Drift, Knox decided to sweep westwards on a broad front, making use of the main railway line. Spreading out his force – the Colonial Division camping at Grootvlei, some distance south of present-day Sasolburg; De Lisle's men at Koppies, then just a station; and Le Gallais at Honingspruit. Knox himself and his staff were with De Lisle. Some false intelligence caused Knox to send the Colonial Division north towards the Vaal River so they were not involved in the drive westwards towards Bothaville.[8]

Le Gallais knew well that Bothaville had been destroyed a few weeks before – he and his men had been part of a force under Lieutenant-General Archibald Hunter which had passed through the area early in August.[9] Nearing the town his men came under fire from Boer artillery across the Valsch River. This was late on the afternoon of 5 November. Two Australian soldiers, Troopers Albert Page and D.R. Fisher of 4th South Australian Imperial Bushmen describe how the Boers opened fire with a pom-pom and a 15-pounder. Another man, Trooper Tom Stott said "not much damage was done on either side", but Fisher said:

> *...shells were flying in all directions. There was a house a little distance off. I got behinds it with four or five others when the enemy put a pom-pom onto us. That gun threw a pound shell, and could fire 25 shells without stopping. They put about a dozen into the house where we were and blew one side down. Stones were flying in all directions. I thought it was all "up a tree" with me. Some of the horses pulled away, but I managed to get mine and he followed me for about a mile. I was well out of the road then. Our big guns next came up and fired a few shots. It then got dark and the enemy cleared. They thought we wouldn't follow them, but we did.*[10]

Le Gallais and his men camped that night in the town square and ascertained that De Wet and Froneman had arrived in the course of the day – presumably from some local black people. Commandant Steenekamp with the baggage and artillery had also passed through. The Boers were camped at Doornkraal a short distance south of Bothaville in a slight depression.[11] In the *Times History of the*

---

[1] Chamberlain and Drooglever *The War with Johnny Boer* p346. Letter from Lieutenant Livingstone-Learmonth of 1NSWMR.
[2] Chamberlain and Drooglever *The War with Johnny Boer* p345. Letter from Captain W. Watson of 1NSWMR.
[3] There is a small monument marking the spot where the wagon exploded – it is in the veld to the south of Parys and difficult to find.
[4] Chamberlain and Drooglever *The War with Johnny Boer* p346. Letters from Captain W. Watson of 1NSWMR and Lieutenant Livingstone-Learmonth of 1NSWMR.
[5] De Wet's version in *Three Years' War* of the events described above differs considerably. De Wet says that they crossed at "Witbanksfontein" on the morning of 26 October. He must have meant Witklipfontein which is a short distance upstream of Schoeman's Drift. There is a long reach in the Vaal River here which is wide and quite shallow – nowadays much deeper because of the weir at the drift. This must have been a lapse of memory on his part. His book was written without notes while on board ship with Generals Botha and de la Rey on their way to England in 1903. De Wet *Three Years' War* p168.
[6] This place is difficult to pinpoint on modern maps – possibly the farm has been renamed. De Wet *Three Years' War* p168.

[7] General Koos de la Rey was supposed to be at this meeting but "was prevented from coming." De Wet *Three Years' War* p169.
[8] Childers *The Times History of the War in South Africa*, Vol V p15.
[9] Childers *The Times History of the War in South Africa*, Vol V p15.
[10] Letters from Troopers Tom Stott and D.R.Fisher, Fisher's appearing in *The Advertiser*, Adelaide 28 December 1900.
[11] The site of the battle is alongside R59 road and adjacent to the monument at the roadside. The layout is clear from reference to

War in South Africa, it is said that "After his skirmish with Le Gallais…De Wet outspanned at Doornkraal farm, about five miles from the river, keeping the Valsch River between himself and the British troops."[1] The Boers had surely been there some days however, as camping in the ruins of Bothaville would have been distasteful. Major-General Knox was with De Lisle's men at Elandsvley, about 10 kilometres north east of the town.

Le Gallais's men crossed the Valsch at 4 a.m. and almost immediately came upon a Boer picket of five men who were all asleep. Major Kenneth Lean and the 8th M.I. were in the lead and they were captured without a shot being fired. The spoor of the Boer guns was also clear and the advance continued. Lean knew that the Boer laager was nearby and sent back for the guns. Three guns from "U" Battery joined them and Lean and 67 men galloped forward to a rise from where they could see the Boer laager not 300 metres distant. The men were asleep, the guns and wagons outspanned and the horses grazing loose. It was now about 5.30 a.m. Lean's men lined the crest of the rise and opened rapid magazine fire on the laager.[2]

Completely surprised, most of the Boers grabbed whatever horses they could find and galloped away, De Wet and Steyn included. De Wet said of his men that "a panic had seized them." Seeing De Wet himself saddling his horse and leaving the scene cannot have induced his men to make a stand and defend their position. Many of the Boers had even galloped away bare-back and De Wet's efforts to rally the men were unavailing.[3] Major Lean and his 5th M.I. spread out with the Worcester company in the centre, the Royal Irish holding a kraal on the left and the Buffs on the right, by now having advanced to a position on the edge of the Boer laager. The 8th M.I. reinforced the 5th, occupying a farmhouse and kraal on the left.

About 130 Boers occupied a garden with a substantial stone wall and fought bravely to save the guns which were unable to come into action, being showered with shrapnel and case by the guns of "U" Battery. The bank of a small dam was also occupied by the Boers who were in a strong position for defence. Colonel le Gallais was soon on the scene and he and second-in-command Lieutenant-Colonel Ross took up position in the farmhouse. As the door of the farmhouse was open, anyone moving around was clearly visible to the Boers only 100 metres away. Le Gallais was mortally wounded and Ross severely wounded. A number of officers were killed and the 170 British soldiers were in a critical situation. Le Gallais had sent his staff officer Major William Hickie to order every available man to the scene. It was an hour before reinforcements arrived. Knox left his camp at 5 a.m. and soon heard Le Gallais's guns in action.[4]

When de Lisle arrived with further reinforcements at about 10 a.m. he took command. The Boers whom De Wet had managed to rally and were trying to counter attack were driven back. De Lisle sent his New South Wales men to the left who were able to fire on the garden and the Boers in the small farm house to the rear. Late reinforcements were some West Australians under Lieutenant Darling. The garden now surrounded, the counter attack beaten back, de Lisle determined on decisive action. The 5th M.I. and Darling's West Australians were ordered to fix bayonets and charge. With the first flash of the steel the white flag went up and the Boers surrendered.[5]

De Wet and Steyn were now in rapid flight and the guns and supplies which they had been accumulating over the last two months were all lost. De Wet claimed that the loss of the guns made little difference to them, "as our ammunition for these pieces was nearly exhausted."[6] For the guerilla warfare now beginning, such hardware would indeed have been of doubtful advantage to them anyway. Wagons and supplies would have been a more significant loss but the Boer casualties were considerable. For the British, the loss of ten officers was serious, especially an officer of proven ability in countering guerilla tactics such as Philip le Gallais.

The British pursued their beaten enemies but "found that the enemy had broken up into small parties and dispersed all over the district."[7] The *Times History* comment was that: "It was yet to be learnt that the capture of guns and supplies was of very secondary importance"[8] in the guerrilla war which was now gathering momentum. The capture of De Wet and President Marthinus Steyn of the Free State, both of whom narrowly escaped the ambush at Doornkraal, would surely have had a significant effect on the progress of the war.[9]

---

the battle map.

[1] Childers *The Times History of the War in South Africa*, Vol V p16.
[2] Both *The Times History of the War in South Africa* Vol V pp16-21 and *The War in South Africa 1899-1902 (the official history)* V4 pp486-89 have more detailed descriptions of the battle.
[3] De Wet *Three Years' War* pp 171-2.
[4] Pakenham *The Boer War* pp475-76 has Hickie's comments that "The General is an old woman" based on the fact that it was eight o'clock before De Lisle's reinforcements arrived.
[5] De Lisle *Reminiscences of Sport and War pp112-13*. De Lisle also describes how Colonel Walter Ross was wounded by a bullet that hit him on the point of the chin. An operation was performed without chloroform in Kroonstad to remove his lower jaw! He lived on soup and milk for some time but later found he could eat mince. He commanded a brigade in the First World War as Brigadier-General Sir Walter Ross.
[6] De Wet *Three Years' War* p171.
[7] Maurice *The War in South Africa* p489.
[8] Childers The *Times History of the War in South Africa*, Vol V p21.
[9] What was truly remarkable however was that a little more than a fortnight after the setback at Doornkraal De Wet had assembled another force. With 1,500 men and a Krupp gun he overcame an entrenched British garrison, 450 strong, and captured the town of Dewetsdorp in the southern Free State and made his way to invade the Cape Colony.

References

1. L.S. Amery and Erskine Childers *The Times History of the War in South Africa*, Vols IV & V Sampson Low, Marston & Company, Ltd. London 1906/7.
2. Henry de Beauvoir de Lisle *Reminiscences of Sport and War* Eyre & Spottiswoode, London 1939.
3. Dr J.C. (Kay) de Villiers *Healers, Helpers and Hospitals* Vol II Protea Bookhouse, Pretoria 2008.
4. Maurice *The War in South Africa 1899-1902*.
5. Max Chamberlain and Robin Drooglever *The War with Johnny Boer Australians in the Boer War 1899-1902* Australian Military History Publications, Loftus, Australia 2003.
6. Christiaan de Wet *Three Years' War* (edition in English) Archibald Constable & Company 1902 (reprint Galago Publishing, Alberton 1986).
7. Thomas Pakenham *The Boer War* Weidenfeld and Nicholson Limited, London 1979.
8. General Ben Viljoen *My reminiscences of the Anglo Boer War* Hood, Douglas & Howard, London 1903 (reprint C. Struik (Pty) Ltd, Cape Town 1973).
9. R.L. Wallace *The Australians at the Boer War* The Australian War Memorial and the Australian Government Publishing Service, Canberra 1976.
10. Craig Wilcox *Australia's Boer War* Oxford University Press 2002 (published in association with the Australian War Memorial).
11. H.W. Wilson *After Pretoria* Vol I Published in parts, London 1900-02.

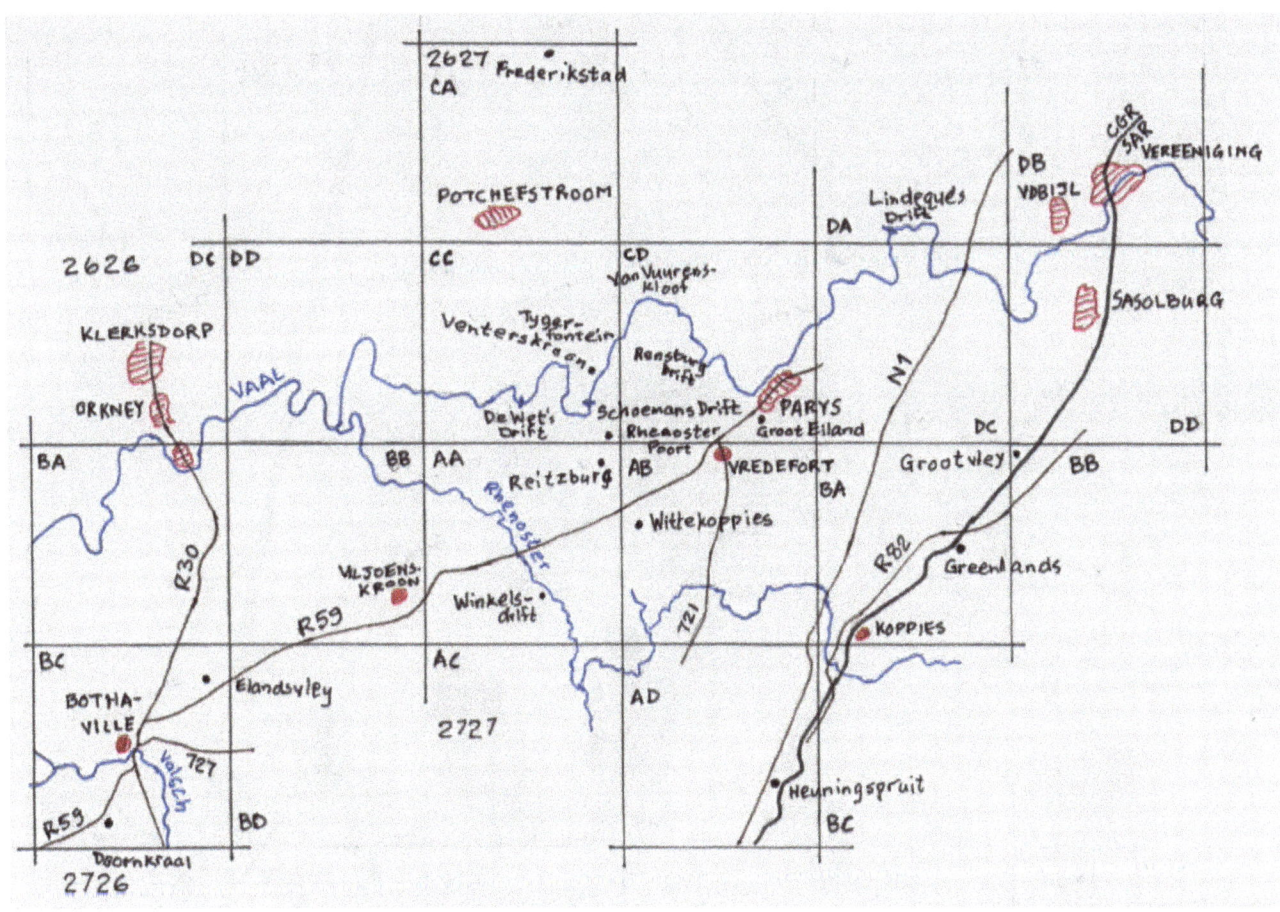

Map based on 1:50k survey maps of the area of the campaign, October-November 1900. All places mentioned in the text are marked with the relevant survey map numbers. Modern roads and railway line are indicated. Initial engagement was at Rensburg Drift after which the British bivouacked for the night at Groot Eiland. Maj-Gen Knox then positioned his force along the main railway at Grootvley (Colonial Division), Koppies (Lt-Col de Lisle) and Heuningspruit (Lt-Col le Gallais) and the two Colonels drove westwards towards Bothaville – the Colonial Division having been sent north towards the Vaal River on a false scent.

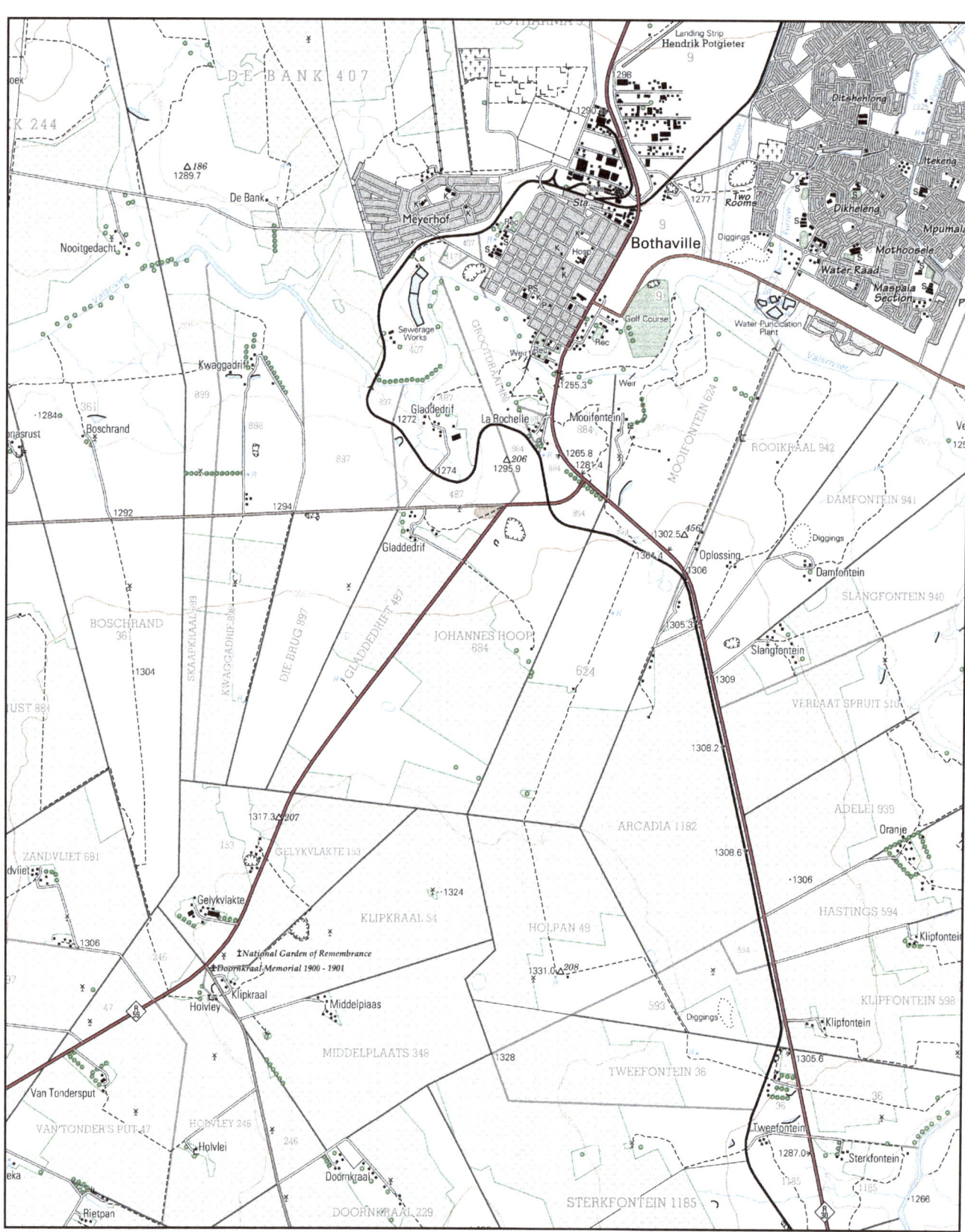

Crop from 1:50k survey map 2726BC: Location of Bothavillle and Doornkraal monument and battle site on R59 south of the town.

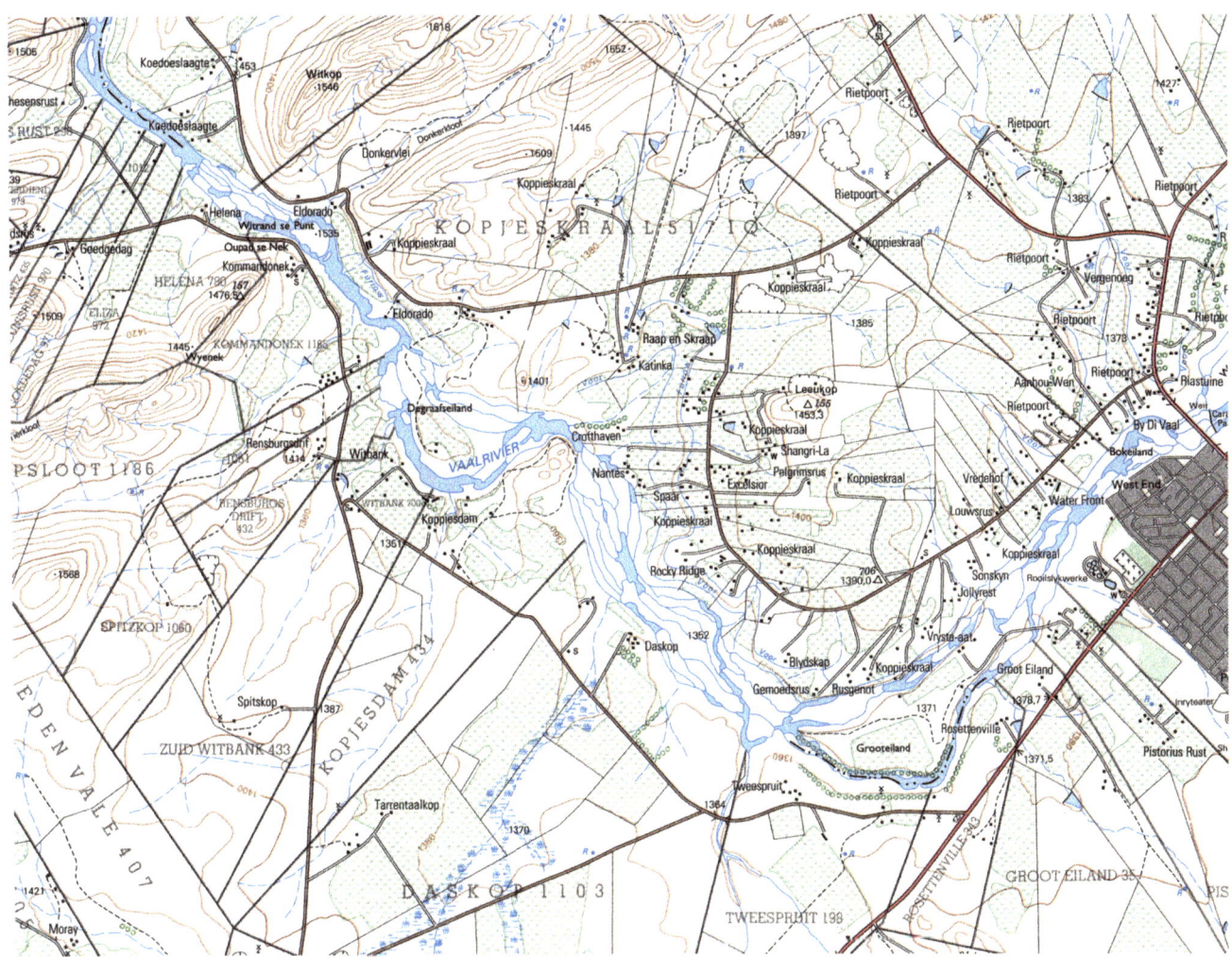

Crop from 1:50k survey map 2627CD: The location of Rensburg Drift is shown at a place where the Vaal River splits into a number of separate streams. The town of Parys is at the right and the British camp on the night of 27 October was at Groote Eiland, just south of the town.

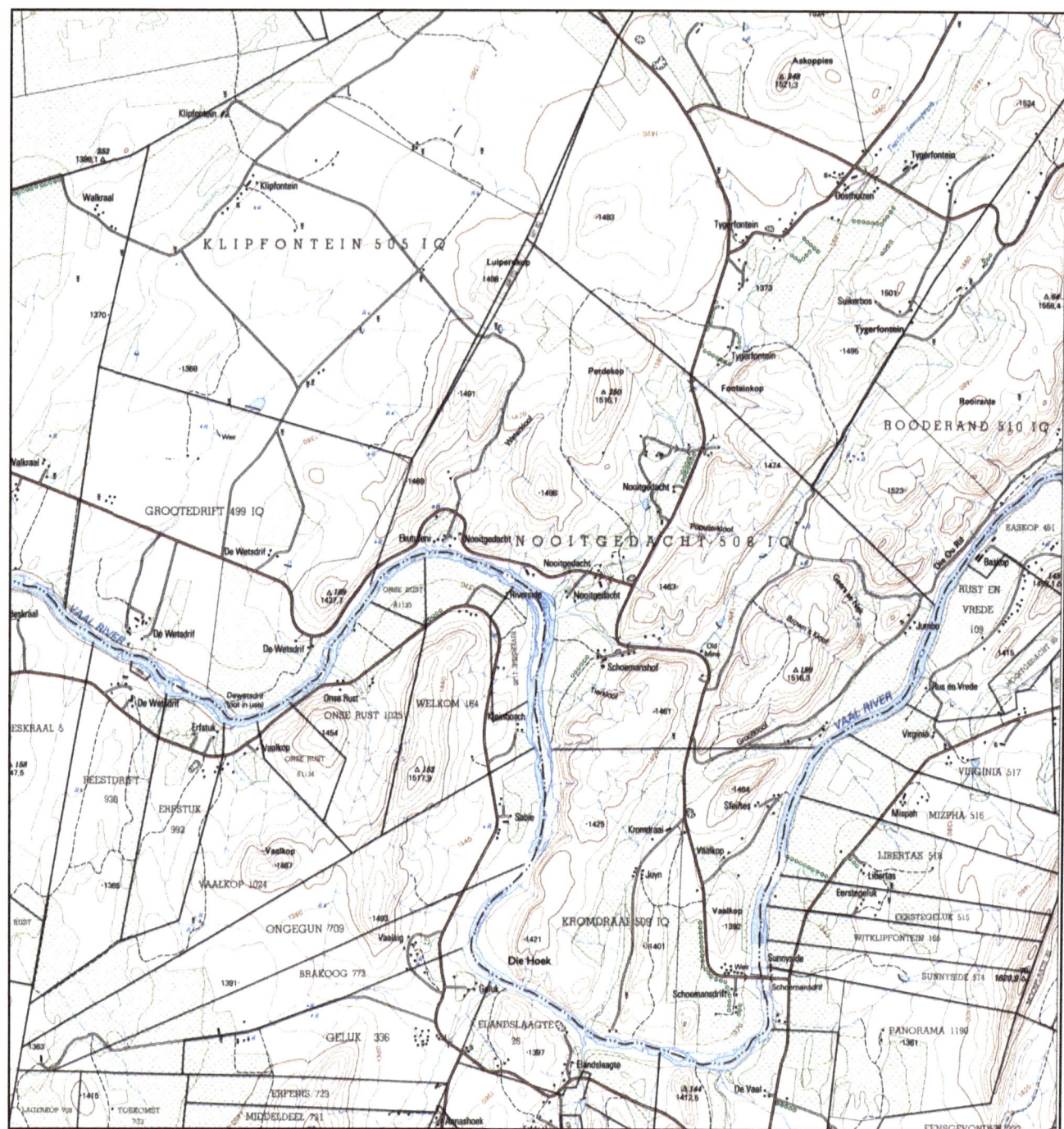

Crop from 1:50k survey map 2627CC: Schoeman's Drift is just north of the sharp bend in the Vaal River with Witklipfontein a little further north. De Wet's account says that he crossed the river here. Near the top right corner is the farm Tygerfontein where Colonel le Gallais was camped to prevent the Boers from crossing back into the Free State over Schoeman's Drift.

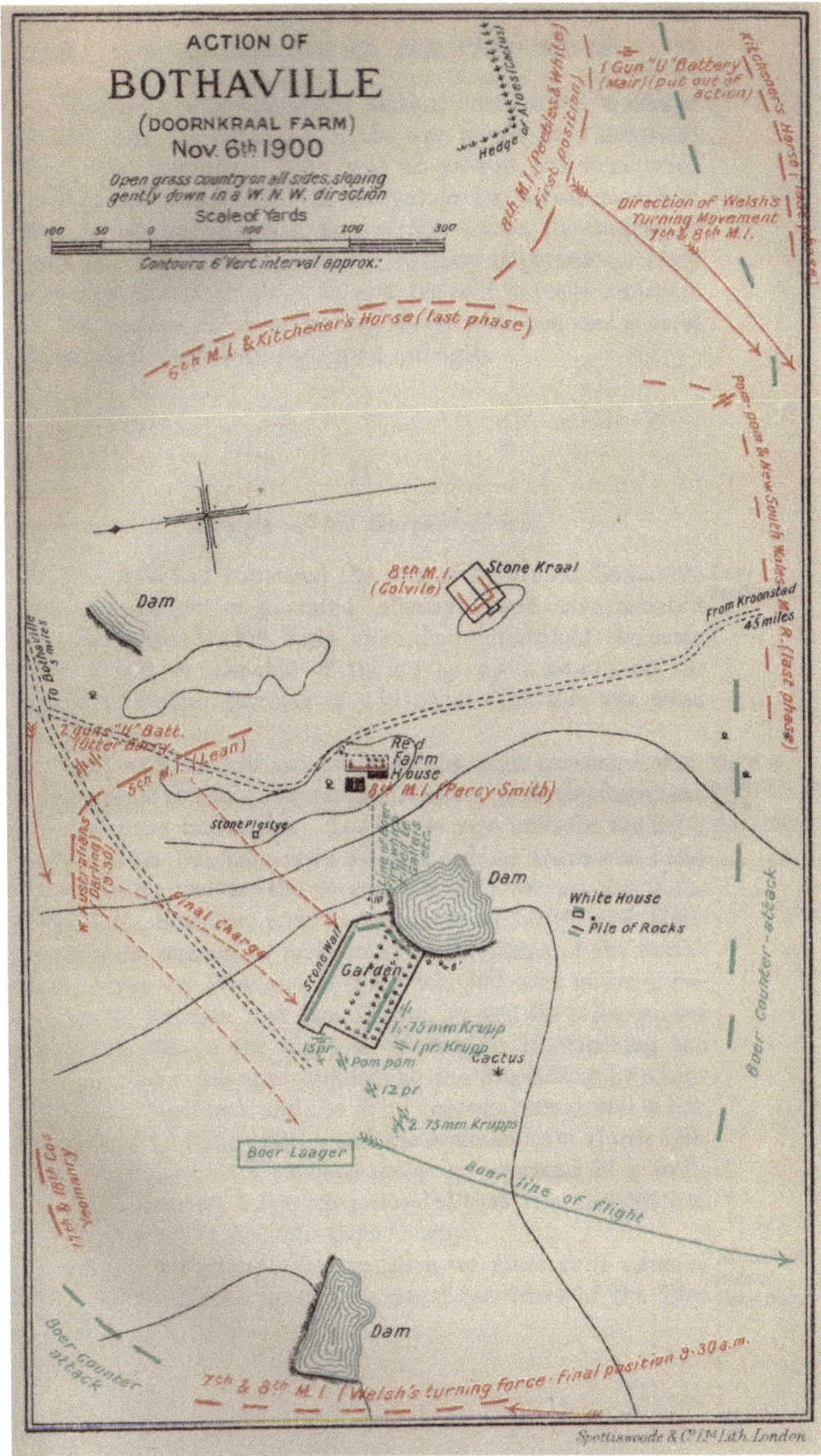

Doornkraal: The battle map from the *Times History of the War in South Africa*. The garden and some of the other features marked on this map are still readily discernible on the site.

General Christiaan de Wet – the picture taken in Potchefstroom when he visited the town in October 1900. He is holding the 200th rifle refurbished by the Boers from the pile of surrendered weapons which was burned by the British when they occupied the town in May.

Colonel Charles Knox who came close to capturing Christiaan de Wet at Doornkraal.

The battle site: The north and west walls of the garden clearly visible. The wall of the small dam is between the two trees on the left.

Doornkraal monuments: The column on the side of the R59 – the battle site is just behind. The Boer memorial in the national graveyard across the road from the battle site.

Graves in the Garden of Remembrance, Bothaville.

The death of Lt Col le Gallais.

Major Kenneth Lean who led the advance.

British soldiers on the firing line – the wounded loading the rifles.

Lieutenant-Colonel Philip le Gallais:
On the staff of Major-General Archibald Hunter in Bloemfontein wearing a forage cap.

In the full dress uniform of an officer in the 8th (Royal Irish) Hussars.

The Bothaville gun: The Krupp gun captured by the Western Australians at Bothaville which is now in King's Park, Perth. Lieutenant H. Darling, 1st WAMI who led the final bayonet charge. (Photos John Sweetman of Perth, WA)

General Christiaan de Wet and President Steyn make their getaway.

Guerrilla Warfare – Tactics and Strategy

Field-Marshall Lord Frederick Roberts decided towards the end of 1900 that the war was "practically over" and handed over command to General Lord Herbert Kitchener. His return to England was somewhat delayed by the illness of his daughter but he and his family were home by Christmas. The last action under Roberts's command was at Rhenosterkop, north of the town of Bronkhorstspruit, east of Pretoria.

A high hill, the Rhenosterkop, overlooks an area to the east of rugged hills and kloofs which could easily hide a Boer commando. The Boers made use of this terrain on a number of occasions in the next two years and the British were hard put to keep the area clear of their Boer adversaries. It was the scene of a pitched battle on 29 November when Boer General Ben Viljoen occupied an extended line along a series of ridges. Furthermore, he attempted to defend his position and held off the attacks of the British for the entire day. Probably he only did that to enable his wagons to get a good start on the inevitable British pursuit.

But the inevitable British pursuit never happened and Viljoen's men escaped. Neither side made any real gain from their exertions around Rhenosterkop. The tactics of British Major-General Arthur Paget in making frontal attacks on the very strong defensive positions of General Viljoen's burghers caused needless casualties. Viljoen and his men disappeared to the northeast.

At that time British columns were ponderous and unwieldy. Besides the mounted men there were infantry as escort for the column's transport and its guns, ambulances, a kitchen and engineers to undertake repairs and build roads and entrenchments. They were well protected against attack but the column moved far too slowly to be able to capture or destroy the much more mobile Boers.

Both sides were learning about a kind of warfare that was new to them. The Boers had never faced the trained soldiers of a regular army and the British were hard put to understand how they were to counteract the tactics of the Boer commandos. Each side had suffered setbacks, the Boers were not yet ready to surrender as Lord Roberts had hoped and Lord Kitchener was forced to reorganize his army and devise a new strategy and different tactics. He had two urgent priorities – protect his vulnerable railway lines and enlist more mounted soldiers in an attempt to match the mobility of the Boers.

For the Boers, demoralized after a series of defeats and the loss of their capitals, it was necessary to persuade their countrymen who had laid down their arms to return to their commandos. Most of these had buried their Mauser rifles and only handed in an old muzzle-loader when they signed Lord Roberts's undertaking to return to their farms and homes, and agreeing not to take up arms again. Many were easily persuaded to tear up the document that they had signed without a qualm. More robust methods were used on occasion but most of those who were thus persuaded took the first bolt hole that offered.

Steyn and de Wet in the Orange Free State and de la Rey in the western Transvaal soon revived Boer spirits and the war took off again after the lull in activity at the end of 1900.

Rhenosterkop

29 November 1900

Commandant Ben Viljoen of the Johannesburg commando was promoted General soon after the battle of Diamond Hill, in the hills east of Pretoria on 11 and 12 June 1900. He took command of the Krugersdorp, Germiston, Boksburg and Johannesburg commandos as well as the Zuid Afrikaansche Republiek Politie (Z.A.R.P.), mounted police.[1] After the Boers were driven into the lowveld, Viljoen trekked with elements of this force and some others to Pietersburg (now Polokwane). His route took him through what is now the Kruger National Park, dry, arid and unhealthy, many of his men suffering and dying of typhoid, dysentery and malaria.[2]

Arriving in the Highveld they were able to recover and replace their clothes and boots. The area was still under Republican control, "all the officials...in their proper places...and the Vierkleur (the Republican flag) flying from the Government buildings."[3] The railway was intact and the telegraph was still operating as far as Warmbad (now Bela Bela). Viljoen travelled by train to Nylstroom (now Modimolle), in November 1900 the southern frontier of republican territory. President Marthinus Steyn of the Orange Free State had arrived in the village a day or two before which caused quite a commotion. A public meeting was called to hear stirring patriotic speeches from Steyn and Commandant-General Louis Botha whereupon Steyn departed for the western Transvaal to meet with General Koos de la Rey.[4] Steyn's "fiery counsels had a strong effect upon the policy of the sister-state".[5] Certainly, Steyn's fervour was a considerable factor in persuading the Transvaalers to reorganise their remaining forces and continue the fight for their independence.

The Boers held a *krygsraad*[6] in a hall at the Nylstroom hotel on 27 or 28 October. Botha ordered Viljoen to march with his command to the area north and east of Pretoria while Botha himself made his way to the Highveld between the Natal and Delagoa Bay railways. Viljoen was to reorganize the commandos there and maintain law and order. This was no easy task as the commandos themselves had differences. Commandant Dircksen of the Boksburg commando had surrendered to the British and negotiated a limited armistice. He returned to his commando, climbed onto a wagon and addressed them, suggesting that they do

---

[1] Viljoen *My Reminiscences of the Anglo Boer War* p105. Viljoen was one of the youngest Boer generals, being only 30 at the time of his promotion.
[2] Viljoen *My Reminiscences of the Anglo Boer War* pp132-145.
[3] Viljoen *My Reminiscences of the Anglo Boer War* p146.
[4] Viljoen *My Reminiscences of the Anglo Boer War* pp149-50. mentions the public meeting and the krygsraad. See also Maurice History of the War in South Africa Vol III pp436-37.
[5] Chilvers *The Times History of the War in South Africa* Vol V p60.
[6] *Krygsraad* — a council of war.

likewise - they refused! Chris Muller, who was to become an able officer, was elected Commandant in his place.

A further problem was the presence of General Daniel Erasmus, Viljoen's superior officer during the early fighting around Ladysmith, a year previously. He was not now inclined to take orders from Viljoen and was no longer respected by the men of the Pretoria commando. Erasmus was apparently planning to surrender and held a *krygsraad* to discuss the eight-day armistice while peace terms were discussed. Muller and numbers of others objected to this and Erasmus found himself no longer Commandant of the Pretoria commando.[1]

In the vicinity were a number of Boers who had surrendered, "hensoppers" as they were derisively named by the fighting Boers. They had passes from the British authorities allowing them to return to their farms but were required to report any burghers or a commando who came close. Viljoen rounded up fifteen of these dissidents and arranged a court martial in the churchyard at Rhenosterkop. The principal offender was one van Schalkwyk who was sentenced to two years imprisonment and the confiscation of all his portable property. As the Boers had no prison, Muller commented that such people merely returned to their families.[2]

Viljoen initially based himself at Witnek on the edge of the rugged area of hills known as the Gouwsberge. He had a force of about 1,200 men at his command.[3] With him were the Johannesburg and Boksburg commandos as well as a detachment of the Zuid Afrikaansche Republiek Politie (South African Republic Police), survivors of their gallant action at Bergendal in September. The Pretoria commando, split up into several groups as a result of their strife with Erasmus, was in the area. The Krugersdorp commando with its very able Commandant, Jan Kemp, had been sent to the west and now took orders from General Koos de la Rey, the Deputy Transvaal Commandant-General.

Attacks on stations on the Pretoria-Delagoa Bay railway line at Balmoral and Wilge Rivier on 19 November alerted the British to the presence once more of a strong Boer force in the vicinity. British accounts say that the attacks "both failed" but the Balmoral station building was damaged, the telegraph instrument was smashed and a stretch of railway line was torn up. An outlying post was captured by the Boers who took 43 men captive but who were soon released.[4]

Major General Arthur Paget was ordered to deal with Viljoen, whose force was reported to be near Rhenosterkop, north of Bronkhorstspruit. Told to cooperate was Major General Neville Lyttelton, commander of a number of columns along the Pretoria-Delagoa Bay railway line. Paget was then at Rietfontein, west of Pretoria after operating north of Pretoria in September and October.[5] At Eerstefabriken, thirteen miles east of Pretoria, he was joined by Brigadier General Herbert Plumer with a mounted column on 21 November. Paget's infantry force comprised seven companies of the 1st West Riding Regiment and five companies of the 1st Royal Munster Fusiliers. The artillery attached to the column was four guns each of the 7th and 38th Batteries Royal Field Artillery and two Naval 12 pounders of the Royal Garrison Artillery.

Plumer commanded two brigades of Australians and New Zealanders: Colonel T.E. Hickman with the 4th South Australian Imperial Bushmen, 3rd Queensland Mounted Rifles, 4th Queensland Imperial Bushmen, 3rd Victorian Bushmen, 4th West Australian Mounted infantry and some men of the 3rd Tasmanian Contingent of 1st Imperial Bushmen as escort for the guns. The 3rd New Zealand Mounted Rifles under Lieutenant Colonel M. Cradock completed the column of mounted men. The whole force numbered approximately 2,500 officers and men with ten guns and two Vickers-Maxims.[6]

Field Marshall Lord Roberts was on the point of leaving South Africa, believing as he did that the war was "practically over".[7] His orders to Paget were about the last that were issued by him as Commander-in-Chief.[8] Paget intended to approach from the north, driving Viljoen and his men south and east. Lyttelton was informed of Paget's operation but coordination was near impossible because of the difficult terrain east of Rhenosterkop.

Paget marched on 25 November to De Wagens Drift and on the following day to Sybrand's Kraal, a familiar place for Paget since his column had camped there at the end of September. Near here the first clash with the Boers took place, the Pretoria commando still seemingly under Erasmus. Paget was able to "compel Erasmus to fall back on Viljoen at Rhenosterkop."[9] This is difficult to reconcile with Poortjiesnek, Viljoen's escape route to the northeast, being watched by Erasmus and 400 burghers of Pretoria.[10] A clash with a patrol of the Pretoria burghers under Max Theunissen is likely what happened. The only evidence for this is scanty but Theunissen's men joined the Johannesburg commando's men on 29 November, the day of the battle of Rhenosterkop.[11] Thus they were not with the other Pretoria burghers who were watching the line of retreat.

Plumer and the mounted men headed north out of Sybrand's Kraal towards Suster's Hoek. Commandant Chris Muller had hastened to this place with the Boksburg commando. Here they clashed with the mounted column. Muller said the "enemy was so strong — there were four thousand mounted men and many guns" that they were forced into a fighting retreat back to Rhenosterkop.[12] Captain

---

[1] Muller *Oorlogsherinneringe* p59.

[2] Muller *Oorlogsherinneringe* p63. Viljoen *My Reminiscences of the Anglo Boer War* p153.

[3] Maurice *History of the War in South Africa* Vol III p438.

[4] Chilvers *The Times History of the War in South Africa* Vol V p61. Maurice *History of the War in South Africa* Vol 3 pp445-46. P.C. Coetzee has compiled British and Boer accounts and drawn maps of the attack on Balmoral Station.

[5] It was Paget who had interviewed Commandant Dircksen about 27 September, accepted his surrender, and permitted him to return under an armistice to his commando. Maurice *History of the War in South Africa* Vol III p374.

[6] Maurice *History of the War in South Africa* Vol III p448. See also Murray *Official Records of the Australian Military Contingents*.

[7] Roberts's own words at a dinner in Durban in December 1900, quoted by Lieutenant Colonel Sir Henry Rawlinson in his diary and in Pakenham *The Boer War* p458.

[8] Chilvers *The Times History of the War in South Africa* Vol V p61.

[9] Maurice *History of the War in South Africa* Vol III p448.

[10] Chilvers *The Times History of the War in South Africa* Vol V p62.

[11] Schikkerling *Commando Courageous* p104.

[12] Muller *Oorlogsherinneringe* p65. Also Viljoen *My Reminiscences of the Anglo Boer War* p159. In Chamberlain and Drooglever *The*

H.L.D. Wilson's letter to his wife bears witness of a fight with artillery at Albert Silver Mine to his left. He says that he was "five miles off on a ridge" and that they "went on a little further and went into camp".[1]

There was no element of surprise; the British shelled the Boers that night and one of their men lost his way, blundered into the Boer lines and was captured. He told them that his general was Paget and that Lyttelton was expected from the east tomorrow.[2]

The British camp was on the farm Hartebeestfontein, about TWO miles away from the Boer laager, which was to the north of Rhenosterkop "in a depression among massive granite boulders, some almost as large as houses."[3] Orders were received by the various units at 8 p.m. on 28 November and the troops moved out at daybreak on the 29th. Viljoen and his officers were able to see the advancing British Infantry and mounted Australians and New Zealanders in a dawn ride along the lines. No doubt influenced by what Muller had told him, he estimated that his enemy was 5,000 strong. His own strength was "500 at the outside"[4] but they occupied very strong positions. The complete Boer line stretched about four miles.

The Johannesburgers, commanded by Viljoen's younger brother, Wynand, occupied a line of small ridges strewn with big boulders. In front of them was a flat plain or glacis which was totally without cover of any sort giving them an excellent field of fire. Behind them was a small ravine and a stream in which they sheltered their horses. The British infantry who advanced towards them would have faced a storm of fire and scarcely seen a single Boer.

It was the British infantry who attacked on their right against the Johannesburg commando, "thinly strewn in twos and threes behind boulders"[5] There would have been several hundred men in this line. They got to within seventy paces before the Johannesburgers opened fire. Those who survived fell flat and were unable either to advance or fall back. A second attempt was made with the same result in spite of the efforts of Lieutenant Colonel G.E. Lloyd of the West Ridings. Apparently wounded in the leg he propped himself up with a rifle and continued to shout his orders until he was shot down.[6] Artillery in the form of two 15-pounder field guns supported them and a number of Boers were hit by shrapnel.[7] The Munsters and the West Ridings were obliged to sit tight in their position for the whole day. Any movement attracted heavy fire and movement forwards or back was thus out of the question.

Nevertheless, part of the Boer line felt themselves to be under severe threat. Some of the Johannesburgers and Field Cornet Max Theunissen's Pretoria burghers were occupying "a stony koppie slightly ahead of our regular front."[8] The Jeppestown commando, who was the furthest to the right of the Johannesburgers, was assailed by "a large body of enemy horse, taking advantage of the concave nature of part of the ground..." — presumably some of the 4th Queenslanders. Other Johannesburgers galloped to their assistance.[9]

In the centre of the Boer position were the mounted police of the ZARP. These men were members of a trained para-military force, some of the best trained men that Viljoen had. They occupied an outcrop covered in enormous boulders which was well-nigh impregnable to a frontal attack. Their commander was Lieutenant D. Smith who was killed a short time after Rhenosterkop. The advance guard, the 4th Queensland Imperial Bushmen, was allowed to get close before the Boers opened fire. The result was that, just like the infantry on their right, they could only lie flat behind what little cover was available. All they could do was to get a message back that they were in a tight place.

The 4th South Australian Imperial Bushmen were with the main body. It was still only 5:30 a.m. when a staff officer arrived to inform their commanding officer, Colonel James Rowell, that the Queenslanders needed assistance. Captain H.L.D. Wilson was ordered to take his squadron forward. They advanced past the Queenslanders and crept up through the long grass to within 300 yards of the Boer police. Wilson's line was stationary and he asked for artillery support. Shrapnel showered the rocks in front but the South Australians could only advance a short distance further as the enemy fire was too hot. Just at dusk, Wilson heard the Boer commandant giving the order *"Voorwaarts!"* ("Forward!") He pulled his men back 50 yards and they poured a volley over the ridge which discouraged any further advance from the Boers.[10]

On the Boer right, placed in more rough ground, were Muller's men. In that position was the Boksburg commando with some of the Pretoria burghers. The Boers' only Krupp gun was placed behind them. "Early in the morning of 29 November, just as it began to get light" Muller led a number of mounted Boers in a sally against the advancing British. They took their Krupp gun with them and opened fire, firing four shots before they were forced to limber up and gallop back to their line. Muller said these made inroads in their ranks[11] but Lieutenant Arthur Bailey of the 4th Q.I.B. says that they were riding in open order and "[12] they could see

---

War with Johnny Boer p355 is a graphic account of that day's skirmishing with the Boers, evidently at Sybrand's Kraal, Suster's Hoek and further, by Captain D.J. Ham of the 3rd Victorian Bushmen.

[1] Wilson to his wife — published in Border Watch, Mount Gambier, South Australia.
[2] Schikkerling *Commando Courageous* p104.
[3] Schikkerling *Commando Courageous* p103. This place can be positively identified.
[4] Viljoen *My Reminiscences of the Anglo Boer War* p160.
[5] Schikkerling *Commando Courageous* p104.
[6] Viljoen *My Reminiscences of the Anglo Boer War* p162 tells of placing flowers on Lloyd's grave some months later. Muller *Oorlogsherinneringe* p66 tells that he had a very loud voice and "we could always hear when he gave the order to charge."
[7] Schikkerling *Commando Courageous* p104: "Three shrapnel bullets lodged in the back of Polly Burger..."

[8] Schikkerling *Commando Courageous* p104.
[9] Schikkerling *Commando Courageous* p105.
[10] Captain H.L.D. Wilson's letter is an excellent account of the 4th SAIB's action that day when they were forced to lie flat for 13½ hours. "When one looks over the battlefield one wonders how we were not all killed."
[11] Muller *Oorlogsherinneringe* p65 says *"Ons skiet paaie in hulle..."*
[12] Chamberlain & Drooglever *The War with Johnny Boer* p352, extract from Lt Arthur Bailey's diary. Quaintly, Bailey names the Boer general "Bill John".

the Boers on the skyline. Suddenly a shell fell fair in No. 1 Division, quickly followed by three more. No one was hurt."

To attack Muller's position the mounted brigades had to advance up an incline with no cover apart from some scattered anthills. Plumer was looking for a gap in the Boer line but their right was protected by a deep ravine. Hickman's brigade with the 3rd Queensland Mounted Rifles, 3rd Victorian Bushmen and 4th West Australian Mounted Infantry and Cradock's 3rd New Zealand Mounted Rifles could only make a frontal attack and quickly lost four men killed and a number wounded. There was sporadic gunfire throughout the day but they could make no forward progress.[1]

When night fell the British dug trenches, expecting to be attacked the following day, 30 November, but the Boers had left during the night. Viljoen had only decided to make a stand in order to allow his guns and wagons to escape to the north to Poortjiesnek and the Langkloof. Viljoen was aware that Lytellton had been informed of Paget's movements. Commandant Thys Pretorius's commando was sent to watch the Waterval Drift, the only feasible crossing over the Wilge River to the east of Rhenoster Kop. Lieutenant-Colonel G.D. Carleton and his column of the 18th Hussars captured his laager, Pretorius himself had a narrow escape, and occupied a position commanding the drift. The Hussars were unable to contact Paget although they were a relatively short distance away.[2]

When the British approached their positions of the previous day they found the Boers had gone. The 3rd Victorians realized then what a strong position the Boers had held. They commented too that the Boer losses must have been great. In the rocks were dead horses, blood-stained clothes and a Boer's head in a hat, the body nowhere to be found.[3]

On 30 November a party of Queenslanders, Victorians and New Zealanders under Major W.H. Tunbridge followed the tracks of the retreating Boers. Muller had placed a rearguard at Engelbrecht's Drift,[4] about three miles from where they had fought the battle. A nervous Boer opened fire when the Australasians were still a thousand yards away. Lieutenant R.H. Walsh of the 3rd Queenslanders said, "they wheeled round and went, as the kiddies say, 'like anything' with bullets flying around us." Tunbridge had strict orders not to bring on a fight and returned to camp.[5]

Paget's losses were 87 with 21 killed and 66 wounded. Viljoen claimed that two Boers were killed and 22 wounded. He said, "the exact loss of the enemy was difficult to estimate. It must, however, have amounted to some hundreds."[6] The Boers headed to the Bothasberg, east of Lydenburg, where they knew they could find good grazing for their horses and where they would not be molested by the British for some weeks.

References

1. Major Charles Burnett *The 18th Hussars in South Africa: The Records of a Cavalry Regiment During the Boer War* Warren & Son, Winchester 1905.
2. Max Chamberlain & Robin Droogleven *The War with Johnny Boer* Australian Military History Publications, Loftus, Australia 2003.
3. Hedley Chilvers (editor) *The Times History of the War in South Africa* Vol V Sampson Low, Marston & Company, Ltd, London 1907.
4. P.C. Coetzee *The Boer attack on Balmoral Station 19th November 1900* unpublished.
5. D.O.W. Hall *New Zealanders in South Africa 1899-1902* War History Branch, Department of Internal Affairs, Wellington 1949. Reprint Naval & Military Press, Uckfield, Sussex.
6. *Len Harvey Letters from the Veldt An account of the involvement of volunteers from Queensland at the war in South Africa (Boer War) 1899-1902* Maryborough sub-branch Returned Services League of Australia, Queensland 1994.
7. Major General Sir Frederick Maurice *History of the War in South Africa* Vol 3. Hurst & Blackett Limited, London 1908.
8. General C.H. Muller *Oorlogsherinneringe* Nasionale Pers, Beperk Cape Town, Bloemfontein and Pretoria 1936 (reprint Bienedell Uitgewers, Pretoria 2002).
9. Lieutenant-Colonel P.L. Murray *Official Records of the Australian Military Contingents to the War in South Africa*, Department of Defence, Melbourne 1911. (reprint Naval & Military Press, Uckfield, Sussex).
10. Thomas Pakenham *The Boer War* Weidenfeld & Nicholson Limited, London 1979.
11. R.W. Schikkerling *Commando Courageous* Hugh Keartland (Publishers) Johannesburg 1964.
12. Richard Stowers *Rough Riders at War* published by the author, Hamilton 2006.
13. General Ben Viljoen *My Reminiscences of the Anglo Boer War* Hood, Douglas & Howard, London 1903 (Reprint by C.Struik (Pty) Ltd, Cape Town 1973).
14. Steve Watt *In Memoriam* University of Natal Press, Pietermaritzburg 2000.
15. Wilcox, Craig *Australia's Boer War* Oxford University Press, Australian War Memorial, Melbourne 2002.
16. Letter from Captain H.L.D. Wilson to his wife — published in Border Watch, Mount Gambier, South Australia, Saturday 12 January 1901.

---

[1] Stowers *Rough Riders at War* p29 has a description of the New Zealanders' fight and the evening counter-attack by Muller's men. See also Muller *Oorlogsherinneringe* p68.
[2] Burnett *The 18th Hussars in South Africa* pp123-25. Maurice *History of the War in South Africa* Vol III p455.
[3] Chamberlain & Droogleven *The War with Johnny Boer* p357. Captain D.J. Ham's account of the 3rd Victorian Bushmen at Rhenoster Kop.
[4] Muller *Oorlogsherinneringe* p69.
[5] Harvey *Letters from the Veldt* p83
[6] Viljoen *My Reminiscences of the Anglo Boer War* p164.

Casualty List[1]

435	Corporal	R. Devereux	2nd New Zealand Mounted Rifles	KIA
394	Private	W.A. Jennings	2nd New Zealand Mounted Rifles	KIA
306	Private	H.E. Oppenheim	2nd New Zealand Mounted Rifles	KIA
418	Sgt Farrier	R.E. Smith	2nd New Zealand Mounted Rifles	DOW
734	Private	G. Hyde	3rd New Zealand Mounted Rifles	KIA
717	Sergeant	F.M. Russel	3rd New Zealand Mounted Rifles	KIA
296	Private	A.E. Wright	4th Queensland Imperial Bushmen	KIA
70536	Driver	J. Blower	U Battery, Royal Horse Artillery	DOW
577	Sergeant	C.E. McCabe	4th South Australian Imperial Bushmen	KIA
48	Trooper	A.S. Page	4th South Australian Imperial Bushmen	KIA
509	Trooper	A.R. Mackenzie	3rd Victorian Bushmen	KIA
1700	Sergeant	A.G.K. Buckingham	5th Victorian Mounted Rifles	KIA
1509	Private	W. Andrews	1*′ West Riding	DOW
5284	Private	W. Edwards	1" West Riding	KIA
1637	Private	T. Gilby	1" West Riding	DOW
5832	Private	J. Harrison	1" West Riding	KIA
	Lt Col	G.E. Lloyd	1" West Riding	KIA
l	Lieutenant	H.J.C. Oakes	1*′ West Riding	DOW
3176	Private	W. Roberts	1" West Riding	KIA
3612	Private	S. Venables	1" West Riding	DOW
5142	Private	J. Wilkinson	1" West Riding	KIA

KIA	Killed in action	15
DOW	Died of wounds	6
Wounded:	4th Queensland Imperial Bushmen	8
	5th Victorian Mounted Rifles	1
	4th South Australian Imperial Bushmen	2
	2nd and 3rd New Zealand Mounted Rifles	17
	1st Royal Munster Fusiliers	13
	1st West Riding Regiment	25
	Total	**66**

BATTLE OF RHENOSTERKOP—HOW COLONEL LLOYD DIED.

---

[1] See Watt *In Memoriam* for complete details.

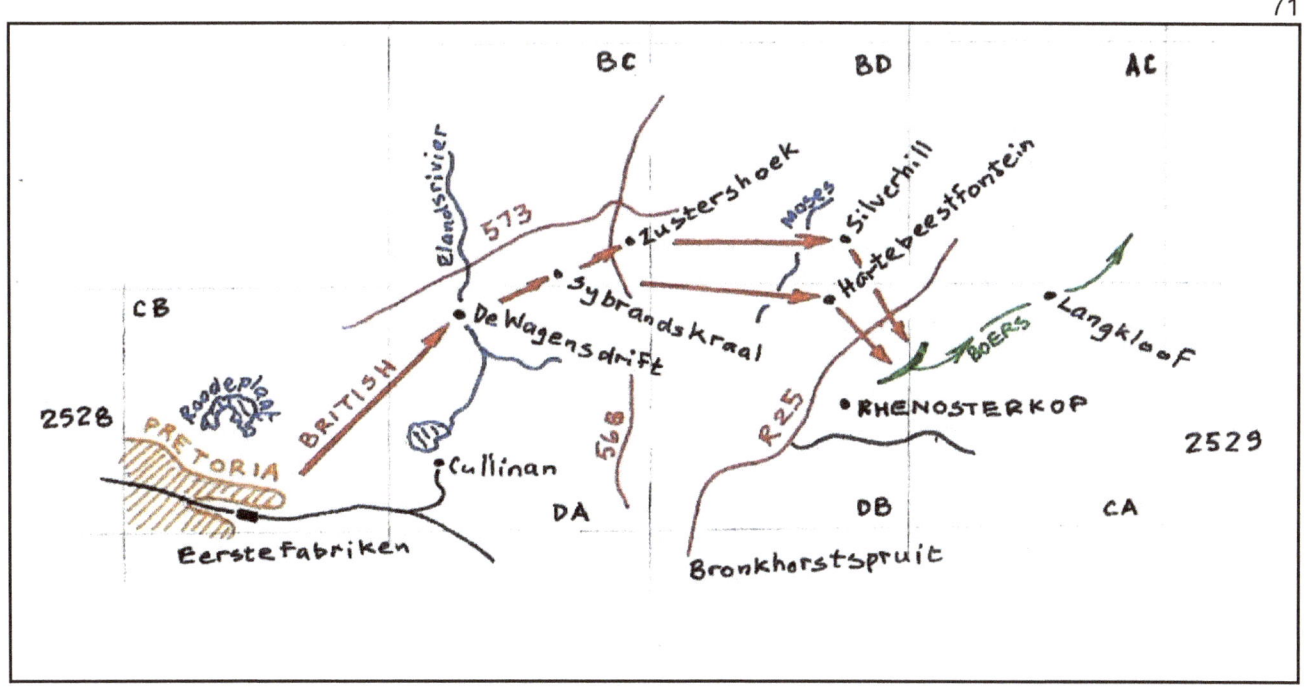

The numbers and letters are those of the corresponding 1:50k topo survey maps
of the South African Surveyor General.

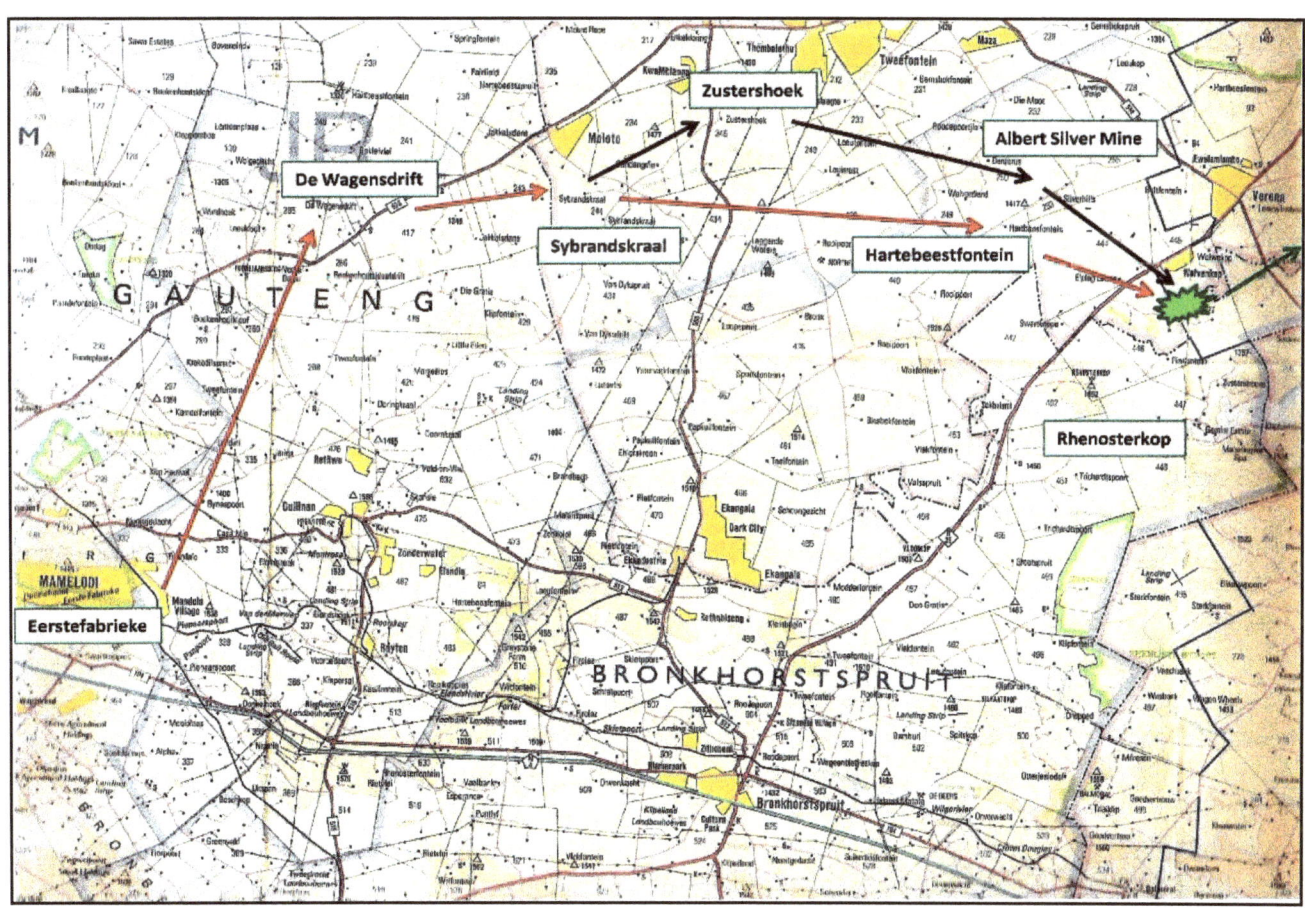

The British advance: Paget's columns assembled at Eerstefabrieken, outside Pretoria on 25 November. They marched to De Wagensdrift on 26th and to Sybrand's Kraal on 27th where Plumer and the mounted men headed north to Zustershoek. On 28th the column marched to Hartebeestfontein while Plumer's mounted men engaged the Pretoria commando of Commandant Erasmus at Albert Silver Mine, now Silverhill. Advancing in the early morning of 29th they engaged the force of General Ben Viljoen to the north of the prominent hill called Rhenosterkop.

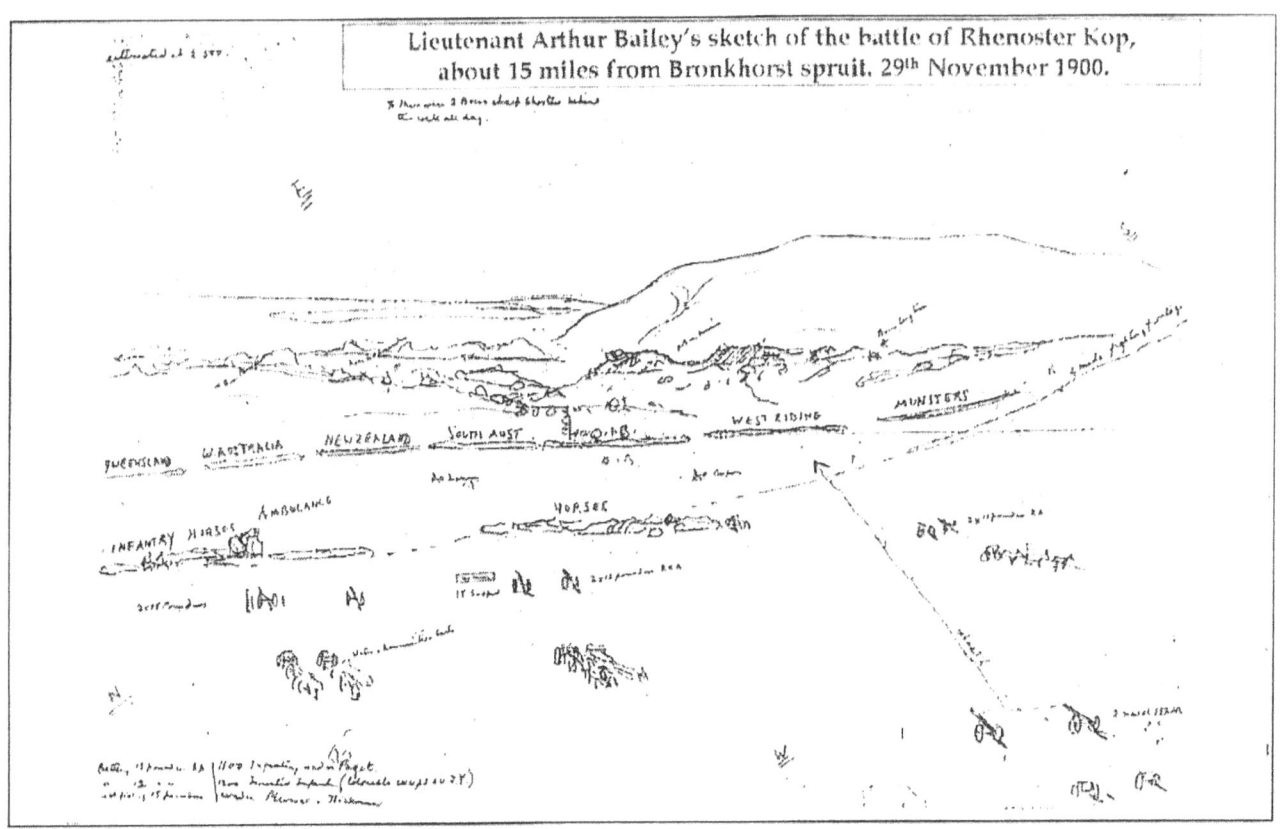

The battle: Lt Bailey's sketch is the only known drawing of the battle. Frank Dadd's picture below shows the 4th Queenslanders in a tight place. The hill to their front is not Rhenosterkop but the kop where Viljoen had located his headquarters and heliograph.

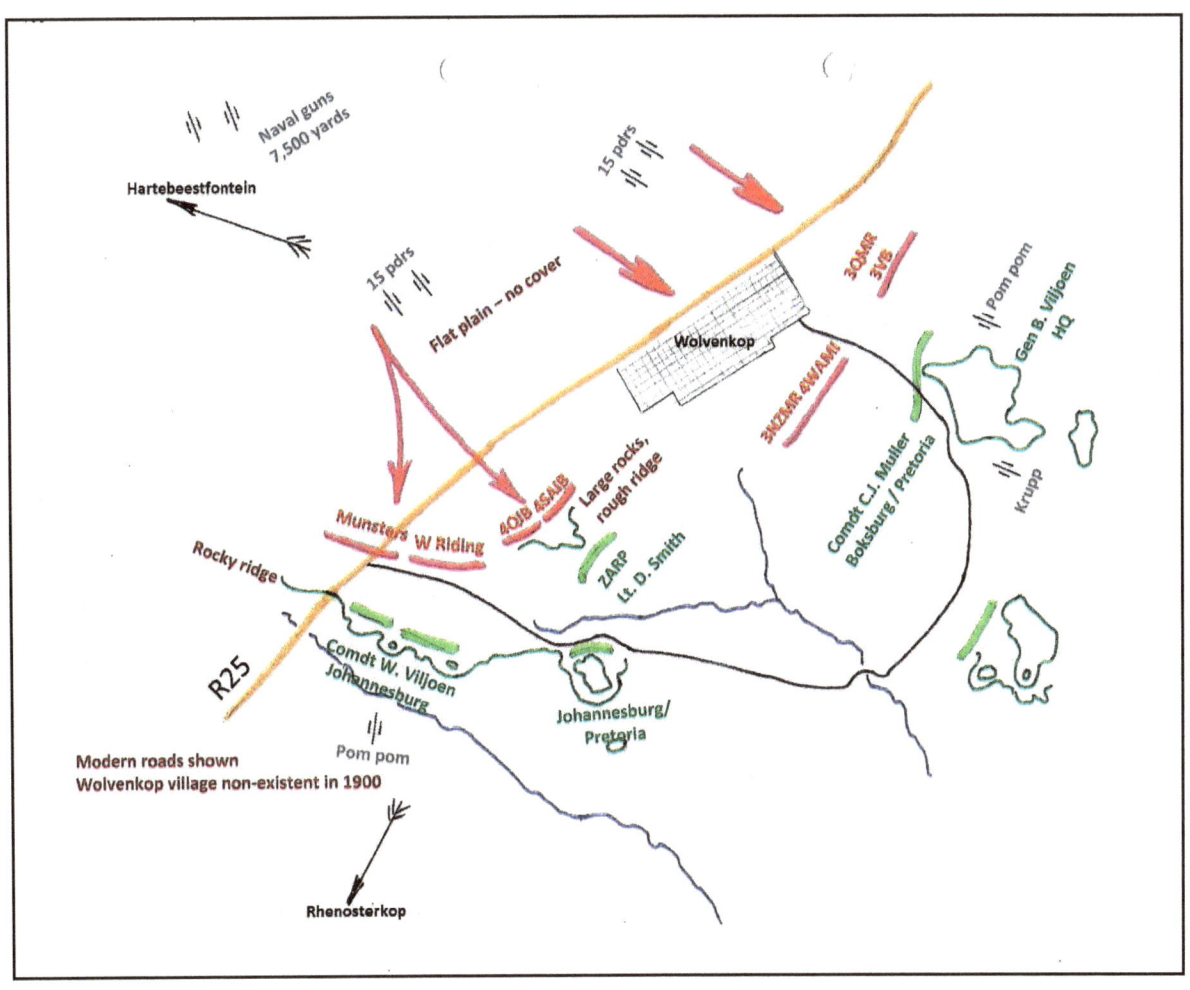

The battle: Scale diagram with British and Boer positions marked and the relevant portions of two 1:50k topo survey maps similarly marked.

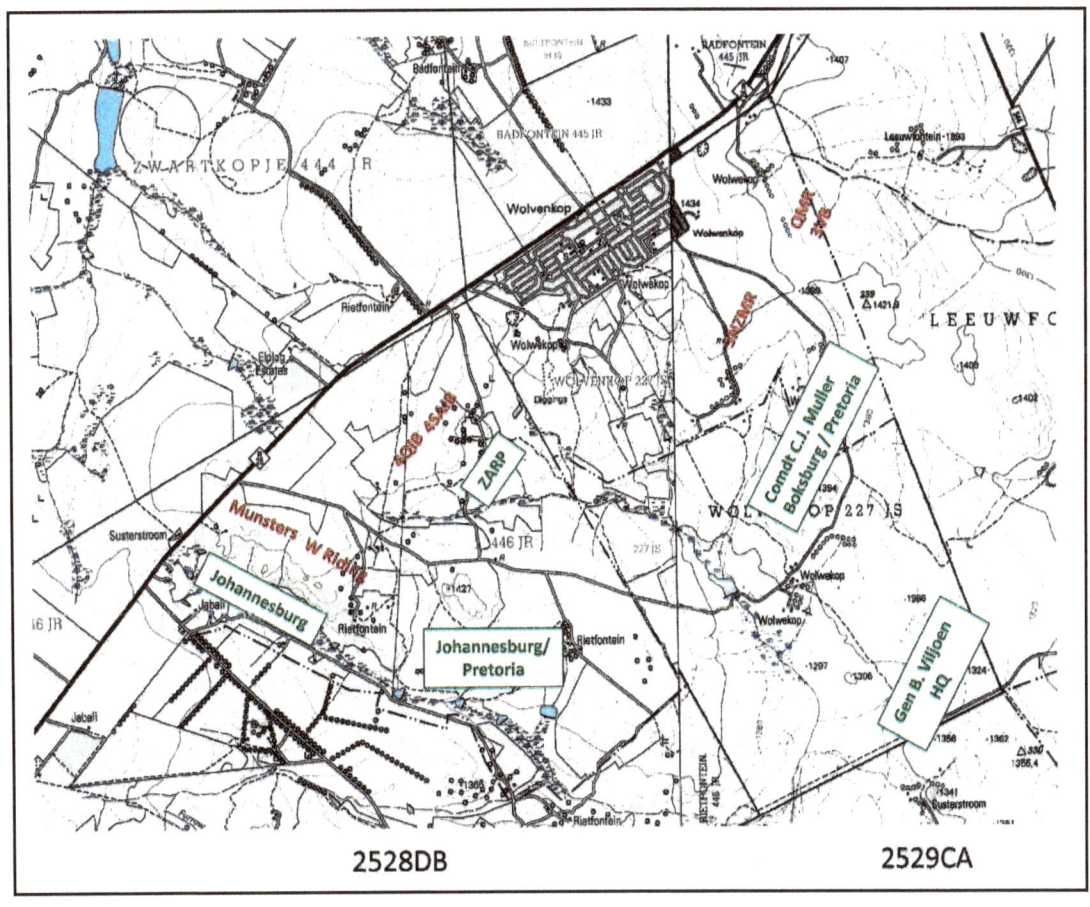

Lieutenant Arthur Bailey
4th Queensland Imperial Bushmen

Major W.H. Tunbridge
3rd Queensland Mounted Infantry

Imperial map of 1900: This map issued by the British Army Intelligence Department in 1900. The red road running diagonally from the bottom left is the course of the modern road 573. The area around Rhenosterkop has little in the way of roads and tracks which is why Viljoen chose it for his laager. Sybrandskraal, Zustershoek, Albert Silver Mine, Hartebeestfontein and Rhenosterkop all marked. The battle took place on Rietfontein and Wolvenkop.

...massive granite boulders, some almost as large as houses...

Ancient Matabele structures were ready-made fortifications.

The small hills where Viljoen located himself with a heliograph. He could see the whole battlefield from there.

The area with the huge granite boulders, the ZARP position. To the right the ridge with the Johannesburgers. Viljoen's HQ visible just right of the tree. Rhenosterkop in the far distance.

Australians

Australian soldiers played a considerable part in the war in South Africa, the Anglo Boer war of 1899-1902. At the start of the war Australia was still not a single political entity but was in the process of forming the Commonwealth of Australia, the country that it is today. Each of the six Colonies sent a number of contingents to South Africa, supporting the British Government in defence of the Empire in its dispute with the two Boer republics of the *Zuid Afrikaansche Republiek* (as the Transvaal had been renamed shortly after their independence was regained in 1881) and the Orange Free State. Australian Commonwealth contingents arrived only after the war was over.

Around 20,000 men and eighty women from Australia went to South Africa with the various contingents as well as to enrol in other British and Colonial regiments. By comparison, 7,500 Canadians and 6,500 New Zealanders took up arms for the Empire.[1] The New South Wales Lancers were the first of the Australians to arrive in South Africa and were in action in the north of the Cape Colony in November 1899. They returned to Australia in December 1900 with a number of other Australian contingents, around about the time that Lord Roberts, in a speech in Durban, proclaimed that the war was "practically over". He was right, the war of set-piece battles was over, but those Boers still in the field and under arms had not capitulated. They were more determined than ever to fight for their independence.

With their capitals in the hands of their enemy, the Boers were dispirited but Paul Kruger, the President of the *Zuid Afrikaansche Republiek*, in exile in Holland, signalled that hostilities should continue. President Steyn of the Orange Free State's determination, invoking the cooperation treaty of 1897 between the two republics, ensured their continued resistance. Boer leaders like Christiaan de Wet and Koos de la Rey were likewise adamant that hostilities should continue.

They had plenty of modern weaponry, much of it now captured British rifles and ammunition, since cartridges for their German Mauser rifles were practically exhausted. Food was never plentiful since the British had resorted to a policy of scorched earth to deny the Boers any livestock or foodstuff. The principal advantage that they had over the British army and its Colonial allies was vastly superior mobility. They were able to operate in the field with an absolute minimum of wagons and carts, the burghers surviving on little more than biltong (dried meat) and green maize.

By early 1901 it was clear that a protracted struggle was in the offing. Retraining took time as did the procuring of thousands of horses, especially as the supply to South Africa had at first been halted altogether in the light of Lord Roberts's pronouncements.[2] Enormous numbers of horses were required for army and Lord Roberts telegraphed to the Secretary of State in February 1900 not long after he had arrived in South Africa to take command: "Please arrange for early and steady supply remounts...Without mobile force I can do nothing in this country." Procuring these huge numbers of horses in Britain alone was impossible and a majority of what was needed came from the United States and some other countries outside the British Empire. Consequently, when Colonial contingents were raised they had of necessity to provide their own horses.[3]

There were almost immediately problems with their horses. Shipped in stalls below decks and then railed upcountry in open trucks immediately on arrival in South Africa, made them unsuitable for hard work without a period of rest and recovery. There was insufficient water and grass on the *veld* for hard-working horses and the army was never able to keep sufficient fodder on hand. Fodder had to be brought by convoy to the various columns operating out in the countryside, imported mostly from Argentina. Horses brought into South Africa had little resistance to horse sickness. "Horses seem well but suddenly drop down and in ten minutes are dead", said Lieutenant James Patterson of the 5th Victorian Mounted Rifles.[4] After just two weeks of campaigning in April 1901, two thirds of the 5VMR's horses were useless or dead.[5] The only remounts available were also in poor condition.

To counter the Boer mobility the British cavalry regiments needed to be retrained for their new role as mounted infantry. Artillerymen and infantry had to be taught to ride horses. The Colonials, Australians, New Zealanders, Canadians and the numerous regiments raised locally, were almost without exception already trained as mounted infantry. These men were used exclusively as front-line soldiers leaving the British infantry to guard lines of communication and to act as garrison troops in occupied towns.

The first Australian contingents arrived back in Australia in November and December 1900. The British commander in South Africa, General Lord Kitchener, who had taken over from Lord Roberts in November 1900 now called for replacements in the last few days of December 1900. All the new recruits were to be mounted and experienced officers and rankers from previous contingents would be offered promotions to stay on. Kitchener was very keen to recruit colonial horsemen as these were "the best men for the work in hand."[6] There was a perception in Australia that the real

---

[1] Wilcox *Australia's Boer War* Preface pXIII gives this figure for Australian involvement which includes enlistments in irregular corps. In a speech at the planting of South African cedar trees at the Anglo Boer War Grove in Canberra, Ms Katy Gallagher, Chief Minister of the Australian Capital Territory, gave a figure of 16,000 men who served a year in Australian units while another 8,000 others served in South African Colonial units.

[2] After Lord Roberts made a speech in Durban in December 1900 when he said the war was "practically over", the Remount Department recalled its buying commission, see *Times History* vi pp436-7.

[3] Anglesey *A History of the British Cavalry* quotes figures from the *Royal Commission on the War in South Africa*. 470,000 horses and 149,600 transport mules were found by the Army Remount department and sent to South Africa. This does not include domestic horses in South Africa and those from Australia, Canada and New Zealand. See also *Times History* vi p419.

[4] Quoted in Wilcox *Australia's Boer War* p131.

[5] Quoted in Wilcox *Australia's Boer War* p134.

[6] Wilcox *Australia's Boer War* p188.

fighting was over, only police work remained. The response to the call for volunteers in all the Australian colonies, soon to be the states in the Commonwealth of Australia, was overwhelming. Several thousand came forward in Victoria and there were even more in New South Wales.

In Victoria the original intention was to form one regiment of five hundred men but so many came forward and so many passed the requirements of riding and shooting that two regiments were formed. These were the 5th and 6th Victorian Mounted Rifles although the designation "6th" was seldom mentioned. There was even an overflow of 256 men who joined the Marquis of Tullibardine's Scottish Horse Regiment.[1] After six weeks' training they left for South Africa, 1,018 strong, on 15 February 1901.

Those who were accepted were "fit young men, more often from towns and suburbs than the bush."[2] Thus, between February and April, 1901 the largest military force to leave Australia before 1914 sailed for South Africa in fifteen ships. They came from all six of the original Colonies now amalgamated into the states of the Commonwealth of Australia. By comparison, in Canada there was a considerable body of opinion that opposed Canadian participation in the war. Their government would only allow 1,248 Canadians to join the South African Constabulary early in 1901.[3] New Zealand, with its small population, in 1901 provided their 6th and 7th Contingents, each 600 strong.[4]

On arrival in South Africa, the 5th and 6th Western Australian Mounted Rifles were attached to the column of Major General Walter Kitchener, based in Middelburg in the eastern Transvaal (today Mpumalanga). The 5th Victorian Mounted Rifles were initially with the column commanded by Major General Stuart Beatson, an experienced general who had been sent to South Africa with Major General Sir Bindon Blood from India. In June part of the 5VMR was ambushed by a Boer commando and overwhelmed at Wilmansrust. Beatson all but accused the Victorians of cowardice and mutinous conduct. Further, a remark was passed that the 5 and 6WAMR had run away at Brakpan. The later awards of two Victoria Crosses to men of the 5VMR, as well as a Victoria Cross and mentions in dispatches to the Western Australians, showed these assertions to be undeserved.

A short while after Wilmansrust they formed part of the column of Colonel W.P. Pulteney. He was quoted as saying that "he had felt trepidation when he learned that the 5th were to be posted to him, but within two days his fears had been dispelled."[5] As time passed and experience was gained, these Australians came to be regarded as excellent soldiers. The 5VMR later took part in a number of successful actions, the relief of the 5th Queensland Imperial Bushmen at Onverwacht on 4 January 1902 being noteworthy. The soldiers soon regained their confidence after these early setbacks, to judge from their letters. Lieutenant J.H. Patterson wrote in his diary that Colonel W.P. Pulteney, under whose orders they fell from late 1901, considered the 5VMR to be the finest irregular regiment in the field.

Two battles east of Johannesburg in 1901: Brakpan Farm and Wilmansrust

In the winter of 1901 two battles involving Australian contingents in the Highveld region of the Transvaal east of Johannesburg caused some controversy. The 5th and 6th Western Australian and the 5th Victorian Mounted Rifles both found themselves accused of being faint-hearted in the face of the enemy, all but cowards.

The 5th and 6th Western Australian Mounted Rifles were 449 strong in four mounted rifle squadrons. Quite soon after their arrival in South Africa at the end of March 1901 the 5WAMR took part in a sweep north of the Pretoria-Delagoa Bay railway. Attached to the column of Major General Walter Kitchener, they saw little, if any, action and were "mostly occupied with capturing cattle."[6] Returning to Middelburg to refit they were joined there by the 6th Western Australian Mounted Rifles. The 6WAMR had left Perth, Western Australia a month after the 5WAMR and arrived in Durban only at the end of April.

The two regiments were amalgamated in May 1901 in South Africa. Commanding the 5th Contingent was Captain H.F. Darling,[7] the 6th, Captain John Campbell. On their arrival in South Africa, Major Jack Royston, ex-Sergeant Major of the Natal Regiment, the Border Mounted Rifles who had distinguished himself in the siege of Ladysmith, took command of the two regiments. "Galloping Jack", as he later became known, commanded Australian troops in the Great War and was a huge success with the Australian Light Horse in Palestine in 1916-17.

One of the officers of the 6WAMR was Lieutenant Frederick William Bell. He had first enrolled as a private in the 1st Western Australian Mounted Infantry and saw action around Colesberg in February 1900. Later in that year he was part of Major General Robert Broadwood's column engaged in the first De Wet hunt. Bell was severely wounded at Palmietfontein, outside Lindley in the Free State. So severely, shot in the abdomen, that he was invalided back to England. He recovered and returned to Perth in February 1901. As a soldier with experience of conditions in South Africa he was given a commission, joined the 6WAMR, and left again for South Africa in April 1901.[8]

Brakpan Farm

The two regiments left Middelburg on 12 May and headed southeast. There was some fighting at Bosmanspruit on 14 May when Campbell and his men moved about six miles

---

[1] Wilcox *Australia's Boer War* p193.
[2] Wilcox *Australia's Boer War* p189.
[3] Miller *Painting the map red* p368.
[4] Hall *The New Zealanders in South Africa* pp54-71.
[5] From the diary of Lieutenant J.H. Patterson, 5VMR in the National Library of Australia, Melbourne and quoted by Chamberlain in his paper *The Battlefield Trials of the 5th Victorian Mounted Rifles*.

[6] Chamberlain & Drooglever *The War with Johnny Boer* p423, account of Corporal Gerald Grave, Perth Morning Herald, 9 July 1901.
[7] The same man who, as a Lieuenant, was in action at Doornkraal on 6 November 1900.
[8] Briggs *The Search for Lieutenant Colonel F. W. Bell, V.C.*.

away from General Kitchener's main column. An attempt to surprise some Boers in a farmhouse at Rietkuil was unsuccessful but one man, Private J.T. Facey was severely wounded, shot in the thigh.[1] Captain Campbell described the incident as "some nasty fighting."[2]

Rejoining the column they moved south, clearing farms on either side of the Klein Olifants River. On Thursday 16 May their orders were to clear a farmhouse on the farm Brakpan.[3] Campbell's men picked up the Boer family and the young Lieutenant Tony Forrest was given charge of the wagon with the Boer women and perhaps some children as well. The Boer women told Campbell about three wagons that were mired in a spruit. Perhaps it should have been no surprise when this turned out to be a trap. When the soldiers dismounted to free the wagons the Boers opened fire from the ridge on the farm adjacent to Brakpan, Boschmanspoort.

It was soon apparent that the Western Australians were severely outnumbered and that the Boers were encroaching on their flanks. Campbell saw no alternative but to withdraw and retire back to the safety of the column. This was achieved with some difficulty but six men were killed and two later died of their wounds. The Boers picked up one man, Private J. Semple, and carried him to the farmhouse at Brakpan. During the retirement, Lieutenant Frederick Bell saw a man dismounted. He galloped back to pick him up but the horse was incapable of carrying them both. Bell gave the man his horse and covered his ride to safety. Campbell appears to have done something similar but it was Bell who was rewarded with the Victoria Cross.[4]

Lieutenant Forrest was killed when some Boers galloped towards the wagon in his charge, possibly to free the women and children. He was only sixteen and could well have enjoyed some family influence to have become part of the 5WAMR. His father, a famous explorer of Australia, Alexander Forrest, had been mayor of Perth and his uncle, Sir John Forrest was Minister of Defence in the Commonwealth Parliament. Alexander Forrest died only five weeks later and the grief caused by the loss of his son was said to be a factor in his death.[5]

The fate of Corporal R.J. Furlong is still unknown but he must surely also have been killed in action. During the withdrawal, Trooper Sizer had his horse shot from under him. He lay in the grass and returned the Boer fire expecting to be captured. A horse, which turned out to be Furlong's, came galloping by. Sizer caught the horse, mounted and returned to the column. Some months later the CWAMR captured some Boers who were in possession of saddles whose numbers identified than as having been Furlong's. The Boers told of how Furlong had been left on the field after the fight and it is an assumption that he was later buried by them.

It seems that the detailed map that we have of the action was drawn by Captain John Campbell for the Forrest family. The map was part of the collection of Forrest Papers but appears to have been removed in 1984. Someone in Australia appears to have the original but copies have since come to light.[6] The map is a great deal more detailed than the sketch maps usually made by eye-witnesses which makes it likely that it was Captain John Campbell's work. It lacks scale and a north arrow.

Positive identification of the site of this encounter has only recently been made. An Australian, looking to locate the missing headstone of a relative, Private J.Semple, wrote to the Middelburg Municipality who turned the letter over to a local journalist. The journalist in turn was looking to preserve the graves on what had been the family farm, Bosmanspruit, taken over by a coal-mining company. The Campbell map was compared with an aerial photo of the area by two local farm owners. Part of the area of the historical Brakpan farm, a subdivision called de Rust is where the Boers defended themselves from the West Australians.

This incident is not described at all in the Times History of the War in South Africa and Maurice in the Official History mentions Lieutenant Frederick Bell only in a footnote.[7] Boer Generals Ben Viljoen and Chris Muller in their memoirs also ignore it, although probably their men were nowhere near. No Boer Commandant is named as the enemy by the Australians but it was likely to have been Commandant Piet Trichardt of Middelburg and his men. The site is on the east side of the Hendrina-Arnot Power Station tarred road.

A neighbouring farm, Groblersrecht, was the site of Walter Kitchener's bivouac that evening and where the funeral of the Western Australians was performed the following morning. As was the custom, Lieutenant Forrest was buried in a separate grave from the mass grave for the N.C.O., Sergeant F.F. Edwards, and the four men. Kitchener's address enjoined them not to be vindictive and to treat the Boer women and children kindly.[8]

---

[1] Chamberlain & Drooglever *The War with Johnny Boer* p424. *Casualty noted in The South African War Casualty Roll*.
[2] Chamberlain & Drooglever *The War with Johnny Boer* p423, report of Captain John Campbell from the *Perth Morning Herald*, 10 July 1901.
[3] There is a town called Brakpan, near Johannesburg, which is not to be confused with this place.
[4] According to Mrs Bell's daughter Cynthia, the man rescued by Bell was his batman.
[5] Chamberlain *The Action at Brakpan* from *Sabretache* Vol XLV No 3 – September 2004 p45.

---

[6] Dr James C. Briggs found Frederick Bell's grave in Bristol, England and embarked upon a search to find out more about him. In the course of the search he acquired a copy of the map, apparently from a contact in Australia. See Briggs *The Search for Lieutenant Colonel F. W. Bell, V.C.*
[7] Maurice *History of the War in South Africa 1899-1902* footnote on page 148 of Volume 4.
[8] Chamberlain & Drooglever *The War with Johnny Boer* p425, account of Corporal Gerald Grave, *Perth Morning Herald*, 9 July 1901.

Casualty list

5WAMI:

Corporal W.F.Bollinger	DOW	Carolina Nr (Grobbelaar's Recht)	17.05.01
Sergeant F.F.Edwards	KIA	Carolina Nr (Grobbelaar's Recht)	15.05.01
Lieutenant A.A. Forrest	KIA	Carolina Nr (Grobbelaar's Recht)	15.05.01

6WAMI:

Private F.T. Adam	KIA	Carolina Nr (Grobbelaar's Recht)	15.05.01
Private A. Blanck	DOW	18.05.01 Carolina Nr	16.05.01
Private B. Fisher	KIA	Carolina Nr (Grobbelaar's Recht)	15.05.01
Private F. Page	KIA	Carolina Nr (Grobbelaar's Recht)	15.05.01
Private J. Semple	KIA	Carolina Nr (Grobbelaar's Recht)	15.05.01

All were buried on Grobbelaar's Recht and re-interred in 1962 to Middelburg Military Cemetery.

Private J.Furlong	MIA	Grave unknown	15.05.01

Wilmansrust

In contrast with the Western Australians, the 5th Victorian Mounted Rifles saw some hard fighting in the sweep north of the Pretoria-Delagoa Bay railway line in April and May 1901 when they formed part of the column commanded by Major General Stuart Beatson. Boer General Ben Viljoen's commando had slipped over the line and headed into the rougher country to the north. On 7 May they were in action near Rhenoster Kop. This was where Viljoen had battled Major General A.H. Paget's force, which included two mounted brigades of Australians and New Zealanders, the previous November. On this occasion the 5VMR found themselves drawn into a trap by what seemed to be just a small number of Boer fugitives. Trying to clear some gullies they lost a captain and a lieutenant killed and three men wounded.[1]

The sweep north of the railway line had been very successful from the British Army's viewpoint. "More than a thousand Boers had been captured or surrendered, hundreds of women and children had been brought in to the concentration camps, a number of farms had been looted and destroyed, and Viljoen was convinced that the war was lost."[2] The 5VMR had seen a great deal of fighting and suffered a number of casualties. One man was listed as missing, eighteen had been wounded, one had died of disease and seven had been killed in action.

The commanding officer of the 5VMR, Colonel Alfred Otter was invalided home to Australia and the regiment was split into two wings, the right commanded by Major Thomas Umphelby and the left by Major William McKnight. The 5VMR was reduced to 700 men with a number in hospital. Their horses had suffered even worse than the men as previously related. On 25 May 1901 the 5VMR was in reserve at Brugspruit[3] on the Pretoria-Delagoa Bay railway line. There were patrols to the south and four men were killed in an action at Trichardt's farm, Middelkraal, on 29 May.[4] It is significant that McKnight blamed, in a letter to his fiancé, not just bad luck but "some curs" in the contingent for the losses. As the left wing was only part of the force, McKnight was not happy about "being ordered about by a gunner" – Major C.J.U. Morris, R.F.A. being in command.[5]

On 6 June Major General Beatson's orders were to move south so as to link up with Major General Sir Bindon Blood's columns at Bethel. Beatson halted at Van Dyk's Drift on 10 June and awaited the outcome of the 5VMR left wing's ride to the east to investigate the report of a Boer laager and a small commando at Boschmansfontein. The left wing was comprised of companies E, F, G, H with two pom-poms, left Hartebeestfontein on 9 June and evidently ran into a Boer convoy. Some cattle were captured and the Australians complained that they were unsupported by Major Morris and the pom-poms who were "two miles in our rear" which allowed the convoy to get away.[6] They camped the night of the 11th at Trichardt's farm, Middelkraal. They were short of rations and next morning Major Morris managed to get in touch with Van Dyk's Drift by heliograph from a farm eight miles to the north of Middelkraal, Wilmansrust.

The rations arrived later in the day, escorted by G Company of the 5VMR, and the decision was made to camp there.[7] They were in what seemed to be a secure position on a flat shelf overlooking the Klein Olifants River, also

---

[1] Chamberlain & Drooglever *The War with Johnny Boer* pp421-23.
[2] Wilcox *Australia's Boer War* p200. Viljoen *My Reminiscences of the Anglo-Boer War* pp 206-10 indicates that matters were critical but does not anywhere give an opinion that the war was lost. This view comes from the diary of A.W. Murray 5WAMR which is in the private collection of Jeff Cossum in Melbourne, Australia.
[3] Now renamed Clewer.
[4] Chamberlain & Drooglever *The War with Johnny Boer* p432-3. Maurice's official history gives the date of this engagement as 28 May.
[5] McKnight papers in the Tasmania Museum and Art Gallery, Hobart, Tasmania. "Some curs" appears only in a letter to Belle, his fiancé.
[6] Chamberlain & Drooglever *The War with Johnny Boer* pp458 – letter from Bugler Jack Carolin published in *The Bendigonian*, 13 August 1901. This incident is reported in neither Maurice's official history nor the *The Times History of the War in South Africa*.
[7] Chamberlain & Drooglever *The War with Johnny Boer* p458, Bugler Carolyn's letter.

known as the Leeuwspruit at that point and scarcely more than a stream. "The camp site was as good as any others in the immediate vicinity but it was not ideal. The main camp was positioned on one of the highest points of the farm but there was higher ground to the north where there was an old cemetery. A short distance away on the downward slope to the west was a farmhouse and a stone cattle kraal. The surrounding countryside was rolling open grassland. The open appearance of the landscape however, was deceptive. Gullies and creek beds provided many areas of "dead ground" where large numbers of men could remain hidden from view. The camp enjoyed good views of the distance but restricted outlooks on the dead ground close by.[1]

The Boers had been watching their movements and sniping whenever they saw an opportunity. None of the Australians had been hit but they were constantly aware of Boers just out of rifle range. Bugler Jack Carolin even said, "The Boers were in great numbers on the skyline in front of us."[2] Some came closer and were driven off with a burst of pom-pom shells. The fact that the two wagons with rations and a Scotch cart with pom-pom ammunition arrived without interference from the Boers seems to have convinced the British that the Boers had fallen back. Beatson had information that there were a number of Boers at Vaalkop on the farm Elandsfontein and sent a message to Major Morris at Wilmansrust that he wished to attack them there the morning of 13 June.[3]

General Ben Viljoen had left his men under Commandants Chris Muller, his brother Wynand Viljoen and Nick Groenewald, while he guided the Transvaal Government to the farm Waterval, near Standerton. There they met with members of the Orange Free State government on 20 June 1901 and resolved to continue the war.[4]

Commandant Piet Trichardt approached Muller with a plea for assistance while a number of Boer commandos were near Elandsfontein. This was the Boer force of which Beatson had intelligence. Vaalkop is the highest hill in the area and was commonly used by the Boers for observation. Muller could see the British force as it moved to Wilmansrust and sent Groenewald with ten men to close with them. The object was to try and draw some of the 5VMR away from the column so as to give the Boers the opportunity to fire on them. All that happened was that the British fired a "couple of pom-pom shells at them and they simply turned their horses and walked towards the skyline again." This was at about 4 p.m. according to Muller.[5]

Trumpeter Carolin also wrote in his letter that Muller, on a splendid grey horse, remained in sight long enough for Major Morris to fire four pom-pom shells at him. Muller does not mention this but he does say that "I had a good pair of binoculars and could see everything that they were doing", as he was not a long distance away from the camp.[6]

The other principal first-person Boer account is from Roland Schikkerling, a young man from Pretoria. He told that the local farmers who were assisting them knew that the men camping on Wilmansrust were Australians who were greatly feared by the locals. He was told that the enemy were six hundred strong with two cannon. Both Schikkerling and Muller say that the attacking Boer force was about 150 strong.[7]

The place that Major Morris had selected for the camp was on a flat grassy shelf which overlooked the river and was protected by a rocky outcrop on the south side. Quite near to the camp on the eastern side, about four hundred yards away, is a small stream. A little further away on the western side is another. A farmhouse and a stone cattle kraal were on the western side of the shelf. The rocky outcrop gave protection on the south side but on east and west the slope is gentle which the Boers knew well. It seems likely that the owner of the farm was one of the Boer guides.[8] Beyond the outcrop on which the camp was situated and about two hundred yards away, was a flat rock ledge which dropped sharply down to the river. This very steep drop, almost a cliff, curves around the camp and forms a hollow which could easily hide 150 horses from view.

With the rations arriving in the late afternoon, about 5 p.m.,[9] the men being "on short rations…we all had big appetites",[10] they were very soon "scattered about the camp cooking scram for breakfast as we never have time in the morning, our rifles and bandoliers lying about the saddles."[11] Letters and newspapers had also arrived with the rations and numbers of the men were around the campfires reading. It seems clear that all were satisfied that any Boers that they had seen during the day had been driven off by the gunfire and a relaxed atmosphere prevailed in the camp. There would also have been considerable noise as the nearly three hundred men and their horses were fed and bedded down for the night. Muller's attack was carefully timed – a little later the camp would have been almost silent and the noise of his men, however stealthy, might have been picked up.

Captain J.C. Watson of the Royal Field Artillery, who was acting Adjutant to Major F. Morris, was given orders to place the piquets for the night. He gave instructions to Lieutenant Thomas Power of the 5VMR and three positions were chosen. McKnight's report gives the positions as follows: "One NCO and 6 men on the right front of the guns and the same number on the left side about 500 yards from our camp; one NCO and 12 men in rear of the camp and one officer and 20 men in a small kopje about 1,000 yards in the right rear." Lieutenant Power reported to Major McKnight that the pickets had been placed just after dusk.[12]

---

[1] This description is from P.J. Gallagher's unpublished manuscript *Wilmansrust* pp17-18. There is today a survey beacon on this high ground but there is no sign of the cemetery.
[2] Chamberlain & Drooglever *The War with Johnny Boer* p458, Bugler Carolyn's letter.
[3] Maurice *History of the War in South Africa* p206.
[4] Ben Viljoen *My Reminiscences of the Anglo-Boer War* p228. Hedley Chilvers *The Times History of the War in South Africa* Vol v pp296-98. Maurice *History of the War in South Africa 1899-1902* Vol 4 p206.
[5] Muller *Oorlogsherinneringe* ("War memories") p87.

[6] Muller *Oorlogsherinneringe* ('War memories') p88.
[7] Schikkerling *Commando Courageous* p219.
[8] Chilvers *The Times History of the War in South Africa* Vol v p296.
[9] McKnight *Report on the Wilmansrust affair*.
[10] Chamberlain & Drooglever *The War with Johnny Boer* pp457-58, Bugler Carolyn's letter.
[11] Chamberlain & Drooglever *The War with Johnny Boer* p462, Private E.S. Johnson's letter from the LaTrobe Collection, Melbourne.

A little after this Commandant Muller was making his plans. He chose two local burghers who knew the area well to act as guides. When it was dark enough the 150 Boers rode towards the British camp taking great care to ride as silently as possible and cleverly using the ground to avoid being seen by their piquets. They got close to the camp without being detected and Muller gave the order that twenty horses should be tethered together so that one man could hold them.[1] Schikkerling's account tells how they "courted every cover, and then while, to my mind, it was still too light, we exposed ourselves riding boldly in the direction of the enemy...until we reached a valley eight hundred yards from him, and at the foot of the slight eminence on which he had camped." Concerned that he might need to make a rapid getaway before a bayonet charge, Schikkerling tied his horse to the rein of the adjacent horse with a bow that would need only a tug to release.[2]

Leaving the horse holders, the rest advanced up the bed of the stream on the eastern side of the camp. The Australian piquets did not see or even hear them in the darkness. They would have had a wide view during daylight but when it got dark were not able to see the Boers in what was now dead ground. They were also too far away to be able to readily communicate with the camp should they have spotted any enemy activity. If anyone was looking out from the camp they did not see or hear anything untoward and no alarm was given. The Boers advanced and stayed about ten yards apart from each other, forming a curved line around the northern and eastern edge of the camp about a hundred yards away. The line of about 140 men covered a large arc around two sides of the camp. This explains the statement from Private Johnson that "they came in from two sides making a crossfire."[3] It was now about 7.45 p.m. Muller's men now lay down preparing to open fire.[4]

Schikkerling had a Mauser rifle, unusual at this stage of the war since ammunition for these rifles was becoming very short – most of the Boers were now carrying British rifles, Lee Metford or Lee Enfield for which plenty of captured ammunition was available. He had turned down the offer of a revolver, preferring his rifle as it could be loaded more quickly. The Mauser was loaded with a clip containing five cartridges. The camp was clearly visible and the horse lines were outlined by the burning campfires. Commandant Nick Groenewald, said Schikkerling, gave the signal by firing the first shot and the Boer line simultaneously opened a rapid fire on the camp and the unsuspecting Australians.[5] Then the Boers charged, Schikkerling says he reloaded twice as he ran, and were in among their enemy within seconds.

The Australians were taken completely by surprise. Bugler Carolin was taking his greatcoat and waterproof sheets off his saddle, preparing to "have a nap." As he drew his carbine from the saddle bucket, two bullets knocked it out of his hand and Sergeant Roberts called out to him to blow the cease fire.[6] Private Johnson had received a newspaper and had settled down to read it at one of the fires. Some of them tried to get to their rifles, Johnson was one of about 20 who did but was unable to open fire. In the darkness and confusion there was as much chance of hitting one of their own men as a Boer.[7] The Boers were at an advantage here since the Australians were silhouetted by the light of the campfires.

Major McKnight was able to get to his carbine but he found himself taken prisoner almost immediately by a group of Boers that he "mistook for Victorians as they were dressed in khaki and wore hats turned up similar to ours." He said this was "seven or eight minutes after the opening of the firing."[8] Captain Miller attempted to organise resistance and Lieutenant Power of the 5VMR tried to rally some of the men in the cattle kraal but to no avail.[9] Major Morris surrendered and the Boers "mustered us all into a mob like a lot of sheep."[10] The Victorian's doctor, Lieutenant Herbert Palmer, was killed and the wounded were attended to by the veterinary officer, Captain Samuel Sherlock, who won the praise of Major General Beatson's senior medical officer who said, "that the forty men wounded were very little prejudiced by the want of a medical officer."[11]

The Boers took everything they could lay their hands on from the camp. The guns and their ammunition were taken but were recaptured in the next few months – these weapons really did not suit the tactics that the Boers were employing at this stage of the war. They found them to be something of a hindrance to their manoeuvrability. The Australians were shocked that "they also took some of our dead chaps' boots."[12] Schikkerling also looked for new boots: "I walked in among the prisoners and asked solicitously what size boots they wore. By way of answer a naked foot was held up, and each toe seemed to say in mocking chorus 'Too late'".[13] British army biscuits seem to have been highly-prized by the Boers as "One Boer remarked that the biscuits were a change from mealie".[14]

Apart from fifteen dead (with four more who would die later of their wounds) and fifty wounded, there were 138 dead horses and mules and numbers of others who would be destroyed in the following morning.[15] Muller quickly asked about the British doctor but was told that he had been killed: "I called the officers to collect their people together and one of the officers I told to take three of their best horses and

---

[12] In June in that area dusk would be just after 6 p.m.
[1] Muller *Oorlogsherinneringe* ("War memories") p88.
[2] Schikkerling *Commando Courageous* p220.
[3] Chamberlain & Drooglever *The War with Johnny Boer* p461, Private Johnson's letter.
[4] Muller *Oorlogsherinneringe* ("War memories") p88.
[5] Muller says it was himself who gave the signal to open fire. Major McKnight's report says "a whistle was blown".
[6] Chamberlain & Drooglever *The War with Johnny Boer* p458, Bugler Carolyn's letter.
[7] Chamberlain & Drooglever *The War with Johnny Boer* p461, Private Johnson's letter.
[8] McKnight *Report on the Wilmansrust affair*.
[9] Hedley Chilvers *The Times History of the War in South Africa* Vol v p296 says this was Lieutenant Wood of the 5VMR.
[10] Chamberlain & Drooglever *The War with Johnny Boer* p461, Private Johnson's letter.
[11] Report of the medical officer to the brigade major of Beatson's column. Quoted in Wilcox *Australia's Boer War* p207.
[12] Chamberlain & Drooglever *The War with Johnny Boer* p459, Bugler Carolyn's letter.
[13] Schikkerling *Commando Courageous* p225.
[14] Chamberlain & Drooglever *The War with Johnny Boer* p459, Bugler Carolyn's letter.
[15] Chamberlain & Drooglever *The War with Johnny Boer* p461, Private Johnson's letter.

two men to fetch a doctor from their nearest camp."¹ The Boers marched the prisoners, anything from 70 to 80 of them, "a mile out on the veld and let them go."² One of the Boer officers, it could have been Muller, Groenewald, Wynand Viljoen or Trichardt, left them with, "Good night lads, our turn tonight, yours some other time."³

The following morning, "four Boers came to within 500 yards of our camp and took cattle away. They went around by Lieutenant Cotton's party, who opened fire on them and shot General Grobler dead and got the cattle back."⁴ *It was not the General but his son.* From McKnight's report is the statement that "We gathered 82 rifles and 5,000 rounds of ammunition and had to defend ourselves next morning killing General Grobler's son and wounding another man."

McKnight said that about 14 men reached the main column, Beatson's force at Van Dyk's Drift, where they had been since 10 June, as related. There are conflicting accounts about Beatson's reaction to news of the disaster at Wilmansrust. The official history says that "At 1.30 a.m. Beatson received intelligence of this disaster and at once hurried to the scene, arriving there before daylight."⁵ However, McKnight states in his report that the doctors did not arrive until 10 a.m. and J.H. Patterson stated in his diary that Beatson feared a night attack and "waited until dawn before hastening to Wilmansrust."⁶

After burying their dead the combined column made its way to Bethel⁷ and then to Ermelo to assist Major General Sir Bindon Blood's columns in their operations. It was only on 27 June, on their arrival back in Middelburg, that the 5VMR were remounted. Carolin said that, "I am pleased to be alive to tell the tale, although it is a wonder".⁸ Private Johnson was concerned that "the cutting up that we got will be all over Australia by now and we will have a bad name."⁹ However, said Carolin, "Major Thomas Umphelby has just informed us, at the General's request, that we were in no way to blame for our disaster on the 12th inst., and also that we have commandeered more stock etc. – cattle, sheep, goats, mules and horses – than the whole of the other columns put together, and to allow our disaster to rest."¹⁰

General Viljoen received Muller's report from a burgher who met him on his return from the council of war at Waterval. Muller reported that they had sustained a "loss of six killed and some wounded." Viljoen said, "Our haul consisted of two pom-poms, carts and wagons with teams in harness, and about 300 horses, the most miserable collection of animals I have ever seen."¹¹ The Boers also captured one of their own people who was acting as a guide for the British. His name was apparently "Drotsky" and he was taken to the farm Waterval where the Boer leaders were meeting. His case was discussed at the conference and "it was resolved that the most stringent measures be taken against all National Scouts".¹² Drotsky was tried and executed on 26 June – Schikkerling was an eye-witness of the execution.¹³

The Boer council of war at Waterval on 20 June resolved to continue the war. President M.T. Steyn and General Christiaan de Wet of the Orange Free State were adamant that the Boer guerrilla tactics should be further pursued. A telegram from President Kruger in Holland ordered a continuance and three recent successful Boer actions – Mooifontein, Vlakfontein and Wilmansrust – caused them to decide that "although overwhelmed by numbers and strategy, they...still possessed a local and tactical superiority. In time they might wear down the patience of their great adversary."¹⁴

On arrival in South Africa the 5VMR was one of the units comprising the column of Major General Stuart Beatson. They were keen soldiers and liked Beatson, their dashing general. To James Patterson he seemed a "grand man" and Major William McKnight said he was "a fine fellow to work under."¹⁵ Colonel A.E. Otter, in command of the 5VMR until he was sent home after a spell in hospital, described Beatson as "one of the most charming men he had served under, who thought a lot of the Australians as they were a workmanlike body of men."¹⁶ That McKnight later did not share this opinion of Beatson seems clear. He described Beatson's staff officer, Major Bertram Waterfield, in one of his letters as "that awful brute".¹⁷ It therefore surprised and shocked the men of the left wing when they heard some time after their arrival back at Middelburg on 27 June that Beatson had made some remarks about the Australians during a dinner in the officers' mess.

There was an enquiry that lasted several days from 20 June when a number of the 5VMR, including McKnight and Carolin, gave evidence. Subsequently, Beatson asked Umphelby to inform the men that they were in no way to blame for the setback at Wilmansrust. However, two further minor incidents that reflected badly on the 5VMR seem to have caused Beatson to change his opinion of the Australians under his command. Near Bethal on 28 June an outpost was overrun and two men, a Corporal and a Lance Corporal, were severely wounded. Again on 1 July, at Middelkraal two troopers were captured while another refused to surrender and died from his wounds a few days later.¹⁸

---

¹ Muller *Oorlogsherinneringe* ("War memories") p89. See also McKnight Report on the Wilmansrust affair.
² Wallace *The Australians at the Boer War* p330.
³ Chamberlain & Drooglever *The War with Johnny Boer* p461, Private Johnson's letter.
⁴ Trooper Frank Halsall's letter written from hospital in Middelburg and quoted in Wallace *The Australians at the Boer War* p332.
⁵ Maurice *History of the War in South Africa* p204.
⁶ Quoted in Wilcox *Australia's Boer War* p208.
⁷ "Bethel" is the original biblical spelling of the name of this town which today is spelled "Bethal".
⁸ Chamberlain & Drooglever *The War with Johnny Boer* p459, Bugler Carolyn's letter.
⁹ Chamberlain & Drooglever *The War with Johnny Boer* p461, Private Johnson's letter.
¹⁰ Chamberlain & Drooglever *The War with Johnny Boer* p459, Bugler Carolyn's letter.

---

¹¹ Viljoen *My Reminiscences of the Anglo-Boer War* pp228-29.
¹² O.J.O. Ferreira *Memoirs of General Ben Bouwer* p125.
¹³ Schikkerling *Commando Courageous* pp233-34. See also Blake *Boereverraier* pp177-180.
¹⁴ Hedley Chilvers *The Times History of the War in South Africa* Vol v p297.
¹⁵ Quoted in Wilcox *Australia's Boer War* p200.
¹⁶ Quoted in Chamberlain *The Wilmansrust Affair*.
¹⁷ Quoted in Wilcox *Australia's Boer War* p205.
¹⁸ See Wilcox *Australia's Boer War* p208 and War Office, London *The South African War Casualty Roll* Sixth printed list, 1902 for

Beatson was reported as calling the Victorians a "fat-arsed, pot-bellied, lazy lot of wasters" and further that they were "white-livered curs". A West Australian officer, Major Samuel Harris overheard the remarks and Beatson added, for his benefit, that "the Western Australian draft contingents seemed suitable companions for the Victorians after running at Brakpan."[1] It was reported in the Melbourne newspaper *Age* in October 1901 that he had also said, "You can add dogs too" when seeing an Australian officer writing the remarks down.[2] Beatson apologised fairly soon afterwards to Harris in person having heard that McKnight "had got his back up" and asked Harris to convey an apology about the Victorians.[3]

McKnight did not accept an apology and immediately went back to Pretoria to complain to higher authority. Beatson removed McKnight and Umphelby from command and McKnight returned to Australia and reported to Major General Downes, the Commandant of the Victorian Military Forces. Subsequently three men of the 5VMR, incensed at Beatson's remarks, were arrested and charged with mutiny. One of them was sentenced to death, the others to long terms of imprisonment. Kitchener immediately commuted the death sentence and the War Office in London had them released since they had not been charged and sentenced in accordance with Army law.[4]

Beatson was sent to the Cape Colony in August 1901 but only a month later Sir Bindon Blood, Beatson and a number of other officers were sent back to India, apparently marked down as failures.[5] Not all the Victorians were happy that they no longer served under him – J.H. Patterson being one of them.[6] Certainly, Beatson's methods and the orders he gave about the placement of piquets that contributed to the Australians' disaster at Wilmansrust were not appropriate for the guerrilla warfare waged by the Boers in South Africa. Beatson's remarks and his attitude towards his Australian soldiers can certainly not have found favour with the Commander-in-Chief, General Kitchener. Bindon Blood, no doubt prompted by Beatson, had also reported that "the chicken-hearted behaviour…of the Victorian Mounted Rifles …was only to be expected."[7] This attitude would certainly not have met with Kitchener's approval.

The two battles of Brakpan Farm and Wilmansrust have thus become linked. Clearly, at Brakpan the Western Australians had conducted an orderly retirement in the face of superior enemy numbers. Lieutenant Frederick W. Bell was awarded the Victoria Cross for his action in rescuing a dismounted fellow soldier at Boschmanspoort. Nor were the 5VMR guilty of cowardice at Wilmansrust as their subsequent record showed. There was too the award of a Victoria Cross to Lieutenant Leslie Maygar of the 5VMR in November 1901 at Geelhoutboom.

On leaving South Africa in April 1902 the Commander-in-Chief, Lord Kitchener, sent them a telegram which read: **"Please convey to the Australians my warm appreciation of their gallant and arduous service in this country. In the name of the Army in South Africa, I wish them good luck and God speed."**

Accompanying the 5VMR was John Frederick Stebbins, now a Lieutenant. He had been an *uitlander* in Johannesburg before the war. When war broke out he made his way to Rhodesia, today Zimbabwe, and joined the Bechuanaland Protectorate Regiment. This was one of the units that were besieged in Mafeking. After that, he returned to Australia around the end of 1900 when the regiment was disbanded. Having had some military experience of South Africa, he was given a Lieutenant's commission in the 5VMR. When the regiment returned home in April 1902, Stebbins remained in South Africa and joined the 6th Australian Commonwealth Horse who actually arrived in South Africa after the war had ended. They did not stay very long!

Lieutenant Stebbins wrote a number of interesting letters, many of which are in the collection housed in the La Trobe Library in Melbourne. Among his papers is a sketch map of the battle site.[8] It is the only map in existence drawn by a participant in the battle. His map bears a slight resemblance to the modern 1:50000 survey map. However, he is mistaken in the way he has shown the river which continues in an easterly direction and does not curve around to the north. His map does clearly show that the British-Australian force camped on a flat piece of ground with streams to east and west. He also shows the Boers in the hollow formed by the river and the attack of the Boers in a long arc around the camp. The "Boer horse holders" are clearly shown in the wrong place in relation to the camp. Stebbins must have drawn the map from memory and it is not a bad effort considering his circumstances on the night. One of his letters says he was "grateful he came out of it without a scratch."[9]

A monument placed on the burial site of the graves of the two officers and fifteen men who were buried there seems to have confused a number of visitors to Wilmansrust. The monument and the graves were removed in the 1960s and are now in the Garden of Remembrance in the Middelburg military cemetery. This site is about a mile (1.6kms) away from where the fight took place and is an open piece of hillside. Long after the battle a barn or large shed was erected near the graves. Later still a small house was built near the road, now the R35, and a main road leading to the power station at Arnot. In the 1950s the road was tarred and a road camp established for the contractors – these buildings are now all demolished. Although nowadays there are some large trees around this burial site, this is an open piece of convex hillside, a more unsuitable piece of ground for a camp site it would be difficult to imagine.

The Boer scout, a joiner as the Boers described him, Drotsky, was from Carolina and would have known the area

---

the casualties.
[1] Wilcox *Australia's Boer War* p208.
[2] Wallace *The Australians at the Boer War* p332. Clearly some of these reports of what was said and when are not entirely accurate.
[3] Wilcox *Australia's Boer War* p208 and McKnight *Report on the Wilmansrust Affair*.
[4] Wilcox *Australia's Boer War* p209 but see also Chamberlain *The Wilmansrust Affair*.
[5] Wilcox *Australia's Boer War* p217.
[6] Diary of J.H. Patterson 10 August 1901 quoted in Wilcox *Australia's Boer War* p209.
[7] Wilcox *Australia's Boer War* p208.
[8] The map is reproduced in Chamberlain & Drooglever *The War with Johnny Boer* p457 as well as in the illustrations to this account of Wilmansrust.
[9] Wilcox *Australia's Boer War* p208.

well.[1] The Australians and the British officers had been patrolling in the area for nearly three weeks and would also have had some knowledge of the area and its features. Major Morris went to the top of the slope behind the camp to send his signal to Beatson on the morning of 12 June and would have observed the suitable camping site around the deserted Wilmansrust farmhouse.

Schikkerling described how they "reached a valley eight hundred yards from him (the enemy), and at the foot of the slight eminence on which he had camped" (as previously related).[2] General Muller says, "Every one of us walked in a long row towards the ridge; the camp stood on the ridge."[3] Wallace describes how "the Boers came to a small valley or depression in the hills (which) brought them to the base of the rise at the foot of the camp without being observed."[4] P.J. Gallagher's unpublished manuscript describes the site as follows:

> The camp site was probably as good as any others in the immediate vicinity but it was not ideal. The main camp was positioned on one of the highest points on the farm but higher ground was to their left on the northern side where there was an old cemetery and a few trees. Behind the camp, a short distance away on a slight downward slope to the west, were an old farmhouse and a stone cattle kraal. The surrounding countryside was rolling, open country with few trees except around buildings. The open appearance of the landscape however, was deceptive. Gullies and creek beds below the general level of the land provided many areas of "dead ground" where large numbers of men could remain hidden from view. The camp enjoyed good views of the distance but restricted outlooks on the dead ground close by posed risks. A hill to the west overlooked the area as did high ground to the southeast and south. The enemy could easily study the layout of the camp without approaching to dangerous range. The British position was surrounded on three sides by downward slopes that ran to a tributary of the Oliphants River. This spruit ran from north to south, east of the farmhouse before turning to the southwest. Unless the slopes were guarded, they provided any attackers with sheltered approaches to the camp. In some directions the nearby ground fell away so that, as Major Morris later reported, anyone approaching from these directions in daylight could be within 250 yards [228m] before being seen. The distant hills to the south were visible but even in daylight; the lower ground was not all visible from the farmhouse area where Morris had decided to stay for the night.[5]

All of these features can be established on the site as detailed in the maps and satellite picture of the site attached. Photographs of the site give further positive proof that the old Wilmansrust farm is sacred ground where the men of the 5VMR were ambushed and where fifteen of them were killed outright.

Where the casualties were buried was not the place where the fight took place. It cannot be known for certain but it seems very likely that the prisoners were marched to this spot and then released after the battle. It is about a mile away from the battle site. Other burials have been made nearby. These seem to be family graves of the local farmers. On one of what remains of a headstone the date 1892 can be made out. Photographs were taken in 1937 during a site inspection when the graves and the monument were still in good condition. In the 1960s, the monument, headstones and remains were moved to the Garden of Remembrance in Middelburg cemetery.

Nearby operations of Anglo American Coal may result in the destruction of the site if action is not taken soon to preserve this piece of our heritage.

References

1. Leo Amery and Hedley Chilvers *The Times History of the War in South Africa* Volumes V & VI. Sampson Low, Marston & Company Ltd, London 1907 and 1909.
2. The Marquess of Anglesey *A History of the British Cavalry 1816 to 1819 Volume IV 1899 to 1913* Leo Cooper, London 1986.
3. Albert Blake *Boereverraier* Tafelberg Publishers, Cape Town 2010.
4. Doctor James C. Briggs *The Search for Lieutenant Colonel F.W. Bell, V.C.* Sabretache Vol XXXVIII Apr-Jun 1997. ("Sabretache" is the Journal of the Military History Society of Australia).
5. Max Chamberlain *The Wilmansrust Affair* Journal of the Australian War Memorial. Numer 6 April 1985.
6. Max Chamberlain *The Action at Brakpan* from *Sabretache* Vol XLV No 3 – September 2004.
7. Max Chamberlain *The Battlefield Trials of the 5th Victorian Mounted Rifles* Paper presented on 9 June 2001 at the Orders and Medals Research Society Convention held at Blackburn, Melbourne, 9-11 June 2001.
8. Max Chamberlain & Robin Drooglever (edited by) *The War with Johnny Boer, Australians in the Boer War 1899-1902* Australian Military History Publications, Loftus, Australia 2003.
9. Erskine Childers (editor) *The Times History of the War in South Africa, Volume V*, Sampson, Low, Marston & Company Ltd, London 1907.
10. O.J.O. Ferreira (editor) *Memoirs of General Ben Bouwer* Human Sciences Research Council, Pretoria 1980.
11. P.J. Gallagher *Wilmansrust* Unpublished manuscript, undated.
12. Albert Grundlingh *The Dynamics of Treason: Boer collaboration in the S.A. war of 1899-1902* Protea Book House, Pretoria 2006 (translation from Afrikaans of Die "hensoppers" and "joiners" 1979).
13. D.O.W. Hall *The New Zealanders in South Africa* War History Branch, Department of Internal Affairs, Wellington 1949.

---

[1] Blake *Boereverraier* p177 says that he might have been one Johannes Marthinus Drodski of the farm Zevenfontein in the Carolina district but it is not possible to be certain.
[2] Schikkerling *Commando Courageous* p220.
[3] Muller *Oorlogsherinneringe* ("War memories") p88.
[4] Wallace *The Australians at the Boer War* p329.
[5] Gallagher *Wilmansrust* p17.

14. Major General Sir Frederick Maurice & Captain M.H. Grant *History of the War in South Africa 1899-1902, Volume 4* Hurst & Blackett Limited, London, 1910.
15. Major William McKnight *Report on the Wilmansrust Affair* Commonwealth of Australia Defence Department correspondence.
16. Carman Miller *Painting the map red, Canada and the South African War 1899–1902* University of Natal Press, Pietermaritzburg 1993.
17. General Chris Muller *Oorlogsherinneringe* Nasionale Pers, Beperk Pretoria 1936 (in Afrikaans).
18. P.L. Murray *Official Records of the Australian Military Contingents to the War in South Africa* Australian Government Printer, Melbourne 1911.
19. R.W. Schikkerling *Commando Courageous A Boer's Diary* Hugh Keartland (Publishers) (Pty) Ltd, Johannesburg 1964.
20. John Stirling *The Colonials in South Africa 1899-1902* William Blackwood & Sons, Edinburgh and London 1907.
21. Ian Uys *Victoria Crosses of the Anglo-Boer War* Fortress Financial Group, Knysna 2000.
22. Ben Viljoen *My Reminiscences of the Anglo-Boer War* Hood, Douglas & Howard, London 1903 (reprint C. Struik (Pty) Ltd, Cape Town 1973).
23. R.L. Wallace *The Australians at the Boer War* The Australian War Memorial & the Australian Government Publishing Service, Canberra, 1976.
24. War Office, London *The South African War Casualty Roll* Sixth printed list, 1902.
25. Steve Watt *In Memoriam, Roll of Honour Imperial Forces, Anglo-Boer War 1899-1902* University of Natal Press, Pietermaritzburg 2000.
26. Craig Wilcox *Australia's Boer War, The War in South Africa 1899-1902*, Oxford University Press. Published in association with the Australian War Memorial Melbourne, Australia 2002.
27. H.W. Wilson *After Pretoria* Volume II The Amalgamated Press, London 1902.
28. Speech at a formal ceremony to plant trees of a South African species (Widdringtonia cedarbergensis – Clanwilliam cedar) at the Anglo-Boer War Grove at the National Arboretum, Canberra by Ms Katy Gallagher, Chief Minister of the Australian Capital Territory.
29. *The South African War Casualty Roll, The "South African Field Force" 11th October 1899-June 1902.*

Casualty list

REGT_NO	RANK	NAME	INITIALS	REGIMENT	CASUALTY	DATE
1359	PTE	BARNARD	SJ	VICTORIA MTD RIFLES,5	KIA	1901/06/12
1438	PTE	BLANDFORD	EH	VICTORIA MTD RIFLES,5	KIA	1901/06/12
1560	PTE	BOND	L	VICTORIA MTD RIFLES,5	KIA	1901/06/12
1691	LCPL	BUTTON	GR	VICTORIA MTD RIFLES,5	KIA	1901/06/12
1007	PTE	COLLINS	J	VICTORIA MTD RIFLES,5	DOW	1901/06/13
1430	PTE	GOUDIE	LJW	VICTORIA MTD RIFLES,5	KIA	1901/06/12
1366	PTE	HARRISON	H	VICTORIA MTD RIFLES,5	KIA	1901/06/12
1380	PTE	HENDY	HH	VICTORIA MTD RIFLES,5	KIA	1901/06/12
1485	SGTFAR	HOULIHAN	JF	VICTORIA MTD RIFLES,5	KIA	1901/06/12
1292	SHSM	MAHONEY	TH	VICTORIA MTD RIFLES,5	KIA	1901/06/12
1404	CPL	NEWLANDS	H	VICTORIA MTD RIFLES,5	KIA	1901/06/12
	LTSURG	PALMER	HA	VICTORIA MTD RIFLES,5	KIA	1901/06/12
1481	PTE	ROWE	EJ	VICTORIA MTD RIFLES,5	KIA	1901/06/12
1550	PTE	SMITH	WA	VICTORIA MTD RIFLES,5	DOW	1901/06/13
1307	PTE	STRATTON	GW	VICTORIA MTD RIFLES,5	KIA	1901/06/12
1602	PTE	THORNTON	RM	VICTORIA MTD RIFLES,5	KIA	1901/06/12
1095	PTE	TOPHAM	R	VICTORIA MTD RIFLES,5	DOW	1901/06/13
	CAPT	WATSON	JC	ROYAL FIELD ARTILLERY,9	KIA	1901/06/12
1610	PTE	MACK	AE	VICTORIA MTD RIFLES,5	DOW	1901/06/13

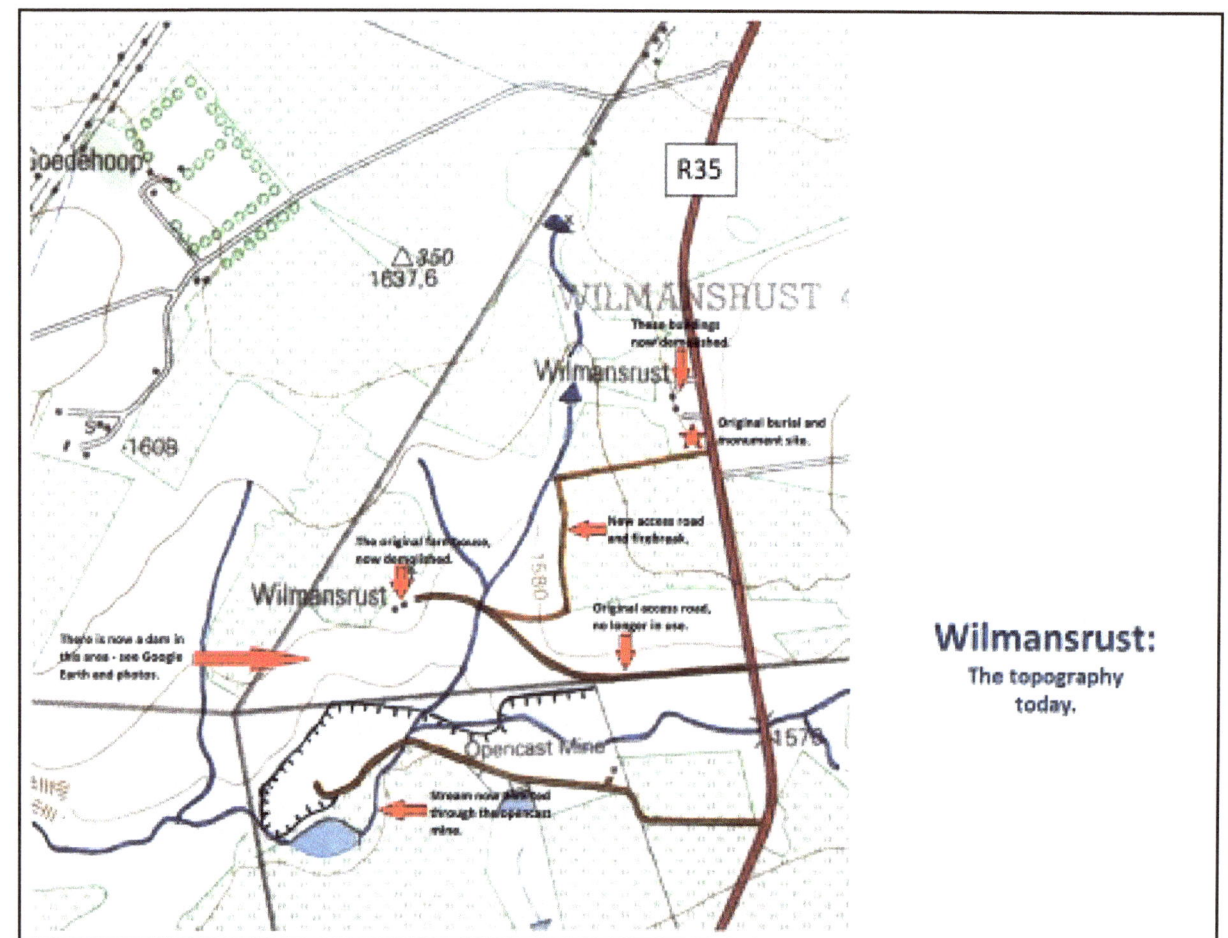

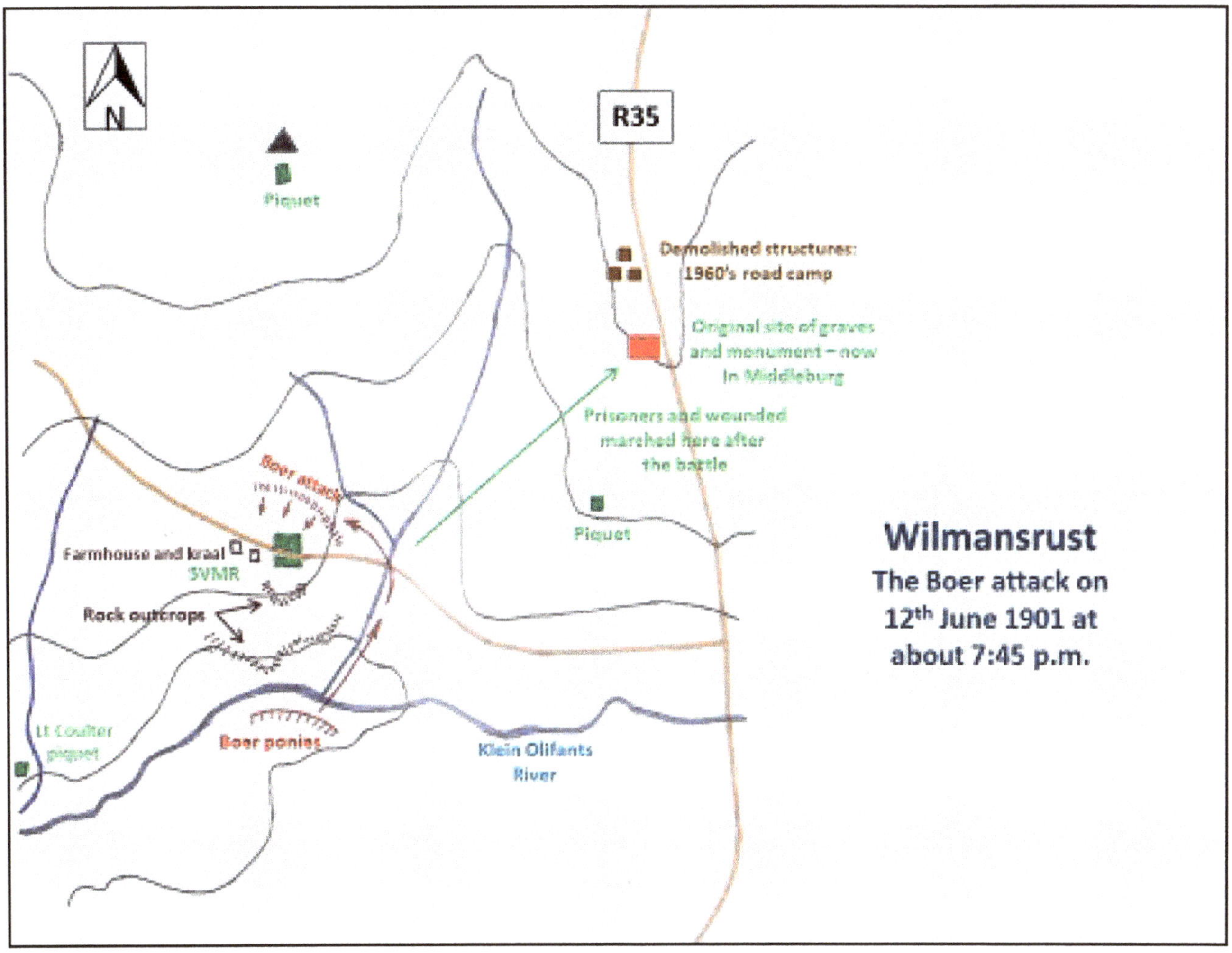

Wilmansrust
The Boer attack on 12th June 1901 at about 7:45 p.m.

General C.H. Muller and a group of his officers in 1902. Commandant Wynand Viljoen, younger brother of General Ben Viljoen standing fifth from the right.

General Christiaan Muller
On commando in 1902.

Shortly after the war.

General Ben Viljoen

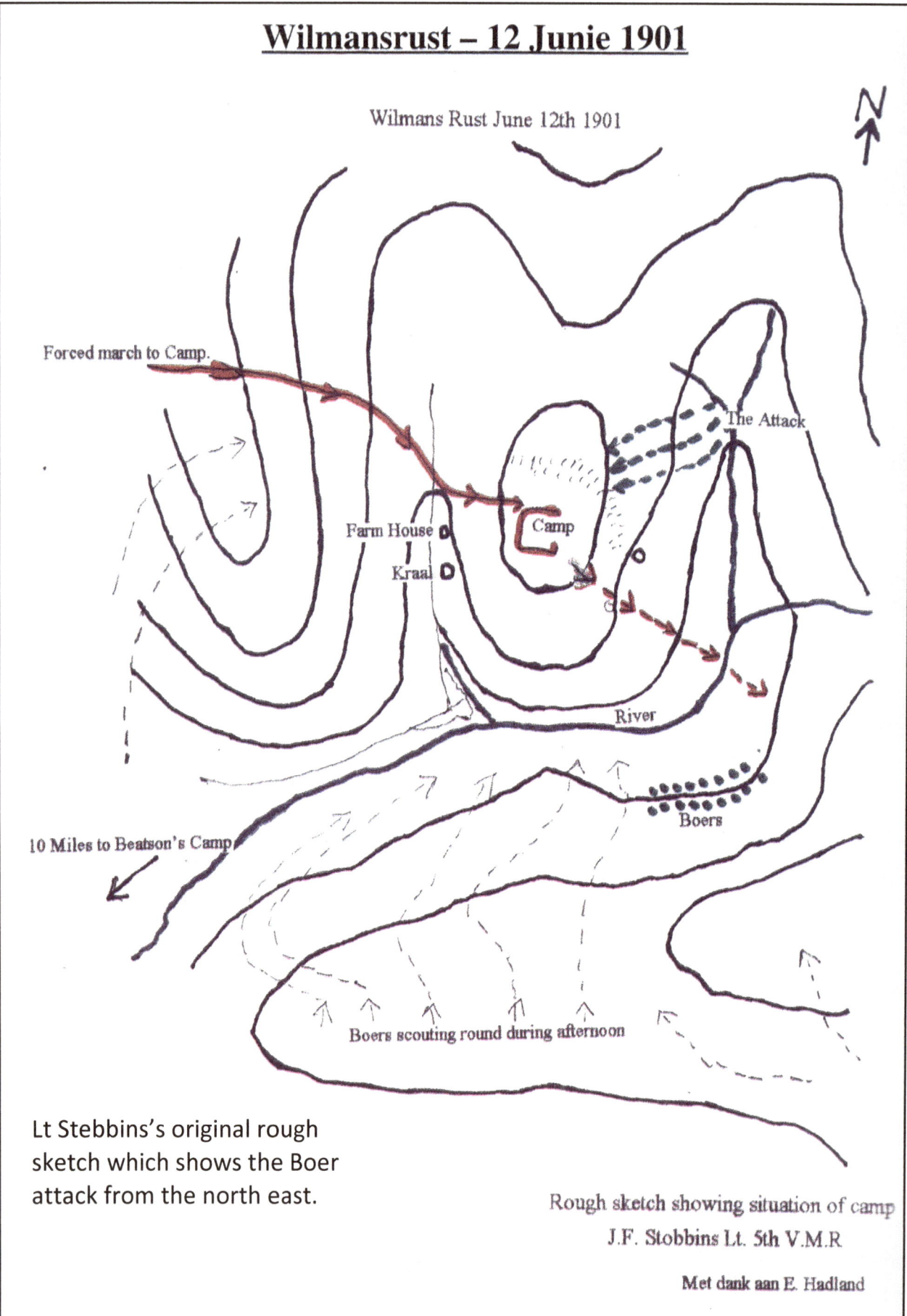

Lt Stebbins's original rough sketch which shows the Boer attack from the north east.

Wilmansrust – the original farm

This view is due west. The river to the left is a tributary of the Olifants River which the opencast mining operation has dammed. The SVMR camped on the flat shelf on top of the gentle rise. They had visibility in all directions although there were two places affording dead ground for Boer attackers on the south side where there was a steep rocky slope rising about 3m.

To the west was a small stream as well as another to the east. There was water for the men and the horses. The small stream east of the camp runs in the hollow just on the near side of the patch of burnt grass. The picture is taken from the approximate position of one of the pickets. The Boer attackers moved up the bed of the stream, in dead ground as far as the picket was concerned, wheeled left, formed a line and opened fire when Commandant Groenewald fired the first shot.

Wilmansrust – the original farm

Looking east from the site of the SVMR camp. The stream runs left to right just past the patch of burnt grass where it forms a pool as it crosses the track. The original road which led past the farm and on to Van Dyk's Drift, now disused, is just visible.

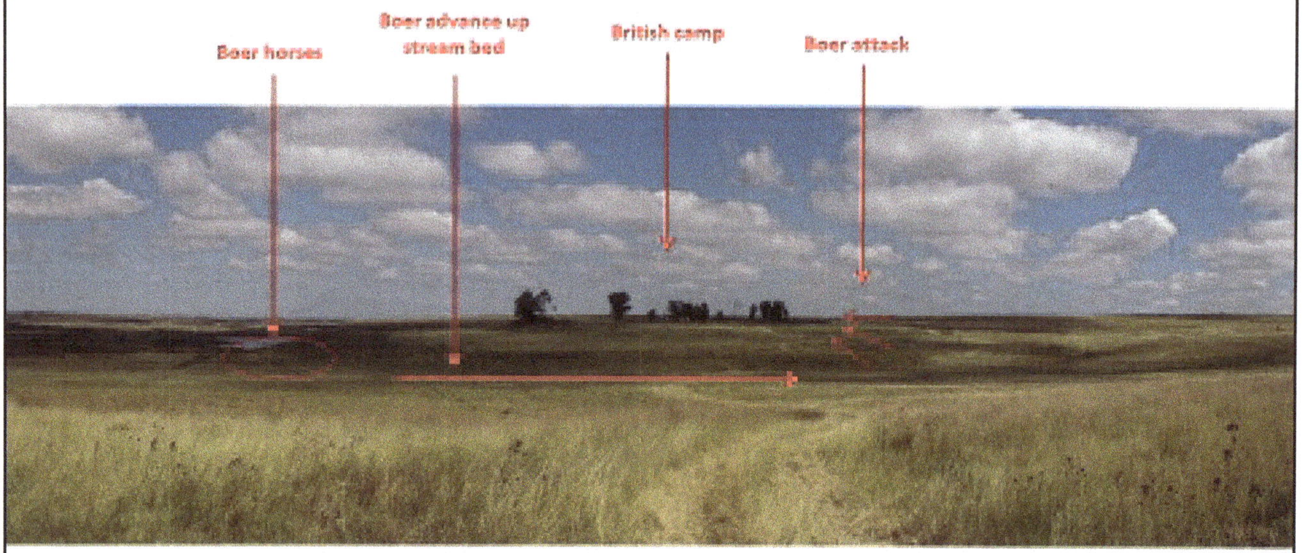

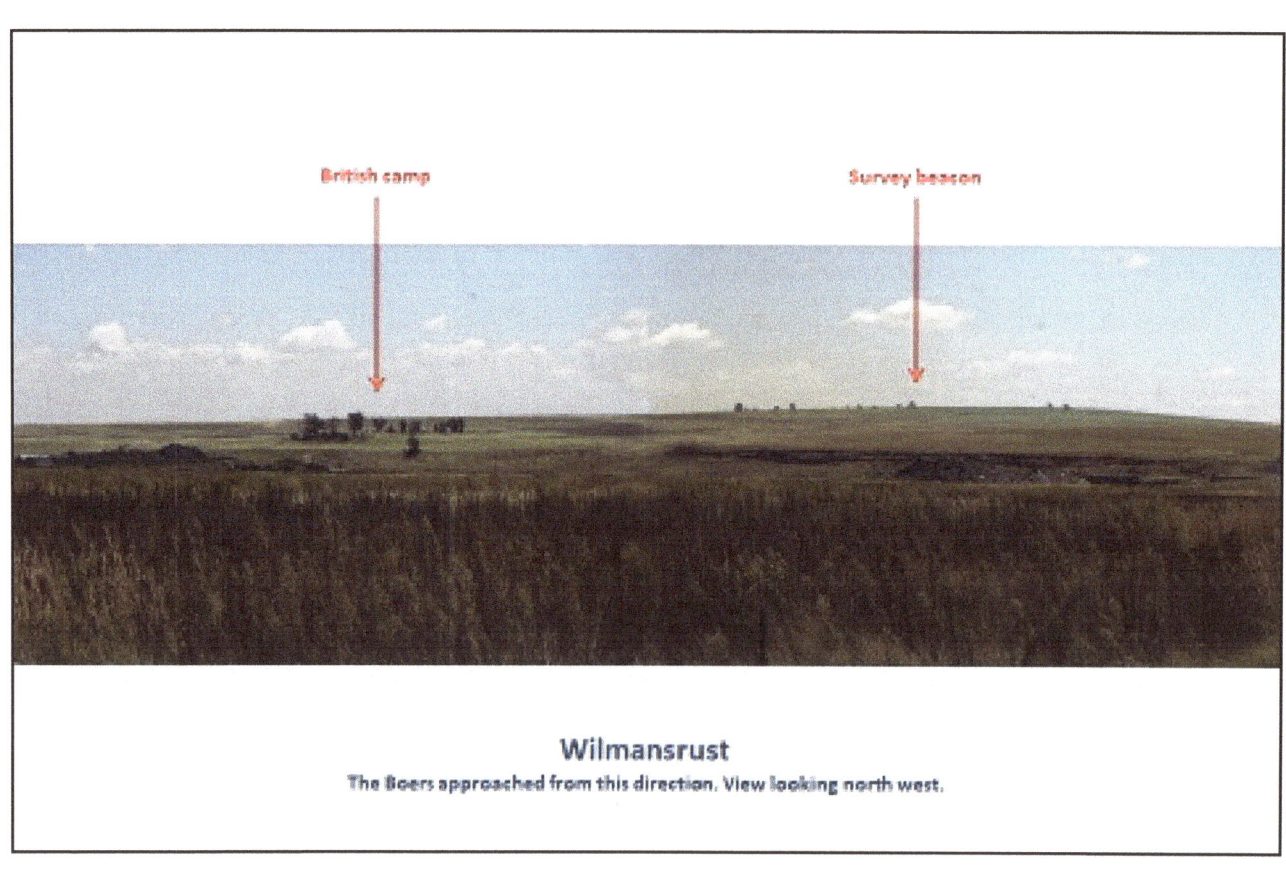

Wilmansrust
The Boer attack on 12th June 1901 at about 7:45 p.m.

Schikkerling described how they "reached a valley eight hundred yards from him (the enemy), and at the foot of the slight eminence on which he had camped." Circled above.

(This view shows the access road made by the mining company.)

Wilmansrust
The Boers approached from this direction. View looking north west.

Botha & Kitchener meet at Middelburg

28 February 1901

It was more difficult to stop the war than to start it. As early as the end of 1900 there were clear indications of war-weariness among participants from both sides. Much earlier of course, Piet de Wet had forcibly expressed himself that further resistance was futile and surrendered. A number of British officers wondered why the Boers were so determined to continue what seemed to be a hopeless struggle.

It was the British General Officer Commanding, Lord Kitchener, who considered early in 1901 that the time was right to meet with the Boer Commandant General, Louis Botha, to explore the possibility of a cessation of hostilities. Contact was made by giving Mrs Botha a letter – she was living in Pretoria – which suggested a meeting with her husband who was somewhere in the east of the Transvaal. Botha clearly realized, unlike some of the Boer hardliners, that win or lose the end of the conflict would have to involve talks between the belligerents. He must have believed even then that there was nothing to lose by having a one-to-one talk with his opposite number.

Kitchener's concern, and that of British High Commissioner Sir Alfred Milner, was to end the war as soon as possible. The longer the war went on, the more bitterness would be engendered. This would make for difficulties in governing the annexed territories once the war was over. The British Government, although determined to bring the war to a successful conclusion, was having misgivings about the cost of waging it. There was also a body of public opinion which included future British Prime Minister, David Lloyd George, who were highly critical of the government and "pro-Boer".

The two commanders met in a house in Middelburg, a town east of Pretoria, which was in use as Major-General Neville Lyttelton's headquarters. It was 28 February 1901 and only Kitchener, Botha and their military secretaries were present at their meetings. Their discussions were carried on in a reasonable spirit and it was an even-handed exchange. It was cordial enough that it has been said that in the evening Kitchener taught Botha the game of bridge. The dinner that was served was likely the best meal that Botha had had in quite a while too.

A set of conditions for a peace treaty were agreed upon with Botha's proviso being that he required to submit the proposals to his own, as well as the Orange Free State, people for ratification. Predictably they turned down the offer. President Marthinus Steyn was highly affronted that he had not been invited to meet with Kitchener. Did Botha go to the meeting with Kitchener without Steyn advisedly? Only 15 months later, near midnight on 31 May 1902, were signatures attached to the document formally ending the conflict, known as the Peace of Vereeniging.

The Waterval *Krygsraad*

20 June 1901

There is a famous picture of the Boer leaders about to take a train from Val Station (on the main line between Johannesburg and Durban, about 20km east of Greylingstad) to Klerksdorp. Boer leaders from the Zuid-Afrikaansche Republiek (the Transvaal) and the Orange Free State were to meet in Klerksdorp to decide on whether to continue with the war or to negotiate peace terms with the British Government. The date was 6 April 1902. Commandant-General Louis Botha had arrived at the station in a Cape cart the previous day, accompanied by an escort of commandos. Botha and a number of Boer officers, now under safe conduct from the British, met in a room of the Val Hotel which still stands on the north side of the station. Hardliners among his officers were against any kind of negotiation with the British and the Boer governments' intentions needed to be clarified.

Ten months previously, another meeting had taken place not very far from Val. On 20 June 1901, a very important day of discussion had brought about some vital decisions on Boer plans for the future. The Boer leaders met in the Branddrift farmhouse (Maurice, 1905, p205; although Childers, 1907, p296) says they met at "the farm Waterval, near Standerton", by which he must have been referring to a farm near the Waterval River since there was no actual farm by that name north of Standerton) alongside the drift of the same name over the Waterval River. At the meeting were Acting Transvaal President Schalk Burger and Orange Free State President Marthinus Steyn, Transvaal State Secretary Francis Reitz, Commandant-General Louis Botha and Chief Commandant Christiaan de Wet, Generals Hertzog, Viljoen, Spruyt, De la Rey, Smuts, Muller, Lucas Meyer and a number of other commandants and officers (Maurice, 1905, p206).

At first, the meeting was convened in a secluded place somewhere along the Waterval River but it was then moved to the nearby Branddrift farmhouse. This was the most secure place they could find in an area criss-crossed by British columns. They kept well away from both railway lines – the main Johannesburg-Natal line and the ZASM line from Pretoria to Delagoa Bay (now Maputo). Blockhouses, only one thousand yards apart and connected by barbed wire, protected the lines. Armoured trains operated on each of these lines and British reinforcements could be rushed to any point where they might be needed.

Boer scouts kept the area around Branddrift under constant surveillance, for security was absolutely vital. (Local oral tradition has it that the Boers even had a sentry on the roof of the farmhouse.) Should the British have managed to locate this concentration of the entire senior leadership of the two republics, the capture of even a few of them would have been disastrous for the Boer war effort.

The Boer *krygsraad* at Waterval had been preceded and indeed precipitated by an earlier meeting between Botha and the British commanding general, Lord Kitchener, in Middelburg on 28 February 1901. Mrs Botha, living in Pretoria, had been given a letter to deliver to her husband (Meintjies, 1970, pp78-81), wherein it was proposed that Botha and Kitchener should meet to see if common ground could be found to arrange terms of peace. Anything and everything was open to discussion "except that the question of independence of the two republics was not to be discussed in any way" (Childers, 1907, pp183-93). It was High Commissioner for South Africa, Sir Alfred Milner's proviso that no discussion was to be made on the subject of independence. (Chapter VII of Leo Amery (ed), *The Times History of the War in South Africa*, gives full details of the terms that were discussed at this conference).

The question of independence, however, was certainly going to be Botha's first point of departure during the meeting, but nevertheless details of a process leading to a cessation of hostilities were discussed in a reasonable and even friendly spirit. Botha clearly realised that, at some time or another, the war could only be ended by negotiation. Meintjies (1970, p81) writes that posters in London announced that Botha had surrendered while a photograph of Kitchener, Botha and their aides was circulated after the Middelburg meeting and certain Boer commandants were convinced that Kitchener was now a Boer prisoner-of-war.

According to Childers (1907, pp183, 191), a letter was sent to the British High Commissioner, Lord Milner, and then to the British Government, who returned it for Kitchener to send a final version to Botha, who declined to negotiate further. Botha then travelled to Vrede in the Orange Free State to meet with General de Wet on 25 March. It is not clear whether President Steyn was also present at this meeting, but a number of matters were discussed and they "parted with the firm determination that, whatever happened, we would continue the war" (De Wet, 1902, p242).

A letter was sent to the Government Secretary of the Orange Free State after a meeting of the Transvaal Government and their generals on 10 May 1901. This letter suggested an approach to Kitchener for permission to send ambassadors to Europe to place before President Kruger "the condition of our country". Furthermore, it was proposed that an armistice be requested so as to decide "what we must do". (This letter, translated into English, is quoted in de Wet, 1902, pp245-7.) President Steyn was very disappointed with the sentiments expressed in this letter and insisted that a joint meeting of the two Republican governments be organised somewhere on the Transvaal Highveld at an agreed venue as soon as possible. (Childers, 1907, p278, describes Steyn's reaction to the letter).

Following representations from Botha and Acting Transvaal President Schalk Burger, Kitchener permitted the Boers to send a telegram to President Kruger in Holland. This was done via the Netherlands Consul and using their cipher. Kruger's reply was to the effect that the Boers should fight on even though there was little chance of any intervention by a European power. He said that there were some signs of public opinion in Britain becoming opposed to the war. As he was now remote from the war, he felt that any decisions should be taken by a joint decision of the two Republican governments. Kruger's telegram was an important document tabled at the meeting in the Branddrift farmhouse (Pakenham, 1979, p513; Hancock and van der Poel, 1966, pp399-400).

The Free Staters set out for the Transvaal on 5 June together with General Koos de la Rey who had joined them from the Western Transvaal. Before travelling further, they had first to attempt the rescue of a Boer women's laager which had been captured by a British column at Graspan, east of Reitz (De Wet, 1902, pp249-51. A more detailed account of Graspan can be found in J. & J.A.J. Lourens, *Te na aan ons hart*, 2002, and there exist also a number of accounts of this clash by Australian soldiers who were involved). The Free Staters, with De la Rey and his staff, headed north from Vrede and crossed the Vaal River near Steele's Drift before striking the main railway line from Natal near Platrand on the night of 14 June. Their escort brought a blockhouse under fire by way of diverting the attention of its small garrison while the rest of the party rushed across the line. De Wet describes how the "first of our men had hardly got seventy paces from the railway line when a fearful explosion of dynamite took place". There were apparently casualties; two dead horses and a rifle were found near the line the following morning. The Free Staters then made their way to Blaauwkop on the Vaal River. This was Commandant Coen Britz's base, where they awaited news of the arrival of the Transvaal party and the site of the meeting (De Wet, 1902, p253. De Wet said there were no casualties, but Maurice, 1905, tells of the two dead horses).

Somewhere along the Waterval River, in an area practically denuded of human and animal population as a result of the British "scorched earth" policy, seemed a likely place to meet. The Transvaalers made their way from the hills around Amsterdam and, with some difficulty, evaded pursuing British columns. General Ben Viljoen provided the escort and the scouts who brought them safely to the farmhouse at Branddrift (Viljoen, 1903, p229). Nevertheless, they had been so closely pressed at one stage they had been forced to abandon all their vehicles (Maurice, 1905, p205).

Alerted by despatch riders, the various parties came together for their meeting. The principal reason for the meeting was to decide whether or not to continue the war, but a number of other matters needed to be discussed too, and important decisions needed to be made. Steyn was in no doubt about his determination to fight on to the bitter end, but recent Boer successes made this matter almost a foregone conclusion for the Boer leadership. Boer successes at Vlakfontein in the western Transvaal (now North West Province) on 29 May (Childers, 1907, pp281-5, gives a map and a detailed account of this action) and Wilmansrust on 12 June (Childers, 1907, pp294-6) had given them encouragement enough. The recent harassment and battering of a British column in a running fight from Rietfontein, near Bethal, all the way to Mooifontein, just north of Standerton, had also been noted (Childers, 1907, p297; Viljoen, 1903, pp225-6).

The map shows Witbank farm, not to be confused with the town of Witbank which is well outside the area of the map. Branddrift, along the Waterval River, is where the meeting took place. The Free Staters and General de la Rey's western Transvaalers travelled from Vrede and crossed the

Vaal River near Steele's Drift. They crossed the railway line near Platrand and spent four days at Bloukop, on the Vaal River. Leaving the meeting, the Boers travelled west to the farm, Witbank, where the Free Staters and the western Transvaalers parted company with General Botha. Generals de Wet and De la Rey then went south along the Waterval River. De Wet crossed the Vaal River near Villiers, while De la Rey headed west and crossed the main railway line near Meyerton.

Thus it was resolved "that no peace shall be made, and no peace proposals entertained that do not ensure our independence and our existence as a nation". More importantly, Botha and Smuts pointed out that although Boer tactics were working well, they did not have a strategy that would bring the war to a conclusion in their favour (See Appendix below for definitions of tactics, strategy and grand strategy by B.H. Liddel Hart). It was unlikely that the Boers could ultimately prevail against the resources and manpower that the British had at their disposal. However, what was needed was a number of big successes that would convince the British of the futility of continuing to fight. The Cape Colony had suffered no devastation and many of its inhabitants were Boers, or at least sympathetic to the Boer cause.

The Free Staters had attempted an invasion of the Cape Colony earlier in the year but Christiaan de Wet's foray over Orange River had not been successful. The Transvaalers were urged to make another attempt. De la Rey made the offer of a commando of experienced men and Smuts was given command of the venture. At the same time, Botha undertook to make a similar foray into the Colony of Natal. (Deneys Reitz's *Commando* is a prime source on Smuts's invasion of the Cape, but see also Shearing [2000] for detail of this remarkable exploit. Botha was less successful in what became merely a raid along the border of Natal – see Childers, 1907, pp334-59). Both caused the British some disquiet and the realisation that some drastic counter-measures were needed.

From Branddrift, the various parties made their way back to their bases. Perhaps to put the British off the scent or because a direct route to the east was barred by British columns, the Boer leaders headed to the west and only split up at the farm Witbank, about 26 miles (42km) east of Heidelberg. From there the Free Staters and De la Rey and his men made for the Waterval River and crossed the railway line near Vlaklaagte guided by Commandant Henk Alberts of Heidelberg. De Wet had farmed at Zilverbank before the war for two years and so knew the area fairly well (De Wet, 1902, p254). He describes Alberts as a "valiant soldier" and a "most sociable man". Near the Vaal River, the Free Staters and De la Rey parted company, the latter crossing the Cape railway line near Meyerton and De Wet and his President entering the Free State at the drift over the Vaal at Villiersdorp (now the town of Villiers).

Viljoen's orders were for him to take his commandos to the north of the Delagoa Bay railway line, which did not please him at all. Having been pursued by British columns, he had crossed the Delagoa Bay railway line with some difficulty and now he was being ordered to repeat the operation and cross back to the north (Viljoen, 1903, p229).

A few months later, on 25 January 1902, Viljoen was captured and sent as a prisoner-of-war to St Helena. The Transvaal Government travelled safely back to the hills and kloofs of the eastern Transvaal.

After this there were no more joint meetings of the two Republican governments until the April 1902 consultations in Klerksdorp when it was agreed to approach the British with a joint proposal for negotiations about peace. By then, many felt that the bitter end had indeed been reached, though many others did not. It took nearly six weeks of hard bargaining from the time that the Transvaal generals had their meeting in the room in the hotel at Val until, near midnight on 31 May 1902, the Peace of Vereeniging was eventually signed, ending a tragic period of South Africa's history.

Appendix: Liddell Hart's definitions of tactics, strategy and grand strategy

Sir Basil Henry Liddell Hart, commonly known throughout most of his career as Captain B.H. Liddell Hart, was an English soldier, military historian and leading military theorist. His definitions of tactics, strategy and grand strategy are as follows:

Tactics: the techniques for using weapons or military units in combination for engaging and defeating an enemy in battle.

Strategy: the art of distributing and applying military means to fulfil the ends of policy.

Grand strategy: to co-ordinate and direct all the resources of a nation, or band of nations, towards the attainment of the political object of the war – the goal defined by fundamental policy.

(For a full discussion, see Liddell Hart's *Strategy*, pp319-33).

References

1. Amery, L S (Ed), *The Times History of the War in South Africa*, Volume II Sampson, Low, Marston & Company Ltd, London, 1902.
2. Childers, E (Ed), Amery, L S (General Ed), *The Times History of the War in South Africa*, Volume V Sampson, Low, Marsten & Company Ltd, London, 1907.
3. De Wet, General Christiaan, *Three Years War* Galago Publishing [Pty] Ltd, Alberton (Reprint of original Archibald Constable & Company, London 1902).
4. Hancock, W.K., & van der Poel, J., *Selections from the Jan Smuts Papers I*, June 1886-May 1902 Cambridge, 1966.
5. Liddell Hart, B.H., *Strategy* Faber & Faber London 1954, 1967 reprint Meridian, 1991).
6. Lourens, J., & Lourens, J.A.J., *Te na aan ons hart: Aspekte van die Anglo-Boereoorlog in die Reitz-omgewing* self-published, Reitz, 2002.
7. Maurice, Major-General Sir Frederick (Ed), *History of the War in South Africa, 1899-1902*, Volume IV (London, 1905).

8. Meintjies, Johannes, *General Louis Botha* (Cassell, London 1970).
9. Moore, Dermot Michael, *General Louis Botha's Second Expedition to Natal* (Historical Publication Society, 1979).
10. Pakenham, Thomas, *The Boer War* (Weidenfeld and Nicholson Ltd, London, 1979).
11. Reitz, Deneys, *Commando: A Boer Journal of the Boer War* (Faber and Faber, London, 1929).
12. Shearing, Taffy and David, *General Jan Smuts and his long ride* (Privately printed by the authors, Sedgefield, 2000).
13. Van der Westhuizen, Gert and Erika, *Guide to the Anglo-Boer War in the Eastern Transvaal* (printed by Transo Pers, Roodepoort, bound by IPS Finishers, Johannesburg).
14. Viljoen, General Ben, *My Reminiscences of the Anglo-Boer War* (Struik [Pty] Ltd, Cape Town 1973 [Reprint of the original Hood, Douglas & Howard, London, 1903]).
15. Wilson, H W, *After Pretoria*, Volume II (Harmsworth, London, 1902).
16. Military History Journal Vol 16 No 2 December 2013.

The participants in the peace conference at Middelburg, Transvaal, on 28 February 1901:
Sitting (left to right): N.G. de Wet, General Louis Botha, General Lord Kitchener, Colonel Hubert Hamilton (de Wet and Hamilton were the Generals' military secretaries)
Standing (left to right); Colonel David Henderson, D.E. van Velden, Major Watson, H. Fraser, Captain F.A. Maxwell, H. de Jager

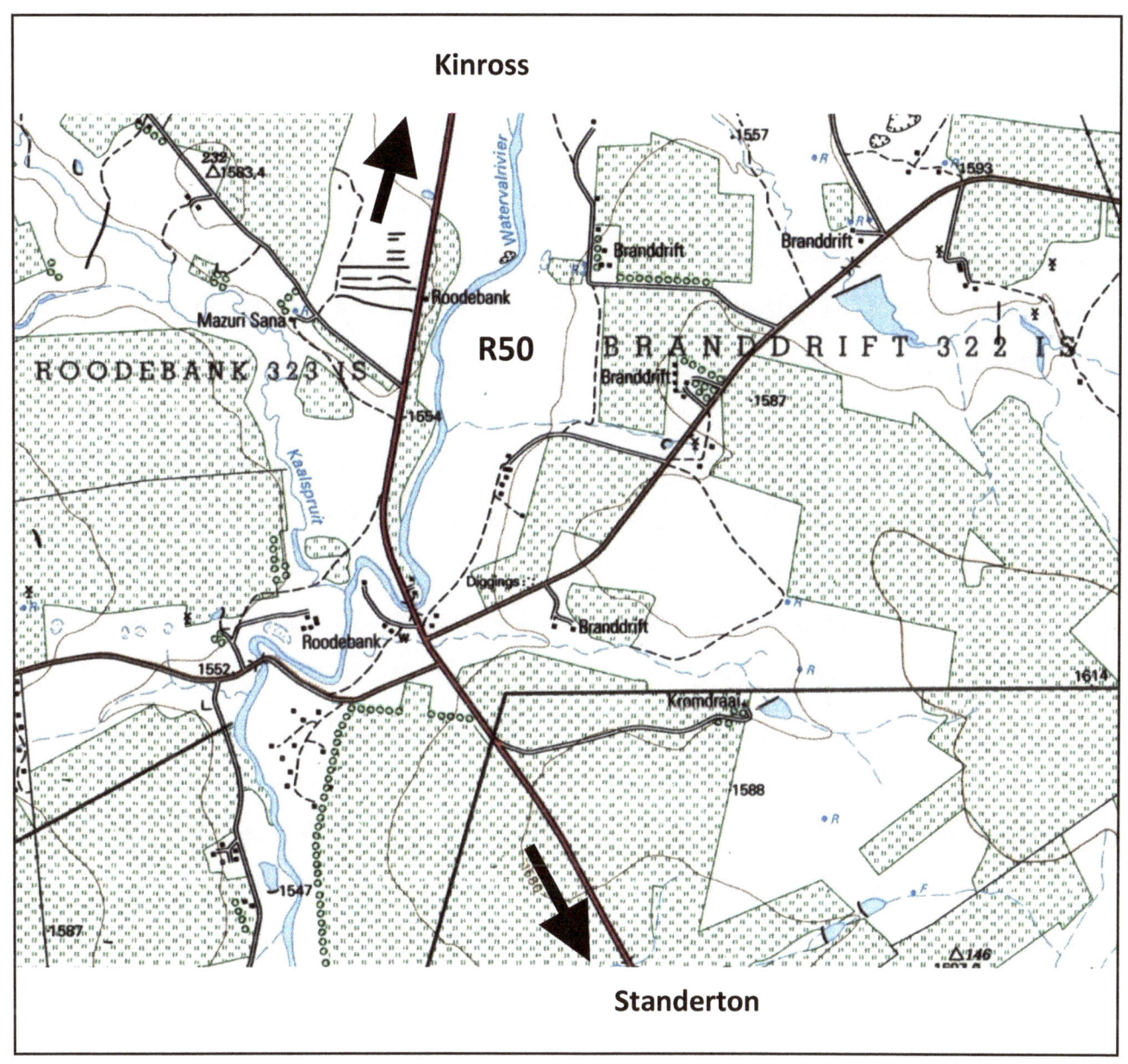

Transvalers:
Schalk Burger, Louis Botha

Free Staters;
Christiaan de Wet, Marthinus Steyn

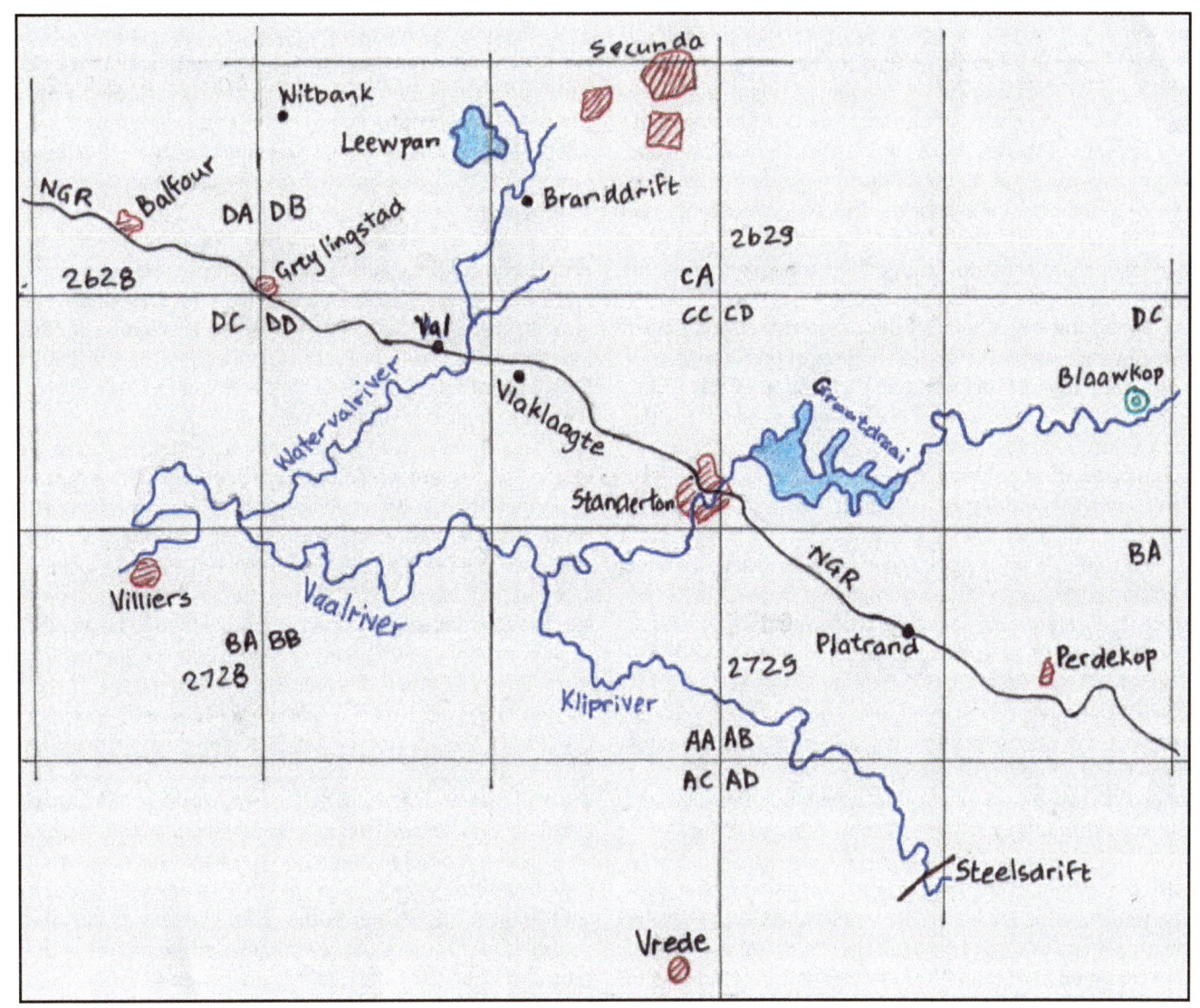

Routes to the "Waterval" *krygsraad* and return.

Hensoppers and Joiners

Boers who disagreed with their governments' policy of going to war fell into two broad categories, "hensoppers" or "joiners".[1] To this day some families carry the stigma of having been hensoppers or joiners, though few were ostracized as completely as Christiaan de Wet's brother Piet. In a number of towns, peace committees were formed and attempts were made to persuade commando members to return to their homes and farms. The example of Meyer de Kock is noteworthy – he left Pretoria and arrived at one of Ben Viljoen's commandos to urge them to cease fighting. He was tried and shot for his pains.[2]

Signing the British amnesty declaration that Lord Roberts hoped would pacify the occupied areas of the Orange Free State and Transvaal did not have the desired effect. Smuts explained that the simple Boer farmers came to the conclusion that the original sin of signing such a document could be absolved by tearing it up and returning to the field. There may have been more robust methods applied to encourage such action in many cases.

It is difficult to establish how many British citizens or English-speakers joined the commandos. Some certainly did since the commando law applied to inhabitants of the Transvaal rather than citizens. Others complied with the Transvaal law but averred that they would not take up arms against their own countrymen. Jack Lane, an English shopkeeper from Wolmaransstad, was commandeered against his will and acted as commissariat controller. However, he refused to take any of the numerous opportunities to desert but still returned to his home as soon as he was able.[3]

Many Natal and Cape Colony Afrikaners sympathized with the actions of the Boer republics in going to war with the British. Some joined the commandos knowing that the death penalty awaited for any of them who were captured and convicted of treason. The examples of Gideon Scheepers and Johannes Lotter, both executed for treason and other crimes, were particularly tragic and considered to be martyrs by their own side. Two English-speaking Cape citizens who joined the Orange River Colony Police, the Allison brothers, were captured by a Boer commando and executed only a week before the cessation of hostilities in May 1902.

By the time that the Anglo Boer war became a guerrilla struggle, it took on many of the characteristics of a civil war, rather than a war between national forces. Quite a number of Boers moved into the concentration camps as a way of avoiding military service. They readily accepted British amnesty offers to take up arms against their own people as members of the National Scouts or the Orange River Colony Police. The pay of five shillings per day and a share of any looted cattle was a welcome inducement too.

Two Joiners – Bouwer and van Emmenes

Executions by the military during time of war might not be considered very remarkable. Spies, deserters and traitors can expect small mercy from their own side. Nevertheless, the case of two young Boers, Pieter Barendse Bouwer and Adolf Jacobus van Emmenes, members of the Heidelberg Volunteers, executed on the farm Rietfontein on 24 August 1901 is particularly tragic.

"Joiners" were Boers who had joined their enemy, the British, and fought against their own people. "Hendsoppers" were Boers who had refused to fight further when the guerrilla campaign began after the British occupation of, first Bloemfontein and then Pretoria, in the first half of 1900. Both were despised as "verraaiers" – traitors to the cause of the Boer struggle for independence.

Pieter Bouwer was a teacher in a Heidelberg[4] school, where the position would have provided him with a better living than the hard struggle for existence on a small farm. His parents farmed in the Klip River district of Heidelberg and were still living at the time of his death. Little more is known about them. After the war, when Bouwer's widow was in some difficulty, they no longer seemed to be around to support her.[5] Sometime in 1901 Bouwer joined the Heidelberg Volunteers and was listed as a private.

Adolf van Emmenes was born on the farm Witpoort near Heidelberg.[6] As a youth he was recommended for training with the *Staatsartillerie van de Zuid-Afrikaansche Republiek*, the only regular military unit in the Transvaal, or the ZAR as it had become known. Heidelberg Commandant Fanie Buys made the recommendation to the authorities and Dolf served almost a year. He was said to have worn his uniform with great pride. At the outbreak of war, his father and several of his brothers were on commando. Sometime in the second half of 1900 they voluntarily surrendered on their farm to a British column. They all then signed the oath of neutrality and may have moved away from the farm to live in Heidelberg. Dolf van Emmenes remained at Witpoort until November 1900. The farm was constantly raided by the fighting Boers. He then fled to the British camp at Greylingstad and sought sanctuary there.[7]

The Van Emmenes farm was never able to provide more than bare subsistence for the family and so their decision to move into Heidelberg may have been dictated by financial considerations. We know that at least two of the Van Emmenes brothers, and probably their father and the others, became members of the Heidelberg Volunteers. This was a

---

[1] "Hensoppers" is colloquial Afrikaans for "hands uppers". Joiners were those who went further and joined the enemy, such as National Scouts of Orange River Colony Police.
[2] Viljoen.
[3] See Lane.
[4] Heidelberg is a small town to the southeast of Johannesburg which had a majority of Boer inhabitants but also a significant English-speaking community.
[5] The dates of death of Pieter Bouwer's parents are not known but they seem not to have survived the war.
[6] No farm by that name is shown on modern survey maps nor on contemporary maps of the area. Possibly the family did not own the land that they occupied.
[7] Blake p79.

volunteer burgher corps organised by the British Heidelberg Commissioner, Major John Vallentin, comprised mostly of English-speaking inhabitants of the town and a few Afrikaners who thus became "joiners".[1] They were known derisively by the Boers as the "Witkop Commando" (the White-headed Commando) because of the white hat bands that they wore.

J.G. van den Heever's memoirs of the Anglo Boer War published in 1941, have much detail of events in the Heidelberg district at this time. While the British were in control of the towns and had blockhouses and wire entanglements along the railway lines, they could only venture into the countryside in daylight with a strong heavily-armed force. The tactics that they employed were to raid the farms in the area after sundown with scouts provided by the Heidelberg Volunteers and local black people. Any unwary Boers would be captured and livestock could be driven back into town or to the nearest railway line before it became light.

One night in July 1901, a farmer, P. du Preez, of the farm Witkleifontein was killed during a night raid on his farm. Some of the Heidelberg "joiners" were apparently responsible for what seems to have been the cold-blooded murder of a decrepit old man who was unable to go on commando.[2] The fighting Boers considered that this crime could hardly go unpunished and they could not be expected to show mercy to any "joiners" whom they might capture.[3] Van den Heever's memoirs were published forty years after the event and must thus be treated with some caution. At that time, the winter of 1901, the countryside was being cleared, the inhabitants relocated and the livestock either utilised by the British or slaughtered out-of-hand.

In order to evade British columns, Boer women organised laagers and tried to hide in places where they thought they would not be found. In July 1901 the women of the Heidelberg district assembled such a collection of wagons. This tactic was seldom very successful although this particular laager may have been something of an exception. The location of such laagers was often given to the British by the local black inhabitants and that was probably the source of Vallentin's intelligence on 24 July. He left Heidelberg some hours before dawn at the head of a strong column, heading for Beerlaagte, the reported site of the women's laager. He may not however, have had intelligence of a Boer force encamped the previous night at Malanskraal, closer to Heidelberg. If he did, clearly he did not consider them to be any kind of threat to his raid. The British force was comprised of regular mounted infantry and a number of Heidelberg Volunteers, including some of the Heidelberg Afrikaners.[4]

The Boer commando's scouts warned the women to move further south and they camped near the Vaal River at Grobbelaarsdrift, now under the waters of the Vaal Dam.

---

[1] Uys pp153-155 has much detail of Vallentin and his volunteer force. Vallentin was killed at Onverwacht (also known as Bankkop) in a skirmish with the commandos of Opperman and Brits on 4 January 1902. See *The Battle of Onverwacht*, South African Military History Journal, December 2004.
[2] Van den Heever p89.
[3] Blake p74 quotes this event from Van den Heever's memoirs. There is no independent confirmation elsewhere of this incident.
[4] Uys p160.

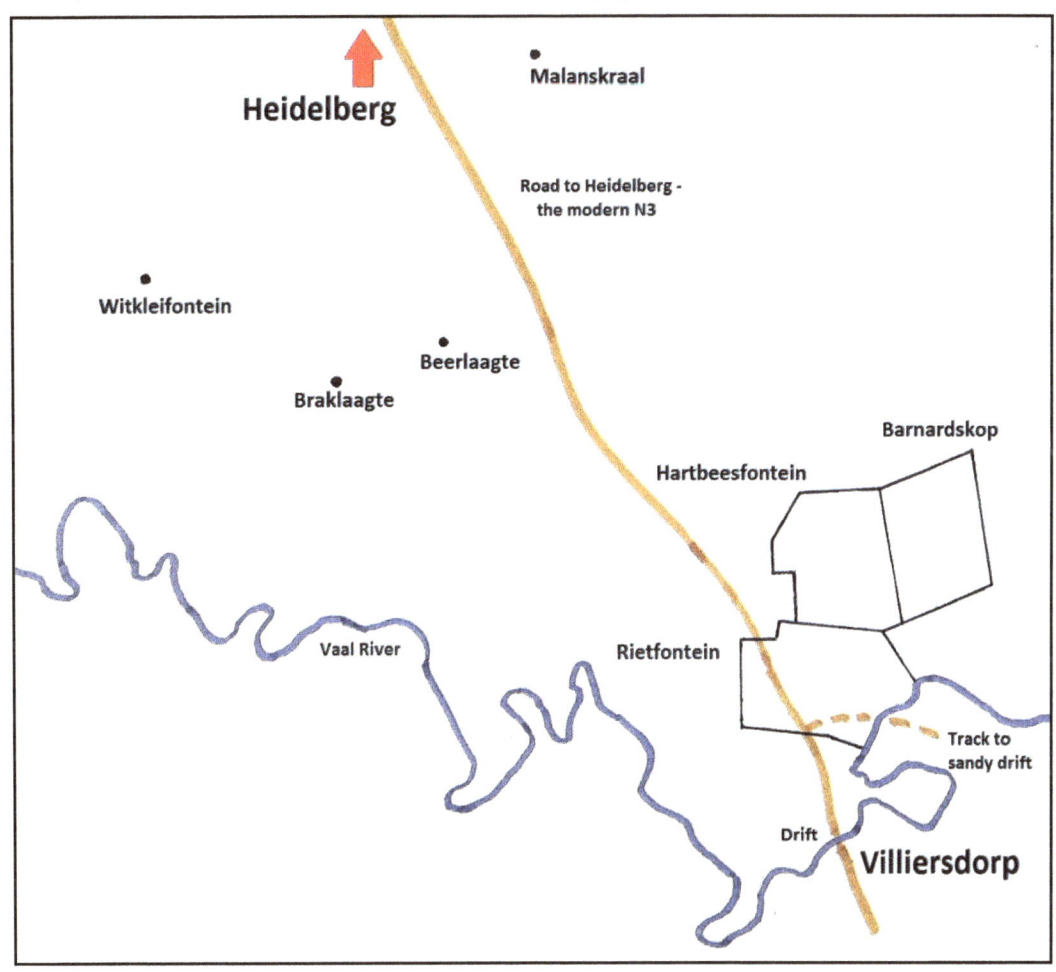

The Boers under Field Cornets Georg ("Org") Meyer and Hendrik Kamffer intercepted and ambushed the British at the farm Braklaagte, causing them to retire back into Heidelberg. The Boer accounts of the engagement at Braklaagte describe a rout of the British force. Nevertheless, Major Vallentin and Scout Gorman covered the retirement back to Heidelberg, rescuing four of their men who had been dismounted. Both men were mentioned in despatches (an honour just short of the award of a medal).[1] Another account says that the battle took place in misty weather, the "joiners" panicked at the prospect of capture by the Boers, and many fled in all directions into the thick mist.[2]

In the course of the engagement four of the Heidelberg Volunteers were killed. One of them was Eddie Morrison, best friend before the war of Louis Slabbert, one of the commando members. Three more of their pre-war friends lay dead too – John Beck, Frederick Nel and Philippus van Eeden.[3] Three prisoners were taken, Pieter Bouwer, Dolf van Emmenes and a man described as "one Scheepers".[4]

Scheepers was wounded, seriously, according to Field Cornet Hendrik Kamffer. Kamffer and Assistant Field Cornet Andrew Brink had chased Scheepers, possibly G.C. Scheepers of the ward Kliprivier who was known to have deserted the Boers,[5] and Brink shot and wounded him. While he lay under guard on the ground, according to Kamffer, a lone rider appeared. He was recognised as Danie Maartens who was very excited and asked if the commandos had captured his brother-in-law, Scheepers. When told that he was lying wounded under guard a short distance away, Maartens rode up to him, dismounted from his horse and shot him between the eyes.

According to Maartens, Scheepers and certain other joiners had, some nights previously, raided Maartens's farm, then occupied only by his wife and small daughter. Mrs Maartens was a sister of Scheepers and she and her little girl were driven into the *veld* about one thousand yards away from the farmhouse which was set alight. Barefoot and clad only in their nightclothes in the bitter July winter weather they were near death from exposure when Danie Maartens found them the next morning. His emotions can well be understood but there is no confirmation elsewhere of this incident.[6]

Another "joiner" was able to evade the commandos and make his way southwards. His name was Piet Jordaan and he had the misfortune to run into the women's laager at Grobbellarsdrift. He denied that he was a "joiner" but was nevertheless made to run the gauntlet. They lashed him with *sjambokke* (rawhide whips) and he sought refuge in the water of the Vaal River, icy cold at that time of year.[7]

A number of the prisoners were released but Bouwer and Van Emmenes, known personally to many of the Boers, were taken with the commando as they moved away from the scene of the engagement, back to one of the numerous places in the area where they could remain undiscovered by their enemy. Unlike Jordaan, soundly beaten by the women-folk, they were probably not physically abused.[8] However, Kamffer repeatedly taunted Bouwer by indicating the sun and saying, "Look carefully, young man, tomorrow you might not see it again!"

A court martial was assembled under the command of Commandant Fanie Buys. The two accused were tried in a stable on the farm Hartbeesfontein in a hearing that took two days. The record of the proceedings of the court has been lost and so it is not known with what exactly they were charged. Van den Heever says that murder was one of the charges – of Du Preez perhaps? – but certainly they must have been accused and found guilty of high treason. Many questions about the trial will remain unanswered. Were the two accused required to conduct their own defence? Even this we cannot say for certain in the absence of any record.[9]

Van den Heever, in a passage that may have been influenced and indeed written by his relative, the well-known Afrikaans author, C.M. van den Heever, described the reaction of the two accused when the death sentence was pronounced. They turned deathly pale and had difficulty holding themselves erect as they were led away, is how he described it. The rest of the passage is an impassioned attempt to justify the imposition of the sentence of death that was given to the two young men. "Cruel but also certain and justifiable."[10] Clearly this paragraph of the "Memoirs" was written by a man of letters.[11]

About half an hour after the court concluded, Van den Heever and another man, H. Bronkhorst,[12] were told to leave that night for the eastern Transvaal. They were to locate the itinerant Transvaal Government who were evading discovery and capture by the British columns scouring the countryside. Somewhere near the Swaziland border they found F.W. Reitz, the State Secretary. The sentence was confirmed, according to a British report, by General Louis Botha himself and Van den Heever and Badenhorst made their way back to their commando.

Presumably these two took with them a written account of the findings, if not a summary of the proceedings, of the court over the two days of the trial. No such documents have survived nor has the document, signed by Botha (?), that authorised the death sentence. The journey there and back took fifteen days, such were their difficulties of evading capture and penetrating the wire barriers between the lines of blockhouses that were now extending over the country.[13]

While awaiting the return of these emissaries, Bouwer and Van Emmenes were held in the jail at Villiersdorp (as it then was – now Villiers).[14] Their jailer was Frans Kruger

---

[1] Uys p161.
[2] Ankiewicz p81.
[3] Ankiewicz p81 also mentions another by the name of Archie Anderson.
[4] See Uys p 161.
[5] Blake Note 13 on p287.
[6] Hendrik Kamffer *Herinneringe* p15 quoted in Blake.
[7] Uys p161 and Blake p75.
[8] Blake p56 quotes Kamffer who says (in Afrikaans) that they were "*goed karnuffel*" which in English is "roughly manhandled".
[9] Blake p77.
[10] Translated from the Afrikaans: "*Wreed maar ook beslis en regverdig...*"
[11] Quoted in full in Blake p77.
[12] Uys p164 quoting Van den Heever p81, Blake p77 says the second man was H. Badenhorst and Ankiewicz p83 names him Hendrik Boshoff.
[13] Van den Heever's account of his journey to find the Transvaal Government describes several meetings with Boer farmers but they apparently did not encounter any British patrols or columns.
[14] The prison where they were held still exists, part of the Villiers

together with a young telegraphist, J.A.C. Kriek. Kruger asked Kriek to give the prisoners the opportunity to escape, this to be done when Kruger was absent getting water for his wife's cooking. Kriek was to indicate an escape route to them but the prisoners refused this offer. They suspected a trap so that they could be shot in a prepared ambush and preferred to stay where they were. Other assertions by Kriek, reported by Uys, were that they were resigned to their fate, whatever it might have been.[1]

Immediately after the return of Van den Heever and his colleague, a message was given to the prisoners that the death sentence had been confirmed and that they would be executed within twenty-four hours. On 24 August 1901 the prisoners were taken by horse cart to the farm Rietfontein, north of the Vaal River and a short distance from the stables where the court martial had sat to try the two men. A Dutch missionary, Mr Poelakker, had visited the men regularly while they were imprisoned and he accompanied them on their last journey.

At this point the various accounts of the execution become somewhat difficult to reconcile with what might actually have happened. According to both Kamffer and Louis Slabbert,[2] the condemned men were required to dig their own graves, were then shot and immediately buried. Neither of them indicate whether they were actually present at the execution. Kriek and Van den Heever, however, both said that the graves were prepared the previous evening and furthermore, that they were blindfolded so that they should not see the open graves. They were led to the head of their graves where they were required to stand. Once again, we cannot be certain that Kriek and Van den Heever were eye-witnesses but their version seems more plausible.

While they stood blindfolded next to their graves, Dominee Poelakker comforted them with a reading of some verses from the bible. He told them of the life hereafter, which they would enjoy "thanks to the mercy of Christ". He is said to have asked them to convey greetings to his dead parents and to tell them that he would soon be joining them. Finally, he shook hands with each of them.[3]

The firing squad of twelve men was assembled, six for each of the prisoners. As usual on these occasions, six rifles were loaded with blank cartridges and six with live rounds. The members of the firing squad were required to choose one of the guns. They would not know whether they had picked up a rifle loaded with a blank or a live round. The signal to fire was given by an officer hitting a stone against a shovel. It was half past nine in the morning.

For the young men of the firing squad this must have been traumatic in the extreme. Bouwer and van Emmenes were personally known to a number of them and some members of the firing squad had been Bouwer's pupils in the school at Heidelberg. Van den Heever said that some of the members of the firing squad were close relatives of the

---

SAPS station, although considerably altered.

[1] We do not know whether Kruger received instructions from a superior Boer officer to allow the prisoners to escape from custody. J.A.C. Kriek, in his old age, was interviewed by Ian Uys. Ludwig Ankiewicz who is local farmer, remembers meeting with J.A.C. Kriek, then a very old man, around the same time.

[2] Louis Slabbert's account appears in an article by H.J. Jooste entitled "Veld Cornet (Field Cornet) Salmon van As" in *Christiaan de Wet Annale* Number 6, October 1984.

[3] Blake p80, Uys p165.

The location of the grave is at S26°56' E28°37' and ruins of the stable at S26°53' E28°36'.

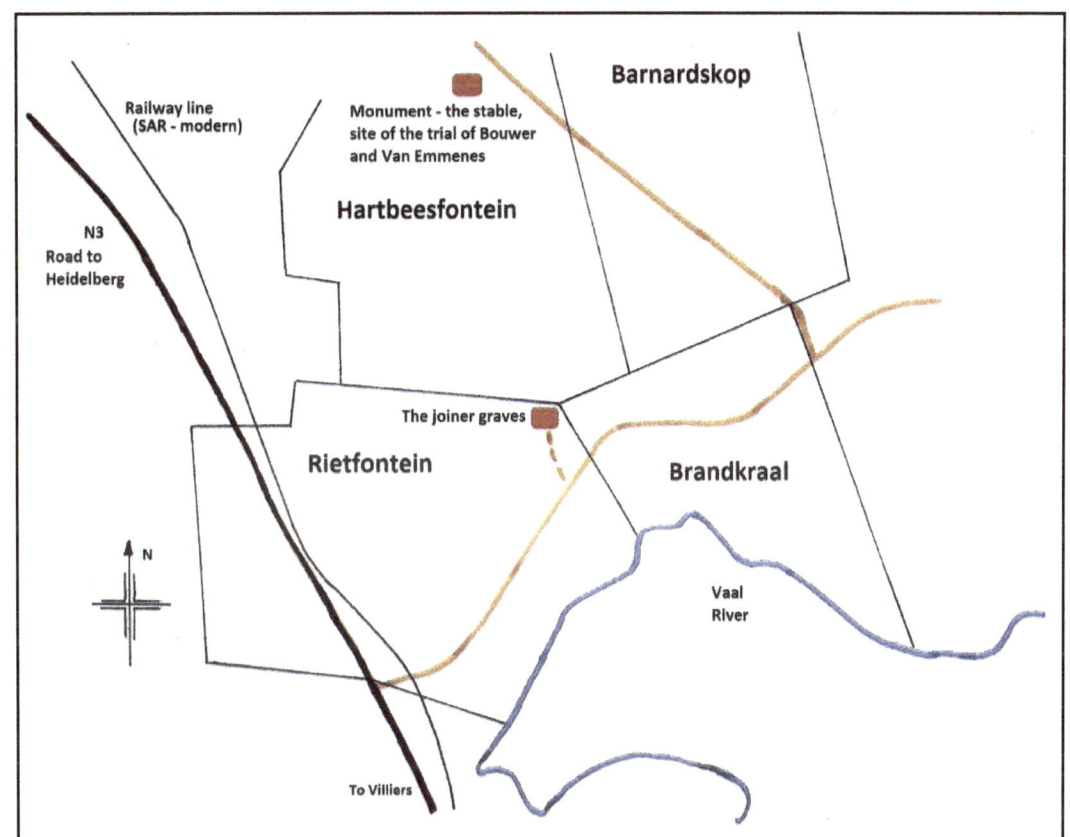

two victims. The psychological effect of this on these young men must have been severe and long-lasting.

It was later said that one of the men, apparently van Emmenes, was not killed instantly. The Boer doctor, a German by the name of Otto Schnitter, was present and required to certify that the prisoners were both dead. It was said that he climbed down into the grave and opened the jugular vein. More normal procedure would have been to check the pulse which would tell whether the heart was still beating. Alternatively, it is relatively simple to establish whether the man was still breathing.

This story emanated from a number of English-speaking members of the Heidelberg Volunteers who had been captured during the fight at Braklaagte and subsequently released. Among them was Sergeant Major Schroeder who reported the capture of Bouwer and van Emmenes by the Boers.[1] Bouwer and van Emmenes were enlisted as privates in the Heidelberg Volunteers and were officially reported as "missing-captured". This required that an enquiry be instituted into the circumstances of their capture and subsequent execution. Assistant Field Cornet Andries Jacobus Greyling of the Heidelberg commando was later captured and reported to the British on 3 May 1902 that he had been an eye witness to the execution. It was he who first mentioned the story of the opening of the jugular artery.[2]

At the subsequent enquiry, a Sergeant Fowlds of the 2nd National Scouts made the declaration under oath that, "I have heard it said that the opening of the artery was for the purpose of allowing van Emmenes to bleed to death."[3] Both Greyling's and Fowlds's reports were hearsay and cannot be taken as absolutely factual. However the story has been repeated in the district for many years even up to the present day. This is according to Ludwig Ankiewicz who grew up on the farm Barnardskop and who is an undoubted authority on the history of the district, as well as a number of other residents of the area.

Evidence presented to Lieutenant Nixon who was responsible for the investigations leading to the establishment of an enquiry concluded that van Emmenes was hit by five bullets but was not killed instantly. Would this therefore indicate that Bouwer in turn was killed instantly by a single shot? The British enquiry did not recommend that anyone be prosecuted in view of the lack of any conclusive evidence.

J.G. van den Heever's detailed description of the whole affair at no time mentions anyone by name. At the time that he wrote his memoirs he was living on the farm Beerlaagte, near to where the joiners were captured. He clearly wished to spare surviving relatives of the two men any further pain. The context of his account means it is unquestionably about Bouwer and van Emmenes.[4]

Bouwer's young wife was almost immediately in difficulties. The couple had a daughter, seventeen months old at the time of Piet's execution, and a son born on 31 July 1901 when he was in prison at Villiers. Less than six weeks after the death of her husband, Nicolina Bouwer's little girl died to be followed only three months later by her baby son.

---
[1] Blake p78.
[2] Grundlingh p294 reports the same information in a manner that it would appear factual.
[3] Blake p81.
[4] Blake p82.

The British authorities were sympathetic and she was granted £80 as compensation for war damages as her husband's estate was worthless. Similarly, van Emmenes's father claimed and was awarded compensation, the British authorities noting that he was "in poor circumstances".

The account in Ian Uys's *Heidelbergers of the Boer War* written in 1981 tells the story of Bouwer and van Emmenes. Much of it is based on an interview that he had with J.A.C. Kriek, as related. Kriek had been a teenager at the time of the Anglo Boer war and was a very old man when Uys learned that he was still alive and living in Heidelberg in 1974. More recent research has been undertaken by Albert Blake for his book *Verraiers* which devotes a chapter to the two young men.

The site of the graves might have been lost were it not for the suicide of Koot Bierman, a 21-year-old who shot himself on the farm Hartbeesfontein. It seems that he had managed to get into serious financial difficulties. Suicide was the reason why his family would not allow him to be buried in the family plot on their farm. He was interred next to "the other two murderers" and stones were arranged over the grave roughly in the shape of a coffin. Because of this the location of the site has not been lost – it is on the boundary line of the farm Rietfontein and Hartbeesfontein.

The grave of Bierman and its coffin-shaped surround was still intact in 2010 although the stones were now somewhat disturbed. The last resting place of Bouwer and van Emmenes was an overgrown mound of earth. During 2010 members of the South African Military History Society led by committee member David Scholtz decided that it would be appropriate to erect granite memorials over the grave and at the site where the court martial took place. While the conduct of Bouwer and van Emmenes in taking up arms against their own countrymen cannot be condoned, the members of the Military History Society felt that the history of this whole affair and their burial place should not be allowed to disappear into obscurity.

Ludwig Ankiewicz, a local farmer and undoubted authority on the history of the district, was very supportive of the project as well as numbers of other local people. English and Afrikaans inscriptions were agreed for the memorials at both Rietfontein and Hartbeesfontein. This is how the English inscriptions read:

> *Here lie Pieter Bouwer and Adolf van Emmenes, two former members of the Republican forces who deserted during the Anglo-Boer War and joined the British forces. After they were captured, they were charged with high treason and sentenced to death. They were executed by firing squad and buried on Rietfontein on 24 August 1901.*
>
> *This is the site of the stable where two former members of the Republican forces, Pieter Bouwer and Adolf van Emmenes, who deserted during the Anglo-Boer War and joined the British forces, were charged with high treason and sentenced to death after they were captured on 24 July 1901. They were executed by firing squad and buried on Rietfontein on 24 August 1901.*

A stonemason was engaged and the granite memorials over the grave and at the stable site were erected on 25 July

2011. The joiners' grave, once the overgrowth had been removed, was found to be a soil mound covered with rocks. These must have been collected from the vicinity and placed (possibly by members of the families) so as to prevent wild animals from digging up the remains. It was thought best to flatten the mound and lay a granite border around the grave. The rocks were replaced over the grave within the granite border and the memorial was erected at the head of the grave. At the stable site the job was easier. There was flat ground, a foundation was laid and the memorial was erected facing the road passing by the remains of the stable.

On 26 August 2011 the memorials to these two tragic figures were dedicated in a ceremony attended by a number of interested people. Ludwig Ankiewicz in a short speech described how these two young men came to be executed by their own people. Nigel Mason, an Anglican lay minister, delivered a short burial service, something Pieter Bouwer and Adolf van Emmenes were not given on the day they died and were interred. The ceremony took place two days after the 110th anniversary of their deaths, and was testimony to the fact that the passing of time has caused much of the bitterness towards the 'joiners' to dissipate.

The decision by these two young men to take up arms against their own people cannot be condoned and yet they deserve some sympathy. No one will know for certain what their motives were. May they now rest in peace, perhaps knowing that their story will not be forgotten.

(The writer must acknowledge that this article has drawn heavily on the chapters in Ian Uys's and Albert Blake's books dealing with this sad event. Ludwig Ankiewicz's booklet on events in the area of the Suikerbosrand has been equally informative.)

References

1. Albert Blake *Boereverraaier: Teregstellings tydens die Anglo-Boereoorlog*, Tafelberg, Cape Town 2010.

2. Ludwig Ankiewicz *Vanaf die Suikerbosrant tot by die Vaalrivier: Diè deel van die Ommidraai Kronkelroete* self-published by the author 2009.

3. *Christiaan de Wet Annale*, Number 6 October 1984.

4. Albert Grundlingh *The Dynamics of Treason: Boer collaboration in the South African War of 1899 – 1902* Protea Book House, Pretoria 2006 (translation from the Afrikaans by Dr Bridget Theron of *Die "Hendsoppers" en "Joiners": Die rasionaal en verskynsel van verraad* Protea Boekhuis, Pretoria 1979).

5. Hendrik Kamffer *Herinneringe* (translation into English as *Memoirs*) Ian Uys Collection in the archives in Pretoria.

6. Ian Uys *Heidelbergers of the Boer War* Ian S. Uys, Heidelberg 1981.

7. J.G. van den Heever *Op Kommando onder Kommandant Buys* Bienedell Uitgewers, Pretoria 2001.

26 August 2011:
Nigel Mason, a lay Anglican minister, reading the burial service. Ludwig Ankiewicz and his wife in the background.

The graves as they were in 2010:
Koot Bierman's grave with stones arranged in the rough shape of a coffin and with no headstone to identify his last resting place.

The grave of the "joiners". Completely overgrown, it was only when the overgrowth was removed that it was realised that the low mound was covered with rocks which preserved it from being eroded away with the weather as well as preventing interference from wild animals.

The monuments over the Joiners' graves on Rietfontein and at the ruins of the stable at Hartbeesfontein.

The gathering at the dedication ceremony. The six people behind the grave are (right to left) David Scholtz in the camouflage cap, Ludwig Ankiewicz, Albert Blake, Ian Uys, Nigel Mason and Bob Smith. The author is on the left in the green cap.

The Boer invasions of the Cape and Natal in September 1901

The Boer deliberations at Branddrift, known as the Waterval *kreigsraad/krygsraad* which reaffirmed their determination to continue the war, also made decisions about strategy. Tactical successes with surprise attacks on British convoys and isolated garrisons were unlikely to weaken the equally determined British resolve. Nevertheless, Botha and Smuts pointed out that a major success was needed if they were to win the war and force the British to the negotiating table. A decision was made for Botha to make an armed incursion into Natal while Smuts, with a commando of experienced fighters from General Koos de la Rey's western Transvalers, was to likewise raid into the Cape.

By the second half of 1901 Boer resources in men and materials were running low. The two republican governments were avoiding detection and capture by numerous British columns traversing the country. The Transvaal Government was hidden in the mountains of the eastern part of their country and the Orange Free Staters were undetected for some time at the Rondebosch farmhouse, east of Reitz. Ammunition supplies were marginal and were now entirely from captured British supplies. Food was in short supply and the commandos were hard put even to live off the land. Clothing was such that British army tunics and breeches were much prized even though anyone captured wearing such stolen kit was liable to harsh treatment.

A major invasion by the combined forces of the two republics to drive the British into the sea was clearly out of the question. Nevertheless, forays into the Cape and Natal Colonies could cause some alarm, divert British troops to defend areas that hitherto had not seen action and perhaps attract recruits to the Boer cause. Botha undertook to lead a raid into Natal, his force about 1,400 strong. Smuts crossed the Orange River into the Cape Colony with 350 men of Koos de la Rey's westerners. Botha was soon driven back into the Transvaal Highveld but Smuts had a long, long ride. His commandos got to see the lights of Cape Town but were driven away north into Namaqualand. They were still active there when the war came to an end in May 1902.

Neither invasion achieved very much in a strategic sense. Smuts's men were never cornered but neither did they do any serious damage to their enemy. The major part of Deneys Reitz's book *Commando* describes their remarkable journey. The two raids, for that is really all that they amounted to, had little strategic significance. Smuts caused Major-General John French some anxiety for his command in the Cape Colony. Botha's men suffered a setback when they failed to overwhelm the defenders of Forts Itala and Prospect on the Natal border but they did manage to capture a supply convoy before they turned back to the Transvaal.

Colonel George Benson, enjoying considerable success in the eastern Transvaal with night raids on Boer laagers, was a marked man. Botha, with a majority of the men who had accompanied him to Natal, managed to catch Benson at a disadvantage. The Boers captured two guns and inflicted more than 130 casualties on Benson's column at Bakenlaagte in October 1901. Thereafter overwhelming British reinforcements drove the commandos into the mountains north of Vryheid. In any case, by the early months of 1902, peace negotiations were starting.

17th Lancer graves at Modderfontein

"Don't shoot – we are the 17th Lancers!"

MODDERFONTEIN

17 September 1901

On the farm Modderfontein in the Eastern Cape, 22 kilometres from Tarkastad, are the graves of those officers and men of "C" Squadron of the 17th Lancers who died in defending their camp against the commando of General Jan Christiaan Smuts on 17 September 1901. Three officers have separate headstones and they and thirty-five men of the regiment are buried in a mass grave. Three gunners of the Royal Garrison Artillery also died there and are named on the memorial. The astounding fact is that the 17th Lancers lost more men killed in action that day than on any other single day in its long history, more even than in the Charge of the Light Brigade at Balaklava in 1854! (*The White Lancer and Vedette*, 1986 p112)

Had the Boer commando not succeeded in overwhelming their opponents that day, the history of the Anglo Boer War and indeed of the world could have been very different. Smuts later became a world figure, a Field Marshal in the British army and a member of the original committee of statesmen who proposed the formation of the United Nations. How did this disaster for the 17th Lancers happen? The writer has made a study of the ground and a number of accounts that exist of the encounter and offers this version of events on 17 September 1901 on the farm Modderfontein in the Eastern Cape.

Denys Reitz wrote a racy version of it all in *Commando* and Ben Bouwer, his Commandant on the day, has more to say in his memoirs. From the other side, Lieutenant-Colonel Douglas Haig, the Lancers' commanding officer, gave a short description in a letter to his sister Henrietta, written a few days after the battle. There are descriptions in the official history and in *The Times History of the War in South Africa*. The officer casualties are pictured in *After Pretoria* and my other references also have accounts but none of these has satisfied me that they give a proper explanation of what happened that day.

The British knew that the Smuts commando must by now have been at the end of their tether. The weather of late had been diabolical, even for that area which nearly ever year seems to have a particularly severe spell in September. Smuts and his men had suffered severely since they crossed the Orange River into the Cape Colony on 3 September at Khiba Drift. Attacked by the Basuto near the Wittenberg Mission they had lost one man killed and three captured in defending themselves but had managed to continue southwards. (Taffy & David Shearing, 2000: *General Smuts and his long ride* pp32-34, Sandy Stretton 2001: *Smuts in the Stormberg* p 21)

Smuts himself had a narrow escape at Moordenaar's Poort, near Dordrecht, on 11 September when he and two companions had been ambushed while scouting the way ahead. British columns practically surrounded them on the Stormberg. Guided by a friendly *bywoner*, the crippled Hans Kleynhans, they had a miraculous escape at Boshoff's Kraal when they slithered down the mountainside on a grassy slope, the only way down and a near-vertical incline. (Denys Reitz, 1929: *Commando* p219). They crossed the branch railway line near Halseton and the main line from East London at Putter's Kraal.

The commando headed along the Klaas Smits River travelling south and west. Making for the farm Rhenosterhoek, they came across the column commanded by Lieutenant-Colonel G.F. Gorringe heading for the same farm. They spent the night "adrift on the open veld", in Reitz's words, as neither side wanted a clash in the awful weather then prevailing. (Denys Reitz 1929, *Commando* p223).

The next day (15 September) they called in at Waterval, a large farm that housed several families. Smuts was most reluctant to stay the night there as he knew that Gorringe's column was not far behind. They pushed on through the night and this was "the night of the big rain", Reitz again. His description of the hardships that they suffered that night is most graphic. After a stop at a deserted farm, Groothaasfontein, they went northwest across the farm Hondeklip, crossed the *nek* to the south of Toorkop and found food and forage on the farm De Hoek, owned by Fanie Venter. (See map showing the commando's route from Putter's Kraal to Modderfontein and Klein Mostert's Hoek).

Next day was 17 September. Going past the farm Rietfontein they came to Ewan's Hope and it was here that Jan Coetzer, a 17-year old youth, came running out of the farmhouse to tell them that British cavalry had a camp in the next valley. Coetzer had seen a patrol of the 17th Lancers come close to the farmhouse earlier that morning. Seeing nothing, the Lancers had returned down the Buysrivierpoort and back to the camp at Modderfontein. Jan Coetzer's warning to the commando is quite factual – some accounts say that Coetzer was feeble-minded but Fanie Venter, who farms in the area, claims this is not so: "You are talking about one of my ancestors!"

The camp of the Lancers at Modderfontein was in a poor position for a determined defence. The regiment had been trained around from Stormberg and had arrived on Sunday 15 September (Haig's letter). Their orders were to guard the passes into the valley – the Buysrivierpoort and the Elandsrivierpoort. Due to the incessant rain of the previous week, the Elands River was running high and was difficult to cross with their transport. The farm of Hendrik van Heerden, a little way back from the two passes offered a sheltered campsite and a comfortable farmhouse for the officers' mess. Mr Van Heerden and his wife were confined to the bedroom so as not to give away any information that might find its way to Smuts or any other enemy in the neighbourhood. (Taffy & David Shearing, 2000: *General Smuts and his long ride* p54).

Haig himself was there to inspect the site the day before, Monday 16 September, and lunched with Captain Sandeman, the Squadron commander, on the dolerite dyke which protrudes from the ground behind the farmhouse. He describes Sandeman as a "most capable officer" and clearly Haig came over from Tarkastad to inspect the position (Haig's letter). Equally clearly he must have told Sandeman to stay where he was (*The Times History of the War in South Africa* v p388).

The next morning, Tuesday 17 September, was foggy and Sandeman sent two patrols out to reconnoiter the passes (Haig's letter). These would have been each a troop in strength, about thirty men, and commanded by a lieutenant in all likelihood. One patrol went through the Buysrivierpoort and onto the open plain near Ewan's Hope. There they expected that they might meet up with Lieutenant-Colonel Gorringe's men. Gorringe was in fact not far away having camped the previous night on the farm Hondeklip being aware that Smuts's men were not too far ahead of them. The Lancers could see a considerable distance across the flat country to the next range of hills, the Toorberg, and north and south, but no Boers or British column was in sight. The other patrol equally drew a blank north of the Elandsrivierpoort and the Elands River could now be reasonably easily crossed by mounted men. The two troops of Lancers returned to camp the way they had come leaving pickets guarding the exits from the passes. The map will make this clear.

Gorringe had captured a number of Boers on Hondeklip on 16 September – Ben Bouwer's account says that they had been sent out from De Hoek as foragers. (Taffy and David Shearing 2000: *General Smuts and his Long Ride* p52 gives some of the names of those captured or wounded in the clash with Gorringe and Bouwer confirms the incident in his *Memoirs of General Ben Bouwer*). Gorringe moved towards Tarkastad, not far away, to get supplies and confer with Haig.

Denys Reitz and his section had been ordered by Smuts to scout the way ahead and it was them who happened across Jan Coetzer (Denys Reitz 1929, *Commando* p225. Reitz does not mention Coetzer by name – his descendants are certain it was him who gave the warning). Bouwer claims to have been with the patrol. Coetzer was a 17-year old who lived on the farm Ewan's Hope. He rushed out to the approaching Boers and excitedly told them that an English patrol had only returned down the Buysrivierpoort a few minutes before. Again, refer to the map.

Reitz sent Edgar Duncker back to report and he returned with General Smuts and Commandant van Deventer. Evidently Smuts had planned to pass through Lelik Poortjie to get over the next range at Klein Mosterts Hoek but he immediately decided to attack the Lancers' camp as they were in desperate need of fresh horses, ammunition and food.

Commandant Ben Bouwer led a party of scouts through the Buysrivierpoort. Commandant Jaap van Deventer took another group who followed a little way behind. Smuts stayed back to organise the rest of the commando including several men who had no horses. It was now late morning. They passed through the poort and were spotted by one of the Lancers' pickets. One of the picket troopers galloped back to the camp and told Captain Sandeman that a party of Boers was advancing towards the camp. Sandeman immediately sent out a troop under 2nd Lieutenant Russel to investigate. The message was probably received in the camp at about noon (Haig's letter says noon, Grant says 12.30 p.m. in *History of the War in South Africa 1899-1902*).

There is mention of a spy in an account in Afrikaans by J.P. Bosman who claims to have seen him in the morning before they left the farm De Hoek. The Reverend John Catling also describes how an English farmer came into the Lancers' camp to warn them of the approaching Boer commando. Captain Sandeman arrested him, according to Catling, as a spy. It is possible that this man was the "spy" seen at De Hoek.

Russel's troop came across Ben Bouwer's group at a stream and a patch of thorn bush. The Boers levelled their rifles at the Lancers and Russel shouted to them, "Don't fire. We are the 17th Lancers." (See H.W. Wilson's *After Pretoria II* p745 for a picture of this incident). Russel and his men expected them to be from Gorringe's column. The Boers opened fire at once and the Lancers suffered several casualties. Realising that these were Boers, Russel sent some of his men back to camp along the road while he circled around to the west with the rest of the troop. The men he sent back to camp were delayed by a gate and suffered several more casualties. (Denys Reitz 1929,: *Commando* p226).

Reitz was one of those who opened fire at the stream. He had dismounted and, as he had no more cartridges for his Mauser he dropped it there, picked up a Lee-Metford and a bandolier from one of the Lancer dead, rushed for his mare and joined in the chase after the Lancers patrol. At the gate in the fence, Ben Bouwer and Jaap van Deventer conferred. Bouwer and his men who included Reitz followed the retiring members of the patrol (Denys Reitz 1929, *Commando* p226).

Bouwer with Reitz, his Veld Cornet Jack Borrius, and about a dozen others made their way up the eastern side of the valley, which is flat and open. Borrius took his men into the rocks and bushes of the dyke. Hidden in the rocks were the two guns – a mountain gun (popular in India – muzzle-loaded, could be quickly dismounted and carried by four or six mules) and a Maxim machine gun. Reitz and his friends dismounted and abandoned their horses. Boer horses were trained to stand still and did not need minders. They found themselves very near the gunners and quickly opened fire on the guns which were in an exposed position although protected by a ring of rocks. Lieutenant Hay-Coghlan was shot by Reitz, two of the other gunners were killed and another, who managed to escape into the camp, was wounded. They were also very close to the tents of the camp and were in a tight position. (This account differs in a number of important respects from the description given in Taffy & David Shearing 2000: *General Smuts and his Long Ride* p55. The account in Sandy Stretton 2001: *Smuts in the Stormberg* pp49-53 seems more plausible).

Commandant Ben Bouwer arrived just behind the Borrius section, dismounted and ran into the yard of the farmhouse on its south side. The guard at the door opened fire and hit young Lawrence Tyner in the head. Bouwer's men spread out in a line to the south of the farmhouse and opened fire on the Lancers' right flank. Van Deventer had circled around even further to the south and approached the farm from that direction. Bouwer's men were already engaging the Lancers. It appears that the latter mistook the oncoming Boers for their colleagues of the "A" squadron who were camped at Hoogstede to the south of Modderfontein. By now, Smuts and Kirsten had taken up a position on a small rise about 800 yards to the west and from this point swept the flat field with rifle fire. The Lancers assailed from all sides, were without adequate cover and suffered accordingly.

When a patrol from the "A" Squadron of the Lancers was spotted in the distance, the Boers on the side of the dyke realised that they would have to finish things quickly before Lancer reinforcements arrived. Reitz and his fellow Boers probably saw Van Deventer's men approaching and made the same mistake as the Lancers! Borrius gave the orders and Reitz and his section charged into the remaining Lancers, only about fifteen of whom were left. Further resistance was hopeless, one or two threw down their arms but several escaped into the tents. Reitz shot an officer who tried to escape on a horse, Lieutenant Russel or Morritt? (Denys Reitz 1929, Commando p229).

With the guns out of action, the rest were quickly overwhelmed. Captain Sandeman rallied some of the men who occupied one of the stone kraals but they were too few to defend the whole perimeter and they too were attacked from all sides having no alternative but to give in. A number of Lancers were forced to retreat to the south through the narrow defile at Thorn Grove. Bouwer says the action took "less than twenty minutes". In view of the serious opposition that the Boers encountered from the Lancers it does seem unlikely that matters were decided quite so quickly. J.P. Bosman and Micholls describe what appears to be a small number of Lancers caught in the open on the right and forced to retreat through a defile, possibly near Thorn Grove farm. Micholls says, "after shooting their horses...having expended all their ammunition."

The Boers now spent not more than a few minutes looting the camp. They replenished their ammunition supplies, took as much food as they could carry and took British uniforms to replace the rags and grain bags that they had been wearing. Reitz now encountered Lord Vivian and the conversation took place is related by Jan Reitz in Thomas Pakenham's introduction to later editions of Commando. (The account as related by Thomas Pakenham in the introduction to 1983 editions of Commando is now discredited as Lord Vivian died in 1940. The Mauser rifle that Denys Reitz discarded before the battle was returned to him when he was in England as South African ambassador.) Reitz now kitted himself out with Vivian's equipment – a Lancer's uniform complete with badges and insignia, Lee-Metford rifle and full bandoliers as well as a superb grey Arab, formerly the property of Lieutenant Sheridan (Denys Reitz 1929, Commando p231 – Ben Bouwer though, acquired Vivian's fine binoculars!)

The Boers were now like giants refreshed in Reitz's words and burned whatever they were unable to carry away with them. Most importantly however their confidence in their leader, General Jan Smuts, was restored. In the foul weather that they had experienced since crossing the Orange as well as the determined and relentless pursuit of the British columns, their faith in Smuts had been wavering and a number had deserted to attempt to get back to the Free State and Transvaal. There was henceforth no more talk of this. In particular, Commandant Piet Wessels took about 100 of his men back to the Free State on 8 September, according to Bouwer.

There was something near to three hundred animals, horses and mules in the camp. A number of these would have been killed and wounded in the fight but there would certainly have been enough to remount the commando. Reitz himself managed to acquire both a horse and a mule. The commando had a string of walkers when they left De Hoek as well as a number of wounded. No wounded were left behind at Modderfontein, although they had at least six more casualties, (D.H. Parry in The Death or Glory Boys has an eye witness account saying that Commandant (sic) Smuts said they "had paid dearly for it") who they took as far as Cradock where there was a Red Cross hospital.

A few blows from Van Deventer (formerly a gunner in the Transvaal Staats Artillerie) disabled the mountain gun and they rode off to the north through the Elandsrivierpoort and over Klein Mostertshoek pass towards Maraisburg (now Hofmeyr). They also captured two Maxim guns but Bouwer said they were too much of a nuisance and so were dumped into the first dam that they came across.

The patrol from "A" squadron was not strong enough to do more than exchange a few shots with the fleeing Boers. They did what they could to rescue the few Lancers who were unwounded. The patrol sent messages back to their camp at Hoogstede. From there a galloper went in to Tarkastad where Haig had two further Lancer squadrons. The news reached him at 4:30 p.m. and he galloped the 22 kilometres to Modderfontein in an hour and a quarter (Haig's letter). This would mean that he arrived there at 5:45 p.m. and much too late for pursuit of the commando. The wounded were taken into Tarkastad – it is said that two of them are buried in the town cemetery but the writer is unable to confirm this.

A squadron of one of the British Army's crack cavalry regiments was overwhelmed, that is undeniable. All previous accounts give the impression that a mob of Boer irregulars descended on the camp which was taken completely by surprise. This I believe to be incorrect and the attack was conducted in a thoroughly professional manner by experienced Boer soldiers. None of the Lancers surrendered in the sense that no white flag was hoisted by anyone. General J.C. Smuts himself, in a speech in England some years later when a guest of Douglas Haig said: "How gallantly those boys fought against us, many being killed because they knew not how to surrender." Several threw down their rifles when confronted with Boers at point-blank range and one at least gave in when he bumped into Reitz at the corner of the kraal (Denys Reitz 1929, Commando p230).

The Lancer camp was in a less than ideal place for defense. They encamped there when they arrived in the area in pouring rain and were unable to cross the Elands River with their transport. The farm's field and the shelter in the lee of the dolerite dyke, to say nothing of the comfortable farmhouse, provided a solution to this problem. Also, they were close to the river which solved the problem of water for men and beasts. Unfortunately it was dominated on all sides by higher ground and the Boers, with their eye for such things, took full advantage.

"C" squadron consisted largely of new recruits and they had little experience of combat. They fought well and in the tradition of the regiment and its motto with the Death's Head and "or Glory". The fact that they suffered more casualties than at any other day in their history is testimony enough to their heroic defense.

References

1. *The White Lancer and Vedette*, 1986 (Regimental magazine of the Queen's Royal Lancers).
2. Shearing, Taffy and David *General Smuts and his long ride*. Privately printed by Taffy and David Shearing, Sedgefield 2000.
3. Stretton, Sandy *Smuts in the Stormberg*. Published by The Anderson Museum, Dordrecht 2001.
4. Wilson, H.W. *After Pretoria II*. Published by Eyre and Spottiswoode, London 1902.
5. Pakenham, Thomas. *The Boer War*. Published by Weidenfeld and Nicholson, London 1979.
6. Childers, Erskine (Editor) *The Times History of the War in South Africa*, Volume V. Published by Sampson Low, Marston, London 1907.
7. Grant, Captain Maurice Harold, *History of the War in South Africa 1899-1902*, Published by Hurst and Blackett Limited, London 1910.
8. Reitz, Denys. *Commando*. Published by Faber and Faber, London 1929. *Commando* was written from notes that Reitz preserved after the war. The original manuscript is in the Brenthurst collection and differs from the published book in a number of respects.
9. Bosman, J.P. *Slaan en Vlug*. Published privately by L.W. Bienedell, Pretoria 1999.
10. Cooper, Duff. *Haig* Published by Faber and Faber, London 1935.
11. D.H. Parry. *The Death or Glory Boys* Published by Cassell, London.
12. Micholls - *History of the 17th Lancers*.
13. Diary of the Reverend J. Catling.
14. Maps based on survey maps from the Chief Directorate, Surveys and Mapping, Mowbray.

Ewan's Hope farmhouse

Modderfontein farmhouse

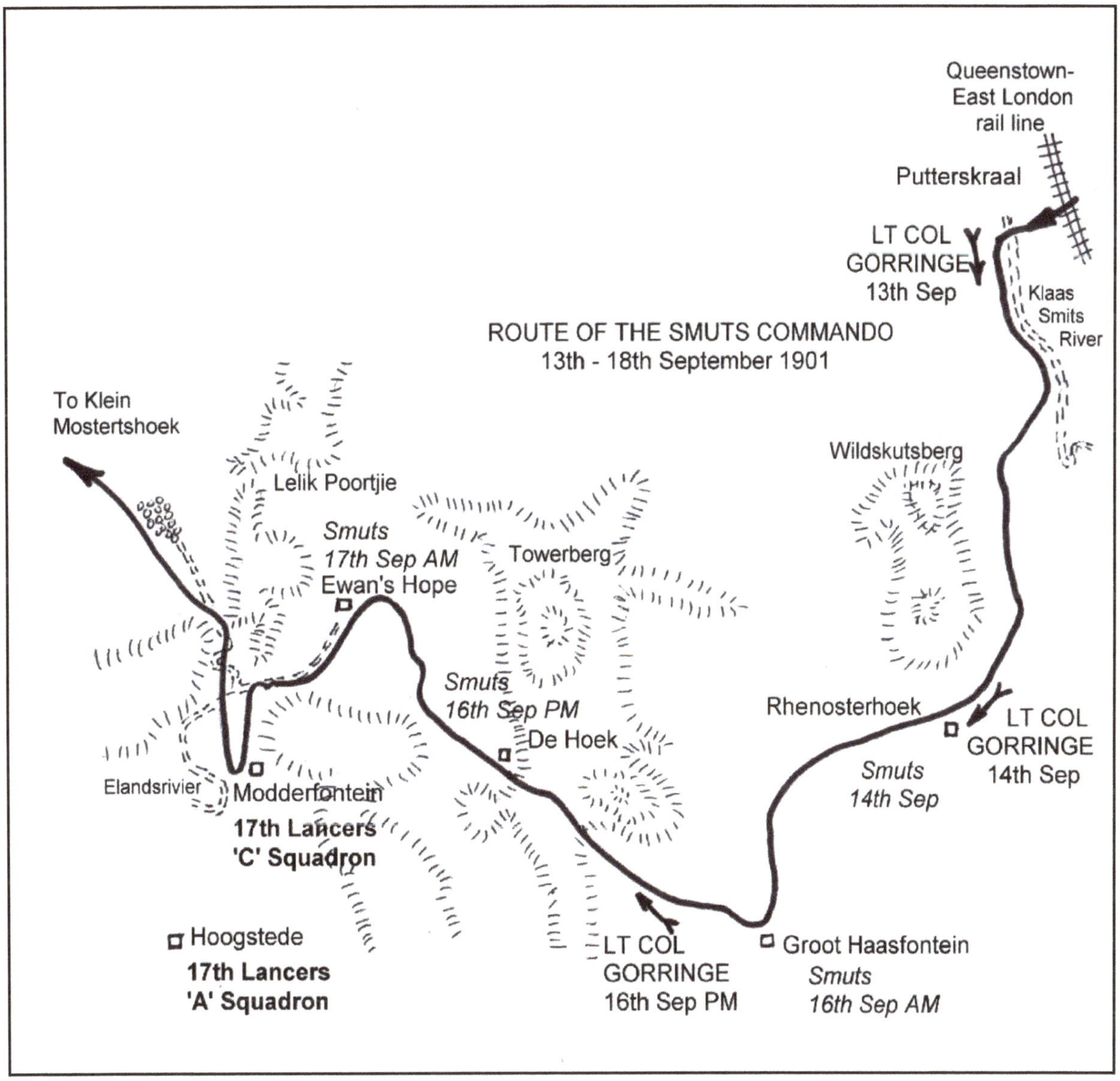

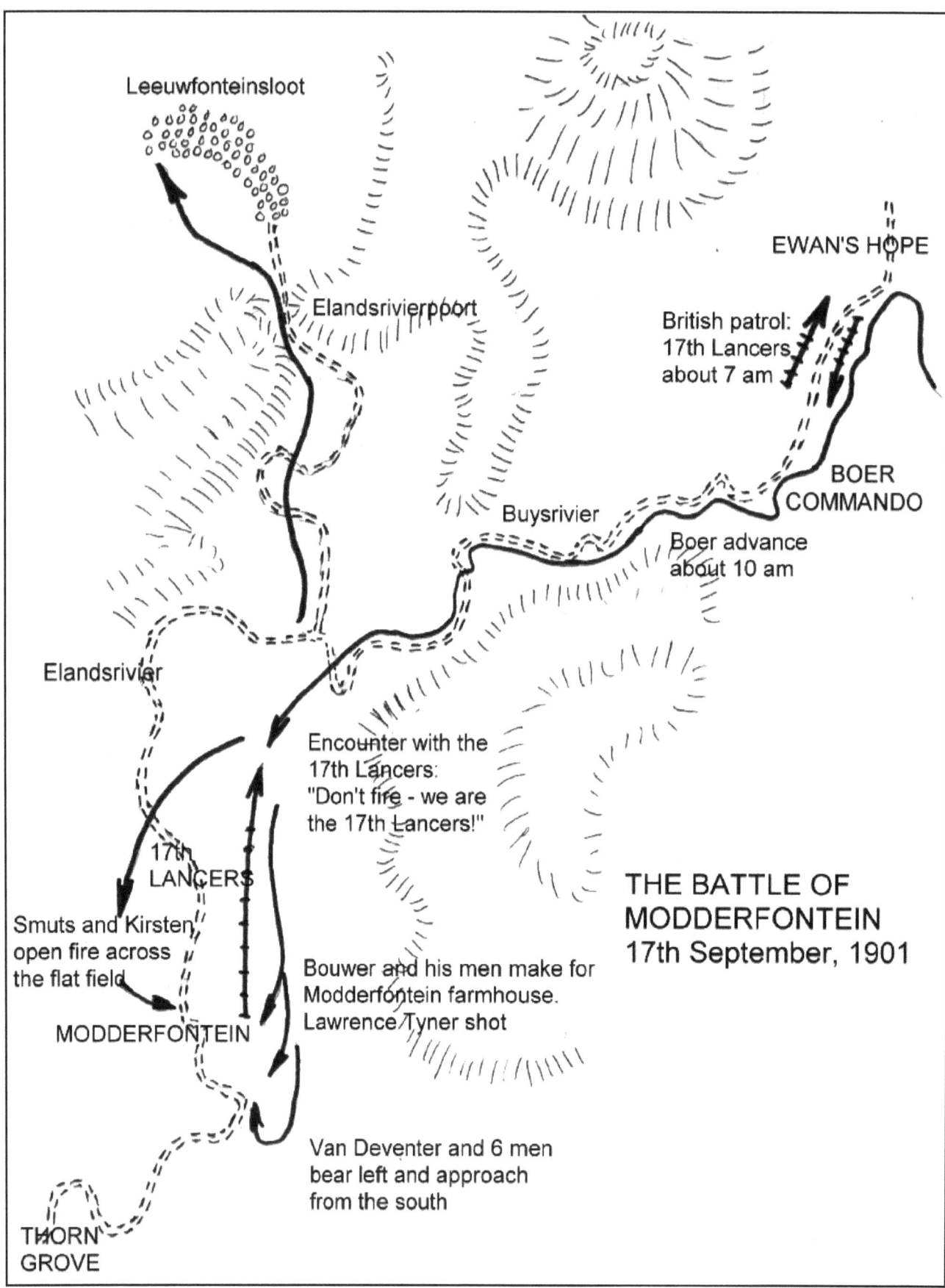

Mokari Drift

Van Stadensrus is a small obscure Free State town near the border with Lesotho. In the local cemetery four Australian soldiers lie buried. One of them has a handsome marble cross headstone with an inscription on the plinth which says, "In loving memory of my dear son Lachlan John Caskey. Killed at Mokari Drift 27 Sept 1901. Erected by his mother." Next to it are the remains of what may once have been a glass-fronted wooden headstone with an inscription for Alfred Ernest Pooley. The glass is long gone and the inscription too is missing. Beside these two memorials are two small pieces of wood, all that remains of the wooden crosses that once graced the last resting places of Benjamin Milner and George Henry White.[1]

The four were casualties of a skirmish with the Boer commando of Commandant Louis Wessels, itself a part of the larger force commanded by General Pieter Kritzinger, on the farm Dewetsdal on the Caledon River. Originally buried in the garden of the farmhouse on Mokari farm they were reinterred in Van Stadensrus in the 1960s during the programme of consolidating farm graves into cemeteries or Gardens of Remembrance in the nearest town. This remote and out-of-the-way graveyard will likely preserve what remains for another century. Details of the Boer casualties are unknown though there must surely have been some in what was a fierce fight typical of the minor actions of that period of the Anglo Boer war as British columns scoured the countryside for their elusive enemy.

In August and September 1901 there was considerable military activity in the south eastern Orange River Colony (the new name for the Orange Free State under British occupation) as the British attempted to locate and capture the commando of Assistant Commandant-General Jan Smuts, heading for the Cape Colony. Taking a sizeable commando from the Transvaal through the Orange River Colony was no easy task but Smuts made it safely to his meeting place at Zastron in the southeast with General Pieter Kritzinger who was to provide guides for the crossing of the Orange River. Kritzinger had been driven out of the Cape only two weeks previously and certainly had valuable information for Smuts concerning the whereabouts of the enemy forces over the river.[2]

Smuts and his commando of about 350 men crossed the Orange at Kiba drift some way upstream from Aliwal North on the night of 3rd September or the early morning of the following day. Accompanying him for a few days was Commandant Louis Wessels and fifty of his men among whose number was an old veteran of the Basuto wars of the previous century who pointed out the crossing place over the river. The British had guarded every drift (every drift but one perhaps?) and Kritzinger was left behind at Zastron to divert pursuit from Smuts with the intention was of joining him later with reinforcements.[3]

This small concentration of Boers, Smuts and Kritzinger together mustered scarcely more than 600 men, caused the British to rush troops to the area from all quarters. Although Smuts and most of his men had managed to evade capture and cross into the Cape Colony, Kritzinger and his men in the Zastron area were a threat that the British needed to eliminate. Major-General Fitzroy Hart was in command of a section of river from Aliwal North to the Basutoland border. He really had insufficient troops to guard every drift but there were in addition three further British columns in the area to the north of him under Colonels Rawlinson and Thorneycroft and Brigadier General Plumer.[4]

Kritzinger was able to avoid the attentions of the columns and used Vecht Kop, a high hill to the east of Zastron to observe his enemy's movements. Guarding the drifts over the Orange at Quaggafontein was Lieutenant Colonel the Honourable A. Murray with a force that included a number of Lovat's Scouts, a Yeomanry company raised by Lord Lovat largely from his estate in Scotland. With Major Lord Lovat and a detachment being absent chasing Smuts across the river, Murray had only 106 men spread over a number of pickets around his camp. The Yeomen were unable to resist the onslaught of Kritzinger's commando around midnight on 20 September. Murray and eleven of the Lovat Scouts were killed as well as eight gunners of the 38th Battery, Royal Field Artillery. Kritzinger's men retired back towards Rouxville with a number of horses, rifles and ammunition and an Armstrong gun.[5]

Kritzinger had now revealed himself. Boer tactics were to split into smaller groups and head in different directions. The country along the Basutoland border provided a multitude of mountain fastnesses with kloofs and ravines where they could stay out of sight for a while. One of these groups headed north with the captured gun and was spotted by the scouts of Colonel Thorneycroft's column. About forty Boers were attacked by the men of Thorneycroft's Mounted Infantry, abandoned the gun by the roadside and were cornered in a donga on the farm Florence.[6]

Another of these small groups, probably no more than eighty in number, also headed north. They crossed to the right bank of the Caledon River and laagered on top of a high hill on the farm Sweetfontein. The summit of the hill was in the shape of a bowl, small streams provided their water, and they were able to see long distances in every direction. They seemed to be safe from detection while they awaited word from Kritzinger about rejoining him for his next foray into the Cape Colony. Their Commandant was Louis Wessels who had returned from guiding Smuts, taken a prominent part in the attack on Lovat's Scouts at Quaggafontein and was described by Kritzinger as "certainly one of the most intrepid and fearless officers of the whole Boer army".[7]

The column of Brigadier Herbert Plumer had been in the vicinity of Zastron and further north, Wepener, since early September. Plumer was well-liked by his Colonial troops, Australians and New Zealanders, which was something of a rarity for a British officer. He had been in South Africa several times before the war from 1894 onwards and at the relief of Mafeking was a Lieutenant Colonel. His column consisted of 980 men, Australians, New Zealanders, gunners from the R.F.A., 7th Mounted Infantry (Royal Hampshire Regiment) from England and some Scottish Yeomanry.[8]

The Australians were the 5th Queensland Imperial Bushmen, mostly from the country districts of Queensland so they would have had much in common with their Boer adversaries. It had become clear to the British once the war became a conflict with bands of highly-mobile Boer guerilla fighters that they needed mounted scouts skilled in bushcraft. The Australian Bushmen therefore were good riders and trackers, able to live off the land and endure harsh conditions, all traits that would enable them to equal the Boers in those respects.

Most of them were from the bush but there were a good many town boys among them. They were all fired up with the patriotism of the day and were keen to fight the Empire's foes. With barely a month's military training they were hardly a match for the Boers now hardened by nearly two years of living in the veld with only their horses and rifles between living or dying or being captured. The Q.I.B.'s marksmanship does not seem to have been very good as they expended thousands of rounds in engagements with the Boers in order to inflict a quite moderate numbers of casualties. Nevertheless, they were much better physical specimens than their British colleagues and this meant that they generally gave a good account of themselves.[9]

In the 5th Q.I.B. were a number of interesting people. Two young brothers, David and William Lilley joined the regiment with David, the elder brother being an acting Corporal and William a private. Because William was only seventeen, David was encouraged by his parents to "keep an eye on William". One of the officers was a Brisbane teacher, Lachlan John Caskey who was a Lieutenant in "K" Company of the Q.I.B. He was almost thirty-one when he arrived in South Africa and had been a teacher at a boys' school whose inspectors described him as "very hardworking and energetic, not intellectual." Another Lieutenant was Alfred Ernest Pooley who had been Sergeant Major in the 4th Queensland Contingent, returned home and then volunteered for another tour of duty, promoted this time to officer's rank. He had been born in England and emigrated to Australia in the 1890s. We do not know his age.[10]

The column had been moved from the eastern Transvaal (now Mpumalanga) to arrive in Bloemfontein on 18 July 1901. By the end of August they had moved south patrolling along the Orange River. Marched to Priors Siding on the main railway line it seemed as if they were about to be returned to the eastern Transvaal. After an inspection by the Medical Officer they were ordered to march eastwards as part of the force trying to prevent Smuts crossing into the Cape Colony. Once it was realised that Smuts had succeeded in crossing the Orange River, Pieter Kritzinger became their quarry but he proved very difficult to find.[11]

From Priors Plumer led his men towards Rouxville and they camped for the night at Jakkalsfontein, near Smithfield. They headed north cooperating with other columns around them and reached Wepener on 13 September without seeing any sign of Kritzinger or Wessels – but no doubt the Boers were aware of the British presence. The Q.I.B. patrolled in the area for three days and then the column turned south and arrived back at Rouxville on 22 September, intelligence suggesting that they could catch sight of the Boers moving northwards after their success at Quaggafontein. The British now seemed to be in a good position to capture the remnants of Kritzinger's commando, scattered around the area after Thorneycroft's success at Florence on the evening of 20 September.[12]

However, in Rouxville was an order sending Plumer hurrying back northwards. On 19 September, a small British force consisting of mounted infantry of the Bedfordshire Regiment and two guns from "U" Battery R.H.A. left their camp at Boesman's Kop, due east and some ten miles from Bloemfontein, and headed south to attack a Boer commando on the farm Vlakfontein. Finding this farm unoccupied they advanced towards another farm, Slangfontein where they were attacked by the Boers from positions where they were unable to respond. The commander was a militia officer, the two guns were in charge of the young Lieutenant Otter-Barry and the foray was made without the order of higher authority. There were only thirty-five Boers involved in the attack on nearly one hundred and seventy British. Otter-Barry was killed and the two guns lost. With an officer and five men were killed, seventeen men were wounded and ninety-four taken prisoner, to say the least, "the whole affair…must be regarded as highly discreditable." Lord Kitchener in Pretoria must have been considerably irked as he urged that every effort be made to recover the guns and find Commandant R.C. Ackerman and his men.[13]

Plumer had time only to restock his wagons and the column marched out again that afternoon marching northwards most of the night. Early on 24 September they were at the farm Stellenbosch where some Boers were sighted but they were unable to overtake them. With the hard marching that had kept them on the move continuously for seven days no doubt their horses were nearing exhaustion. On Thursday 26 September they entered Wepener again and there Plumer met with Lieutenant Colonel Lowry-Cole whose orders were to guard the crossings of the Caledon River from Jammersberg southwards. There was a report that a force of Boers about two hundred strong had passed between Plumer and Lowry Cole the previous night. Plumer managed to get in touch with Lieutenant Colonel Louis du Moulin who had been rushed to Slangfontein and had continued on to Jammersberg. He had discovered what looked like a new grave at Slangfontein which was found to contain fifty-seven of the rifles captured in the debacle of 19 September. Clearly the British were expecting to find a large commando responsible for the attack on Slangfontein, not just a few stragglers who were the actual force, and it was unlikely that du Moulin would have encountered anyone in his sweep towards Jammersberg Drift. He left before Plumer arrived in Wepener and spent the night at Droogfontein on the road from Bastard's Drift.[14]

Plumer's plan was to make a sweep southwards on the left bank of the Caledon River and his orders to du Moulin were for his force to head southwards along the right (or western) bank. It was expected that the Boers would cross the river at one of the drifts the next day. A night patrol left Wepener on the evening of Thursday 26 September – fifty men of the 7th Mounted Infantry (Hampshire Regiment), fifty men of the 5th Q.I.B. under Lieutenant William Hunter, fifty New Zealand Mounted Rifles and fifty Imperial

Yeomanry under the overall command of Major A.W. Andrew. This was one of Plumer's usual tactics and the patrol was to reconnoitre the drifts over the Caledon for the column to cross the following day.[15]

The patrol marched through the night and camped at 3 a.m. "about a half-mile from the drift" which would have been Bastard's Drift. Major Andrew sent nine men of the 6th NZMR under a Corporal Hemphill to the river where there was a wagon drift. Clearly expecting to find it occupied by du Moulin's men on the other side they ran into some Boers who opened fire and Hemphill's horse was shot. Trooper I.E. Baigent turned his horse around, took Hemphill up on his own horse and rode to safety under heavy fire. This was the sort of brave deed that would merit the award of the Victoria Cross but only a D.C.M. was awarded. This engagement held up Andrew's force for some hours and Lieutenant P.L. Tudor's New Zealanders eventually secured the drift.[16]

These Boers were probably a picket sent by Wessels at Sweetfontein to make sure that he would not be surprised and attacked from the rear. Major Andrew sent forward the 5th QIB to the next drift, Mokari (the Basuto name for the Caledon River) where there was a recognised crossing point that had been in use since the first Boer settlers arrived in the area in the 1830s. Lieutenant Hunter was in command with his own "M" Company, Lieutenant Jack Caskey with "K" Company and Lieutenant Alfred Pooley with "L" Company. This little force arrived at Mokari, around noon on Friday 27 September.[17]

Between Mokari on the eastern or left bank and Sweetfontein and Dewetsdal opposite, and upstream from the actual Mokari drift, is another place where the river can easily be crossed unless the water is unusually high. Hunter, in the lead, led his men up onto a small koppie overlooking this spot, a wise and cautious step to take in view of the small force that he had with him. From here they noticed a number of Boers walking around on a koppie on the other side of the river. Hunter seems not to have given the order to cross the river to investigate as he told the Court of Enquiry some days later that he saw Lieutenants Caskey and Pooley going very fast on his left and heading in the direction of the drift. They had decided to investigate the Boers on the western side and crossed over the drift which led them into a semi circle of koppies. Caskey had clearly assumed that du Moulin was nearby on the other side of the river and that these Boers might have scattered to avoid an attack by him. In fact du Moulin had diverted westwards and was that day some distance away to the west near the farm Vermaak.[18]

Almost immediately they came under fire from the hill on their right and galloped hard for some broken ground about five hundred yards to their front. The seven Boers they had seen turned into a force of about fifty and Caskey and Pooley and their men had to seek shelter in the broken ground between the two hills. Pooley went to the left with eleven men who were able to occupy some low rises and keep out of the direct line of fire. Caskey went to the right with Private D. Maloney and was fired on from the front and then from behind as well. He said to Maloney, "They seem to be all around us – hold my horse" and as he dismounted was shot through the chest and killed. Maloney kept firing but then surrendered when the Boers advanced to within twenty-five yards of him.

Pooley's men returned fire but the Boers gradually surrounded them using the broken ground and several deep dongas. They ran short of ammunition but Lieutenant Loynes tells of how two men of the 7th M.I. (Hampshire Regiment) managed to get across the river with two haversacks full of ammunition. Fifty of the M.I. had arrived from Bastard's Drift after Hunter had sent a message by heliograph that they were under fire. Some forty Boers were seen galloping from the right hand koppie which is on Dewetsdal across to the slightly higher hill to the left on Sweetfontein. Besides firing down into the broken ground sheltering the Australians, they would have descended the hill and used the cover of a donga to approach to within a few yards of their adversaries. The Boers came closer and closer but the Q.I.B. "fought like demons at bay." Paton was shot in the arm and Gatfield got a bullet through the ankle, shattering the bone. The Boers called on them to surrender and Pooley was shot through the head by the Boer commandant with a Mauser pistol. "Our gallant little crowd – only nine strong – kept at them refusing to surrender when called upon. White stood up to get a shot and actually got six bullets into him." "Milner was shot some distance to the front...racing for cover." With only twenty rounds left the survivors gave up and handed over their rifles and bandoliers to the Boers. The prisoners were stripped of all their clothing and possessions, rifles, bandoliers, trousers, hats and one man even told that they took his razor. Wessels told them: "Never since I have been fighting have I seen such dogged resistance as shown by you men, and as for that man (pointing to the body of Pooley) he is the bravest man I have seen." Once it got dark the prisoners were released one at a time to make their way back to their own side.[19]

Substantial reinforcements took some time to arrive as Hunter had insufficient men to tackle the Boers across the river. He heliographed messages to Andrew who in turn contacted the column which had only left Wepener that morning. Major Andrew at Bastard's Drift had less than one hundred and fifty men and was concerned about a Boer attack from across the drift. Plumer sent the rest of the Q.I.B. with two guns and a pom-pom to gallop the ten or twelve miles to Mokari. "And such a gallop!" enthused Lieutenant Dods. "Our horses were pretty well done, but they kept going remarkably well, urged on by our men, who reckoned they were to have a decent scrap at last with three hundred Boers." The guns were taken up onto the hill overlooking the scene of the battle via an easy path leading from the garden of the Mokari farm house. The guns (or certainly the pom-pom) let off about a dozen shots and "the Boers could just be discerned in the moonlight trekking away for all they were worth, and we – our horses after that mad gallop could not move beyond a walk to give chase."[20]

The two Lilley brothers were along with them and William Lilley wrote to his parents about the events of the day in similar vein to Lieutenant Dods. Except that young William was less than impressed to find some New Zealanders sitting down having tea "when our blokes was in a tight corner." Some of Major Andrew's men, including his medical officer had already been over the river to treat the wounded and were able to tell a shocked Lieutenant Dods about his good friend: "Caskey – good old Jack! – killed?" The bodies were recovered that night, Caskey's only the next morning since he had ridden further up the rise to the right, and buried in a common grave in the garden of the abandoned Mokari farmhouse.[21]

Plumer's column continued on its course southwards and on 11 October were sent by train back to Volksrust in the south eastern Transvaal. Louis Wessels rejoined Kritzinger and in December they crossed back into the Cape Colony where misadventure befell Kritzinger. He was wounded, captured and faced a court martial but survived to tell his story in a book written by his secretary. Wessels joined Smuts in the Western Cape and survived the war, intensely angered that Smuts had been party to an agreement to end the war. William Lilley was killed at Onverwacht on 4 January, 1902 but David returned home safely to his family. The fight at Mokari Drift was typical of the sharp engagements with small roving bands of Boers at this period of the war. This time the British force was taken by surprise but there were occasions when the reverse was true. Lieutenant Jack Caskey was mentioned in Lord Kitchener's despatch of 3 December 1901 "for great gallantry" but Alfred Pooley who was equally gallant seems to have been forgotten. Lieutenant P.L. Tudor is also mentioned in the same despatch for the action at Bastard's Drift.[22]

The farmhouse is long gone and a newer farm building occupies the spot where it formerly stood. The original gravesite is next to the little stream that seeps out of the dolerite and which provided the water supply for the house and its orchard of peach trees. There is an easy path from the garden up onto the flat-topped hill overlooking the Caledon River and the place where Caskey and Pooley and their men of the 5th Q.I.B. crossed over. Crossing the river at this point is easy, even by foot across a shelf of rocks, except when the river is in flood. The small ridges and gullies where Pooley and his men held out for all that time are easily discernable. They must have convinced themselves that there was no more than a handful of the enemy to contend with. It was a disappointment that there were no spent cartridges to be found – more than a century of rain seems to have washed them all away. Finally, what happened to the two men of the Hampshire Regiment who braved the hostile fire to bring ammunition to the defenders? There is no mention of them as casualties or prisoners. Perhaps they made their way to safety after delivering their burdens.

Notes on sources

1. These names are given in Watt *In Memoriam* and in the official South African War Casualty Roll. Also listed are Lance Corporal J.J. Hall and Private J.T. Gatfield both severely wounded, Private T. Paton slightly wounded and Private F.W. Window who fell from his horse.
2. Reitz *Commando* pp200-202.
3. Reitz *Commando* correctly names the leader of the guiding party as Commandant Louis Wessels. The name of the guide, the old veteran of the Basuto wars, was Piet Wessels. Shearing *General Jan Smuts and his Long Ride* p26.
4. Amery *Times History* v p318. Maurice *History of the War in South Africa* volume 4 p286.
5. Maurice *History of the War in South Africa* volume 4 pp288-289. Kritzinger *In the Shadow of Death* p34.
6. Maurice *History of the War in South Africa* volume 4 p318. Kritzinger *In the Shadow of Death* p36.
7. Kritzinger *In the Shadow of Death* p71.
8. The formal rank of Brigadier General in the British army was not established at that time. It was therefore a local or temporary appointment granted typically to a full Colonel when commanding a brigade or column at this stage of the war. Fogg *The 5th Contingent Queensland Imperial Bushmen* Chapter 4 p2. Maurice *History of the War in South Africa* volume 4 p269 and Amery *Times History* v p385 for some detail concerning Plumer's column.
9. Fogg *The 5th Contingent Queensland Imperial Bushmen* Chapter 2 p7.
10. Alan Lilley *Only one brother returned from the war* from the "Australians at War" web site. Peter Doherty Lachlan John Caskey 1870–1901 article concerning memorial to Lt. L.J. Caskey.
11. Fogg *The 5th Contingent Queensland Imperial Bushmen* Chapter 9 p1. Maurice *History of the War in South Africa* volume 4 pp317-8.
12. Fogg *The 5th Contingent Queensland Imperial Bushmen* Chapter 9 pp4-5.
13. Maurice *History of the War in South Africa* volume 4 p318-9. Amery *Times History* v p386. See J.C. Loock and P.H. Roodt *Die Geveg te Slangfontein* for complete detail of this engagement. It is no surprise that the first two accounts are somewhat misleading.
14. Maurice *History of the War in South Africa* volume 4 p319. du Moulin *Two Years on Trek* pp278-9. Du Moulin was at Jammersberg Drift on 25 September, the day before Plumer.
15. Trooper A.W. Walker's letter, *The War with Johnny Boer* p500. Major Andrew was seconded from the Indian Army, commanded the New Zealand Tenth Contingent who arrived in South Africa as the war was ending, and attained the rank of Brigadier General in the Great War. D.O.W. Hall *The New Zealanders in South Africa* p58.
16. D.O.W. Hall *The New Zealanders in South Africa* p60. Bastard's Drift now lies beneath the waters of the Welbedacht Dam.
17. Lieutenant J. Loynes's letter, *The War with Johnny Boer* p498. When a Court of Enquiry was convened after the incident that is about to be described, every single witness declared that it was "about noon."
18. Fogg *The 5th Contingent Queensland Imperial Bushmen* Chapter 10 p1. Maurice *History of the War in South Africa* volume 4 p320.
19. Lieutenant J. Loynes and Trooper A.W. Walker in *The War with Johnny Boer* pp497-501 have graphic descriptions of the fight on Dewetsdal which must have taken about five hours in all.
20. Lieutenant T.H. Dods, letter published in *The Brisbane Courier*, 27 November 1901.

21. Letter to "Dear Edith and Bob" from Volksrust and dated 6 October 1901 from William Lilley. Collection of the author.
22. Cited in the *London Gazette* for 3 December 1901.

References

1. L.S. Amery *The Times History of the War in South Africa* volume V. Sampson Low, Marston & Company, Ltd, London 1906.
2. Max Chamberlain & Robin Drooglever *The War with Johnny Boer* Australian Military History Publications, Loftus, Australia 2003.
3. Lieutenant T.H. Dods, letter published in *The Brisbane Courier*, 27 November 1901.
4. Lieutenant Colonel L. du Moulin *Two Years on Trek: Being some account of the Royal Sussex Regiment in South Africa* Murray & Co., London 1907.
5. Alan L. Fogg *The 5th Contingent Queensland Imperial Bushmen in South Africa 1901–1902*. Published on the internet on the PC User's Group (ACT) but withdrawn in 2006.
6. D.O.W. Hall *The New Zealanders in South Africa 1899-1902* War History Branch, Department of Internal Affairs, Wellington, New Zealand 1949.
7. General P.H. Kritzinger & R.D. McDonald *In the Shadow of Death* William Clowes & Co, London 1904.
8. J.C. Loock and P.H. Roodt *Die Geveg te Slangfontein* (The Fight at Slangfontein) Friends of the War Museum, Bloemfontein 2005.
9. Maj-Gen Sir Frederick Maurice *History of the War in South Africa* volume 4. Complied by direction of His Majesty's Government.
10. Thomas Pakenham *The Boer War* Weidenfeld and Nicholson Limited 1979.
11. Denys Reitz *Commando* Faber & Faber Limited, London 1929.
12. Taffy & David Shearing *General Jan Smuts and his Long Ride* Cape Commando Series No. 3. Privately printed by Taffy & David Shearing, Sedgefield. 2000.
13. Steve Watt *In Memoriam Roll of Honour Imperial Forces 1899-1902* University of Natal Press, Pietermaritzburg 2000.
14. Craig Wilcox *Australia's Boer War* Oxford University Press (In association with the Australian War Memorial) Melbourne 2002.
15. Letter to "Dear Edith and Bob" from Volksrust and dated 6 October 1901 from William Lilley. Collection of the author.

Casualty list

Bastard's Drift – 27 September 1901

6th New Zealand Mounted Rifles

3423	Private	H. Strawbridge	Killed in action
3277	Private	W.F. Raynes	Killed - accident
3631	Private	W. Matthews	Drowned
3248	Private	R. Letts	Missing - rejoined

Mokari Drift – 27 September 1901

5th Queensland Imperial Bushmen

Lieutenant	A.E. Pooley	Killed in action
Lieutenant	L.J. Caskey	Killed in action
Lance Corporal	J.J. Hall	Severely wounded
Private	B. Milner	Killed in action
Private	G.H. White	Killed in action
Private	J.T. Gatfield	Severely wounded
Private	T. Paton	Slightly wounded
Private	F.W. Window	Injured – fall from horse

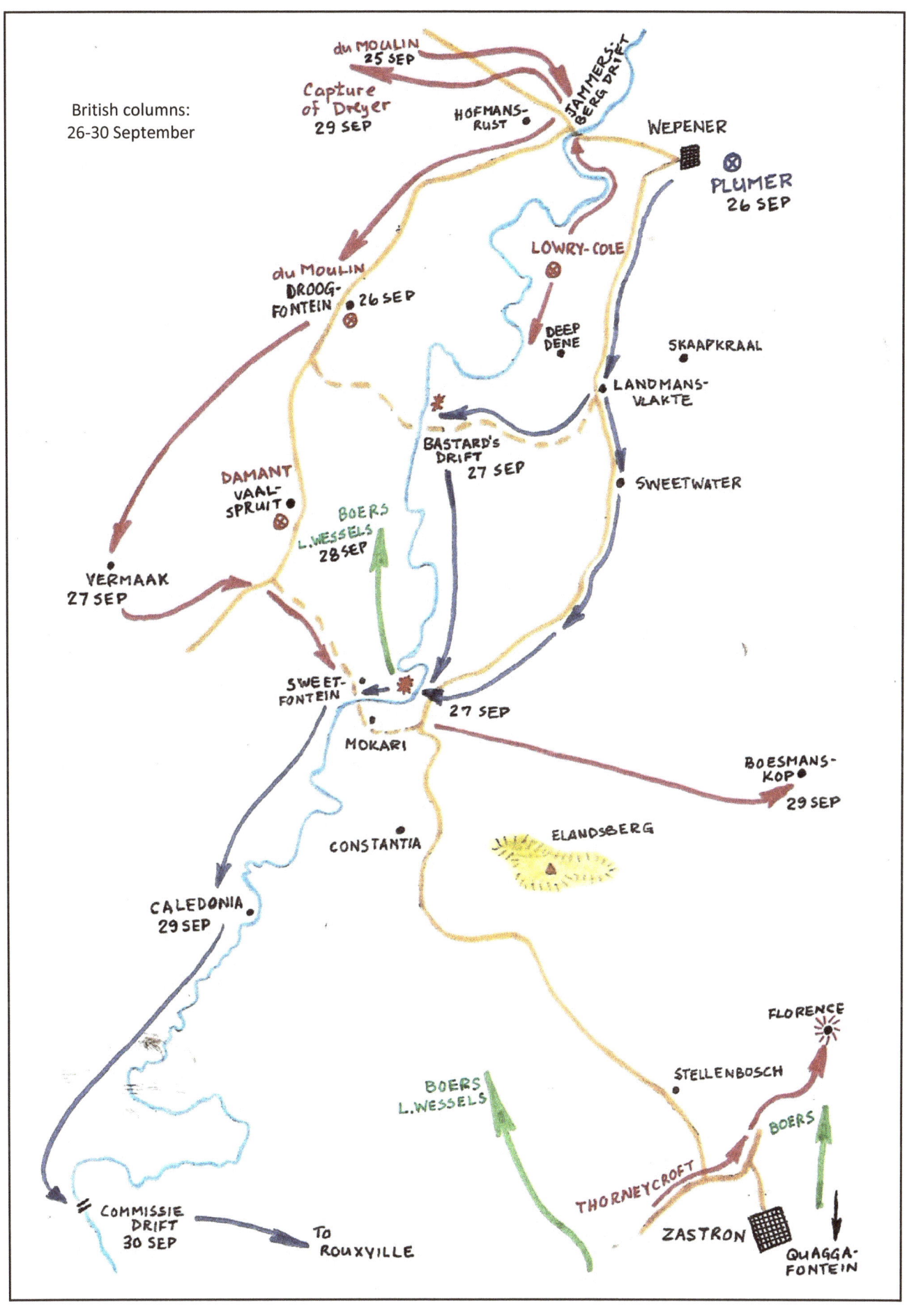

Plumer's column:
2 September to 7 October

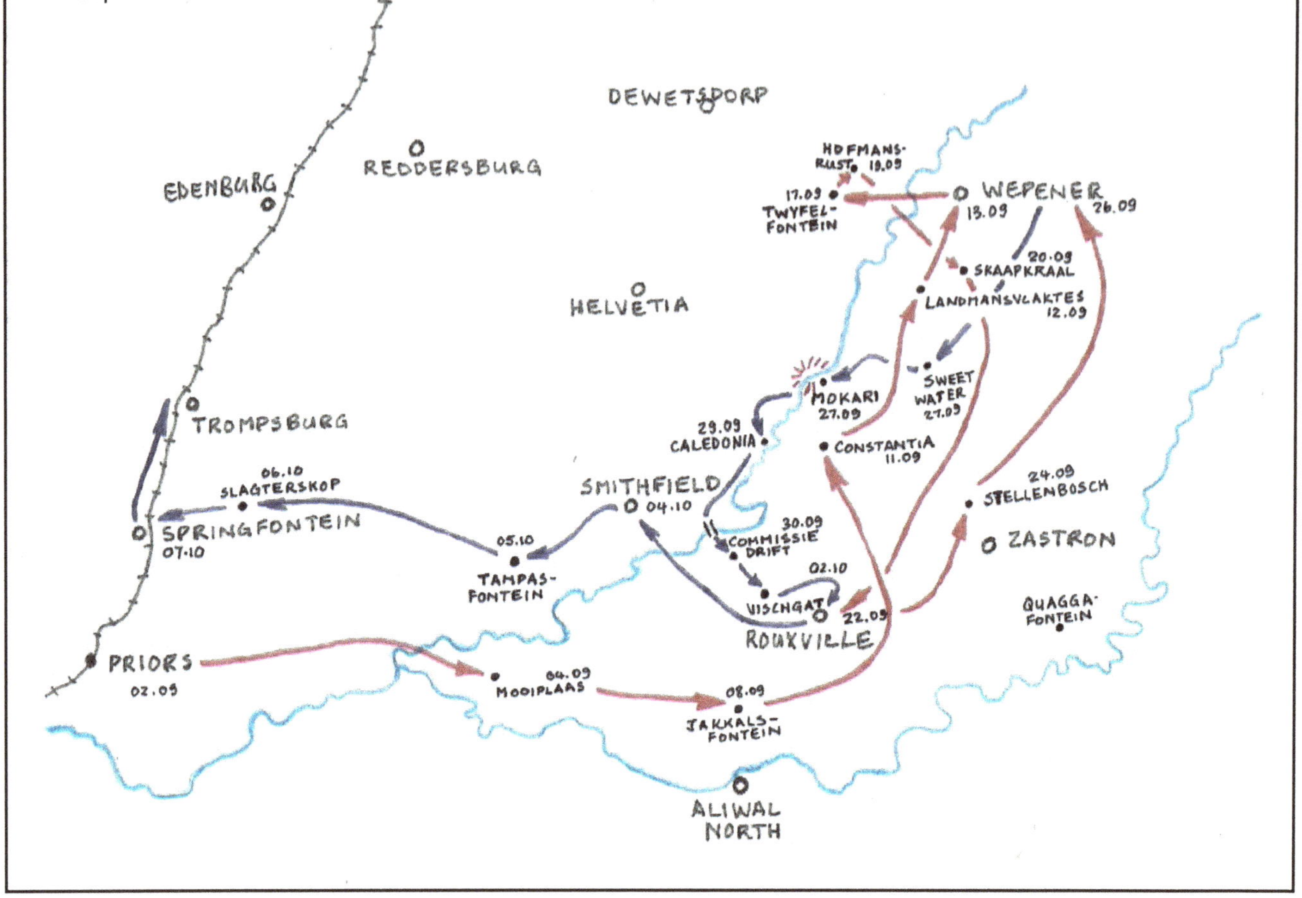

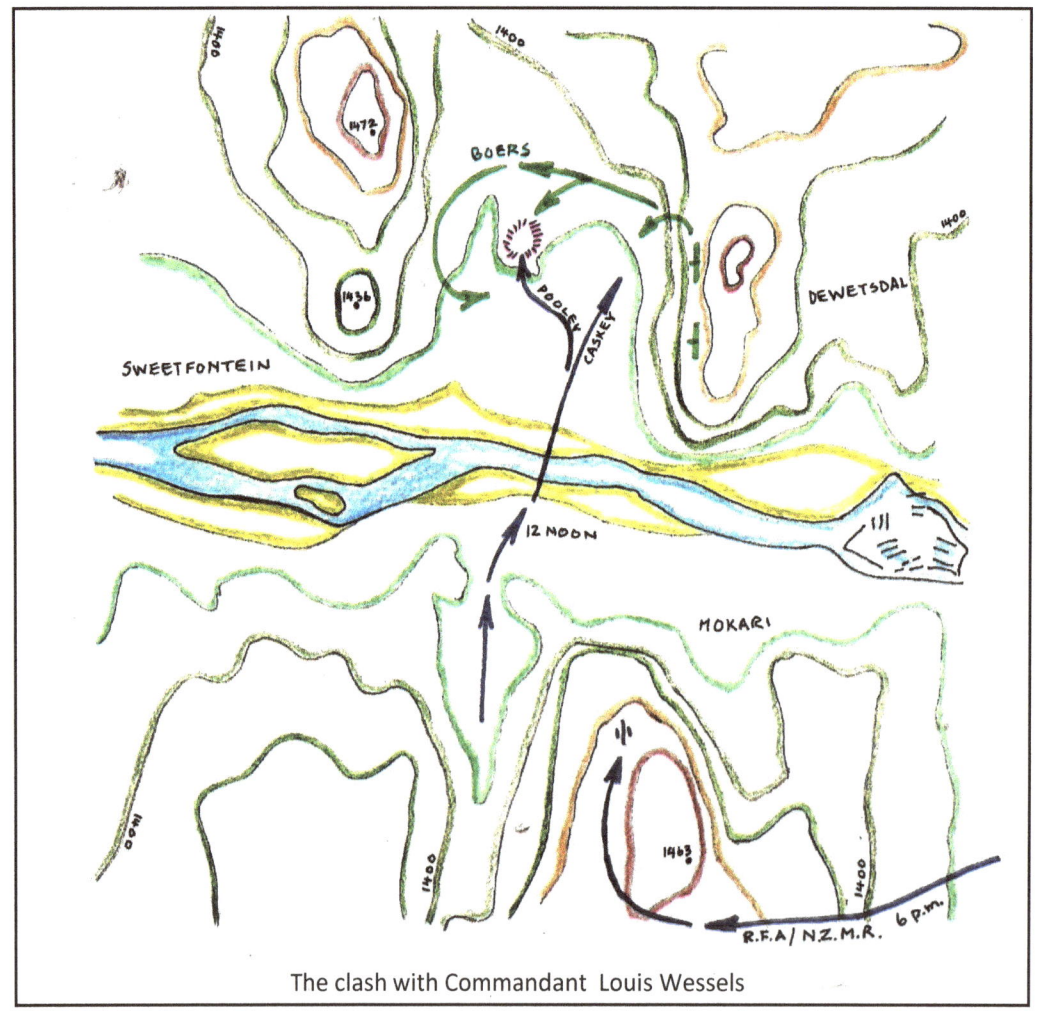

The clash with Commandant Louis Wessels

The graves of Lieutenants Caskey and Pooley.

Where Lieutenants Caskey and Pooley and their men crossed the river. Pooley's men defended the outcrop in the centre just over the river. Caskey went off to the right as shown on the map.

Bakenlaagte
30 October 1901

Major George Elliot Benson was one of a number of officers sent to South Africa on "special assignment" before the outbreak of the Anglo-Boer war. He was one of the British army's more promising young officers and clearly earmarked for promotion.[1] For these officers, intelligence about local conditions was their special assignment and they became a major source of this vital information.

At the start of hostilities, Major Benson was attached to Lieutenant-General Lord Paul Methuen's force advancing from the Orange River to relieve Kimberley, besieged by the Boers under General Piet Cronjé. He led the Highland Regiments as guide as they advanced in darkness before dawn on 11 December 1899 to attack the Boers entrenched at the foot of the hill at Magersfontein. When they were close to the Boer line, Benson advised Scottish Major-General Andrew Wauchope to have his men deploy into open order. Wauchope wanted to get closer before giving this order with the result that the Boers opened fire while they were still closed up. Magersfontein was the second of the three British reverses in December 1899 that became known as Black Week.

At first as staff officer to Lord Methuen his performance was such that Methuen was loath to lose him. Benson was advanced to Lieutenant-Colonel and D.A.A.G. (Deputy Assistant Adjutant General) at Headquarters in Pretoria. He had first come to the notice of Lord Kitchener in the campaign to recapture Khartoum in 1898. In 1899 Kitchener, now the Commanding General in South Africa, determined that Benson should be deployed in the field rather than as a staff officer. In May 1901 he was given command of a column, operating first in the western Transvaal, but was soon put under Lieutenant-General Sir Bindon Blood operating north of the Pretoria-Delagoa Bay railway line. Operations by Blood's columns against General Ben Viljoen along the Olifants River caused the Boer general to retreat northwards into the bushveld.[2]

Colonel Sir Henry Rawlinson was probably the first to adopt the method of night raiding.[3] During daytime it was difficult, indeed nigh impossible, to locate and trap the scattered Boer commandos who could easily evade the British columns sent against them. In July 1901, Kitchener issued orders for the formation of a small number of special columns, noting that "The enemy are now so reduced in numbers and dispersed that greater mobility is required to deal with them." Benson took charge of one of those columns and was promoted full colonel. This technique of raiding Boer laagers at dawn, after intelligence was acquired of the location of such places the previous day from African scouts, then had official sanction at the highest level.[4]

By the middle of 1901 the British system of night raids was garnering 1,500 Boer prisoners per month as well as their wagons, carts and weaponry. These losses the Boers could not replace. Their rifles and ammunition were almost all British Lee-Enfield weaponry captured in the field. Clothing and food were not plentiful. The two Boer governments were fugitives in the field not stopping for very long in any one place.

Benson was particularly successful. His men were well-trained with scouts who had intimate knowledge of the locality and its people. There were infantry and artillery to protect his campsites and mounted men to ride out nightly to targets pointed out by scouts directed by his intelligence officer. It took some months for his column to become fully-trained and by October 1901 his very success caused the Boers to want to find some way to eliminate him.[5]

In the resulting battle of Bakenlaagte on 30 October 1901, Benson was mortally wounded and more than 130 of his men were killed and wounded in the fierce action that began in misty and rainy weather. As usual the Boers were reluctant to risk the serious casualties which would have been the inevitable result of an assault on the British column, camped and fortified around the farmhouse of Nooitgedacht.[6]

In September 1901 Boer Generals Jan Smuts and Louis Botha acted upon the resolutions taken at the Waterval *krygsraad* in June to undertake raids into the British colonies of the Cape and Natal. Smuts gathered up 300 experienced men from Koos de la Rey's western Transvalers and made his way through the Free State evading pursuing British columns. Botha's foray was on a rather larger scale – as many as 2,000 of his burgers wanted to take part but there were not that many horses in the necessary condition to undertake such an arduous expedition. In the end the force comprised scarcely 1,400.[7]

This meant that there were very few commandos left in the Highveld of the eastern Transvaal. Ben Viljoen was left

---

[1] See Captain G.E. Benson *Smokeless Powder, and its probable effect upon the tactics of the future* Aldershot Military Society, Aldershot 1893.
[2] Amery *The Times History of the War in South Africa* Vol V p299.
[3] Shortly after his return to South Africa (he had left for England with Lord Roberts when he thought the war was practically over) Rawlinson was involved in the ambush of a Boer laager on the farm Goedvooruitzicht, twenty kilometres north of Klerksdorp. This was one of the first dawn raids on a Boer laager which became such an effective tactic when good intelligence of the whereabouts of such a laager was available. In the confusion of the attack, some of the Boers managed a counter-attack and Rawlinson was actually in the hands of his enemy for a short while. His horse had been shot from under him and he was probably not wearing any rank insignia so that the Boers were unaware of the identity of their distinguished prisoner. Rawlinson managed to escape when the guns of "P" Battery of the R.H.A. opened fire. The story is in the *Times History*, Volume V p228 but I have not been able to find another reference.
[4] Amery *Times History* V p322.
[5] See Amery *The Times History of the War in South Africa* Vol V pp330-31 for some detail of Benson's raids in the area. Also Ash *Kruger's War* pp455-56 for Benson's methods of night raiding.
[6] The battle, although fought almost entirely on the farm Nooitgedacht, goes under the name of Bakenlaagte, the adjacent farm. Probably this was to avoid confusion with the battle fought on Nooitgedacht in the Magaliesberg between de la Rey, Beyers and Smuts and Major-General Ralph Clements on 13 December 1900.
[7] See Moore *General Louis Botha's Second Expedition to Natal*.

in command of the area and given instructions to act decisively which he did not do, handicapped as he was by difficulties with his subordinates. Botha made his way south, bypassing the as yet incomplete line of blockhouses and forts between Wakkerstroom and Pietretief.

With only a few scattered commandos in the area, the most successful of the British column commanders, Colonel George Benson, made several raids into the Highveld in September and October 1901. The area was practically swept clean of inhabitants and livestock and the fragmented commandos seemed to be keeping their distance.

Benson's method of approach was to advance with a large column with more than 2,000 fighting men. The column was equipped for a long stay away from their base with wagons and carts, an infantry component and a strong contingent of mounted men. Some artillery completed the force, their function being solely to protect the nightly bivouac. With intelligence gained by black scouts, armed with a rifle and well-mounted, a strong mounted force would ride out at night and surround and attack the Boer laagers as dawn was breaking. The whereabouts had been located by the scouts using their knowledge of the area and gaining their intelligence from the local black inhabitants. The raiders could ride as much as seventy or eighty kilometres from the main column.

The intelligence chief under Benson was Colonel Aubrey Woolls Sampson, the former commanding officer of the Imperial Light Horse Regiment. Found wanting as a combat commander, Woolls Sampson became the consummate intelligence officer by virtue of his knowledge of the local languages, Afrikaans as well as the Bantu tongues, and the topography. He had been involved in prospecting and mining in the Transvaal for all of his life, resident in Johannesburg in the last few years. A prominent British citizen he was a member of the Reform Committee and his involvement in the abortive Jameson Raid caused his arrest and imprisonment in 1896. He refused to pay the fine and elected to serve his sentence but President Kruger ordered his release as a gesture of respect on the occasion of Queen Victoria's Diamond Jubilee in 1897.[1]

Raiding at night became standard procedure for the British columns engaged in locating and eliminating the scattered and elusive fragments of Boer commandos. The technique was very effective and the majority of Benson's operations over the previous few months were successful. His men captured more than 600 burgers, secured huge quantities of captured wagons and equipment, horses, herds of cattle and flocks of sheep. Kitchener formed four large columns, with small, highly-mobile contingents of mounted men in support. Four commanders were given command of these units, Benson was one of them.

On 12 October Benson went into Middelburg to refit his column and exchange some of his units for fresh men. Some of the replacements were men who had been for some months engaged in garrison duties and were not entirely conversant with Benson's methods. He left on 20 October,[2] heading towards Bethal and acting on intelligence, raided a Boer laager at Klippoortjie. Thirty-seven Boers were captured but Benson's men suffered no casualties in fighting off a counter-attack by those Boers who had recovered from the dawn surprise.[3]

Botha's raiders had returned by now from their unsuccessful foray to Natal. The commandos had largely split into smaller detachments, as was their usual practice. Botha, before he left on the raid, had sent the Transvaal Government across the Pretoria-Delagoa Bay railway line and they were in relative safety near Roos Senekal. Botha and some of his men were at Schimmelhoek and the adjacent farm Mooifontein at Bakenkop, east of Ermelo. British intelligence discerned their presence from a document captured from a Boer *rapportryer* and Rawlinson's and Rimington's columns were sent from Standerton to descend on this valuable quarry.

The Boer scouts managed to decoy the two columns although Botha had a narrow escape galloping away to the north in such haste as to leave some of his papers and his hat in the Mooifontein farmhouse. This was on 25 October and a few days later Rimington and Rawlinson were back in Standerton and Volksrust. On that same day Benson's men had a sharp encounter with Boer commandos at Rietkuil, some distance north of Bethal.[4] Benson's Australians in the 2nd Scottish Horse gave a good account of themselves against determined Boers on ridges along the Steenkool Spruit.

Botha's return from his raid stiffened resistance with the instructions he had given that Benson's column, isolated and alone on the Highveld, should be attacked with determination. Bethal (and Ermelo too) was in ruins and deserted but British patrols met with unusually sharp resistance. Around Bethal at Mooifontein and Kafferskraal (this offensive farm name appears on contemporary maps but has now been expunged from modern surveys) there were clashes. Benson's camp at Kaffirstat (another offensive colonial name) was closely watched by Boer riders and Woolls Sampson was unable to conduct his usual scouting manoeuvres – it was inadvisable for his scouts to venture out. If captured, they would be shot out of hand.

It was now obvious to Benson that he was in a position of some danger. He was isolated at a considerable distance from his base along the railway line to the north. Other columns were still making their way back from Natal, needing to rest their horses and replenish their supplies. In the event of a serious attack relieving columns were too far

---

[1] Amery *Times History* vol I p 179.
[2] Benson's column: 3rd MI (King's Own Yorkshire Light Infantry) 501, 25th MI (King's Royal Rifles) 462, 2nd Scottish Horse 434, 84th Battery RFA 82, CC and R Sections Vickers-Maxims 36, 2nd East Kents ("The Buffs") 650, making 2,165 fighting men. In addition there must have been a considerable number of drivers and servants.
[3] These 37 Boers captured there: were they commandos or "joiners", men who went over to the British and acted as guides? In Ackermann *Opsaal* p63 it is described how 37 prisoners were taken; later on p87 these 37 are described as National Scouts, members of Boers who acted as guides and scouts for the British Army. There were frequently Boer "joiners" acting as guides in British columns but there is no mention of any in Benson's column.
[4] Wilsworth *Diary of Willie Wilsworth* entry for 25 October describes an action but does not name a place. His grandson's edit of the entry says Rietkuil. Ackermann *Opsaal* pp66-67 describes an action around Ystervarkfontein and Mooifontein, north of Bethal.

away. It had been a risk to venture into the area but with the better Boer fighting men away in Natal with Botha it had seemed more of an opportunity than a risk.

Botha and his commando leaders recognised that there was now a rare opportunity to strike at the lone column. Normal tactics were for the commandos to fragment into small entities. This way they could more easily evade the attentions of British columns. It was always possible for the various small units to concentrate to tackle a worthwhile target. Now was just such a time and Botha returned to Schimmelhoek to give orders for his commandos to come together. He gathered together a force of 500 men from Carolina, Standerton and some of the Swaziland Police. Perhaps even more important he had with him three generals who would be able to organise an attack on Benson's column. They were Johan Grobler, Coen Britz and Koot Opperman, all of them experienced and aggressive leaders

Commandant Hans Grobler of Bethal, Piet Trichardt of Middelburg and Piet Viljoen of Heidelberg with their commandos had more than 700 men in the area around Bethal. They did not think themselves strong enough to launch an attack on Benson's column without further assistance. By 28 October, Botha with reinforcements was not far away, having spent that night at Vaalkop, north of Bethal on the farm Elandsfontein. This was a place that the Boer commandos commonly used, for the hill offered sweeping views of the surrounding countryside and a site for a heliograph. Importantly, Grobler's close surveillance of the British camp meant that Woolls Sampson had been unable to conduct his usual scouting activities and the arrival of Botha's force had remained undetected. Around 1,200 determined and well-mounted Boers were now in the vicinity.

Benson sent a runner to Brugspruit station on the Pretoria-Delagoa Bay railway line informing the army command that he was returning and that he would be there in a few days' time. On 29 October the column marched to Zwakfontein where they camped overnight. This had good water supplies and must have resembled a small town that night with more than 2,000 soldiers and their artillery and wagons. Two soldiers are listed as wounded at Zwakfontein so that there were Boers close enough to snipe. Orders were that the march to the next camp would commence at 4 a.m. It rained during the night and was misty in the early morning.

The next morning the going was not good after the overnight rain. The mule wagons and the marching infantry had no difficulty but for the heavily-laden ox-wagons it was slow going. There was only one stream of any significance to negotiate, the *Dwars-in-die-Weg Spruit* which would have been running quite strongly. Right from the start Boer commandos were visible on the flanks of the column which in itself was not unusual. What was unusual was that they were clearly present in much larger numbers than usual and were more aggressive than expected. In the misty conditions at the early part of the march they were able to get quite close.[1]

Because of the slow going the convoy became extended with the mule wagons getting to Nooitgedacht, where they were to make camp, as early as 9 a.m. All except one wagon made it through the *spruit*, some probably needing double spans to pull them out, but one got seriously bogged down and resisted all efforts at extraction.[2] The rear-guard came under more and more fire as the Boers realised what had happened. The officer in charge was Major Gore Anley of the Essex Regiment with 180 men of the 3rd Mounted Infantry (King's Own Yorkshire Light Infantry, Dublin Fusiliers and Loyal North Lancashires). In addition there was infantry support with a few men of the East Kent Regiment and a pom-pom, quick-firing gun.

Anley sent word back to camp of his difficulty, abandoned the bogged-down wagons and retired to the next rise. The pom-pom came into action but then jammed and was sent into camp with a small escort. Benson himself arrived with an escort of Scottish Horse and endorsed Anley's decision to abandon the wagon. His orders at camp had been for defenses to be set in strong picquets at intervals around the camp and on an arc of about 800 metres distance. In line with this, two guns of the 84th Field Artillery Battery had unlimbered somewhat earlier on a rise later to be known as Gun Hill. They were positioned there so as to protect the left flank of the convoy. With them was an escort of the 25th M.I. (King's Royal Rifles) under Sergeant Anfield.

Anley and his men were sent back to man one of the positions on the eastern perimeter of the defensive arc. Benson with the Scottish Horse and the 3rd M.I. now started to go back to Gun Hill. As they did so, a swarm of Boer riders appeared over the skyline to the south. Hidden in the folds of the ground, a large Boer force had concentrated and Botha's generals had deployed them into a long line that extended for nearly two kilometres. They saw their opportunity and charged towards Benson and his retiring men, overlapping them on both sides. A number of the unmounted East Kents were overwhelmed in the charge but the mounted men made it to the ridge where the guns were positioned.

A defensive line was formed around the guns – guns have to be held at all costs, their loss is unbearable for artillerymen! On Gun Hill were 180 men spread out on each side of the guns, Scottish Horse, a few of the East Kents, and K.O.Y.L.I. The left wing of the Boer charge continued on to attack a company of the 25th M.I. under Captain Crum who were on a rocky outcropping to the north west of Gun Hill. They were able to organise some rudimentary cover for themselves and had another of the 84th Battery's guns.

Benson was now in harm's way and unable to exercise central control over the fighting. In the Nooitgedacht farmhouse were Colonel Woolls Sampson and Major Dauglish of the East Kents, the latter being the senior Imperial officer present. Woolls Sampson took command and Dauglish's infantrymen threw up defenses and dug trenches. With the defenders spread around the camp in a wide arc there were few men left to provide reinforcements for the defenders of Gun Hill.

On Gun Hill a close-range fight took place with the defenders, mostly the Australians of the Scottish Horse,

---

[1] The mist and rain in the morning had cleared up by midday according to the entry for 30 October in the Wilsworth diary.

[2] The bogged-down wagon evidently contained foodstuffs of various sorts – Ackermann *Opsaal* p85 quotes a Boer describing how he had found a bottle of wine, a pudding and some tinned food in the wagon.

King's Royal Rifles and K.O.Y.L.I. It was on Gun Hill that the Boers concentrated their efforts with the two guns as prizes. What use they could make of such weaponry is moot since they were later discovered hidden away on the farm Kaffirstat in December. Almost all the defenders of Gun Hill were killed or wounded and a few made their way back to camp. Several accounts say that British wounded were stripped of their clothing and boots in spite of orders from General Johan Grobler to his men that such behaviour would merit severe punishment.[1] Only wounded were left on the hill including Benson with a mortal wound, enough of them still capable of driving away Boers looking for loot.[2]

Once the firing died down the Boers took possession of the two guns on Gun Hill. They were swung around and it is possible that shots were fired at the camp.[3] Once the Boers came over the crest of the hill, the artillery (which must have been the two guns in the outposts to the west) put down a rain of shrapnel which caused them to take cover once again. At nightfall ambulances came out from the camp to succour the wounded, Benson among them. He was taken back to camp and gave Woolls Sampson orders for the camp to be held at all costs. He died at 6 a.m. the next morning.[4]

With the camp surrounded and numbers of their animals killed or taken by the Boers, the British were not in a happy position. The Boers made no attempt to assault the camp. A night attack would have been very hazardous, besides which they had insufficient manpower and no heavy guns of their own. It was said that Botha was reluctant to attack since the camp contained numbers of Boer women and children, certainly there were a number of non-combatants there including the thirty-seven men captured at Klipppoortjie a few days previously. As Bethal was deserted and most of the buildings destroyed it seems doubtful that the column had made many captures on this particular foray.[5]

Relief arrived on 1 November from Standerton, Allenby and de Lisle, and from Leeuwkop, east of Springs, Barter.[6] One of Kitchener's senior staff officers, Colonel Gilbert Hamilton, took command of what was now practically a force of brigade strength in the area. Botha did not attempt to press home his advantage and merely complimented his men on their courageous conduct, returning back to the east and the Schimmelhoek farmhouse. The Boer commandos once again scattered into their various sanctuaries.

Kitchener in Pretoria was somewhat disheartened by the setback to Benson's column and wrote to Secretary of State for War, St. John Brodrick that, "The Boers observe the movements of a column from a long way off, then having chosen some advantage, in this case it was the weather, then charge in with great boldness, and the result is a serious casualty list."[7] Bakenlaagte was not an overwhelming victory for the Boers although the British loss of more than eighty killed in action and died of wounds and two guns was certainly an unwelcome setback. After two years in the field the Boers were clearly not yet beaten. Their own loss of more than sixty was a serious blow, experienced fighting men who were irreplaceable.[8]

Command in the eastern Transvaal was now given to Major-General Bruce Hamilton, another of the younger, more vigorous leaders. In this revitalized campaign, Botha and his staff had a number of narrow escapes from capture until they were driven into the mountains north of Vryheid. Bruce Hamilton, in command in Vryheid, was ordered not to engage in active operations against the Boer commandos known to be in the area. The war was not yet over but both sides were now making overtures of peace.

---

[1] Wilsworth Diary entry for 27 October tells that a letter was received from General Johan J.N.H. Grobler: "It has caused me great annoyance and displeasure, to see that some of my men, stripped your wounded soldiers of their clothing, which was against all orders of my leaders and officers, and everything will be done to find the offenders, who will be severely punished." This after the engagement at Rietkuil.

[2] See W.H. Wilson *After Pretoria:The Gureilla War* II pp833-34 concerning the looting and murder of wounded. Notwithstanding General Grobler's letter, with clothing difficult to acquire it was difficult for Boers to ignore a uniform jacket or a fine pair of boots on one of their dead or wounded enemy soldiers.

[3] Ackermann *Opsaal* p80 says that artillerist Kotie Naudé was helped to turn the guns around and fired two shots at the camp. The first shot went way over the camp but the second hit its target. The account of E.J. Weeber says that "among the burgers were a couple of ex-artillerymen who quickly took possession of the guns and turned them onto the centre (camp) of the enemy". It is not known how many shots were fired.

[4] Amery *Times History* Vol V pp360-376 has a long and detailed account of the fighting and the individuals involved. Maurice *The History of the War in South Africa* Vol IV pp304-315 has another version.

[5] Ackermann *Opsaal* p69 says that "all the old people, women and children who were still on the farms Rensburghoop, Witbank and Kafferstat were collected together" and taken with the column. Blake *Boerekryger* p168 has a quote about Boer civilians in the British camp. Apparently one was a Mrs Grobler, a relative of Commandant Hans Grobler.

[6] See Maurice *History of the War in South Africa* Volume IV p315 for the strength of these columns: Allenby 1,288 mounted and 5 guns, de Lisle 1,004 mounted and 5 guns, Barter 531 mounted and 762 infantry with 5 guns.

[7] Kitchener letter to Brodrick 1 Nov quoted in Pakenham *The Boer War* p536.

[8] Blake *Boerekryger* p173: "On the Boer side, again, Bakenlaagte is mistakenly held up to be a famous and complete victory, especially to promote nationalism." ("Aan Boerekant, weer, is Bakenlaagte verkeerdelik as 'n roemryke and en volkome oorwinning voorgehou, veral om nasionalisme te voed.")

Casualty List – British

(This casualty list is from Steve Watt's *In Memorium*, University of Natal Press, Pietermaritzburg, 1999)
DOW - Died of Sounds, KIA - Killed in Action, KAS - Killed accidentally

REGT_NO	RANK	NAME	INITIALS	REGIMENT	CASUALTY
2528	RFM	APPLEGARTH	R	KINGS ROYAL RIFLES,4	KIA
7276	SGT	ASHFIELD	W	KINGS ROYAL RIFLES,1	KIA
31716	LCPL	BELL	J	SCOTTISH HORSE,2	KIA
	COL	BENSON	GE	ROYAL ARTILLERY	DOW
4900	PTE	BOWEN	A	EAST KENT,2	KAS
5029	PTE	BOWSTEAD	J	YORKSHIRE LIGHT INFANTRY,2	KIA
30989	TPR	BRADFORD	T	SCOTTISH HORSE,2	KIA
31831	SGT	BRADSHAW	S	SCOTTISH HORSE,2	KIA
8317	LCPL	BRINDLEY	E	KINGS ROYAL RIFLES,1	KIA
	LT	BROOKE	EVI	YORKSHIRE LIGHT INFANTRY,2	KIA
33321	TPR	BUESDEN	WM	SCOTTISH HORSE,2	KIA
25886	TPR	CAMPBELL	B	SCOTTISH HORSE,2	DOW
2159	SGTMAJ	CASSEN	JJ	YORKSHIRE LIGHT INFANTRY,2	KIA
31603	TPR	CLARK	G	SCOTTISH HORSE,2	KIA
2647	RFM	CLARKE	F	KINGS ROYAL RIFLES,4	DOW
	CAPT	COLLINS	CW	CHESHIRE,2	DOW
5890	PTE	COPPINS	CD	EAST KENT,2	KAS
	2LT	CORLETT	AJ	EAST KENT,2	KIA
24886	BDR,ACTG	CUFF	A	ROYAL FIELD ARTILLERY,84	KIA
30994	TPR	CUNNINGHAM	A	SCOTTISH HORSE,2	KIA
3851	LCPL	DAGNALL	H	KINGS ROYAL RIFLES,1	KIA
3846	RFM	DAVEY	EGA	KINGS ROYAL RIFLES,1	KIA
31584	LCPL,SAD	DAVIES	DW	SCOTTISH HORSE,2	KIA
31587	LCPL,SAD	DAVIS	MJ	SCOTTISH HORSE,2	KIA
8087	RFM,BUG	DOUGLAS	J	KINGS ROYAL RIFLES,1	KIA
5007	CPL	DUGGAN	FJ	YORKSHIRE LIGHT INFANTRY,2	KIA
29111	TPR	DUNS	G	SCOTTISH HORSE,2	KIA
2385	RFM	FAWCETT	E	KINGS ROYAL RIFLES,4	KIA?
33829	TPR	FERRIS	C	SCOTTISH HORSE,2	DOW
6551	PTE	FORBES	J	SEAFORTH HIGHLANDERS,1	DOW
1907	RFM	FOSTER	F	KINGS ROYAL RIFLES,4	KIA

REGT_NO	RANK	NAME	INITIALS	REGIMENT	CASUALTY
2961	PTE	GALLAGHER	J	YORKSHIRE LIGHT INFANTRY,2	KIA
7062	RFM	GENT	G	KINGS ROYAL RIFLES,1	KIA
24647	GNR	GILHESPY	C	ROYAL FIELD ARTILLERY,84	KIA
64556	SGTMAJ	GLASTONBURY	GE	ROYAL FIELD ARTILLERY,84	KIA
33821	TPR	GRANT	R	SCOTTISH HORSE,2	KIA
	LTCOL,BREV	GUINNESS	E	ROYAL FIELD ARTILLERY,84	KIA
33907	DVR	HALL	F	ROYAL FIELD ARTILLERY,84	KIA
73204	GNR	HOBSON	J	ROYAL FIELD ARTILLERY,84	DOW
6365	LSGT	HOUSMAN	GH	KINGS ROYAL RIFLES,4	KIA
	CAPT	INGLIS	AW	SCOTTISH HORSE,2	KIA
4706	PTE	JOHNSON	W	NORTHUMBERLAND FUSILIERS,1	DOW
4077	LSGT	JONES	W	YORKSHIRE LIGHT INFANTRY,2	KIA
33467	TPR	JORDAN	A	SCOTTISH HORSE,2	KIA
	LT	KELLY	JB	SCOTTISH HORSE,2	KIA
4700	PTE	KELLY	J	YORKSHIRE LIGHT INFANTRY,2	KIA
4781	PTE	LAWRENCE	JJ	YORKSHIRE LIGHT INFANTRY,2	KIA
1946	CSGT	LAWTON	H	YORKSHIRE LIGHT INFANTRY,2	DOW
6000	PTE	LEE	A	EAST KENT,2	KAS
	CAPT&ADJ	LINDSAY	MWH	SCOTTISH HORSE,2	KIA
	CAPT	LLOYD	THE	COLDSTREAM GUARDS,2	DOW
5914	PTE	LOVE	C	EAST KENT,2	KAS
	LT	MacLEAN	JM	ROYAL FIELD ARTILLERY,84	DOW
31858	TPR	MARKS	AH	SCOTTISH HORSE,2	KIA
4769	PTE	MARPLES	H	YORKSHIRE LIGHT INFANTRY,2	KIA
22431	TPR	MARSHALL	JG	SCOTTISH HORSE,2	KIA
29095	TPR	MARSHALL	G	SCOTTISH HORSE,2	KIA
	2LT	MARTEN	LH	YORKSHIRE LIGHT INFANTRY,2	DOW
25869	TPR	McGREGOR	M	SCOTTISH HORSE,2	KIA
31364	TPR	McKENZIE	AL	SCOTTISH HORSE,2	KIA
30059	SGT	MORGAN	AB	SCOTTISH HORSE,2	KIA
9856	RFM	MORRELL	G	KINGS ROYAL RIFLES,1	KIA
30795	LCPL	MURRAY	A	SCOTTISH HORSE,2	KIA
	MAJ,BREV	MURRAY	FD	SCOTTISH HORSE,2	KIA

REGT_NO	RANK	NAME	INITIALS	REGIMENT	CASUALTY
74493	GNR	NEWELL	W	ROYAL FIELD ARTILLERY,84	KIA
6347	PTE	NUGENT	E	R DUBLIN FUSILIERS,2	DOW
6260	PTE	PACKHAM	F	EAST KENT,2	KAS
17722	DVR	PAINE	WT	ROYAL FIELD ARTILLERY,84	KIA
6101	PTE	RICHARDSON	F	EAST KENT,2	KAS
3562	PTE	RIGBY	R	LOYAL NORTH LANCASHIRE,1	KIA
4261	SGT	ROWAN	F	EAST KENT,2	KAS
26419	SGT	SAUNDERS	JM	SCOTTISH HORSE,2	KIA
8768	RFM	SCRIMSHAW	H	KINGS ROYAL RIFLES,1	KIA
30985	TPR	SHEPHERD	J	SCOTTISH HORSE,2	KIA
	LT	SHEPHERD	RE	YORKSHIRE LIGHT INFANTRY,2	KIA
30063	SGT	SIMPSON	RS	SCOTTISH HORSE,2	KIA
31839	SGT	SMITH	GB	SCOTTISH HORSE,2	KIA
37104	TPR	SMITH	W	SCOTTISH HORSE,2	KIA
9307	RFM	TEW	A	KINGS ROYAL RIFLES,1	DOW
	CAPT	THOROLD	FT	YORKSHIRE LIGHT INFANTRY,2	KIA
33425	TPR,SHSM	TREMLETT	H	SCOTTISH HORSE,2	KIA
33831	TPR	WALKER	F	SCOTTISH HORSE,2	KIA
5981	CPL	WAYMAN	W	KINGS ROYAL RIFLES,1	KIA
31308	GNR	WOODHOUSE	S	ROYAL FIELD ARTILLERY,84	DOW
	LT	WOODMAN	C	SCOTTISH HORSE,2	DOW

Analysis of casualties (fatalities)

Regiment

Cheshire	1
Coldstream Guards	1
East Kent	10
Kings Royal Rifles	15
Loyal North Lancashire	1
Northumberland Fusiliers	1
Royal Dublin Fusiliers	1
Royal Artillery	1
Royal Field Artillery	10
Scottish Horse	33
Seaforth Highlanders	1
Yorkshire Light Infantry	13

Casualty

Died of wounds	18
Accidentally	8
Killed in action	62

88 killed in action or died of wounds

Boers

63 killed in action or died of wounds.

References

1. W.H. Ackermann *Opsaal: Herinneringe van die Tweede Vryheidsoorlog* Voortrekkerpers, Johannesburg 1969.
2. Chris Ash *Kruger's War* 30° South Publishing Pinetown, South Africa 2017.
3. Captain G.E. Benson *Smokeless Powder, and its probable effect upon the tactics of the future* Aldershot Military Society, Aldershot 1893.
4. Blake, Albert *Boerekryger 'n Seun se Hoogste Offer* Tafelberg, Paarl 2012.
5. Amery *The Times History of the War in South Africa* Vol V Sampson Low, Marston and Company Ltd, London 1907.
6. Jacques Malan *Die Boere Offisiere* J.P. van der Walt, Pretoria 1990.
7. Major-General Sir Frederick Maurice *History of the War in South Africa* Volume IV Hurst and Blackett, London 1906.
8. Dermot Michael Moore *General Louis Botha's Second Expedition to Natal* Historical Publication Society, Cape Town 1979.
9. Thomas Pakenham *The Boer War* Weidenfeld and Nicholson Limited, London 1979.
10. H.J.C. Pieterse (editor) *My Tweede Vryheidstryd: Herinneringe van P.C. Joubert* Nasionale Pers Beperk, Cape Town 1943.
11. G.D. Scholtz *In Doodsgevaar: Die Oorlogsvaringe van Kapt J.J. Naudé* Voortrekkerpers Beperk, Johannesburg 1940.
12. Robin Smith *We Rest Here Content* Privately published 2018.
13. John Stirling *The Colonials in South Africa* William Blackwood & Sons, Edinburgh and London 1907.
14. Steve Watt *In Memoriam* University of Natal Press, Pietermaritzburg 1999.
15. W.H. Wilson *After Pretoria: The Guerrilla War Vol II.*
16. Clive Wilsworth (editor) *Diary of Willie Wilsworth* SQMS, 2nd Scottish Horse. Privately published.
17. Articles that appeared in the magazine *Die Huisgenoot*:
18. Johannes Buhrnan *Bakenlaagte: 'n Grootse Wapenfiet op 'n Klein Skaal* 29 November 1935.
19. Evert Domisse *Bakenlaagte Nogeens* 12 May 1939.
20. E.J. Weeber *Die Slag van Bakenlaagte* 10 June 1938.

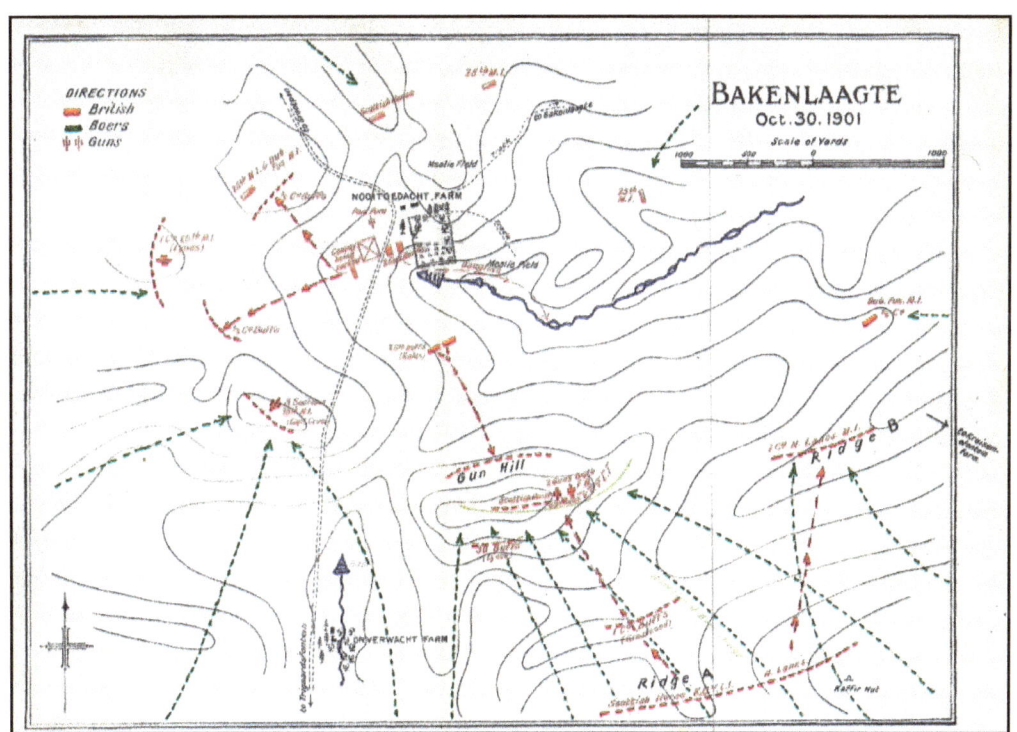

Battle of Bakenlaagte from *The Times History of the War in South Africa.*

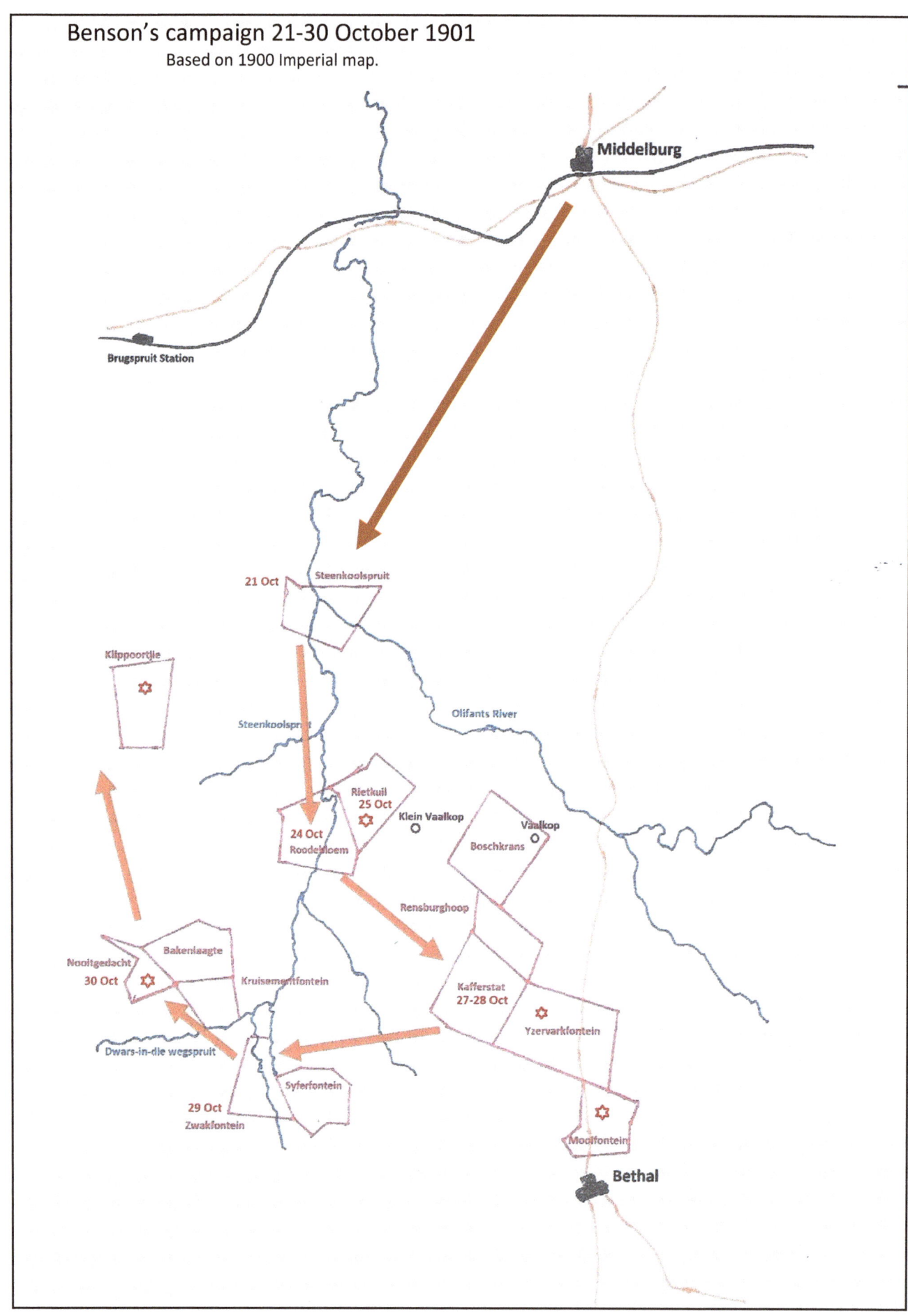

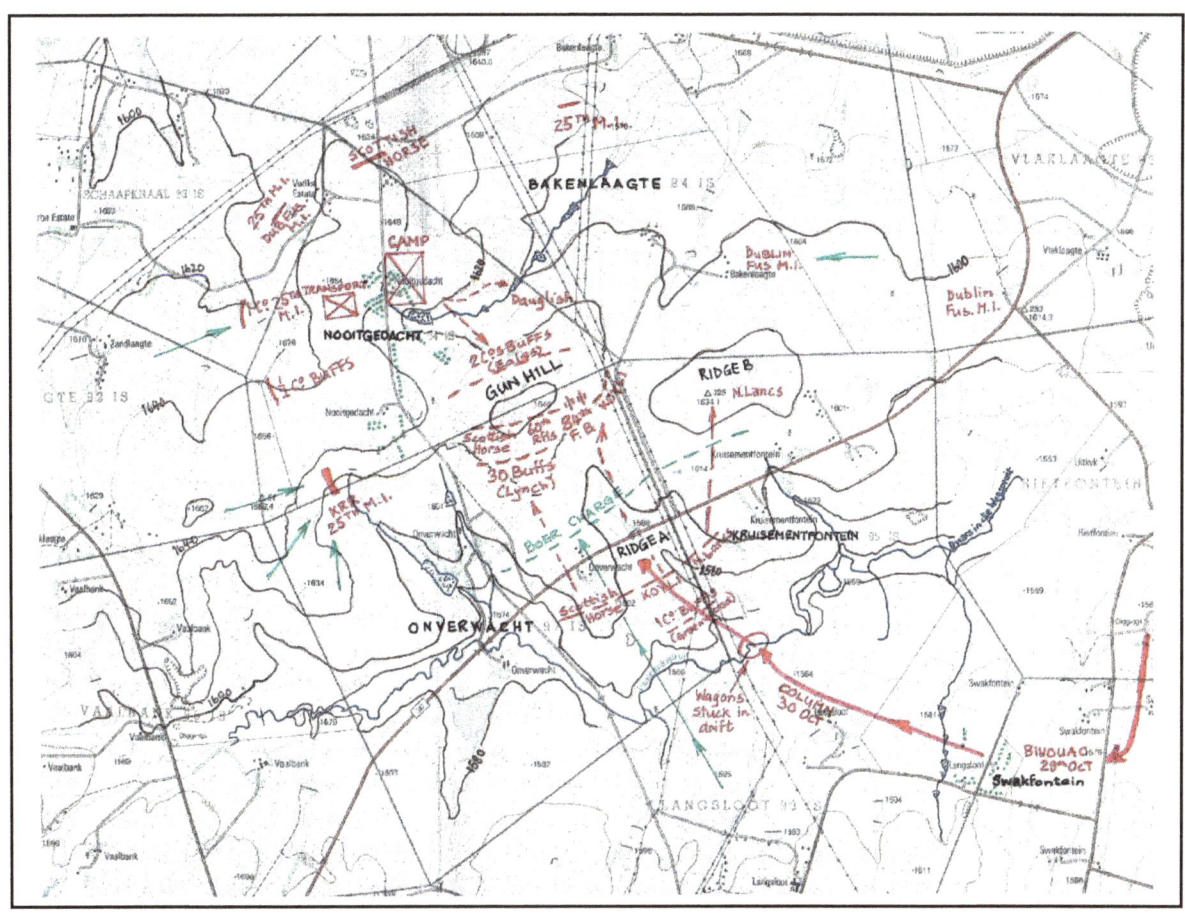

Battle of Bakenlaagte: Map transposed onto modern 1:50k topographical map.

Panorama looking south from the Nooitgedacht farmhouse.
Gun Hill is the clump of trees on the skyline to the left.

Panorama looking north from Gun Hill – farm house building just visible in the clump of trees in the distance (on right).

Louis Botha, Coen Brits, G.E. Benson, Aubrey Woolls Sampson

ONVERWACHT
Bankkop as the English call it
4 January 1902

On a ridge overlooking a fertile valley, the farm Onverwacht, on 4 January, 1902 the advance guard of a British column settled down for a midday meal. The commander of the detachment, 110 men of the 5th Queensland Imperial Bushmen together with a company of mounted infantry of the Hampshire Regiment and some Imperial Yeomanry, was Major John Maximilien Vallentin of the Somerset Light Infantry. Major Vallentin had been in South Africa since before the war and was brigade major in Ladysmith when hostilities began. He had enjoyed a varied career in South Africa, behaving with "conspicuous gallantry" at Elandslaagte on 20 October, 1899 and later, while inside Ladysmith serving as A.D.C. to Brigadier General Ian Hamilton. He contracted enteric fever but recovered to rejoin Hamilton later in 1900 in Bloemfontein. Then as Commissioner of Heidelberg he lived with a Boer commando in that neighbourhood for a week while Field Marshal Lord Roberts's Proclamation was under discussion.[1] He was four times mentioned in dispatches and described in the *Times History* as an "officer of proven gallantry and capacity".[2]

Vallentin had halted his men on a flat area on the summit of the Bankkop range of hills, thirty kilometres east of Ermelo. Pans, small depressions where water collects since the underlying strata does not allow it to drain away, provided some refreshment for the horses and the men and so they off-saddled and prepared a meal. In order to protect against surprise, Vallentin placed pickets along the ridge running a few hundred metres to their front in a line stretching about three kilometres. This was a very strong position, secure from attack in front by the steep ridge while behind them were the soldiers of the Hampshire Regiment and the rest of the 19th Company of Imperial Yeomanry, Scots from the Lothian and Berwickshire. Attack from behind across the flat ground was highly improbable therefore. Not far away, in the direction of Ermelo was the column of Brigadier General Herbert Plumer, nearly a thousand men with mounted infantry and artillery. Even closer, to the east of them, was another column commanded by Scots Guardsman Colonel William Pulteney with a similar complement.

For two months now eight British columns under the energetic leadership of Major General Bruce Hamilton had been searching for General Louis Botha who was known to be in the area with a force of about 700 men. Botha had been leading something of a charmed existence of late, coming close to capture on the 4 December, 1901 when Colonel Sir Henry Rawlinson raided the farm50

Oshoek at dawn and captured more than a hundred Boers, wagons and supplies. Botha's men were driven eastwards and Plumer and Pulteney made contact again at Kalkoenskraal on 6 December but Botha once again evaded capture.[3]

The British now knew Botha to be somewhere along the upper Vaal River, a well-watered area of hills and ravines and the search for Botha's force now intensified. Hamilton and four columns were to the east of Ermelo. Two more columns moved south from Carolina and a number of small laagers were successfully raided during December. However, General Coen Brits managed to ambush part of Brigadier General J. Spens's column on the farm Holland on 19 December and inflict 140 casualties, most of them captured.[4] Brits evaded encirclement a few days later as three columns, Plumer, Pulteney and Spens, closed in on him and on 26 December he joined up with Botha.

On 1 January 1902 the three British columns headed south east out of Ermelo. Spens returned to Begin-der-Lyn to guard the blockhouse line between Ermelo and Standerton while Plumer and Pulteney moved along the Piet Retief road. On the night of 2 January the two columns, more than two thousand men with guns and transport, camped on the farm Maviristad, uncertain of the precise whereabouts of their enemy. That night the Boer force was not far away, camped on the farm Windhoek owned by the widow Ernst, whose husband had been killed early in the war in the fighting along the Tugela River.[5]

The next morning patrols were sent out into the hilly surrounding countryside, its kloofs and gullies affording ideal hiding places for the Boer commando. One of the patrols comprised of men of the New Zealand Mounted Rifles, was surprised and surrounded by Boers from General Opperman's commando on the farm Rotterdam. Twenty-eight of them were captured, disarmed and released. It is said that Opperman gave their officer a horse to make his way back to the camp at Maviristad.[6] Another patrol was attacked that day on the farm Vlakfontein, along the Vaal River, and five of their number were cornered in a kraal and forced to surrender.[7] The intelligence gained from these two incidents gave Plumer a clear indication of where Botha's force might be hiding. On the morning of 4 January Plumer's column marched north along the Vaal River while Pulteney followed the lower road that would take him past the farms Waaihoek and Vlakplaas and onto the eastern edge of the Bankkop range of hills. The intention was to encircle the Boers in the Bankkop hills.

The events of 4 January have been well documented. The letter of a young private of the 5th Queensland Imperial Bushmen, David William Priest, to his father and brother also has a sketch map. This, as far as is known, is the only diagram of the action in existence. Exploration of the site turns up a number of the features described on Priest's map and this has proved to be the key to understanding what happened that day. Priest states in his letter that they "moved off at 5 a.m. with light transport and guns only. QIB's advance guard on left and Pulteney's corps on the right about 6 miles from us, snipers were shooting at us all morning. No one hit." Clearly the Boers were watching the advance closely, but not too closely if they could not hit anyone all morning.[8]

The Boers had slept that night on the farm Schimmelhoek where there is a sheltered kloof. Five or six hundred horsemen and their mounts were easily accomodated.[9] In the morning General Botha told Brits, Opperman and Chris Botha that he had received information that the advance guard of a British column was approaching and he advised withdrawal. His generals were not in favour and advocated a strike against the enemy. In true Boer democratic fashion the three juniors prevailed over their commander and Brits planned the attack and the placing of the commandos. They were from Wakkerstroom (Chris Botha), Swaziland (Koot Opperman), Standerton (Brits) and Ermelo (Commandant Bosman). Brits, as the originator of the plan would be in field command.[10]

The trap was carefully planned and as Vallentin's force arranged their pickets along the ridge, General Brits deployed the Boer force. About 500 of the men were hidden in a kloof which today has been dammed and stocked with fish. In another ravine to the south east was another force with yet another body of Boers hidden in another fold in the ground further to the south east. Below the ridge where the British pickets were watching for any sign of Botha's force was a flat shelf about a kilometre square. There were ravines on two sides and the western edge dipped down to the small river running north westwards to join up eventually with the Vaal River.

A decoy was arranged, fifty cattle with a few Boers to herd them along the flat ground and down over the rim towards the stream. The Boers in the kloofs were out of sight of the Queensland men on the ridge but the decoy was spotted and reported to Major Vallentin who determined to investigate. Leaving some of the men on the ridge in a secure position, the rest headed off down a roadway leading over the ridge and down onto the lower level. (David Priest's sketch clearly shows the road which can be identified today although now disused – a pom-pom gun mounted on artillery wheels and with horses to draw it could not just be dragged over the veld, some kind of road or track was needed). The decoy had disappeared over the edge of the plateau a bit more than a kilometre away and Vallentin's force chased after them with the Yeomanry as the advanced screen. The Queenslanders followed with orders to support the Yeomanry. Suddenly from the right flank the Boers opened fire and emerged from the ravine where they had been hiding. They made for the pom-pom but Lieutenant Reese of the Q.I.B. was ordered to dismount his men and form a defensive line. They opened fire with the pom-pom but it jammed after firing only five shots. Lieutenant H.R. Johnstone of the Yeomanry was shot and Major Vallentin was hit as they tried to get the pom-pom away. Two of the gun horses were shot but Q.I.B. Sergeant Major Frank Knyvett rallied the men in its defence (apparently including Private David Priest) and the gun was dragged back up the road and hidden in a small donga.

Major F.W. Toll of the Q.I.B. was now the senior officer present and he managed to organise a defensive line and send some of the horses back up the ridge. A group of men on the left flank under Lieutenant B.W. Cook were taken prisoner but the rest of the force was pushed back up the ridge to a spur on the north east. The Boers heavily outnumbered the Queenslanders and the few Yeomanry as well as some of the men of the Hampshire Regiment, the rearguard who had arrived to assist. On the right some of the Q.I.B., among them the wounded Captain Carter and Lieutenant Higginson, managed to retire up the ridge and join those of the force who had remained on the right of the picket line. A galloper was sent to summon the columns and Colonel W.R. Pulteney's column on Bankkop to the east was closer than Plumer's who had followed the line of the Vaal River.[11]

Major Toll and his men were now cut off from the rest of the force. The Hampshires had left their horses in a little hollow behind the spur but the Boers managed to work their way around and attack from the rear. There was absolutely no cover and nine of the Bushmen and eight of the Hampshires were killed before the Boers managed to get in so close that further resistance was suicidal. On the Boer side the loss was heavy and the attacks were pressed home with great bravery and even desperation. They certainly knew that they had little time before more than two thousand men from the two British columns appeared on the field.

General Koot Opperman was killed, shot in the forehead as he urged his men forward. His body lay on the field and the General's Adjutant, M.W. Coetzer and Willem Collins battled to load the 120kg body onto a horse. The British columns were now arriving on the top of the ridge and the Boers were subject to artillery fire. In spite of all their efforts they failed to recover the body which was left on the field although Opperman now lies buried in Vryheid cemetery.[12] Another casualty was the young Mosie Van Buuren who was in charge of Louis Botha's young son. Shot in the stomach he died later in the day and is buried on the nearby farm Mooiplaas. During the last assault on the spur, Field Cornet Manie Swart complained to General Brits that they could not shoot at the English because they could not see over the edge of the ridge. Brits ordered them to throw stones over the ridge to make the enemy keep their heads down. The Boers then were able to climb over the ridge and jumped right in to the few remaining British soldiers.[13] The Boers had captured thirty unwounded horses but very few rifles and little ammunition for the Queenslanders and the British had hurled their weapons into the long grass and there was no time to search for them.

Sergeant-Major Weston of the Hampshires was wounded, fatally as it turned out, hit by a bullet coming over his shoulder striking his bandolier and bursting two or three cartridges. Taken to hospital in Charlestown, he died there on 22 January. Louis Botha himself was on the field and although he allowed no looting he asked the wounded Hampshire Regiment's Captain Leigh for his binoculars. Apparently he was much amused to discover that they had been smashed by a bullet.[14]

Boer casualties were heavy and almost certainly more than the twenty-three killed on the British side (one Imperial Yeoman officer, eight Hampshire Regiment and thirteen Queenslanders as well as Major John Vallentin, their commander). Only five Boers were named as casualties. Jackson states that Sergeant Major Weston told him that the British prisoners, some seventy-nine of them, were used as a burial party and to get the wounded away, "a favourite game of theirs". Priest too tells how the Boer doctor whose offer of assistance was refused by the British said the Boers had forty-seven killed and sixty-eight wounded.

By now the balance of Vallentin's force, perhaps forty Queensland Imperial Bushmen, together with a number of Hampshire Regiment some distance away from where Major Toll and the few survivors were captured, had rescued the pom-pom from the donga. They unjammed it and opened fire on the Boers now retreating down the valley towards the farmhouse of Onverwacht. The leading elements of Pulteney's column had arrived on the scene having ridden in from the east over the Bankkop hills. The Boers charged the Queenslanders once again but were driven away by Pulteney's Victorian Mounted Rifles under Major Vialls. Shortly after, Brigadier General H. Plumer and Lieutenant Colonel F. Colvin and the remainder of the columns arrived from east and west.

Lieutenant Colonel Vialls with the Victorians and other mounted men was ordered to give chase but the Boers had scattered in various directions. Viall's men made contact some four kilometres away, were charged by the Boers but easily drove them off. Some of the Boers headed for the Vaal River and headed off to the north where they spent the next day on the farm Smitfield, not to be disturbed by the British (who probably had no idea they were there). Jan Moerdyk's diary for Sunday 5 January says that "after the punishment meted out to them yesterday the enemy left us in peace today", which seems to epitomise the indomitable Boer spirit for their cause which was now clearly hopeless.[15]

During the month of January, the British under Bruce Hamilton continued with their night-raiding tactics but Lord Kitchener's focus was now shifting to efforts to capture Christian de Wet in the eastern Orange Free State and deal with Koos de la Rey in the western Transvaal. Columns were reorganised and manpower reduced. Louis Botha remained in the area but soon realised that the denuded landscape with the few farms still standing was not able to adequately support his force. The British recognised that to surround and capture him was not even to be attempted. In mid-February Botha and his followers by-passed the Wakkerstroom-Piet Retief blockhouse line by marching through Swaziland and headed into the mountains around Vryheid. Brits went back to the Standerton area and his base at Bloukop. Onverwacht was the last aggressive action of Botha's commando in the eastern Transvaal and they remained at large in the Vryheid area until the commencement of peace negotiations in April 1902.[16]

After the battle four graves were dug on the ground near the spur – eleven men of the Q.I.B in one, seven from the Hampshire Regiment in the second, five Boers in the third and the fourth for Major Vallentin. Some years later Vallentin's family arranged for a monument to be erected over the grave which was organised for the family by Captain Siemssen, one of General Louis Botha's personal staff. In 1962 the bodies were moved from the mass graves on the Onverwacht spur and reinterred in a Garden of Remembrance in Ermelo Cemetery on Saturday, 5 May. Monuments that been erected over the original graves were also moved and now stand in Ermelo. Members of Major Vallentin's family and a representative from the Australians were present at the reinterment ceremony.

In February 2002 local people erected an impressive monument on the original grave site made from stone corner posts and with the names of the five Boers who were buried on the field. The 2/14 Australian Light Horse Regiment laid an impressive brass plaque with the names of their dead. Only a fragment of the original cast iron cross with the inscription "For King and Empire" which was erected over the Hampshire Regiment dead remains, cemented into the base of the monument. The monument site is on private land and carefully guarded by the local farmer so vandalism has so far been avoided. It is a fitting memorial to the brave men of both sides who fought it out along the ridge more than a century ago.

Only one brother returned

Two Lilley brothers, William and Dave, joined the 5th Queensland Imperial Bushmen to fight in the Boer War but only one of them returned. Both brothers were popular with their colleagues, William being a private and Dave, the older brother, an acting Corporal. In fact because William was only 17 when he enlisted, Dave was encouraged by his parents to enlist as well to "keep an eye on William".

Details on how William died are sketchy but he was killed during fierce fighting with the enemy near Onverwacht in Northern Transvaal on 4 January 1902. Before that he'd certainly been in the thick of things. In a letter to his sister Edith and brother-in-law Bob dated 6 October 1901, he described some of the action:

> Well a little bit about the war we have had a good deal of fighting lately. We had a bit of a go the other day at a place called Weapener there was 3 boers shot dead & 17 boers wounded our loss was nill and about a week after that there was 50 of QIB & 150 New Zealanders went out on patroal away from the colum & they struck about 400 boers and had a good cut in with them but the boers had the best part of it, they was getting all around our fellers and soon would have had the lot of them. But General Plumer got wind of it & made a bid for it, we were 10 miles off when he heard of it & he sent Col. Jervis & about 200 of us & 2 big guns & Pompom to assist them we galloped the 10 miles & our horses were done in when we got there it was just dusk when the guns & pompom started playing on to them they were all larged up in the camp the shells fell right in amongst them & then there was a bit of a flutter amongst the boers there was little peices flying all roads the shells killed about 4 boers the losses on our side was 4 killed & 2 wounded the men killed were Leiut Kaskey, Leiut Pooley, Private G H White & Private Milliner the men wounded Private Gatfield & another man. The New Zeal never came near our fellers they was sitting down having tea when we came up with the guns & our blokes was in a tight corner the boers [unreadable] of our fellers & they would have had the lot if we hadn't have came up quick they stripped our fellers and let them go. The boer loss was 10 killed & a good few wounded. The name of the place was Makarie Drift. 1 have no more time to write any more,

we are goeing to have a cut at Botha now. I have had no sickness yet Remember us to all up there.

I Remain, Your Brother, W Lilley, South Africa.

(No changes have been made to the spelling or grammar of the original letter)

Although the Lilley family would have learned of William's death through brother Dave, a company commander of the *5th QIB*, Captain Charles Gehrmann wrote a condolence letter to the family. The letter was in a beautiful script:

Dear Sir, It is with great regret that I have to write to you on so sad a matter. No doubt by now you have been advised officially and Dave will have written to you. Your son No 127 Pvt W Lilley met his death bravely in an engagement on January 4th when our regiment suffered severely.

He was one of my best men and was the life of all his troop. His death has cast quite a gloom amongst us. His cheerful manner made him a favourite with both officers and men and I regret his death very much. He was always willing for any work and although not present myself at the time of his death, his example on the field was a lesson many a man could follow and be a credit to his country. Allow me to sympathise with you and your family in your sad bereavement and I pray for the Almighty to be with you in your sad affliction and make it easy to bear.

I trust nothing will happen to your other son and that he will be spared to return to you safe and sound. He is also a credit to his company and is a very promising young officer.

I must apologise for not writing earlier, but I have been in hospital since beginning of the month, hence this delay.

Hoping that the Almighty will be with you in your trouble and that Dave may be spared to you.

I remain, yours sincerely, Chas G. Gehrinann, Capt 5th QIB

The material for this article was supplied by Mr Alan Lilley of Queensland.

Captain C.G. Gehrmann – 5 Queensland Imperial Bushmen

References

1. Pamphlet compiled by Mrs Gretchen Celliers and issued on the occasion of the unveiling of the monument at Onverwacht.
2. R.L. Wallace *The Australians at the Boer War* The Australian War Memorial, Canberra, 1976.
3. Leo Amery *The Times History of the War in South Africa* Vol v.
4. *The South African War Casualty Roll* J.B. Hayward & Son 1982.
5. F.P. du P. Robbertze *Generaals Coen Brits en Louis Botha 1899-1919*.
6. W.H. Wilson *After Pretoria – The Guerilla War II*
7. Private David W. Priest 5th Queensland Imperial Bushmen. Letter to his father now in the hands of his son, Bill Priest.
8. C.C.Eloff (editor) *Oorlagsdagboekie van H.S. Oosterhagen* Raad vir Geesteswetenskaplike Navorsing, Pretoria, 1976.
9. Albert Schmidt *Jacobus Daniel (Koot) Opperman*, article written for the unveiling of the monument on Onverwacht farm in 2002.
10. C.G. Stolp article in *Fleur* 1948 quoted in the inauguration pamphlet.
11. P.L. Murray *Official Records of the Australian Military Contingents to the War in South Africa*.
12. Murray Cosby Jackson *A Soldier's Diary* The Royal Hampshire Regiment Museum Trustees 1999 (reprint of 1913 original).
13. Jan Leendert Moerdyk's *Diary of the First War of Independence* translated from High Dutch by his son Pieter Cornelius Moerdyk.

Notes on sources

1. M.G. Dooner *The Last Post* pp393-394.
2. Amery *The Times History of the War in South Africa* Vol V p456.
3. Amery *The Times History of the War in South Africa* Vol V p453-454.
4. Amery *The Times History of the War in South Africa* Vol V p455. See also F.P. du P. Robbertze *Generaals Coen Brits en Louis Botha 1899-1919* Chapter 20 – "A challenge for an English Officer is accepted." His colourful account is worth reading and bears comparison with British accounts of the incident who acknowledge it to have been a rout. There is another account of the action in *After Pretoria* p938.
5. Eloff *Oorlagsdagboekie van H.S. Oosterhagen* p16.
6. Albert Schmidt article.
7. Robbertze Generaals *Coen Brits en Louis Botha 1899-1919* p74 describes this incident and the wounding of an Ermelo man, one Erasmus, who was taken that night to the farm Schimmelhoek. See also *Oorlagsdagboekie van H.S. Oosterhagen* p16.
8. Letter to his father, Private David W. Priest 5th Queensland Imperial Bushmen.
9. F.P. du P. Robbertze *Generaals Coen Brits en Louis Botha 1899-1919* p74.
10. F.P. du P. Robbertze *Generaals Coen Brits en Louis Botha 1899-1919* p76.
11. Private David Priest's letter as well as the reports of Major F.W. Toll and Lieutenant J.B. Higginson.
12. C.G. Stolp article in *Fleur* 1948.
13. F.P. du P. Robbertze *Generaals Coen Brits en Louis Botha 1899-1919* p77.
14. Murray Cosby Jackson *A Soldier's Diary* pp308-313.
15. Jan Leendert Moerdyk's *Diary of the First War of Independence*.
16. Amery *The Times History of the War in South Africa* Vol V pp459-460.

Monument on the farm Onverwacht.

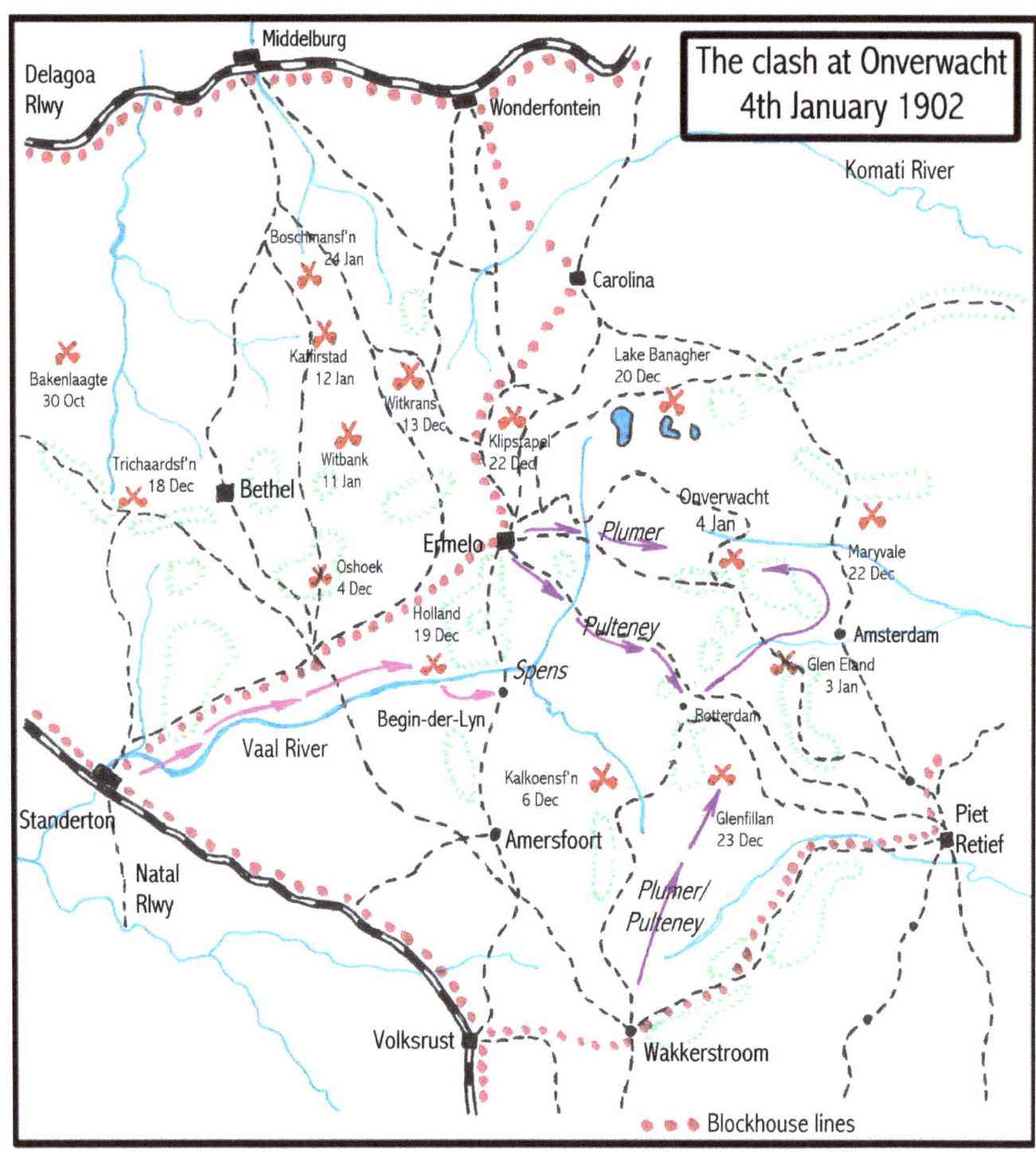

The eastern Transvaal in December 1901 and January 1902.

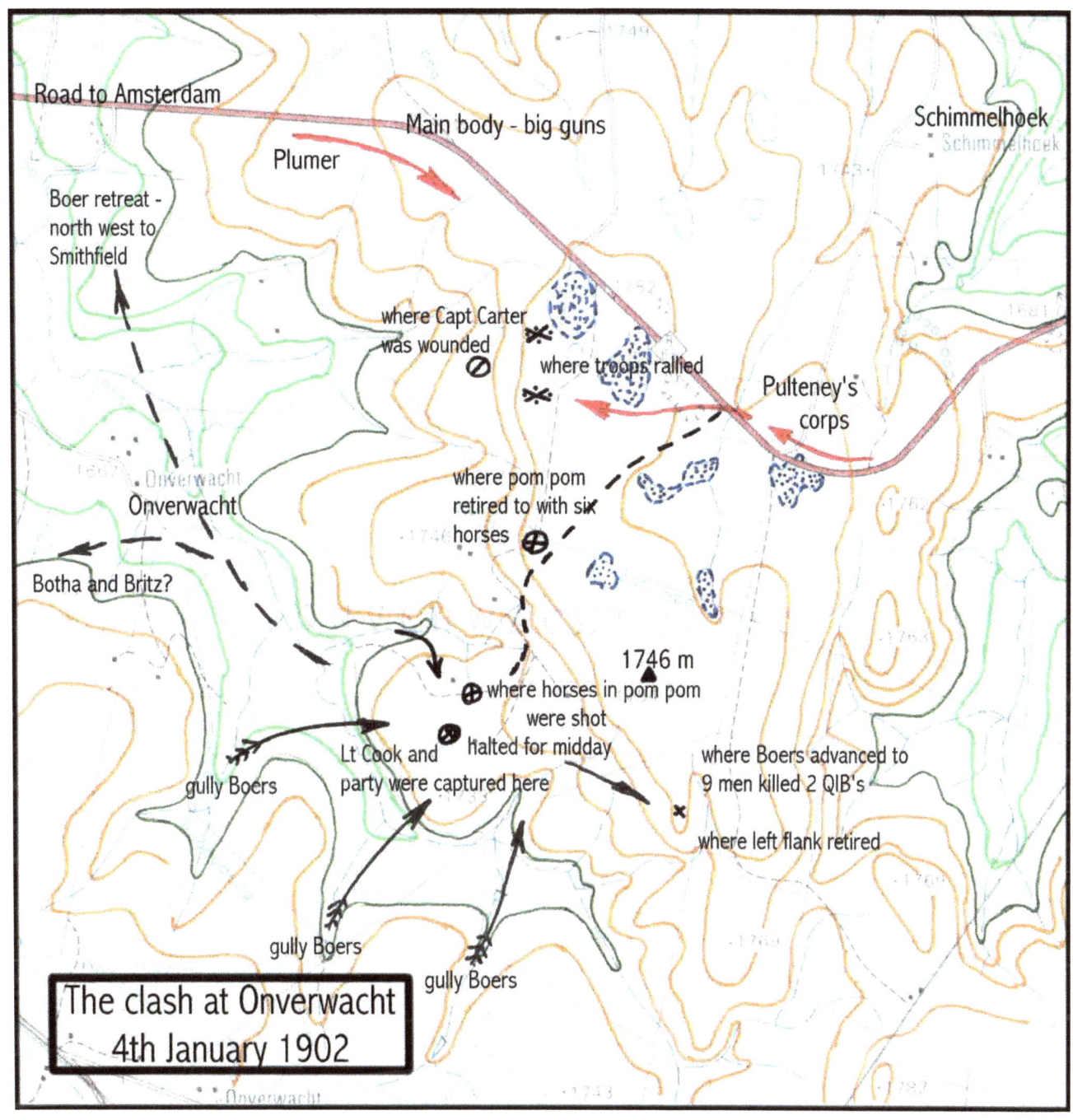

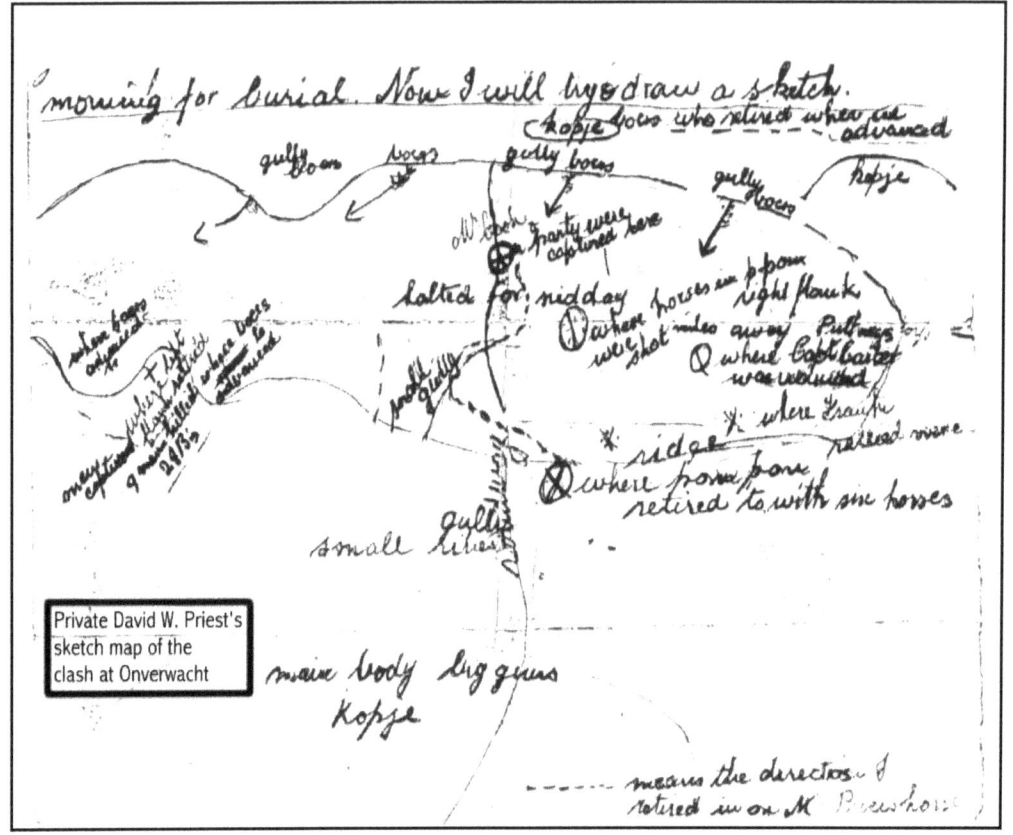
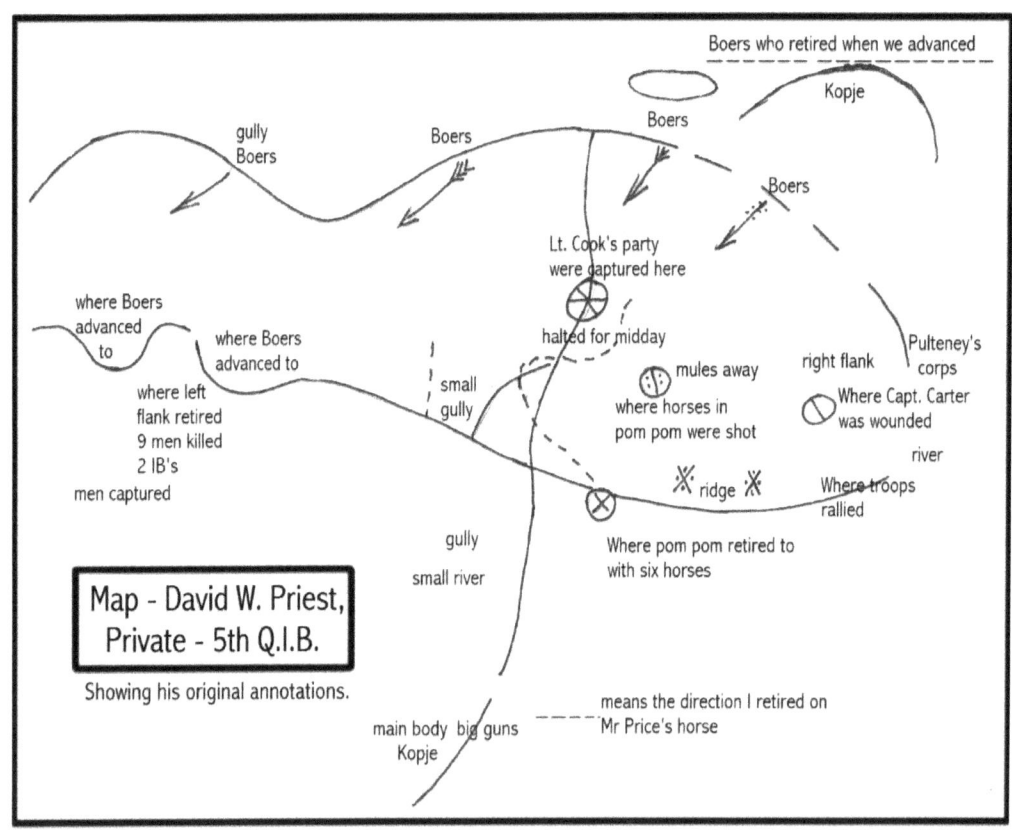

David Priest's map and his annotation.

Boer Generals: Louis Botha (above)
Commandants Koen Brits (top right), Koot Opperman (far right) and Chris Botha (right).

GENERAL SIR BRUCE HAMILTON AND GENERAL SPENS.

Colonel H.C.O. Plumer.
Major J.M Vallentin.

Abram's Kraal
27/28 January 1902

Under the waters of the Kalkfontein dam in the district of Fauresmith in the southern Free State lie the ruins of the farmhouse of Abram's Kraal.[1] It was here in the early morning of 28 January 1902 that Boer commandos under the command of General Charles Nieuwoudt attacked a British column. The column, which was composed principally of soldiers of the Royal Sussex Regiment under the command of Lieutenant-Colonel Louis du Moulin, had chosen this deserted farmhouse and its outhouses, walled garden and kraals for their bivouac that night.

Abram's Kraal farmhouse faced north a short distance from a small rocky ridge along the right bank of the Riet River. The owner had built two kraals to hold his cattle, and perhaps some sheep, as well as a small walled garden where fruit and vegetables were grown. These Boer farm gardens almost invariably contained a small orchard of peach trees. Two barns were used by the soldiers that night while the officers occupied more comfortable quarters in the farmhouse. The close proximity of a shallow *vlei*[2] where they could water their horses and mules was an important factor which governed their choice of this place for their night's halt. Biesiesvlei, a quite extensive shallow pan or pond was nearby. The column almost certainly did not take their horses and mules down to the river for water. That number of horses would be much more easily watered as a large crowd in the *vlei*, rather than in the river. There they would have to have occupied a long stretch of river frontage. As a tactical consideration, at the river and out of sight of the camp around the corner of the ridge, this would have been a difficulty. There were 350 men in the column,[3] all of whom would have been mounted, as well as a number of carts and wagons drawn by mules. They also had a pom-pom gun[4] on a carriage which had its own team of four mules. It seemed a secure place to spend the night.

The Royal Sussex Regiment was stationed in Aldershot, the British Army's headquarters in Hampshire, when war broke out in South Africa in October 1899. They were on the roster for foreign service but that turned out to be Malta and not South Africa. Eventually the call came for them to embark for South Africa after a period of intensive training. The regiment was with Lord Roberts's advance through the Orange Free State and they were in action at the Zand River before entering the Transvaal. They again saw action at Doornkop, outside Krugersdorp, after which Johannesburg was occupied. They were present at Diamond Hill when Louis Botha sought to halt the advance of the British army along the Delagoa Bay railway line, but then spent much time in garrison duties until February 1901 when they were formed into a mounted column.[5]

Louis Eugène du Moulin was of French descent although hailing from New Zealand. He was related to the French settlers who founded the town of Akaroa in South Island. He passed through Sandhurst and joined the 107th Regiment in 1879 which became the 2nd Battalion of the Royal Sussex Regiment in 1881. His service experience was in various campaigns in India from 1888 to 1897. Major du Moulin was promoted to the local rank of Lieutenant-Colonel in June 1901, taking command of the column.

From July 1901 onwards there was considerable activity in the southern Free State in the British army's attempt to find and destroy the commando of General Jan Smuts, on his way to invade the Cape Colony. The British were unable to prevent him crossing the Orange River and moving south and west, eventually getting into the western Cape and close enough to see the lights of Cape Town. The southern Free State had been relatively quiet for most of 1901 but British columns, having been outwitted by Smuts, sought to find General Pieter Kritzinger, some of whose men had acted as a guide to Smuts. Kritzinger's energetic and aggressive Commandant Louis Wessels descended on Lovatt's Scouts at Quaggafontein on 20 September 1901, a farm on the right bank of the Orange River which included several drifts. Wessels took possession of the enemy's camp in a surprise attack at midnight. Then, unaccountably, he and his commando retreated back the way they had come, not taking advantage of the opportunity to cross the Orange into the Cape and add to the disorder there.[6]

Du Moulin's men might have engaged and captured Louis Wessels and his small band of about 80 men but for a miscommunication with Colonel Herbert Plumer. Plumer's Australians had a sharp encounter with Wessels at Mokari Drift on the Caledon River on 27 September 1901 but du Moulin's force was too far away to intervene.[7] By this time the area of the southern Free State east of the railway line between Bloemfontein and De Aar had become untenable for the Boers. Commandant George Brand reported to the Vereeniging Meeting of Commandants in May 1902, "that everything had been carried off – there was not a sheep left."[8] West of the railway line the land was less rugged but more arid. There was general movement of the Boer commandos into this area and the British columns followed. Even the British did not have overmuch in the way of supplies. Captain R.C. Griffin complained that he was "getting tired of nothing but tinned food with an occasional slice of newly killed goat."[9]

---

[1] This is the proper name of the farm in Afrikaans as spelled throughout this article. The name was anglicised to "Abraham's Kraal" in du Moulin's book *Two Years on Trek*.
[2] "*Vlei*" – a pond or marsh.
[3] Du Moulin *Two Years on Trek* p300 says du Moulin had "350 mounted men" but a footnote on p 303 says "about 300, with a pom-pom".
[4] Pom-pom: Nordenfelt 37mm large calibre belt-fed machine gun which fired explosive projectiles. The name comes from the sound the gun made when fired. The British and the Boers both made use of this weapon. It was highly inaccurate and its effect was more to demoralise the enemy than to cause real damage.

[5] Du Moulin *Two Years on Trek* gives a full account of their activities in South Africa.
[6] Maurice *History of the War in South Africa* Vol 4 pp287-89. Kritzinger *In the Shadow of Death* pp33-36.
[7] An account of this action is in *Mokari Drift*, South African Military History Journal, December 2008.
[8] Du Moulin *Two Years on Trek* p296.

Du Moulin's column was moved into Edenburg on 19 December 1901 and continued south to Jagersfontein Road on the main railway line on the 22nd. Intelligence placed Boer commandos at Jagersfontein, 25 miles to the west.[1] On the evening of the 24th the column moved out with 350 men of the Sussex Regiment and a pom-pom gun, the wagons following later. They halted for a short while at Boomplaats Hill[2] and then continued on over the broad flat plain stretching across to Jagersfontein. At the farm Vlakfontein, just as the sun was rising, they encountered a Boer commando. The Boers were not prepared for an attack and numbers of them were caught asleep in a donga[3] and rolled up in their blankets. At the cost of two wounded the column had made a very successful raid:

> Heaps of rifles, saddles, bandoliers and other equipment were brought in and piled against the veranda of the farmhouse, the Colonel and the other officers assembled on the veranda, the horses were picketed in lines in front of the house, the men started to brew their coffee over little fires, and a general air of cheerful satisfaction pervaded the place; for it had been a very successful raid. Besides twenty-eight prisoners, the column had taken 52 rifles, 78 bandoliers, 2,500 rounds of ammunition, 105 horses, 96 saddles, 130 blankets, 25 cloaks and 8 bags of wheat.[4]

One of the captives was dressed in a complete British uniform with regimental badges and slouch hat. To deceive their enemy into thinking that an approaching group of riders was friend and not foe was a tactic adopted by the Boers. Wearing captured British uniforms and arranging themselves so as to look like a British formation was quite frequently successful, enabling them to get to close range before, too late, the ruse was discovered. Commander-in-Chief, General Lord Kitchener, had issued orders in September 1901 that any Boers captured wearing British uniforms were to be tried by Court Martial and shot. Griffin's comment:

> *One Boer caught in khaki was tried and shot in the afternoon. Very horrid business! He was made to dig his own grave and then shot before a full parade of all the troops and the other prisoners, one of whom was his own brother.*[5]

Concerned that the Boers might take revenge with an attack on Christmas morning, du Moulin and his men stood to arms at 3 a.m. and soon after sunrise heard gunfire from the south. This was the action of Colonel A.C. Hamilton who scattered a laager near Heen-en-Weers Kop and took sixteen prisoners. He and his men had outdistanced their wagons which had an escort of only sixty men. Judge Hertzog and General Charles Nieuwoudt pounced at Kok's Kraal, a short distance away, with their 250 men and overpowered the guards. Three African drivers were shot out of hand and four of Hamilton's men were killed and four wounded. The prisoners, and some of the slightly wounded, were stripped and made to walk to Springfontein, "an officer among them", according to the Official History.[6]

Du Moulin's column made its way to Fauresmith which they found to be deserted. They enjoyed the apricots, figs, mulberries and peaches from the gardens behind the houses – paradise they said. They moved into Jagersfontein on 26 December and found the diamond mines, the richest in the world, to be deserted. Next day they headed back to Vlakfontein. Griffin's diary told that:

> On arrival there we found the notice to the effect that we had shot a Boer for wearing British uniform, which we had posted on the door of the farm, had been removed – looks as if Boers had been here again.[7]

Vlakfontein was made the headquarters for the columns operating in the district,[8] those of Lieutenant-Colonel W.G.B. Western and Major D.P. Driscoll's Scouts. Colonel A.N. Rochfort, in overall command of the district, came to Vlakfontein to organise a combined move of the three columns against the Boers who were now to the west of them. Du Moulin's men left Vlakfontein on the 3rd January 1902 and reached Luckhoff on the 11th. Griffin describes how they made that journey with stops at Metz, where they found "traces of late occupation by Boers."[9] At Doornfontein on the Orange River, they were fired at from the opposite Cape Colony bank. At du Plessis dam the column camped at the place where the Boers halted after the capture of Hamilton's baggage. Griffin said that "the well water is beastly and smells and tastes of horse" – evidence that the Boers had dumped a dead horse into it.[10] Luckhoff was totally wrecked.

Into the Cape Colony they rode, crossing the border at Ramah's Spring where they were "most hospitably entertained by an English farmer." Even better was The Grange at Witteput (now Wiput) where they played lawn tennis in the afternoon and went into the farm to "hear some very feeble attempts at music in the evening."[11] At Belmont, site of one of the early battles of the war as Methuen advanced towards Kimberley, a patrol got in touch with 300 Boers moving south and accordingly followed them back into the Orange River Colony.[12] (Intelligence indicated that this commando was that of General Charles Nieuwoudt, in command of the district and under Judge J.B.M. Hertzog). They were back in Luckhoff on the 18th and had to stay there for the day to rest the horses, unable to move although they

---

[9] Entry in Griffin's diary for 16 December.
[1] According to du Moulin *Two Years on Trek* p296, "It was known that the Commandants had been summoned by de Wet to a conference in the north". No such conference occurred – du Moulin is mistaken.
[2] Boomplaats is the site of an engagement between Sir Harry Smith and the Orange Free State Boers under General Andries Pretorius on 29 August 1848.
[3] Donga – a small ravine, sometimes caused by erosion, called a nullah in India.
[4] Du Moulin *Two Years on Trek* p298. A photograph from 2nd Lieutenant R.E. Paget's collection of photographs portrays this scene and shows the recaptured rifles stacked against the veranda of Vlakfontein farmhouse.
[5] Entry in Griffin's diary for 24 December. Du Moulin *Two Years on Trek* p298 also mentions this incident.
[6] Maurice *History of the War in South Africa* Vol 4 p430.
[7] Entry in Griffin's diary for 27 December.
[8] Du Moulin *Two Years on Trek* p300. Vlakfontein
[9] Entry in Griffin's diary for 6 January.
[10] Entry in Griffin's diary for 9 January.
[11] Entries in Griffin's diary for 12 and 13 January.
[12] The British annexed the the Orange Free State and renamed it the Orange River Colony on 28 May 1900.

knew the Boers were only 10 miles away. On the 20th Griffin's men recovered 13 mules and 11 horses near Liebenberg's Pan, some of Hamilton's losses.

Resupply was necessary and so the column headed to Fauresmith and on to Jagersfontein. On the way, Griffin met up with Driscoll "who had just caught 2 Boers and 250 sheep". Griffin took the prisoners to Jagersfontein – "I brought in 3 prisoners of Driscoll's (the 2 he had taken in the morning and the brother of one of them, who had been given away by his brother as Driscoll told him he would shoot him if his brother was not caught)."[1]

The Boers had moved north and on the 23rd du Moulin started after them. That night the column halted at Armoedsfontein and crossed the Riet River the following morning at Jagersfontein Drift.[2] That night at Olievenkloof it rained and Griffin said it was "the worst night I can remember".[3] The march took them to Tafelkop and on the 26th they were at Klipnek in the afternoon, camping that night at Witdam where there was evidently enough water for Griffin to have a bath!

On 27th they marched west and at 8:30 a.m. four Boers were seen by the intelligence officer, Captain Beale, on the farm Vaalpan about five miles away. Vaalpan belonged to Judge Hertzog. Griffin's horses were "quite done up" and the Boers were watched from a high koppie.[4] They circled around and joined a laager about five or six miles away. Griffin estimated that "there were about 400 Boers with 3 Cape carts[5] and about 50 head of cattle and a lot of spare horses."[6] The Boers moved off and du Moulin's men followed, passing through De Dam where the Boers had camped. By the evening the column was at the farm of Abram's Kraal on the right bank of the Riet River with a low ridge between the farmhouse and the river. This is how the farm has been described:

> At Abraham's Kraal, the farm houses are at the open end of a semi-circle some 200 yards in diameter, formed by a low ridge that rises here and there into small koppies covered with large stones. Beyond the buildings and facing the semi-circle is a garden with a stone wall. Standing with ones' back to the garden and buildings, on the right is a large stone kraal divided into several compartments. In front is the highest part of the ridge, beyond which the ground drops very quickly to the Riet River. On the left, the ridge ends in a conical rocky mound, with a small kraal at its foot. On the outside of this mound a donga leads up from the river, and curls in towards the farm.[7]

The Boers having crossed the river were nowhere to be seen. They had circled around to the west and were hidden in the hills around Poortjie. Their scouts told them of Western's column approaching from the west and they also knew that Driscoll was to their south. If they were to avoid encirclement they would have to attack one of them and du Moulin looked to be numerically inferior and close at hand. Commandant M.A. Theunissen was given command of the attackers.[8]

Piquets were placed on top of the low ridge and on left and right on small mounds. The colonel and his staff slept in the farmhouse and the other buildings were utilised by the men. The transport and the horse lines were along the garden walls. Fortuitously, at 1 a.m. one of the Sussex's sergeants "got up to put the nose-bag on his horse, as a patrol was to go across the river at 3 a.m." He was walking back to his place when he heard a shot fired from the piquet and shouted, "Stand to!" In the darkness the Boers had climbed the steeper southern slope but did not surprise the wakeful piquet who saw them and one of whose members probably fired the shot. Crossing the drift at Poortjie, the Boers had worked their way along the river bank until they were below the picquet. Some of them then climbed the steep southern slope of the ridge, and a number of them made it down the lesser northern slope and into the camp. Their guide, the owner of the farm, clearly knew every inch of the ground but was killed early in the assault. The Boers occupied the large kraal coming around over the saddle to their left of the ridge.[9]

Officers and men were quickly awake and soon recovered from the sudden shock attack. Major Gilbert moved to the small kraal where the pom-pom was placed. Lieutenant Thorne was sent to the garden wall to get men to come over to the small kraal. These men maintained a steady fire along the ridge. Du Moulin collected together some of the other men who cleared the Boers out of the large cattle kraal. Leading a charge to clear the Boers from the further side he was shot through the heart, the two men following being mortally wounded. The British were now firmly established and fighting back. Griffin and two other officers were held at gunpoint as "the bullets of friend and enemy alike were rattling among us."[10] The Boers were then being contained and even pushed back although the fighting must have been terribly confused. At about 2 a.m. Commandant Theunissen decided to call off the attack. A whistle sounded several times, apparently from the position of the piquet on the ridge – the signal to withdraw. Griffin's captors bolted and the Boers scrambled back over the drift leaving two dead behind them.[11]

Thirteen men died in the action, eleven men of the Royal Sussex Regiment and two of their Boer adversaries. Seven of the British were killed in the action and four others died later of their wounds. Eight of the Sussex men were buried at the farmhouse, the seven who were killed in action and Private Gaston, who was fatally wounded. Three graves were

---

[1] Entry in Griffin's diary for 21 January.
[2] Although this drift is referred to as Jagersfontein Drift, on Jagersfontein farm on the north bank of the Riet River, the crossing point was almost certainly at what is now called Banks Drift on an adjacent farm.
[3] Entry in Griffin's diary for 24 January.
[4] Koppie – literally a "small hill".
[5] Cape cart – a small two-wheeled cart with a canopy top that can hold two passengers.
[6] Entry in Griffin's diary for 27 January.
[7] Du Moulin *Two Years on Trek* p302. The sketch map shows the marches of du Moulin's column and locates all the farms named.
[8] In a footnote on p303 of Du Moulin *Two Years on Trek*, Nieuwoudt commanded a force of 400 men.
[9] A more detailed account of the attack is given in Du Moulin *Two Years on Trek* pp303-07.
[10] Entry in Griffin's diary for 28 January.
[11] Griffin gives the name of one of the Boer dead as Field Cornet Myburgh. He does not name the other fatality, the owner of the farm.

dug, one for Colonel du Moulin, another for the two sergeants and the men as well and a third for the two Boers killed. "At half past seven, all the available men paraded, Captain Montrésor read the burial service, and the last post was sounded over the grave of the man to whose initiative and energy the column owed its existence, and who had died most gallantly in its defence."[1]

A major loss for the British was a large number of dead horses and mules killed in the crossfire that swept the horse lines in the darkness.[2] The attack was abortive for the Boers – although they had killed a number of the column's animals as well as its commanding officer, they had lost two dead and a number had suffered wounds.[3] One of the Boer wounded was serious enough that he was sent into the British camp under a flag of truce at 8 a.m. just as the column was leaving – he later died.[4] There seem to have been a good many more wounded and later it was heard from prisoners that Nieuwoudt considered night raids to be too risky after his sortie at Abram's Kraal. Certainly, the Boers would never have attempted their bold assault in daylight. An attack timed to open just as dawn broke, as had been so successful for the British in night raids on Boer laagers, would have had a much better chance of success, rather than their desperate charge in total darkness.

Then began, at 8:30 a.m. that morning, the return to Jagersfontein Drift and Vlakfontein. Many of the men were dismounted but nevertheless the column marched nearly thirty miles and camped "at a farm about two miles south of Jagersfontein Drift."[5] One of the wounded, Private B. Gaston, died before the column set out. During the march three more died and were buried along the way, one of them the wounded Boer. Privates Light and Clarke died on the journey and Brackpool on arrival at their camp on 29 January.[6]

A number of African drivers had some adventures:

> Several of the African drivers had bolted at the first alarm in the morning, two of them with nothing on at all. They had made a bee-line through the barbed wire, cactus hedges and mud holes; and, during the march, sorry figures came limping back to the column and rejoined the wagons. One got right through to Vlakfontein, doing the 45 miles in ten hours, and said the column had been wiped out. The garrison there had an anxious time until runners arrived from Major Gilbert on the following morning.[7]

On 22 February Griffin was back at Abram's Kraal but remarked that there were "too many of our dead horses there to be pleasant."[8]

The Royal Sussex Regiment was sent northwards and became part of Lieutenant-General Ian Hamilton's force in the western Transvaal. They took part in the actions in that area in April 1902 just before peace was concluded on 31 May, 1902.

In 1937 the Kalkfontein dam on the Riet River was completed. The dam wall was built across the narrow neck between the hills at Poortjie. The Abram's Kraal farm was inundated by the water of the dam. The remains from the graves at Abram's Kraal were disinterred before that happened and reburied on a hill near the dam wall. Only one metal cross remains which bears the inscription, "In Memory of 9 British soldiers who died during the war". This cross was probably moved from the original burial site to the Kalkfontein Dam cemetery and is still in place there. Nine might be an error as only eight were interred at the farm.

In 1983 the South African War Graves Board in the person of Maurice Gough-Palmer visited the Kalkfontein cemetery. Correspondence was opened with the County Archivist of the West Sussex Records Office, custodian of the records of the Royal Sussex Regiment which was amalgamated with a number of others in 1966 and today forms part of the Princess of Wales's Royal Regiment. The South African War Graves Board expressed surprise that the Regiment had not erected any monument at Kalkfontein. The reaction from the West Sussex Archivist was to the effect that the members of the Regimental Association "will be delighted to know that this omission is being rectified."[9] In fact, it took 25 years before the omission was rectified. On 15 April 2008 a granite memorial was unveiled at Kalkfontein Dam cemetery by Brigadier Andrew Mantell, British Defence Adviser in South Africa in the presence of a number of invited guests. The Regimental flag was flown out to South Africa in the diplomatic bag and The Royal Sussex Regimental Association was represented by former officers of the Regiment, Major Bazil Carlston and Captain Charles Wilmot. The project to erect the memorial was initiated and managed by a group of South Africans led by David Scholtz. His work in doing this was described as "devoted and imaginative" by the Royal Sussex Regimental Association in expressing their gratitude.[10]

It was not possible to examine the actual battle site until 2015 when the level of the dam had fallen to only 6.6 per cent of capacity. Even so, the entire site was not above water. South Africa was experiencing one of the periodic droughts that occur from time to time. This area of the country is particularly prone to these very arid periods. There was in December 2015 absolutely no flow at all in the upper reaches of the Riet River and it would take prolonged and incessant rainfall over some months to get it flowing again.

When the writer and friends were taken to the site in December 2015 by Mr Attie Roodt whose family own the farm Kraaipoort, the farmstead and most of the other buildings were still submerged. Photos of what can be seen

---

[1] Du Moulin *Two Years on Trek* p307.

[2] Estimates vary as to how many horses and mules were killed. Du Moulin *Two Years on Trek* p 304 says "ninety" and on p306 "120" while Maurice *History of the War in South Africa* Vol 4 p433 says "nearly 150."

[3] Lieutenant-Colonel Louis Eugène du Moulin is described as a remarkable leader and organiser in a preface to by a fellow officer of the Royal Sussex Regiment, Colonel J.G. Panton, written in 1906. The book was written by du Moulin but clearly not the last two chapters which deal with Abram's Kraal and later.

[4] Du Moulin *Two Year on Trek* p308 and Griffin's diary entries for 28 and 29 January

[5] Entry in Griffin's diary for 29 January. It has not been possible to establish exactly where they camped and exactly where Light, Clarke and Brackpool were buried. S.A. Watt *In Memoriam* merely shows "Fauresmith District".

[6] Letter from the County Archivist of the West Sussex Records office, 27 June 1983.

[7] Du Moulin *Two Years on Trek* p308. Major Gilbert took over command of the column.

[8] Entry in Griffin's diary for 22 February.

[9] Letter from the West Sussex Records office dated 3 June 1983.

[10] Press release from the Royal Sussex Association.

show the small kraal in an excellent state of preservation and the large kraal, but not the farmhouse or the walled garden. The slope from the camp piquet on the top of the ridge is quite gentle. The slope down to the river, although much steeper, would not, indeed did not, offer a very difficult obstacle to the attacking Boers. A stone water tank on the knoll above the farmhouse was clearly built after 1902. The top of the ridge behind the farm buildings, site of the camp piquet, is always visible, even when the dam is full to capacity. It is then an island surrounded by water. As always, an appreciation of the real scale is only possible with a visit to the actual site. After so many years of waiting it was a salutary experience to see the site of this fierce encounter between some determined Boers and their equally-determined British opponents. It may well be some years before such an opportunity to examine the site happens again.

Finally, the Vlakfontein farmhouse where the British columns based themselves from December 1901 to February 1902 is still intact. It is therefore possible to see exactly where Lt-Col du Moulin and his officers assembled to view their recaptured rifles as described in Du Moulin *Two Years on Trek* p298, the extract reproduced earlier in this account.

References

1. Lieutenant-Colonel L.E. Du Moulin, *Two Years on Trek – Being some account of the Royal Sussex Regiment in South Africa* Murray and Co., The Middlesex printing Works, London 1907.
2. Erskine Childers, (editor) *The Times History of the War in South Africa* Vol V Sampson Low, Marston and Company ltd, London 1907.
3. Captain R.C. Griffin, *Typewritten diary* from the records of the Royal Sussex Regiment held in the West Sussex County Museum, Brighton.
4. Major-General Sir Frederick Maurice, *History of the War in South Africa* Vol 4.
5. General Pieter Kritzinger, *In the Shadow of Death* Originally printed for private circulation in 1904 but available in Project Guthenberg on the internet.
6. S.A. Watt, *In Memoriam* University of Natal Press, Pietermaritzburg 2000.

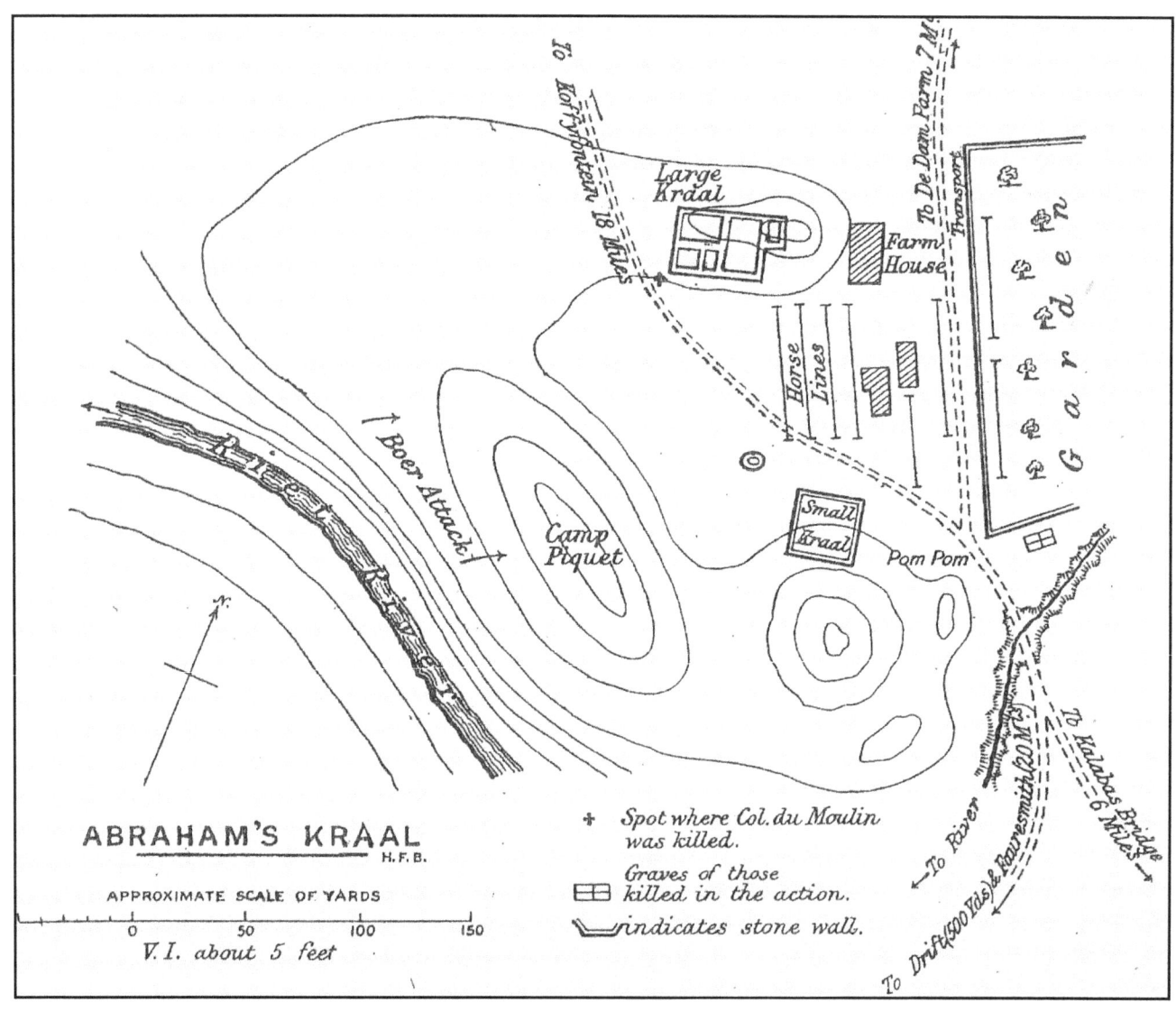

Casualties (Abram's Kraal)

Lieutenant-Colonel L.E. du Moulin	KIA	28 January 1902	Buried at Abram's Kraal *
Colour Sergeant A.E. Weston	KIA	28 January 1902	Buried at Abram's Kraal *
Sergeant C. Green	KIA	28 January 1902	Buried at Abram's Kraal *
Private W. Covington	KIA	28 January 1902	Buried at Abram's Kraal *
Private T. Hill	KIA	28 January 1902	Buried at Abram's Kraal *
Private R. Pimm	KIA	28 January 1902	Buried at Abram's Kraal *
Private G. Tomlin	KIA	28 January 1902	Buried at Abram's Kraal *
Private B. Gaston	DOW	28 January 1902	Buried at Abram's Kraal *
Private J. Clarke	DOW	28 January 1902	
Private T. Light	DOW	28 January 1902	
Private A. Brackpool	DOW	29 January 1902	
Private T. Bostock	Severely wounded		
Private G. Langley	Severely wounded		
Sergeant E. Simmins	Slightly wounded		
Drummer S. Sproston	Slightly wounded		
Private J. Coles	Slightly wounded		
Private A. Cox	Slightly wounded		

* Reinterred at Kalkfontein cemetery.

Casualties (Kok's Kraal)

Lieutenant A. Phillips (49th I.Y.)	KIA	25 December 1901
Lance-Corporal H. O'Donnel	KIA	25 December 1901
Lance-Corporal C. Rigby	KIA	25 December 1901
Private B. Bell	KIA	25 December 1901
Private H. Darwin	KIA	25 December 1901
Private H. Fort	Severely wounded	
Private J. Chalk	Slightly wounded	
Private D. Hart	Slightly wounded	
Private J. Ferris	slightly wounded	

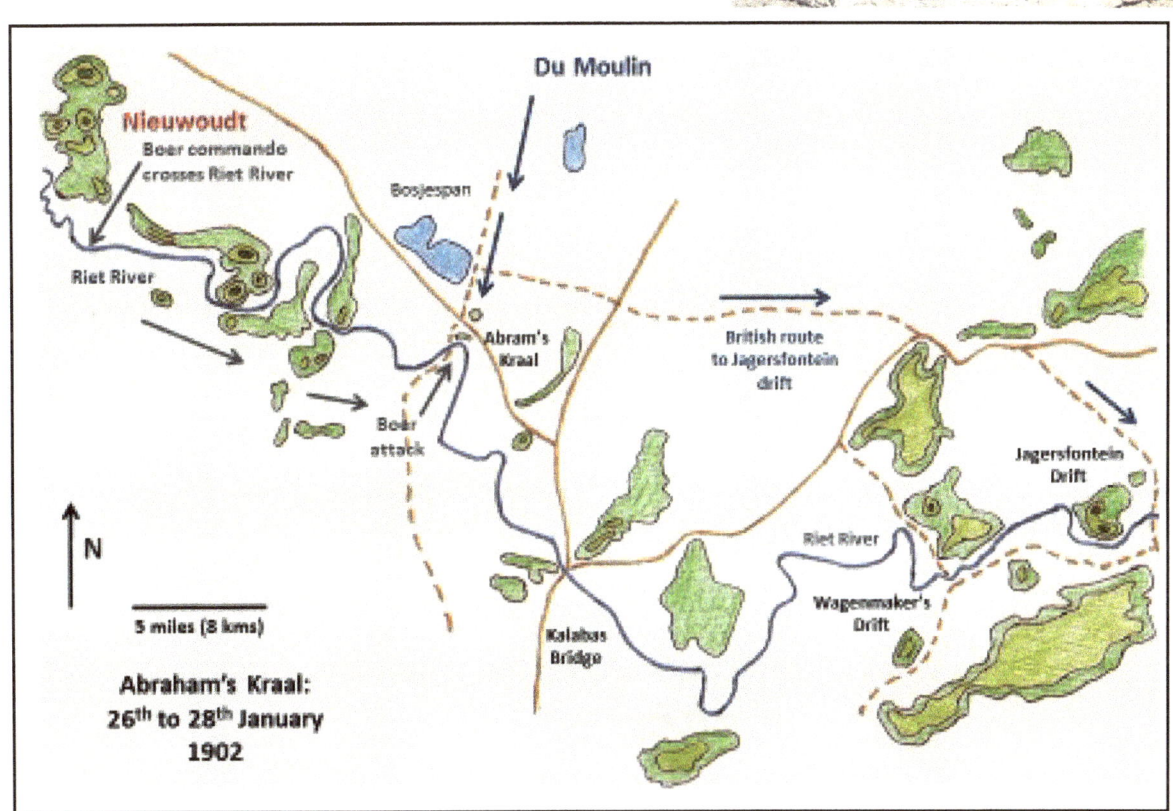

This map traced from the 1924 series and shows the British route of their retirement.

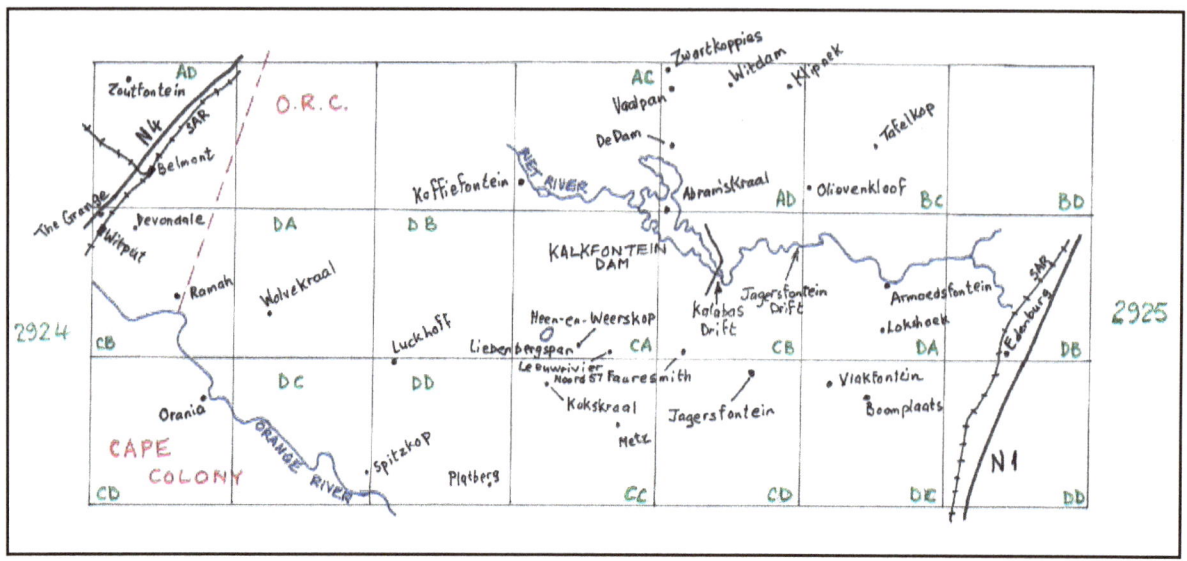

1:50k survey map numbers shown with farm and place names marked. Modern Kalkfontein dam shown.

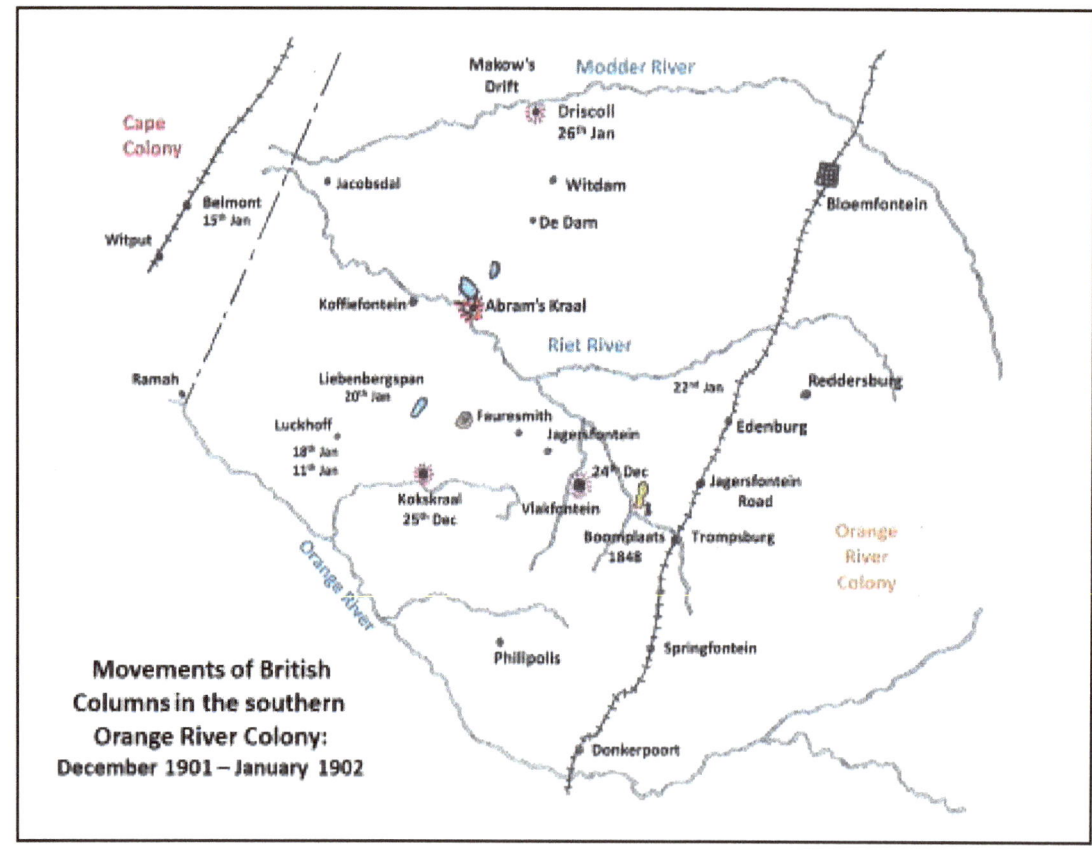

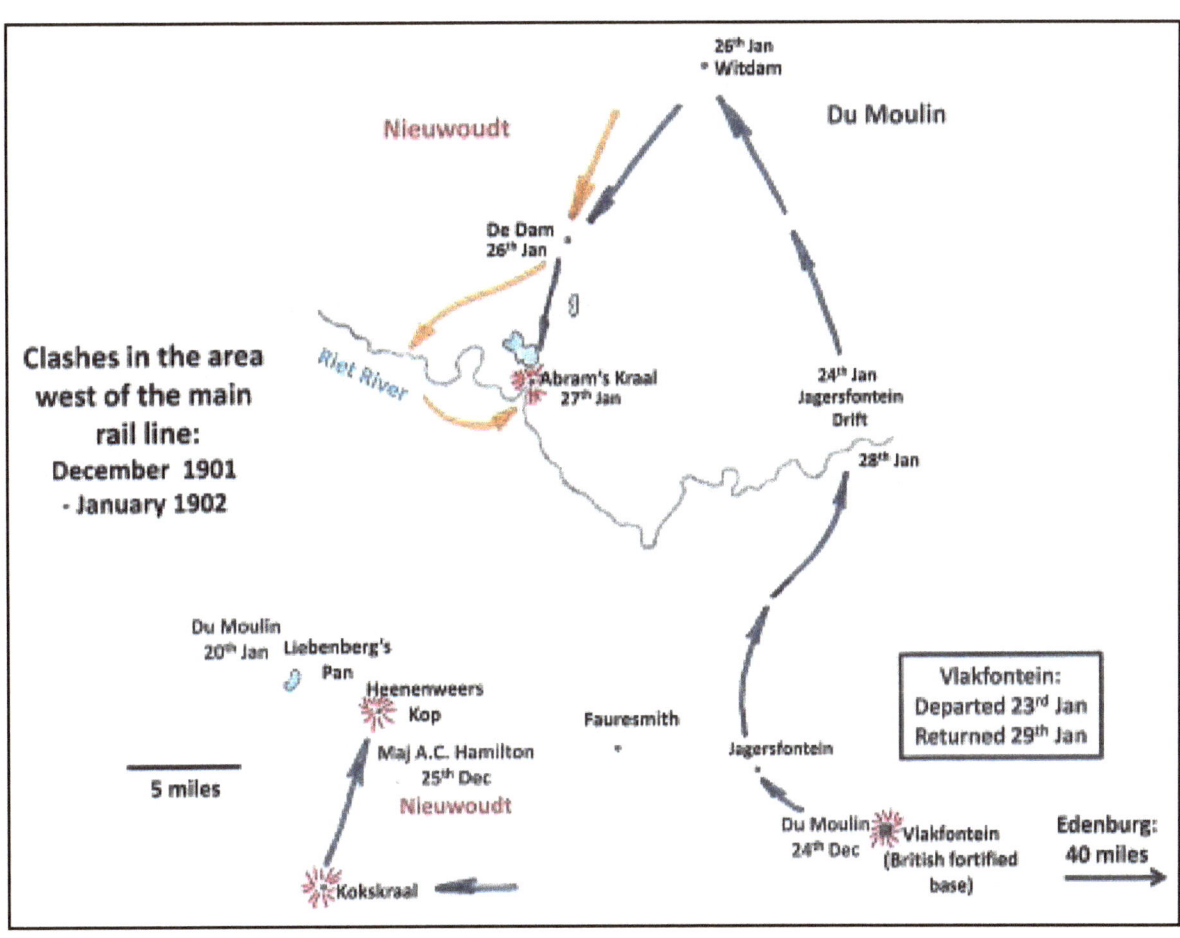

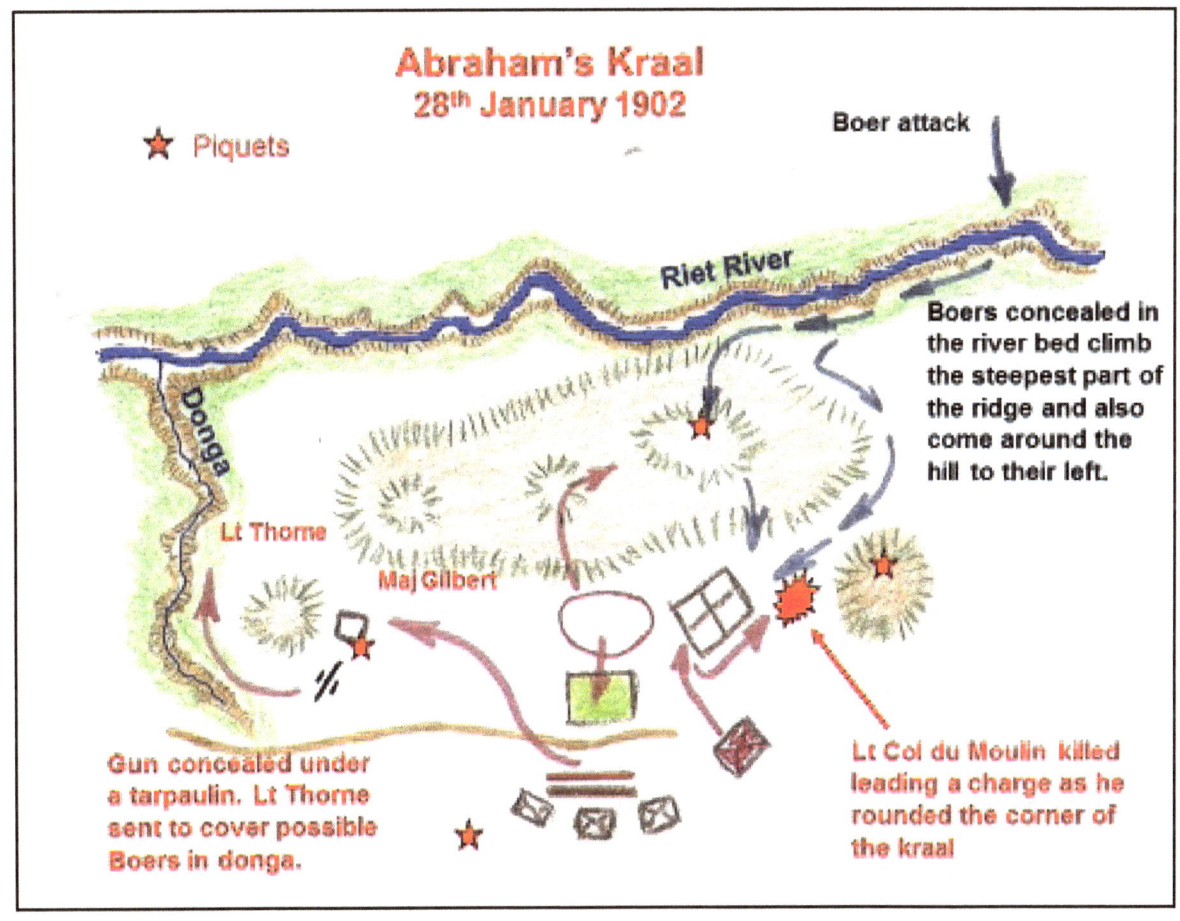

Sketch of the battle following the description in *Two Years on Trek*.

Boer weapons captured after the clash with Field Cornet du Toit at Vlakfontein on 24th December 1901. This the verandah of Vlakfontein farmhouse.

Abram's Kraal on the morning of 28th January 1902.

View in the direction of the picture above – the horse lines.

Lieutenant Colonel
Eugène du Moulin

General Charles Nieuwoudt

Abram's Kraal farmhouse under water in front of the kraal just visible above water.

The Riet River beyond this outcrop at the foot of which was the Maxim gun.

The First Double V.C.

The search for the site where Surgeon Captain Arthur Martin-Leake won his first Victoria Cross

The Victoria Cross is Britain's premier award for gallantry. It was instituted by Royal Warrant on 29 January 1856 for award to both officers and non-commissioned ranks of the Royal Navy and the Army who, in the presence of the enemy "shall have performed some signal act of valour..." Subsequently it has been awarded to members of the other armed forces. It is worn before all other decorations or orders.[1]

Arthur Martin-Leake twice performed such signal acts, in the Anglo Boer War in 1902 and again in the Great War in 1914. He was the first man to be twice honoured so as to earn the award of the Victoria Cross for each of his exploits. Only two others have since managed to emulate Martin-Leake's feat, Noel Chavasse in 1915 and 1916 and Charles Upham in 1941 and 1942.

As Medical Officer to the South African Constabulary, Martin-Leake accompanied a patrol seeking to locate a Boer laager that had encroached into the protected area around Johannesburg and Pretoria. The laager was discovered on the farm Van Tondershoek but the outnumbered policemen were forced to retire back to their base. In one of the two desperate rearguard actions, Martin-Leake moved up and down the firing line attending to the wounded. All the men of this small section of the force were either killed or wounded, including Martin-Leake. For his bravery under heavy fire, Martin-Leake was awarded his first Victoria Cross.

This happened on 8 February 1902, as the Anglo Boer war was winding down and both sides were considering making overtures about bringing hostilities to an end. No memorial or marker has ever been placed to indicate the area of this action and thereby recognize its importance. To correct this, a number of people for whom this was a concern, undertook an investigation to see just what could be identified about the movements of the S.A.C.'s reconnaissance patrol that day. The intention is to erect a substantial marker at a suitably significant location.

The South African Constabulary was formed under the leadership and command of Major General Robert S.S. Baden-Powell. He had become famous after his celebrated defence of Mafeking. Besieged by the Boer forces of the Zuid Afrikaansche Republiek of the Transvaal, he held the town for 215 days until relieved in May 1900. Promoted to Major General, he was given the responsibility of recruiting and training the South African Constabulary, a police force for the maintenance of law and order in the Transvaal and Orange Free State, by then annexed as British territory.

The S.A.C. was formed in October 1900 and had a strength of 7,500 men when it was ready to take the field in May 1901. Although nominally under the civilian control of the High Commissioner, Lord Milner, the force was also to serve "as a military force in times of war". By the end of the war the force had grown to 9,500, including men recruited especially for the S.A.C. in Canada and Australia.[2] There were four divisions, A to E (D was the headquarters staff), located in Krugersdorp, Rustenburg, Standerton and Edenburg in the Orange River Colony, as it then was.

Baden-Powell had approval from the Commander-in-Chief, Lord Roberts, to obtain officers, N.C.O.s and men from the army as well as horses and supplies. Baden-Powell's S.A.C. paid better wages than the army and his training methods produced "intelligent young fellows who could use their wits".[3] Members of the S.A.C. had a distinctive uniform, designed by Baden-Powell with stove-pipe leggings, serge jackets with green stripes and an American Stetson hat with a flat brim, which to this day is used by the Boy Scouts movement. In spite of the army's reluctance to let go of their good men, and though horses and supplies were never abundant, the S.A.C. consisted of a "remarkably high stamp of men."[4] There was no urgency to commit the force to the field since at the time of its formation in October 1900, it was thought that the war was almost over. Intended for peacetime police duties, they consequently took the field only in May 1901 and then were used only to man fortified posts within areas already enclosed by blockhouses.[5]

Arthur Martin-Leake was born in 1874 to a family in comfortable circumstances. He entered the University College Hospital in London in 1893 and qualified as a doctor in February 1899. As a student, Martin-Leake worked under Victor Horsley, the foremost neuro-surgeon of his age, assisting or witnessing numbers of his operations on the brain and spinal cord. He qualified as a doctor in February 1899 and obtained membership of the Royal College of Surgeons.

Martin-Leake was House Surgeon at the West Hertfordshire Infirmary when war was declared in South Africa. In Britain there was great enthusiasm for the war and the Martin-Leake family shared this patriotic spirit. There were six Martin-Leake brothers. Stephen, the eldest, was an engineer working in India. William, also in India was with the 1st Cheshire Regiment as was Richard, an engineer. Francis was in the Royal Navy and Theodore was training for the balloon section of the army at Aldershot. There was a widespread feeling that the war would be over by Christmas and Arthur was concerned that he might miss this great adventure. Leave from his duties was readily given by the hospital authorities who clearly shared his patriotic spirit.[6]

A new force, the Imperial Yeomanry was to be raised and Martin-Leake joined the 42nd (Hertfordshire) Company. They embarked for South Africa on 3 March 1900 and finally arrived in Bloemfontein in time to march with Lord Roberts to Pretoria. The 42nd Company I.Y. was part of Major General Broadwood's column chasing the Boer leader, Christiaan de Wet in the area of Pretoria. They were attached to the column which relieved the Australians and Rhodesians

---

[1] The original Warrant is dated 29 January 1856 to which a number of additional warrants were added, the most important being that of King Edward VII in 1902, providing for the posthumous award of the medal.
[2] Miller *Painting the Map Red* pp368-78.
[3] Baden-Powell *Lessons* p218.
[4] *Times History Vol v* p82.
[5] *Times History Vol v* pp325-26.
[6] Clayton *Martin-Leake* pp11-23.

besieged at Elands River but Martin-Leake was intent on gaining a position as a doctor. He left the Yeomanry and was attached to the army as a civil surgeon moving around a number of hospitals including Pienaar's Poort, near Pretoria and then Barberton in the eastern Transvaal (now Mpumalanga).

Disgruntled with his pay and conditions, lack of facilities for study, prospects for advancement and reluctant to join the Royal Army Medical Corps, Martin-Leake managed to join the S.A.C. in May 1901 and one of his letters shows how pleased he was:

> I now hold the rank of Captain. This is a bit of a knock, rather too sudden a rise from nothing. I am moving to Swartkop (near Johannesburg) which is held by the SAC. Nurses have arrived here, so I am delighted to go.[1]

The S.A.C. had a Medical Corporal for each troop of one hundred men whose function was first aid. There was a doctor allocated to any area where a number of troops might be stationed. S.A.C. hospitals were established at each Divisional Headquarters.

Martin-Leake was for some time at an S.A.C. hospital in Meyerton, south of Johannesburg where he was less than satisfied with conditions but he decided to stay on after his three months trial period expired in August. In October 1901 he was transferred to Syferfontein, a short distance north of Val, a station on the main railway line from Johannesburg to Natal, as medical officer of "C" Division of the South African Constabulary. He seems to have been fairly satisfied with this posting:

> They have made me into a travelling M.O. with about 50 miles of line to look after. I like the job, carry a shotgun and have lots of good duck shooting.[2]

His comments about the conduct of the war indicate that he was less than satisfied with this aspect. Writing about the officers in command:

> It seems to me that these people are worse than useless...the only thing they do understand is to dress and to have a good time. I cannot understand how we can ever expect the war to ever come to an end; no wonder the Boers can walk all round us. The line of blockhouses...is a perfect farce; the country behind, which is supposed to be clear, is full of Boers. We must have captured and killed, during the last year, more Boers than ever existed, but yet their numbers in the field seem to increase rather than diminish. Their army as an organised force (has) ceased to exist...but yet we hear now that De Wet has 5000 men and guns in the Free State.[3]

The commanding officer of "C" Division of the S.A.C. was Major J. Fair of the 21st Lancers based at Heidelberg. The "C" Division manned a line of police posts which stretched between the two main railway lines, the line from Johannesburg-Natal and the Pretoria-Delagoa Bay line. Originally the line of Constabulary posts connected the railway lines from Eerstefabrieken, east of Pretoria to Heidelberg. In September 1901 the line was moved further east to between Wilge River Station and Greylingstad. In November the line was moved still further east from Brugspruit on the Delagoa line to Waterval on the Natal railway, with an extension to Villiersdorp (today Villiers). The area west of the line was the so-called "protected area" and was supposedly clear of Boers.[4]

Intelligence reports, probably from local African inhabitants, persistently indicated that a Boer force had encroached into the protected area. Although these were mostly discredited, an order from the Commander-in-Chief, General Lord Kitchener for the line of posts to move further forward, caused Major Fair to order a reconnaissance preparatory to making such a move. The party consisted of 150 men drawn from three troops of "C" Division under the command of Captain Algernon Essex Capell.

They assembled at the farmhouse of Syferfontein (or Cyferfontein), a large farmhouse that had been taken over by the S.A.C. as a fortified post. The stone-built house which still stands was close to the Waterval River which meant a reliable supply of fresh water. It was a very large house with many rooms. A lady of the house once complained that the food was cold by the time it reached the dining room from the kitchen! The ground around was flat and the house was fortified, probably with sandbag redoubts as there is little stone within easy reach.

The patrol set off from Syferfontein at 4 a.m. on 8 February 1902 at which time it would be at least another forty-five minutes before it would even start to get light. They proceeded north east towards the neighbouring farm Vlakfontein[5] and on towards Van Tondershoek. The intelligence was specific that it was on this farm that they might find the Boer laager. The intelligence proved to be accurate. The Boers were hidden in a deep hollow fed by a stream which, even today, has running water summer and winter. A short distance from the hollow was the original Van Tondershoek farmhouse.

These Boers were the men of General Piet Viljoen. After suffering severe losses from British raids at Trichaardsfontein and Witkrans, he had returned to his base at Vaalkop, north of Bethal. Thus his strategy was to move west into the protected area. With 200 men, Commandant Joachim Prinsloo and Field Cornet J.C. Duvenhage made the first incursion into the protected area to be followed on 24 January by another 400 men of the Pretoria, Germiston and Heidelberg commandos. This force, now consisting of perhaps 600 rifles was what was uncovered by Captain Capell's patrol.[6]

Capell's men seem to have rather injudiciously opened fire on the laager but his 150 men were greatly outnumbered. How many Boers were in the laager is a matter of some conjecture. Some accounts say 800, almost certainly an exaggeration – but 600 is credible. If Capell's patrol was able to get as close as 400 yards without detection it is likely that the Boers lay hidden until the last possible moment.

---

[1] Letters quoted in Clayton *Martin-Leake* p59.
[2] Letters quoted in Clayton *Martin-Leake* p61.
[3] Letters quoted in Clayton *Martin-Leake* p62.
[4] *Times History Vol v* pp361 and 398.
[5] Vlakfontein is an extremely common farm name and there must be more than twenty farms in the Transvaal with this name. It is not to be confused with another Vlakfontein to the west of Johannesburg where there was a battle on 29 May 1901.
[6] *Times History Vol v* pp460-61.

When it became obvious that their lair had been detected, they returned fire and attempted to outflank the policemen on both sides.

Now came an orderly retirement back to base at Syferfontein. There were experienced fighters on each side and the running fight took them back over Vlakfontein. There the left and right flank guards were fiercely attacked by the Boers and found themselves unable to join the rest of Captain Capell's men who got away safely. Capell managed to get most of the left flank away but eight men, a Sergeant and an Officer and the Medical Officer, Captain Martin-Leake were unable to find a way to escape. They were engaging some Boers at a distance of 1,600 yards and seemed to be secure until a group of Boers crept up a small donga and opened fire from a flank. All eight men were quickly killed or wounded.

Martin-Leake attended to a number of the men, dressing their wounds and controlling bleeding, all that could be done while under fire. Sergeant Waller was hit in the leg and severely wounded. Martin-Leake attended to him, apparently oblivious of the heavy close-range fire. When Lieutenant Abraham was wounded, a mortal injury, Martin-Leake ran over to him in an attempt to make him more comfortable and ease his pain. It was here that the doctor was shot three times, being wounded in the right hand and left thigh.

The Boers overran the little group but were not inclined to take prisoners. They left them where they lay, expressing regret that they had shot the doctor, and disappeared back the way they had come. The wounded and dead lay where they had fallen for some hours. Help arrived, probably after dark, bringing stretchers, blankets, bandages and water. Men when severely wounded quickly develop a raging thirst and lying for hours in the hot sun must have been agonising. There was at first a limited amount of water but Martin-Leake refused to take his share until all the others had been served.

The right flank was under the command of Lieutenant Swinburne who apparently had twenty-four men with him. A message from Capell did not reach him, the orderly entrusted with its delivery having been shot, but Swinburne's force managed to hold the Boers off until nightfall when they made their way back to Syferfontein. Nevertheless, there were casualties here too, Lieutenant Blackett being killed and a number wounded.[1] The dead and wounded were brought back to Syferfontein where the dead were buried.[2]

Martin-Leake was taken to hospital in Heidelberg where his thigh wound healed easily as did his hand except for the fact that the ulnar nerve had been severed, causing the hand to be paralysed. This would be a disabling wound for a man wishing to become a surgeon but an operation in England in June by Sir Victor Horsley joined the nerve ends and seems to have been partially successful, leaving him with a permanent loss of flexibility. The Victoria Cross was conferred on Martin-Leake by King Edward VII at Windsor Castle on 2 June, the very first post-war ceremony for the presentation of awards and medals.

The Boers did not pursue the S.A.C. patrol. Their hiding place had been discovered and they moved away from Van Tondershoek to the north west where the same men were involved in a much larger clash with the Scots Greys at Klippan on 18 February.[3] This force was later joined by more Heidelbergers under General Hendrik Alberts at the end of February. On 1 April 1902 a patrol of the Queen's Bays, newly arrived in South Africa, "stumbled to their great astonishment on a large Boer laager".[4] Severely outnumbered, they made their way back to base at Boschman's Kop after suffering severe loss.

General Lord Kitchener then mounted an extensive operation in the area in March-April 1902. The British undertook a drive with nearly 15,000 men to trap the elusive Piet Viljoen and his men. The operation failed to net either of the Boer generals or any of their men and by now negotiations were underway to end the war.

The facts concerning the battle where Martin-Leake won his first V.C. are fairly well documented. There is a short account of the action in the official history,[5] while the *Times History* makes no mention of it. Ian Uys's *For Valour* has a good description gleaned from a number of sources, and even a reproduction of a painting from the Royal Army Medical College. Ann Clayton's *Martin-Leake Double VC* has even more detail and makes use of evidence presented to a board of officers convened by Major Fair "for the purpose of enquiring into the reported gallant behaviour of Capt Leake M.O. S.A.C." Nowhere does a sketch map of the scene of the engagement appear.

Maps in the *Times History* and other publications show the lines of police posts stretching between the two main railway lines of the Transvaal. The posts themselves were placed "several miles apart at convenient strategic points". They merely allowed the S.A.C. to maintain a presence in the area since "as a physical barrier they were valueless".[6] The "protected area" was not made totally secure by the line of police posts which was easily penetrated by the Boers.

The various posts utilised a variety of buildings and structures which were in the nature of police stations. The farmhouse at Syferfontein was ideal for the purpose. From there, the exact route of the S.A.C. patrol can only be inferred but certainly they proceeded from Syferfontein, across Vlakfontein to Van Tondershoek. These farms have today been subdivided for modern commercial farming. The deep hollow where the Boer laager lay hidden has now been dammed to exploit the stream which always has water. The Boers would have had very few wagons, if any, and the body of horsemen would have been hidden to any but a close-up observer. There are a number of trees in and above the hollow, some of which clearly date from before the time of the Anglo Boer war. One massive bluegum in particular has a girth and height of exceptional size. Even several hundred men and their horses would have been invisible from a distance among the trees.

---

[1] From accounts of the battle in in Clayton *Martin-Leake* pp64-65 and Uys For Valour pp179-184 who also quotes from a report by Baden-Powell.
[2] In about 1965 the remains were reinterred in Standerton cemetery in the Garden of Remembrance.
[3] *Times History Vol v* p462.
[4] *Times History Vol v* p559.
[5] *History of the War in South Africa Vol IV* pp512-13.
[6] *Times History Vol v* p325-26.

The exact locations of the rearguard actions are well-nigh impossible to locate with any certainty. The Boesmansspruit runs in a south westerly direction along the Vlakfontein boundary. Its high banks would have been the sort of area which would offer numbers of defensible positions. There are several small streams that branch off the Boesmansspruit which could also have afforded cover to the policemen and their Boer adversaries.

Members of the South African Military History Society intend to erect a granite monument at the entrance to Syferfontein farm with the following inscription:

Surgeon Captain Arthur Martin-Leake
1874-1953

In the early morning of 8 February 1902, a patrol, consisting of about 150 policemen of "C" Division of the South African Constabulary, set out from here on Syferfontein to establish the whereabouts of a Boer force under the command of Commandant Piet Viljoen. They came upon Viljoen's men hidden in a deep hollow on the farm Van Tondershoek. The S.A.C. men opened fire, but finding themselves outnumbered, were forced to make a fighting retirement back to their base at Syferfontein. Two rearguard actions took place on Van Tondershoek and Vlakfontein. Surgeon Captain Arthur Martin-Leake was present with a force of eight men commanded by Lieutenant Abraham. Abraham and his men fought until all had been either killed or wounded. Martin-Leake tended the wounded under heavy fire and was himself shot in three places while attempting to make Lieutenant Abraham, who had suffered a mortal wound, more comfortable. The Boers expressed their regret at having shot the doctor. When relief arrived after some hours, Martin-Leake refused water until all the others had been attended to. For this action he was subsequently awarded Britain's highest award for valour, the Victoria Cross.

While serving as a lieutenant in the Royal Army Medical Corps at Zonnebeke in Belgium, Martin-Leake was awarded a second Victoria Cross in 1914 for rescuing, while exposed to constant fire, a large number of wounded who were lying close to enemy trenches. The Bar to his VC was presented to him on 24 July 1915 by King George V at Windsor Castle. He was the first man to be honoured with two V.C.s and only two others have been similarly decorated.

Robin Smith
Howick, June 2011

References

1. R.S.S. Baden-Powell *Lessons from the Varsity of Life* Herbert Jenkins, London 1928.
2. Erskine Childers (Editor) *The Times History of The War in South Africa Vol V* Sampson Low, Marston and Company Limited, London 1907.
3. Ann Clayton *Martin-Leake Double VC* Leo Cooper, London 1994.
4. Captain Maurice Harold Grant *History of the War in South Africa Vol IV* Hurst and Blackett Limited, London 1910.
5. Hertford Library Archive. Letters of Martin-Leake.
6. Karl Köhler *Some Aspects of Lord Baden-Powell and the Scouts at Modderfontein* Military History Journal, Vol 12 No 1, June 2001 South African Military History Society.
7. Jaques Malan *Die Boere-Offisiere 1899–1902* J.P. van der Walt, Pretoria 1990.
8. Carman Miller *Painting the Map Red: Canada and the South African War 1899-1902*, McGill-Queen's University Press, Montreal & Kingston 1993.
9. Ian S. Uys *For Valour* Ian S. Uys, Johannesburg 1973.
10. Wellcome Collecton, London. Letters and documents of Arthur Martin-Leake.

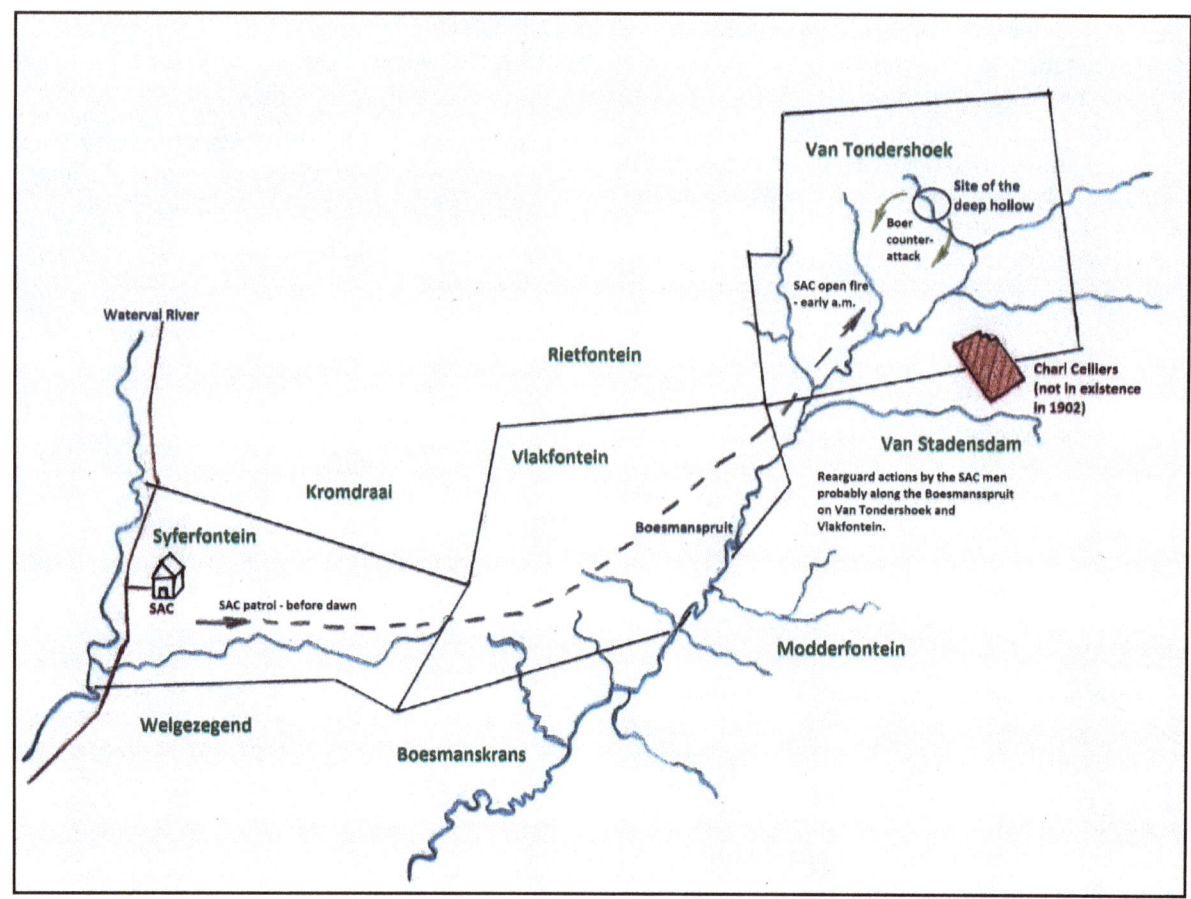

Route of the S.A.C. patrol on 8 February 1902 over the farms Syferfontein and Vlakfontein to Van Tondershoek. The deep hollow where the Boer laager was concealed is a short distance to the north of the small town of Charl Cilliers. The S.A.C. retired back to Syferfontein and their rearguard actions probably were running fights along the Boesmanspruit on Van Tondershoek and Vlakfontein farms.

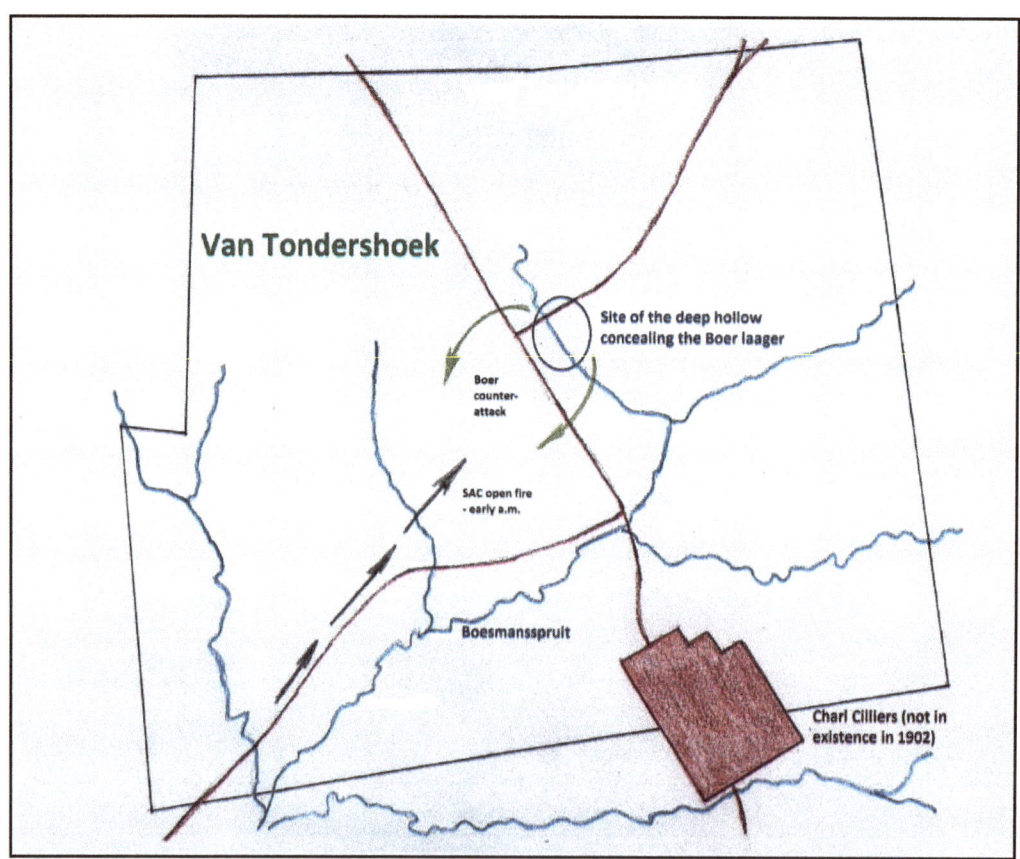

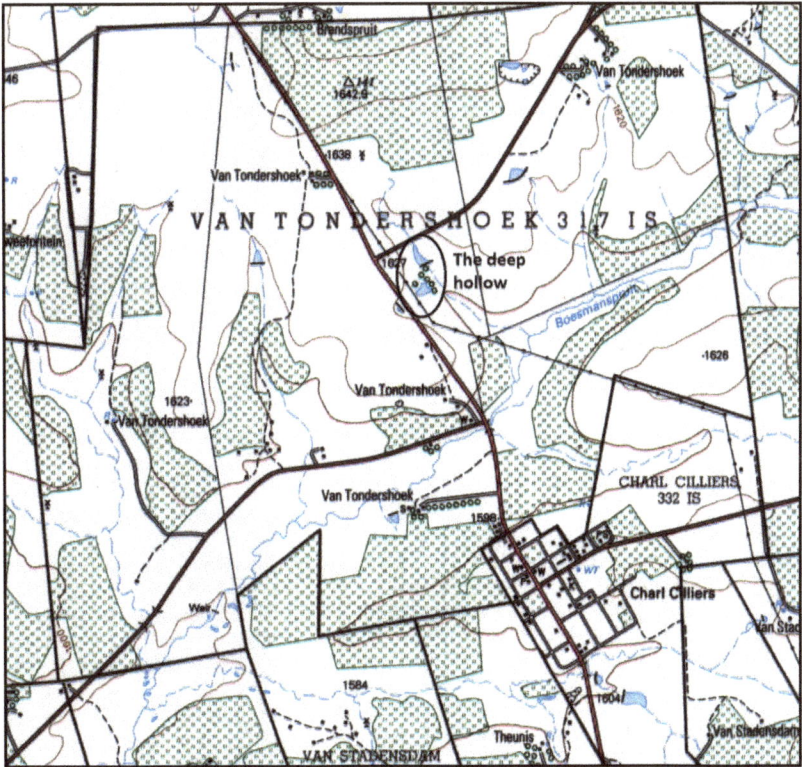

The deep hollow shown on the 1:50 000 ordnance survey map.

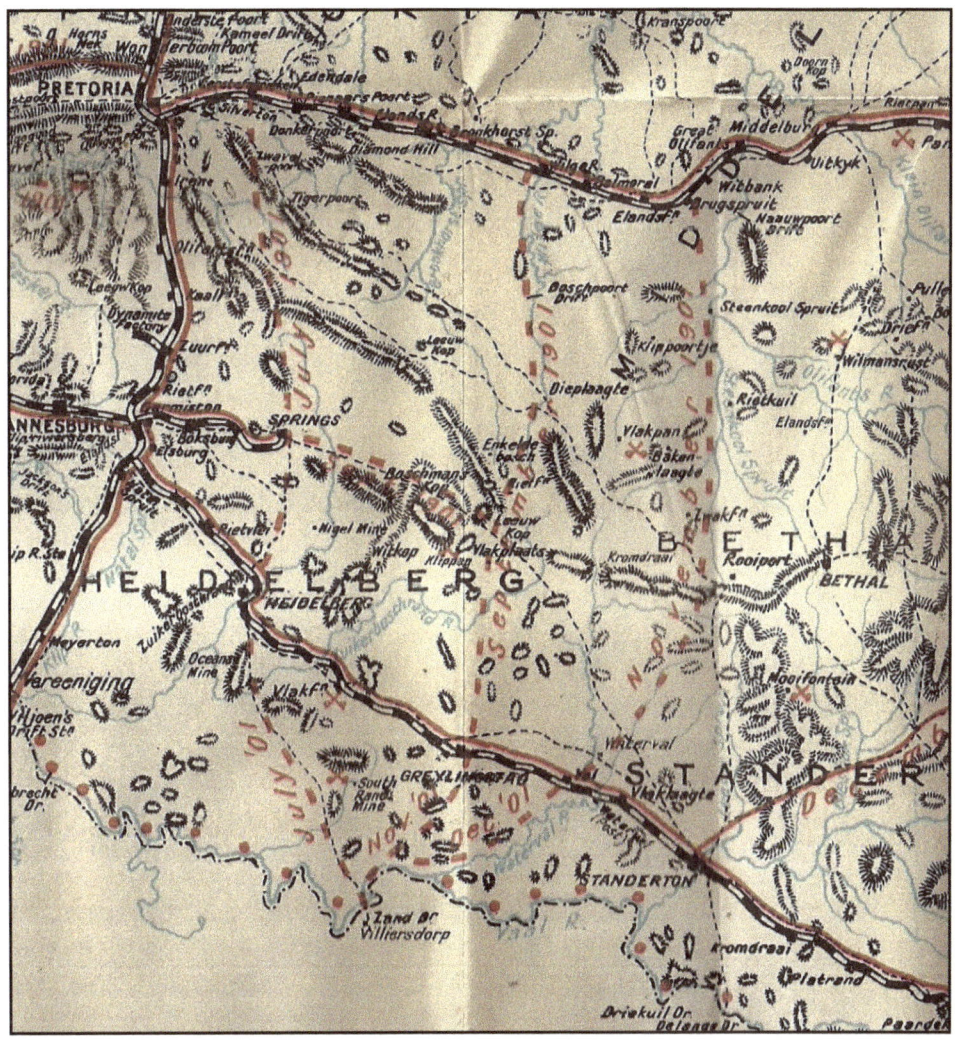

The line of S.A.C. police posts – from the *Times History of the War in South Africa*, Vol V.

Lieutenant Colonel Arthur Martin-Leake, R.A.M.C. – Medals and Decorations:

Victoria Cross and Bar, Queen's South Africa Medal, Clasps: Cape Colony, Transvaal, Wittebergen, King's South Africa Medal, Clasps: SA 1901, SA 1902

1914 Star: Clasp: 5th Aug-22nd Nov 1914, British War Medal 1914-1920, Victory Medal with MID 1914-1919

George V – Silver Jubilee Medal 1935, George VI – Coronation Medal 1937,
Elizabeth II – Coronation Medal 1953

Colonial Aux Forces Officers Decoration, Order of the Red Cross – Montenegro

Martin-Leake wins his first V.C. painting by Cooper in the Army Medical Museum, Aldershot, England.

Trooper Arthur Martin-Leake, Hertfordshire Yeomanry, South Africa, 1900.

Trooper – South African Constabulary.

The Boer commanders: Commandant Joachim Prinsloo and Field Cornet J.C. Duvenhage.

Standerton cemetery, Garden of Remembrance: S.A.C. casualties shown as killed at Van Tonder's Hoek and the memorial headstone of Lieutenants Algernon Blackett and Thomas Abraham. They were all originally buried near the Syferfontein farmhouse.

The abandoned farmhouse at Syferfontein which was one of the police posts of "C" Division of the S.A.C. The S.A.C. casualties were buried nearby until reinterred in Standerton sometime in the 1960s.

The deep hollow on Van Tondershoek where Commandant Prinsloo's Boer commando lay concealed from sight for more than two weeks.

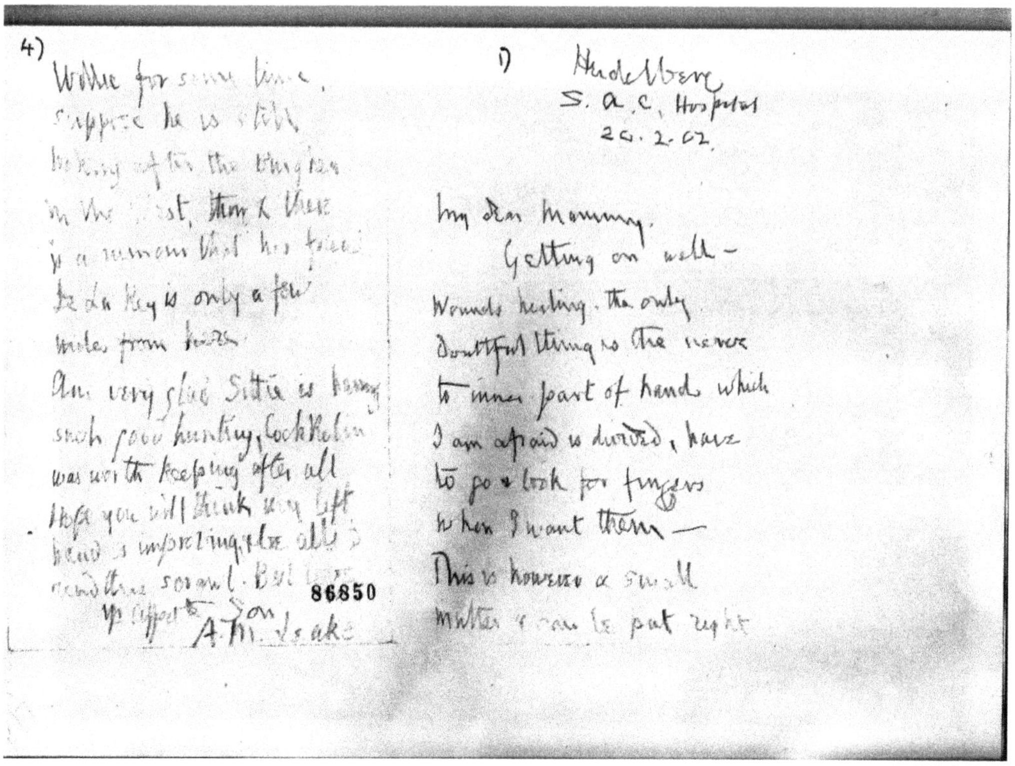

1)
Heidelberg
S.A.C. Hospital
26.2.02.

My dear Mummy,
Getting on well – Wounds healing. The only doubtful thing is the nerve to inner part of hand, which I am afraid is divided, have to go & look for fingers when I want them — This is however a small matter & can be put right

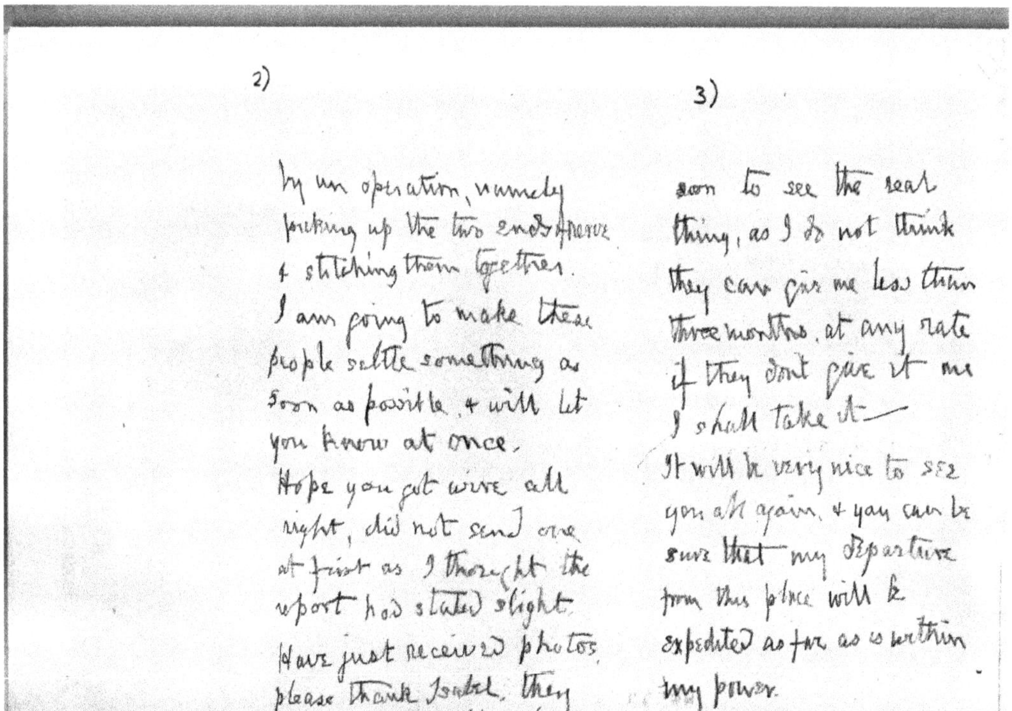

2)
by an operation, namely picking up the two ends of nerve & stitching them together. I am going to make these people settle something as soon as possible & will let you know at once. Hope you got wire all right, did not send one at first as I thought the report had stated slight. Have just received photos, please thank Isabel, they are very good — I expect

3)
soon to see the real thing, as I do not think they can give me less than three months, at any rate if they don't give it me I shall take it —
It will be very nice to see you all again, & you can be sure that my departure from this place will be expedited as far as is within my power.
Have had no news from

4)
Willie for some time, suppose he is still looking after the burghers in the ____, there & there is a rumour that his force De La Rey is only a few miles from here.
Am very glad Sittie is having such good hunting, Cockhalen was worth keeping after all. Hope you will think my left hand is improving & be able to read this scrawl. Best love & regards,
Son
A.M. Leake

86850

Martin-Leake's letter to his mother, written while in hospital at Heidelberg with his left hand since his right hand was paralysed as a result of his wound.

St James's Church, High Cross, Hertfordshire:
Commemorative brass plaque inside the church, the Martin-Leake family plot in the churchyard, Arthur Martin-Leake's grave.

Baden-Powell

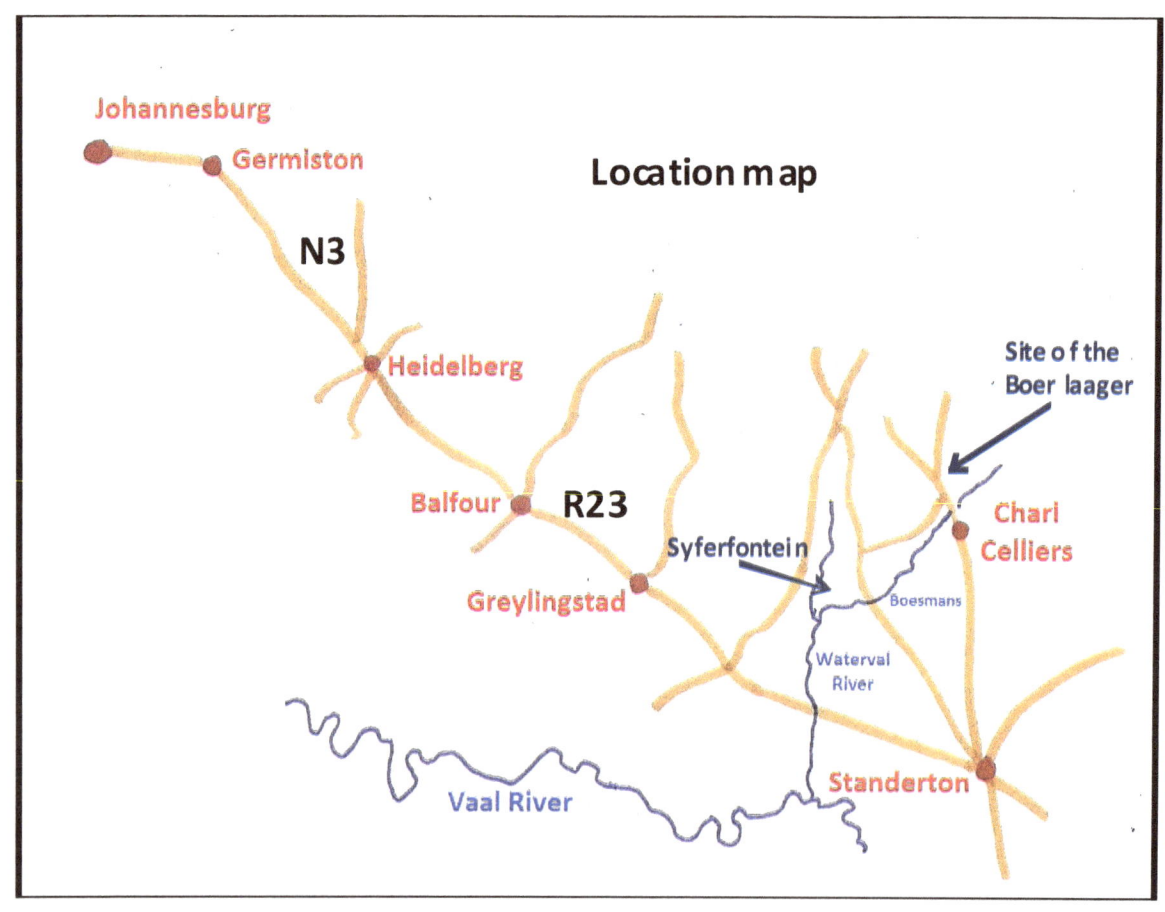

Location map

LANGVERWACHT
23 and 24 February 1902

On the farm Langverwacht, some thirty kilometres south of Vrede, stands the ruined monument to the twenty-three men of the 7th New Zealand Mounted Rifles who were killed nearby on the night of 23 February 1902. They had been part of a British column engaged in sweeping the area so as to flush out the Boer commandos operating in that region. Their quarry was Boer General Christiaan de Wet who had eluded capture for more than two years. He was not to be captured on this night either, as his commandos punched a hole in the British line and disappeared into the night.

By early-1902 the Anglo Boer war was coming to an end but was very far from over. Faced with the highly mobile Boer commandos and their guerilla tactics, the British had evolved new technologies which were taking a serious toll of their adversaries. The eastern Transvaal had been virtually cleared of population and Louis Botha's men had mostly withdrawn to the hills around Vryheid. In the western Transvaal, Koos de la Rey still fell on British columns and convoys whenever an opportunity arose. Jan Smuts was in the north-west Cape and tying down numbers of British troops around O'Okiep. Hertzog and Malan and others operated in the eastern and northern Cape defying every effort to surround and capture them.

It was in the Free State where the most successful of the Boer guerilla leaders, Christiaan de Wet, operated. De Wet may be said to have been the first to advocate and demonstrate the hit-and-run strategy that the British at first found very difficult to counter. That de Wet remained at large was an astounding feat since he was always in the thick of the fighting and many times had been very close to capture. His principal tactic was that of surprise and when he managed to surprise his enemies he was invariably successful.

To protect the railways, the British built small stone forts or blockhouses at strategic points along the railway lines. These were usually two storeys high and had a garrison of thirty men under a sergeant. They were proof against artillery but took too long to build, about three months, and were far too costly at £800 to £1,000 each. As the Boer attacks on the railways became more numerous, something cheaper and more quickly and easily erected was needed. Major Spring Rice of the R.E. then in Middelburg devised a blockhouse made of two concentric cylinders of corrugated iron filled with shingle which was proof at least against rifle bullets and cost but £16. By June 1901 lines of these small forts extended along the railway lines and a start was made on cross-country lines which had a different purpose. They were to be barriers to the free movement of the Boer commandos who were now to be driven and cornered against them.[1]

At first, British strategy was to raid the Boer laagers so as to arrive at dawn. This needed good intelligence of Boer whereabouts and highly mobile columns which could cover long distances at night so as to surprise the Boers at daybreak. De Wet and President Marthinus Steyn with the Free State government had a number of hiding places in the north eastern area of the Free State, centred on the small village of Reitz and with heliograph communications from some of the prominent hill tops. They were able to concentrate their forces when necessary and scatter if a large British force appeared. Places that they frequented in the Reitz area were de Wet's own farm Blijdschap and Slabbert's farm, Rondebosch. The ailing Free State President was able to rest at Rondebosch for some weeks and busy himself with the business and correspondence of the Free State government.

Early in February 1902 a new system of sweeping was attempted. Up until then the Boers had been able to pass the British lines when night fell and gaps in the line opened up as the troops bivouacked. With the blockhouse lines now complete and reinforced for the occasion of a drive, the mounted troops would now form a continuous line ninety kilometres in length. The flanks of the line would be on a blockhouse line and the horsemen would maintain the line riding straight ahead by day. At night every officer and every man would be on picket duty in a continuous entrenched line of pickets. In theory in this way there would be no holes in the net and every Boer commando would be hedged in by the line of horsemen, the blockhouses with their wire entanglements and armoured trains on the railway lines. To maintain such a line over broken country with hills and rivers to be crossed required discipline and skill, not to mention endurance since the drives covered fifteen to twenty kilometres per day for a week or more.[2]

De Wet's whereabouts needed to be established before a decision was made by the British as to the direction of the first attempt at the new model drive. His base near Elandskop, today's village of Petrus Steyn, was well-known but all attempts to nab him there had thus far failed. Colonel Julian Byng camped at Fannie's Home on a bluff overlooking the Liebenberg's Vlei river early in February 1902. Sending Lieutenant Colonel Garatt to Roodekraal and Armstrong Drift on the Liebenberg's Vlei river they came across the rear-guard of a Boer force under Commandant Walter Mears on 3 February. Mears had been ordered to bring the guns captured by de Wet at Groenkop on Christmas Day 1901 across the blockhouse line between Lindley and Bethlehem. Garatt's men included the 7th New Zealand Mounted Rifles who had "a hard gallop and a running fight of some miles" in succeeding to rout the Boer rearguard and recapture the lost guns. Major Bauchop, their commander received a personal telegram from Lord Kitchener and Garratt, "gratified the New Zealanders by assuring them that it was one of the best mounted charges he had ever seen." The guns would have been valuable to the Boers had they but had the chance to use them.[3]

With intelligence that de Wet was in the vicinity of Elandskop, the British line was formed along the Liebenberg's Vlei River in a line ninety kilometres long. The sweep to the west as far as the main railway line was detected by de Wet's scouts and he moved south with his force of seven hundred men who had joined him at Slangfontein. Managing to avoid the advancing British line they crossed the Kroonstad-Lindley blockhouse line on the farm Doornkloof on the night of 6 February heading for the Doornberg, north west of Senekal. The British swept on westwards and closed off the area between America Siding on the main line and Heilbron on the night of 7 February. Several hundred Boers were known to be within the cordon and every possible means was used to ensure their capture. Some managed to cut their way out but nearly three hundred were killed, wounded or captured.

Lieutenant Edward Gordon of the R.S.F. wrote in his diary of the last night of the drive: "Firing almost continuous all night. There were undoubtedly a number of Boers trying the line at various places all along to find good places for breaking thro'. About eight armoured trains could be counted on the main line and the Heilbron branch line, by their searchlights going all night. It was a wonderful sight, like a great display of fireworks with the beams of searchlights flashing all over the sky and a continual roar of rifle fire, punctuated by the rattle of a Maxim or the report of a field gun. It was about the most wonderful night I've ever spent and didn't sleep a wink all night."[4]

The first drive had failed to capture their principal target but a second, much larger scale drive was now planned. A segment of the Transvaal to the south of the Natal railway would be the initial target when the line would wheel right and sweep down the north eastern Free State between the Wilge River and the Drakensberg. This time nearly thirty thousand troops were involved and the drive would take nearly two weeks. De Wet, hearing that the coast was clear, had returned to Elandskop, crossing the blockhouse line once again but this time under fire and losing two killed and eight wounded. In preparation for the second drive, Major-General Elliot reached Lindley on 16 February, making for the Wilge River as his men were to form the line along the river. Receiving intelligence of de Wet's whereabouts near Elandskop, he sent Lieutenant-Colonel de Lisle to capture him but once again de Wet was not where he was supposed to be.

The following day de Wet rode eastwards and joined the government at Rondebosch. President Steyn had remained there and had been well outside the limits of the first drive. De Wet's intelligence, for once was faulty and on the approach of Elliot from the west he made the decision to cross the Wilge River and break through the British line somewhere near the Drakensberg. President Steyn and the government would have to come too as Elliot's men approached. The government documents were hidden in a cave not far from Rondebosch, together with de Wet's clothing and some ammunition.[5]

On the night of 22 February they had reached the Cornelis river and Commandant Manie Botha and his Vrede commando joined them. Botha told them of the British force sweeping in a line from the Wilge to the Drakensberg. They were thus in danger of being trapped against the Bethlehem-Harrismith blockhouse line. All manner of people had fled the British sweep and joined up with de Wet and his commandos. Shortly they were joined by two more Commandants, Alexander Ross and his men from Frankfort as well as Hendrik Alberts and some men from Heidelberg. There were also significant numbers of people and their animals who had left their farms and were fleeing southwards. On the 23rd the crowd followed the commandos as they moved along the left bank of the Cornelis River. By late afternoon they had arrived at the farm Brakfontein to the south of the Witkoppe. De Wet had intended to skirt the Witkoppe to the east and travel north up the valley to Strydplaas but his scouts told him that the British held a strong position at the head of the valley.[6]

Unable to delay until the next morning, de Wet resolved to break through the British line at Kalkkloof. Colonel Michael Rimington's line stretched from Pramkop, which practically overlooked the Wilge River, to Mooifontein where it joined with Colonel Julian Byng. From Vrede southwards the country is rolling grassland and the columns were able to maintain their line with little difficulty. The line swept over the Bothasberg, low hills rather than mountains as their name would seem to imply, but the Kalkkloof provided something more of an obstacle. The left of Byng's line, the 7th New Zealand Mounted Rifles, filed down across the valley of the Holspruit and formed their line along the crest of the next high ground to the south on the farm Langverwacht. To join up with the left of Rimington's line, Lieutenant-Colonel Cox's 3rd New South Wales Mounted Rifles, they had to stretch their line so as to reach up a kloof leading to the farm Mooifontein and Rimington's line which was north of the Holspruit. At the head of the kloof Captain R.A Begbie of the Royal Artillery placed a pom-pom in a small redoubt of stones that they quickly erected.

The Boer scouts, seeing this kink in the line, assumed that there was a gap but there was none. The New Zealanders were entrenched in pickets of six men but inevitably there was a small gap where the line crossed the Holspruit. This stream, like all the rivers and streams in the vicinity, has high banks which constitute something of a barrier to the easy passage of horses and vehicles.

The Boer multitude left Brakfontein once it was dark and retraced their steps of that afternoon along the valley of the Cornelis River. The commandos led the way followed by the crowd of carts and spiders and the herds of cattle and horses. They arrived at the Holspruit at midnight and de Wet and Steyn and his mule wagon crossed over at a ford where today there is a bridge over the river. The commandos had skirted the road to the east and moved towards what they supposed would be an undefended portion of the line. The three commandos would have constituted a force of seven hundred men and they were mostly veteran soldiers. They advanced in two groups, one quietly up the bed of the Holspruit.

The New Zealanders had heard the noise of the Boer multitude for some time and were alert. The sentries had heard the "lowing of cattle, the rumbling of wagons and the voices of women" and roused the men who were sleeping after a good meal of roast sheep. The Boers in the donga, the bed of the Holspruit managed to get in behind the line while the rest of the force rushed one of the pickets. Of the six men in the trench, five were killed. Ross and Manie Botha and their men now turned left and advanced along the line of trenches in a half-circle. The New Zealanders were concerned about hitting their own men if they fired along the trench line but soon put up a stout resistance although under fire from all sides. "The fire was something terrific. Bullets! They were just like hail stones falling on cabbage leaves", wrote Trooper Lytton Ditely from the hospital in Harrismith where he was taken after the fight.

Sergeant Minifie of the 7th New Zealand M.R. was stationed with the pom-pom and had run out of ammunition but heard that a new case of ammunition was coming up. He rallied his men and managed to hold on for about another fifteen minutes. The pom-pom fired twenty or more rounds and then jammed. Captain Begbie was killed and the Boers came close to capturing the gun but Minifie and his men managed to run it down the hill where it ended up in a small ravine. The further advance of the Boers up the kloof and onto the high ground of the farm Mooifontein was stopped by the 3rd New South Wales M.R. Colonel C.F. Cox "fought like a tiger" and had formed a line across the head of the kloof with four of his pickets. No medals were awarded for this action but Kitchener's chief of staff, Lieutenant-General Ian Hamilton wrote to Lord Roberts on 27 February to say that "the New Zealanders, who are about our best men...did not belie their reputation on this occasion."[7]

De Wet had tried to get all his men to charge the line and resorted to his sjambok to persuade the slackers to move forward. Notwithstanding this, many of them fled probably because of the unexpected resistance. There was now a gap in the line and many of the fighting men were able to get through with some of the cattle and horses. They rushed along the flat ground on the right bank of the Holspruit and up a valley which took them to safety and onto the high ground. De Wet and Steyn were with them and the two men in charge of de Wet's little wagon also managed to get through the gap. They headed for the Bothasberg and spent the night on the farm Bavaria where a wounded member of President Steyn's bodyguard died as well as a young boy named Olivier. The next day they returned to the site of the fight to find that the British had departed after burying the Boer dead.

Twenty-three New Zealanders were killed and forty-four more were wounded, most of them from Canterbury and Otago in the South island. They were buried in a mass grave on Langverwacht farm and in 1903 a monument was erected on the burial site.[8] Captain A.R.G. Begbie of the R.G.A. was killed as too was Bombadier J. Ryan. Colonel Cox apparently had three men wounded but there is no record of this in the casualty roll. Boer casualties were also considerable. De Wet admits to eleven dead and twelve wounded but the Boer practice of carrying away their dead could mean that several more were killed.

Only three days later nearly six hundred Boers under Commandant Jan Meyer surrendered to the Imperial Light Horse, part of Colonel Sir Henry Rawlinson's column, on the farm Strathnairn in the Harrismith district. Langverwacht was thus the last engagement of any consequence in this part of the Free State. De Wet and the President, who was now seriously ill, managed to break through the blockhouse lines in their path and cross the Vaal River to meet up with Koos de la Rey. Steyn was suffering ataxia or lack of control of the limbs caused by some kind of neurological disorder and de la Rey's respected doctor von Rennenkampf was unable to give much relief.[9] Lacking the inspired leadership that de Wet had provided, the commandos in that part of the Free State could do little more than avoid capture in the last three months of the war.

Apart from the monument on the burial site at Langverwacht, there are two places in New Zealand where their men are remembered. Farrier Leonard Retter was from Johnsonville, now a suburb of Wellington in the North Island and his father was the blacksmith. Two other of his sons served in New Zealand contingents in the Anglo Boer war. A monument now stands in Moorefield Road in Johnsonville and a short distance away are memorial gates at the entrance to the public park. In Amberley, still a small village north of the city of Christchurch in the South Island, there is a monument to Farrier Sergeant O.H. Turner. The inscription reads, "To thine own self be true" which was written on a piece of paper found on his body. No monument exists for the Boers who died at Langverwacht but the names of those members of the Vrede commando who died in various places during the war are inscribed on the monument in the Vrede Dutch Reformed church garden.[10]

De Wet and the President left Rondebosch on 5 March heading north to the western Transvaal. Before he left, the mule cart was abandoned at a farm, presumably General Wessel Wessel's Lovedale. His personal effects were concealed in a cave together with the government documents as already related. On 4 March Elliot's column started on a sweep northwards on both sides of the Wilge River. Major Charlie Ross and his Canadian Scouts held one portion of the line and they stumbled upon the cave to unearth "310 000 rounds of small-arm ammunition, several hundred shells for field artillery...three sets of field signaling apparatus, all this from under the feet of a British garrison of long standing."[11] Two weeks previously, on 22 February, the South African Light Horse from Elliot's column guarding the Wilge River had skirmished along the Rus se Spruit without finding the cave. Ross also found de Wet's embroidered sash of office which now belongs to author Neil Speed in Australia. De Wet, on his journey northwards "had only the clothes that I was then wearing. I would have sent for another suit had I not heard that the enemy were encamped close to the cave where our treasures lay hidden."[12]

Sources and notes

1. The blockhouse system is the subject of a complete chapter in *The Times History of the War in South Africa* (see v pp396-412). See also *Britain's Last Castles* by Richard Tomlinson in the *South African Military History Journal* Vol 10 No 6 of December 1997.

2. See *The Times History of the War in South Africa* v pp467-473 for a description of the new system. Colonel M.F. Rimington's orders are detailed on v pp476-477.

3. There are numerous accounts of this action but it is impossible to establish exactly where the clash took place. See J. Lourens and J.AJ. Lourens *Te na aan ons hart* pp49-52, *The Times History of the War in South Africa* p475, Christiaan de Wet *Three Years War* and *New Zealanders in the Anglo Boer War* from the internet for various versions.

4. From Lieutenant E.I.D. Gordon's diary now in possession of his son, Major Antony Gordon and unpublished.
5. This "cave" is well-known locally and is a hollow within what was once an overhang. Hundreds or thousands of years ago the shelf fell down and access is through and over the rubble of the rockfall.
6. The name of the farm Brakfontein was changed some years later to Blijdskap, presumably in recognition of de Wet's short visit on 23 February.
7. There exist a number of accounts of this fight. See *The Times History of the War in South Africa* v pp489-490, Christiaan de Wet *Three Years War* and *New Zealanders in the Anglo Boer War* from the internet. Also Chamberlain and Drooglever *The War with Johnny Boer* has an extract from Major G.K. Ansell's staff diary of Rimington's column and letters from members of Cox's 3rd NSW MR. Hamilton's letter to Lord Roberts is given in full in *Lord Roberts and the war in South Africa 1899-1902* editor André Wessels. J.G. Kestell *Through Shot and Flame* contests some versions that contend that the Boer attack was behind a large herd of cattle.
8. The monument remained intact until 2003 when one of the oaks, evidently planted when the monument was built, collapsed after a grass fire, demolished the stone column and damaged the marble plaque with the names of the fallen. Hopefully it will be rebuilt as it forms an important link with the heroic actions of all concerned that night in 1902.
9. See Meintjies *President Steyn* p172.
10. See Willem L.E. Naude *Maar doodkry is min* pp146,153 and 155.
11. See *The Times History of the War in South Africa* v p476.
12. Christiaan de Wet *Three Years War* p307 and see J. Lourens and J.A.J. Lourens *Te Na Aan Ons Hart* pp54-59 for detail of the action along Rus-se-Spruit and Neil Speed *Born to Fight* pp126-130 concerning the discovery of the cave.

Bibliography

1. L.S. Amery *The Times History of the War in South Africa* Volume v. Sampson Low, Marsten and Company, London 1907.
2. J. Lourens and J.AJ. Lourens *Te na aan ons hart* Privately published in Reitz, Free State 2002.
3. Willem L.E. Naude *Maar doodkry is min* Privately published in Vrede, Free State 2001.
4. Christiaan de Wet *Three Years War* Archibald Constable and Company, London 1902.
5. Max Chamberlain and Robin Drooglever *The War with Johnny Boer* Australian Military History Publications, Loftus, Australia 2003.
6. André Wessels editor *Lord Roberts and the war in South Africa 1899-1902* Sutton Publishing Limited, Stroud, Gloucestershire, 2000 for the Army Records Society.
7. J.D. Kestell *Through Shot and Flame* Methuen and Company, London 1903.
8. Johannes Meintjies *President Steyn* Nasionale Boekhandel, Cape Town 1969.
9. Neil Speed *Born to Fight* The Caps and Flints Press, Melbourne, 2002.
10. Unpublished diary of Lieutenant E.I.D. Gordon of the 2nd Batallion, Royal Scots Fusiliers.
11. *The South African War Casualty Roll* J.B. Hayward & Son, Polstead, Suffolk 1982. Reprint of War Office document of 1902.
12. D.O.W. Hall *The New Zealanders in South Africa 1899-1902* War History Branch, Department of Internal Affairs, Wellington 1949.

Commandant Alexander Ross, Colonel Michael Rimington.

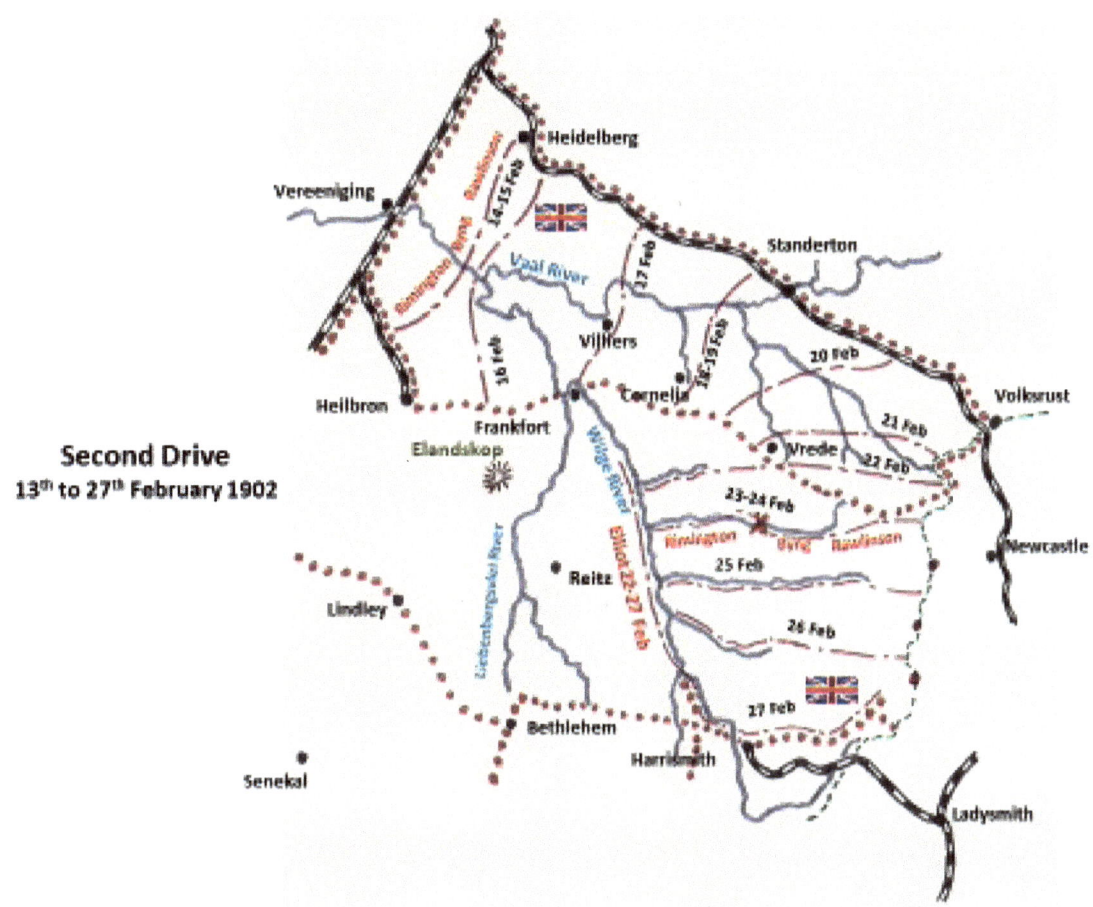

Red dots are blockhouse lines.

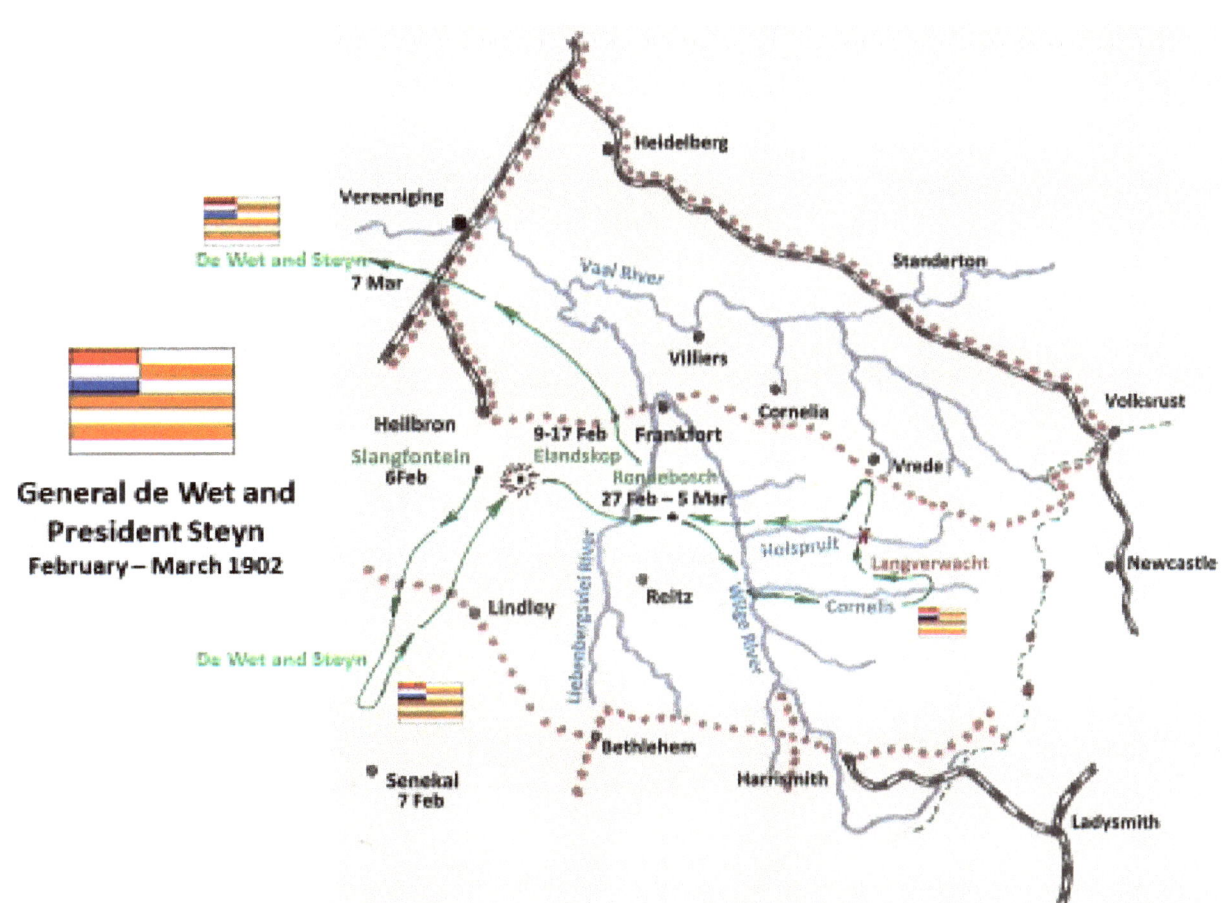

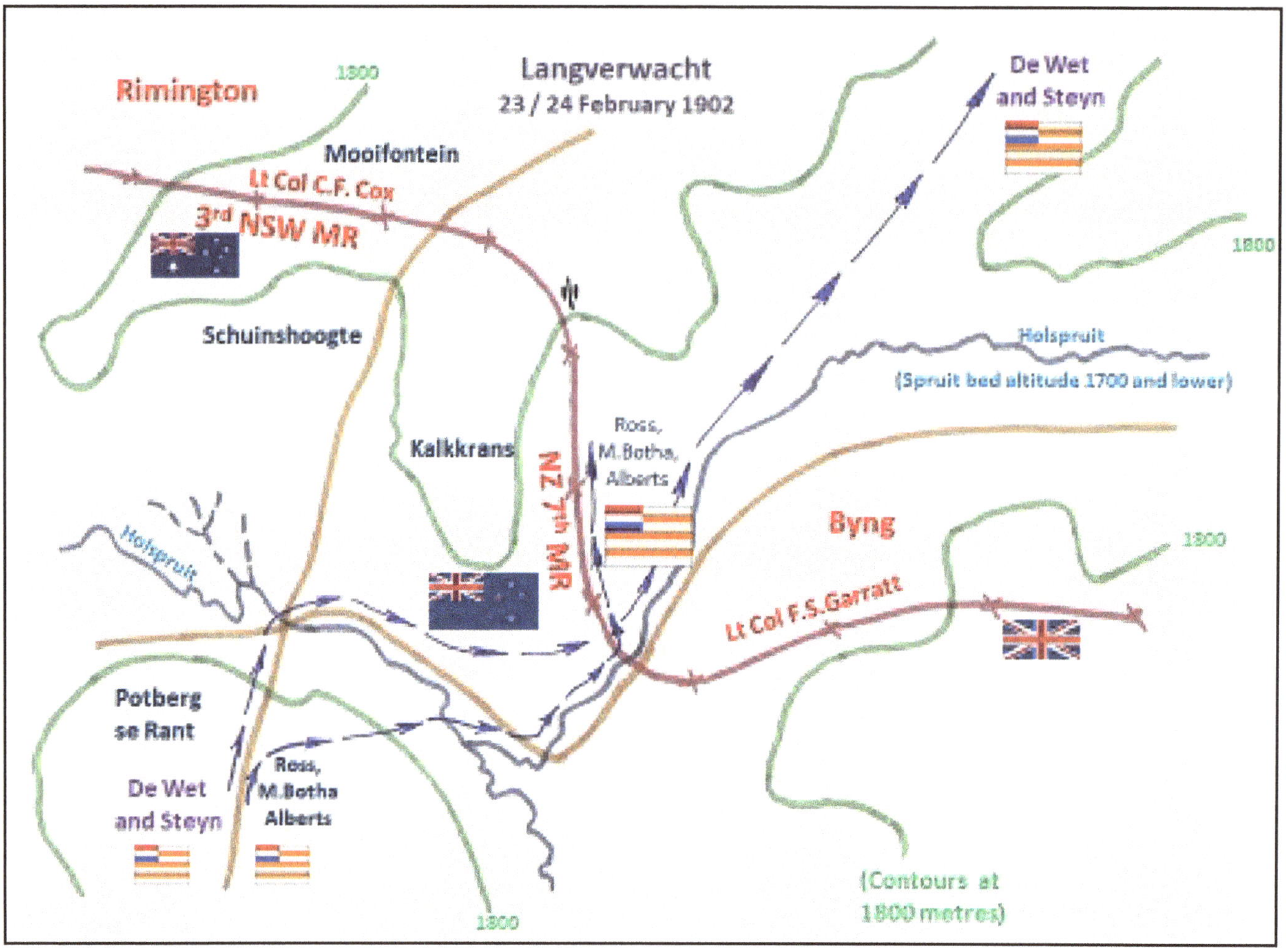

The ruined monument in 2006.

The mass grave in 1903 – on the site of the present monument.

General Christiaan De Wet, President Marthinus Steyn,
Colonel JulianByng, Lieutenant-Colonel F.S. Garrett.

The Final Struggle with de la Rey

How the battle sites – and the graves of those who died there – look today

By March 1902 the war seemed to be in its last phase. Most of the action had moved to the western Transvaal (now North-West Province). General Louis Botha's principal commandos had moved from the eastern Transvaal (now Mpumalanga Province) and settled in the mountainous country to the north of Vryheid. The British scorched earth policy had almost completely denuded large areas of the eastern Highveld of crops and livestock. Even the Boers, renowned for their ability to live off the country, could not survive under these conditions.

Christiaan de Wet was concerned about the health of the Orange Free State Republic President, Marthinus Steyn. On the night of 23/24 January he and some men of the Heidelberg and Vrede commandos had broken through a British line of drive at Langverwacht, on the Holspruit south of Vrede. In the next two weeks De Wet and the seriously ill President evaded British columns, crossed a blockhouse line, forded the Vaal River, and crossed into the western Transvaal.[1] General Koos de la Rey had a German doctor, Karl Gustav von Rennenkampf,[2] who, it was hoped would be able to treat the President but he was unable to provide much relief.[3]

De la Rey controlled most of the vast area between the Zwartruggens and the Vaal River and the British had only three small columns operating in this area while they concentrated on Botha and de Wet. On 30 September de la Rey attacked the column of Colonel Robert Kekwich, the defender of Kimberley during the siege in 1899, at Moedwil. Lieutenant Colonel von Donop was attacked at Kleinfontein, east of Zeerust on 24 October. There was sporadic action in the area, both sides having successes and failures, until February. Commandant Sarel Alberts's commando was pounced on and Alberts and 132 of his men were captured at Gruisfontein, fifteen miles east of Lichtenburg on 4 February 1902.

Shortage of ammunition caused de la Rey's inaction but, by early 1902, both Botha in the east and de Wet in the Free State were hard pressed, and appealed to de la Rey to take to the field.[4] Lieutenant General Lord Methuen left for Vryburg to attend to some administrative work on 8 February leaving Colonel S.B. von Donop in field command. His orders were for Von Donop "to occupy the town of Wolmaransstad and use it as a base of operations."[5] That night, the newly-promoted Colonel acted on intelligence that a concentration of Boers under Commandant F.J. Potgieter was at Elandslaagte, eleven miles west of Klerksdorp. Attacking at dawn he captured 36 of them, Potgieter narrowly escaping by riding bareback clad only in his shirt.[6]

Wolmaransstad was isolated and was not on a railway line so that it was dependent for supplies on convoys. It was fifty miles from the railhead at Klerksdorp. The first supply column left Klerksdorp on 11 February, discharged its load and returned on the 18 without incident. A second convoy started its three-day return journey on the 23rd and camped that night at Kareeboomskuil. On the following evening the convoy camped on a gentle western slope on the bank of the Yzerspruit on the farm Elandslaagte. Under the command of Lieutenant Colonel W.C. Anderson, it did not seem likely that there would be any danger attending the short march into Klerksdorp.[7]

Accompanying the convoy, but not really part of the escort, were seventy-eight men of Paget's Horse, proceeding on special duty to Klerksdorp. They did not camp at Elandslaagte but continued on their march. De la Rey had concentrated his forces under Commandants Liebenberg, Celliers and Kemp at Jakkalsfontein, expecting the British column to take a more northerly route. He was on the lookout for an opportunity to replenish his ammunition. His scouts had reported the departure of the convoy from Wolmaransstad, and he planned to capture, not the wagons which he must have known to be empty, but the guns and ammunition.

In the early morning of the 25 February De la Rey attacked the moving column. Liebenberg, with a frontal attack on the front of the column, was to attract most of Anderson's troops to defend the wagons. Celliers was to assault the rear, now only lightly defended while Kemp was to make a flank attack and drive the column into disorder. Anderson organized a strong defence but was overwhelmed by De la Rey's superior numbers. The Boers captured 145 mule wagons and some ammunition as well as two field guns and three machine guns.[8] J.F. Naudé, of Kemp's staff acquired a Kodak on the battlefield and there after took numerous pictures of historical interest – he must also have acquired a number of roll films as well, judging from the number of his snapshots that have survived.[9] No less than 187 of the 490 British were killed or wounded while the Boers lost 51, "including their young General Lemmer."[10]

Von Donop from Wolmaransstad, joined by reinforcements from Klerksdorp and Bothaville, met at the Wolvespruit to find no trace of the Boers and the captured wagons. He returned to Wolmaransstad to be joined by Colonel R.G. Kekewich who had marched from Hartebestefontein. It was decided that holding Wolmaransstad had become precarious and the town was evacuated and its fortifications destroyed. Plans were set in motion to recover

---

[1] See Robin Smith *Langverwacht* SA Military History Journal, December 2006
[2] Davidson and Filatova *The Russians and the Anglo-Boer War* has biographical details of von Rennenkampf.
[3] de Villiers *Healers, Helpers and Hospitals* Vol II pp167-170 gives details of President Steyn's illness.
[4] Childers *The Times History of the War in South Africa* Vol V p498.
[5] Childers *The Times History of the War in South Africa* Vol V p497.

[6] Maurice *History of the war in South Africa* Vol. 4 p410.
[7] Maurice *History of the war in South Africa* Vol. 4 p410.
[8] Maurice *History of the war in South Africa* Vol. 4 p412.
[9] J.F. Naudé *Veg en Vlug van Beyers en Kemp* p289.
[10] Maurice *History of the war in South Africa* Vol. 4 p415. Malan *Die Boere Offisiere* p40 has General H.R. Lemmer killed in December 1900 in an attack on a column commanded by Lieutenant C.G. Money between Lichtenburg and Marico.

the convoy lost to the Boers. Kekewich gave Lieutenant Colonel H.M. Grenfell command of a column of 1,654 horsemen with four guns and sent them to Rietfontein, west of Hartbeesfontein. Methuen took the field from Vryburg, the strategy, according to his orders, being to prevent de la Rey from moving north into the Marico district.

Methuen's column and that of Grenfell were to concentrate at Rooirandjesfontein,[1] south of Lichten-burg, where two main roads cross, on 8 March. Grenfell was at Leeuwfontein on 6 March and at the rendezvous as agreed on the 8th. Colonel A.N Rochfort's column was to advance from the south to drive the Boers towards this concentration. Methuen's column of 1,300 men was assembled from his Vryburg garrison and railway guards. The mounted troops, 900 in number from a number of different units, police as well as some "surrendered Dutchmen" and "for fighting against de la Rey's veterans they were wholly unsuitable." The column was unwieldy with 39 ox-wagons and 46 mule wagons and set out for a "long journey through one of the most desolate districts of the Transvaal."[2]

Hampered by oxen in poor condition and lack of water, the column only covered twenty miles in the first two days, camping at Grootpan and then Barber's Pan. Methuen wired Kekewich that he would be late. The column crossed into the flat, featureless country at the junction of the two Harts Rivers and made for Tweebosch rather than Leeuwkuil where his scouts reported that there was no water. J.A. van Zyl with a small force from Bloemhof hovered around the rearguard all day. At one stage they fired on Methuen's rearguard who behaved badly under fire and Methuen himself had to restore order so as to disperse the Boers.

The next morning, 7 March they now headed towards Leeukuil.[3] De la Rey was at Doornbult with intelligence about the two columns that were to converge on Rooirandjiesfontein. Grenfell's mobile force of more than 1,500 men was the sort of enemy to be avoided but Methuen's cumbersome slow-moving column was likely prey. In the early morning of the 7th his skirmishers attacked the rear of the column near De Klipdrift. With the same force and generals who had attacked Anderson at Yzerfontein, Kemp, Celliers, Vermaas and van Zyl who had shadowed Methuen for the last few days, de la Rey handled his riflemen with great skill.

There was scattered resistance along the column which had spread out on leaving the camp at Tweebosch and now stretched out over several miles. Methuen did his best to close his men up into a more compact formation and the guns of the 38th Battery kept some of the Boers at bay for a while. Methuen's horse was shot and his leg was badly broken when the horse rolled on him. A rout ensued and the guns were left unguarded. Lieutenant Nesham, in command of the section, was shot down refusing an offer of surrender.

Major Paris rallied about forty men in a stone kraal and held out for about two hours until the Boers brought into action the guns captured at Yzerspruit.

Casualties were surprisingly less than at Yzerspruit a fortnight before, 68 killed and 132 wounded. There were numbers of fugitives scattered over the veld making for Kraaipan and Maribogo on the western railway line and Methuen's column was completely destroyed. Lieutenant General Lord Methuen was the highest ranked officer captured by the Boers. He had suffered an open fracture of the thigh and de la Rey's Russian doctor, Karl Gustav von Rennekampf, set his leg and made him as comfortable as he could. Von Rennenkampf was a German from Tallinn, Estonia then part of the Russian Empire. He was "not only a very good doctor but clearly also an extremely good organizer and a man of real humanity."[4]

Many of de la Rey's men were against releasing Methuen and returning him to hospital at Klerksdorp which is what the gentlemanly Boer general proposed to do. Certain of the Boer burghers were unhappy about this and were against releasing such a high prize but his generals did not oppose de la Rey's course of action and Methuen, after a cordial meeting with Mrs Nonnie de la Rey, was sent off to hospital in Klerksdorp. Kemp himself said, in an interview with G.F. Gibson of the I.L.H.:

> *Lord Methuen's wound was dressed by General de la Rey's doctor, V. Reinkamp and by Dr Mathuen, a military doctor, and he was put into his wagonette and sent to Klerksdorp. He was later stopped by a militant Predikant (Minister) who harangued the Burghers: "Why should we release this leader of the Amalekites, whom the Lord hath delivered inot our hands; we should keep him as a hostage of war." General de la Rey got to hear of this and called a meeting of the Commando the following morning. The General in an address said: "Burghers, I note that you don't want the English Lord released, but don't forget that harshness and brutality begets harshness and brutality, just in the same way as chivalry and humanity begets chivalry and humanity. Now in the future I or General Kemp may be wounded and fall into the hands of the English – then, what would you think if we were badly treated?" On this the Burghers agreed with their General and Lord Methuen was sent into Klerksdorp.[5]*

Tweebosch was certainly a serious setback and the Commander in Chief, Lord Kitchener was disturbed by it.[6] However, these two Boer successes were tactical and did not greatly disturb the British strategy in the western Transvaal. Neither Botha nor de Wet were now capable of

---

[1] The modern survey map gives the name of this place as "Rooijansfontein".

[2] Childers *The Times History of the War in South Africa* Vol V p502.

[3] Childers *The Times History of the War in South Africa* Vol V p504 says that "Methuen, having learnt that there was water at Leeuwkuil,…" while Maurice *History of the war in South Africa* Vol. 4 p417 has "Learning that the place was waterless…" about Leeuwkuil.

[4] Davidson and Filatova *The Russians and the Anglo-Boer War* p155.

[5] Gibson *The Story of the Imperial Light Horse* pp335-6. See Meintjies *De la Rey Lion of the West* pp239-44 for more detail of this episode. Meintjies also quotes from Davitt *The Boer Fight for Freedom* but has reservations about Davitt's objectivity. Wessels *Lord Kitchener and the War in South Africa* pp204 and 318 has some detail of Methuen being held at Gestoptefontein while the decision about his release was further debated in the democratic Boer fashion.

[6] Pakenham *The Boer War* p549.

offensive action and overtures were being made for peace. In fact, even before Yzerfontein, the Vice President of the Transvaal had been given a safe conduct to travel to Kroonstad to meet with the Orange Free State government with a view to forthcoming peace negotiations. De la Rey scattered his men after Tweebosch and, with 300 men, rode to Zendelingsfontein for a meeting with Steyn and de Wet.[1]

Kitchener decided to reinforce the west with 14,000 troops which were now sent to Klerksdorp. The new model drive system of sweeping had been reasonably successful in the Free State but the vastness of the western Transvaal made its operation vastly more difficult. In the third week of March the first sweep was organized and the orders were for 11,000 men to march westwards. After marching forty miles by night to the westward of the commandos, known to be thirty miles west of the Schoonspruit, they were to turn about, form into driving formation, and in one day return to the Schoonspruit line of blockhouses.[2]

To return in one day proved impossible but General Liebenberg's men were closely pursued. They abandoned their wagons and guns at Buisfontein, managed to hide in the Rhenosterhoekberg, but managed to steal out between the camps of Kekewich and Rawlinson at midnight on 24 March.[3] Kitchener himself arrived in Klerksdorp on 26 March and a plan was evolved to try and establish the whereabouts of de la Rey and his force, now combined and somewhere to the west of Klerksdorp. Kekewich was ordered to Middelbult, F.W. (Walter) Kitchener (the younger brother of the Commander in Chief) to Driekuil, Rawlinson to the Rhenosterspruit and Rochfort was to guard the Vaal River crossings. They were all to build fortified camps and scout westwards.[4]

Walter Kitchener's reconnaissance in force discovered the Boers at Boschpan and was checked further west at Boschbult. The column under Colonel G.A. Cookson barely managed to beat off the attacks of Liebenberg and Kemp. The Boers withdrew on the arrival of de la Rey who was reluctant to incur losses in storming the entrenched farmhouse. There was a woman in the house and, according to Kemp, she told that all the British officers in the house were on the point of surrendering. [5] Kitchener arrived with reinforcements on 1 April and the force was withdrawn to Driekuil. British casualties were 178 killed and wounded but 400 horses and mules were killed so that the force was no longer mobile.

The location of the main Boer force now seemingly established, an overall commander was needed to coordinate the movements of the three columns. Colonel Kekewich was not part of Methuen's command and reported direct to Pretoria. Major General F.W. Kitchener also was not given overall command. Lieutenant General Ian Hamilton, Kitchener's Chief of Staff was therefore sent to take overall command. Colonel Rochfort, along the Vaal River, was not part of Hamilton's command for a further month.

On 5 April de la Rey left to attend the meeting of the Boer governments in Klerksdorp, the British operational base, arriving there on the 9th in company with President M.T. Steyn. A day later it had been resolved to negotiate and the Boer entourage travelled to Pretoria to present a proposal for peace. Just at the moment when the British command in the west gained a general, the Boers lost theirs.[6]

Ian Hamilton got to work and a raid to Barber's Pan was organized on 6 April but returned empty-handed. He now resolved to sweep round to the south and east in a great semicircle. The movement would start with an entrenched line along the Brakspruit, with the right touching the Great Harts River. The columns would then march south, swinging round to the east when the right touched the Vaal. Kekewich would form the right of the line, Rawlinson the center and F.W. Kitchener the left. It took some time to organize this and by the evening of the 9th Rawlinson's line stretched from Oshoek to Doornpan and Kitchener from Driekuil to Kliprif. Kekewich, who had reached Noodshulp the previous evening, had reached Boschbult and was thus to the rear of Rawlinson.[7]

During that day Kemp, now in command in place of the absent de la Rey, sent a large Boer force towards Kitchener but no action resulted. Later that evening Kekewich moved in towards the Great Harts River, reaching the eastern part of the farm Roodewal. On the morning of the 11th Kemp's men, at first being mistaken for Rawlinson's men by von Donop in command of Kekewich's advance guards, charged the British line. Kekewich and Grenfell wheeled left and advanced a short distance. Commandant Potgieter, conspicuous in a blue short led the advance. The British shooting was not enough to completely annihilate the Boers charging in the open without cover but none of the Boers managed to approach closer than 70 yards. Potgieter was shot in the head and fell dead as did fifty of his men, another thirty being badly wounded. Kekewich lost seven killed and 56 wounded.

Pursuit took some time to organize although Lieutenant Colonel Briggs with the Imperial Light Horse from Rawlinson's column forced the Boers back to Broderick's Vlei and Simonsvlei. A general pursuit followed but the Boers, severely outnumbered, scattered. Some headed towards Schweitzer-Reneke, followed closely by Kekewich. Two field guns and a pom-pom, captured by the Boers at Tweebosch, were recovered at Nooitgedacht after a long chase.[8]

The Boers lost 110 killed, wounded or captured at Roodewal. The result was sent to Pretoria and certainly would have influenced the discussions about the question of peace. Kemp and his men needed to get through to Rustenburg and Marico and therefore had to cross the blockhouse line between Lichtenburg and Mafeking where "we would fight for the last time."[9]

---

[1] Childers *The Times History of the War in South Africa* Vol V pp507 and 509-12.
[2] Childers *The Times History of the War in South Africa* Vol V p514.
[3] Childers *The Times History of the War in South Africa* Vol V p517. Gibson *The Story of the Imperial Light Horse* p338.
[4] Childers *The Times History of the War in South Africa* Vol V p518.
[5] Kemp *Vir Vryheid en vir Reg* pp458-9.

[6] Childers *The Times History of the War in South Africa* Vol V p526 says "The two Governments, who, although they were treated with all kindness and courtesy, were closely watched...."
[7] Childers *The Times History of the War in South Africa* Vol V p528.
[8] Childers *The Times History of the War in South Africa* Vol V p535.

Battle Sites and Monuments

(The sketch map will be of assistance in locating all the places mentioned in the histories. It is entirely based on the Department of Land Survey's 1:50,000 and 1:250,000 series of maps. GPS coordinates are included for a number of places as well.)

Lambrechtsfontein   GPSS27°28.006 farm entrance

The grave of Lieutenant G.H.B. Coulson is on this farm. A granite headstone memorial was erected on the site and unveiled on 18 May 2003. Since that time the site has become overgrown and the memorial has fallen over – the foundation would appear to be inadequate to support the heavy column. It has since been placed upright on the concrete block and supported with two steel fencing posts and some fencing wire. The Commonwealth War Graves Commission is due to make a proper repair in due course.

Doornkraal (Bothaville)   GPSS27°27.492

This is the site of a battle on 6 November 1900 when Colonel P.W.J. le Gallais was killed in action.[1]

Bothaville

The Garden of Remembrance is on the R59 in the centre of the town. A granite column has the names of all those buried there and Colonel le Gallais's headstone is on the south-east corner.

Yzerspruit   GPSS26°58.967

The site of the battle is on the unpaved Leeudoringstad-Regina road. Some distance after crossing the Jagdspruit the road comes to a rise. On the north side of the road is a survey beacon mounted on an elevated stand so as to rise above the trees. There is a small monument nearby which marks the center of the position held by Liebenberg, the point where the column was first attacked. A British monument used to be on site but has now been moved to the Old Cemetery at Klerksdorp as has the mass grave of the British dead.

The Old Klerksdorp Cemetery

Once badly neglected, this historical site, is the last resting place of generations of people who established the town, industries and mines of Klerksdorp as well as military graves in an Anglo Boer war Garden of Remembrance. The casualties of Yzerspruit were exhumed and moved her in the 1960s during the period of consolidation of military graves into the nearest urban center. The grave of 2nd Lieutenant Eric Sutherland of the Seaforth Highlanders is here – the son of the Chairman of the P. & O. Shipping Line, then the largest shipping line in the world. He was killed in action on 29 May 1902, just two days before the peace agreement was signed.[2] Four graves of Boers executed for treason are also to be seen.[3]

Hartbeesfontein (old name Hartebeestefontein – in Dutch)

Here there is an Imperial Light Horse obelisk as well as the grave of Lieutenant W.C. Wilson of the 15th (Northumberland) Yeomanry.

Ottosdal

There is a small Garden of Remembrance in Ottosdal cemetery where Lieutenant Thomas Nesham is buried. Most of the casualties of Tweebosch were brought to Ottosdal, others buried at Leeukuil or De Klipdrift.

Boschbult   GPSS26°47.800

The farmhouse defended by the British is long gone, a newer house now occupies an area a little further west and there is a simple monument to the Boer dead at the farm entrance. It is on R507, the road connecting Ottosdal and Delareyville, between the turnoff to Sannieshof to the north and Welverdiend to the south.

Roodewal   GPSS26°50.022 graveyard
             GPSS26°50.207 access gate and sign
             GPSS26°50.047 first sign

The graveyard is not easy to find in spite of being signposted. Local people know it as "Potgieter's place" as it is supposedly the site of the Boer charge led by Commandant F.J. Potgieter. He was shot through the head and died close to the place where he is now buried.

---

[9] Kemp *Vir Vryheid en vir Reg* p469.
[1] Childers *The Times History of the War in South Africa* Vol V pp15-21. Maurice *History of the war in South Africa* Vol 3 pp486-89.
[2] See Dooner *The "Last Post"* p371.
[3] Blake *Boereverraaier* pp89-115.

Tweebosch/De Klipdrift   S26°34.318 Monument
S26°34.763 Turnoff and signpost

Not far off the Rostrataville-Sannieshof road to the west is a collection of monuments supposedly near the spot where Lord Methuen lay with his leg broken after his horse was shot under him. The original monument, made of golden bricks, was put up in 1943. There is a granite monument with the names of the Boer dead and another commemorating the centenary of the battle in 2002. In 1938 the Great Trek was commemorated with a wagon trek around South Africa. At many places a wagon was driven across a panel of wet concrete to preserve the tracks – there is a set of wagon tracks at Tweebosch.

Lichtenburg cemetery

In addition to military graves there is here the grave of Jacobus Hercules (Koos) de la Rey with the headstone by sculptor Stefanus Eloff.

Treurfontein cemetery   S26°19.616

This small military cemetery stands at the junction of N14 and 503 outside Coligny.

Ventersdorp

There is a small Garden of Remembrance in the Ventersdorp cemetery. Also interred there is Private G. Shaw, shot as a traitor.[1]

---

[1] Milne *Anecdotes of the Anglo-Boer War* pp137-140.

References

1. Childers, Erskine (editor) *The Times History of the War in South Africa* Vol V Sampson Low, Marston and Company, Ltd London 1907.
2. Maurice, Major General Sir Frederick *History of the war in South Africa* Vol. 4.
3. Johannes Meintjies *De la Rey Lion of the West* Hugh Keartland Publishers, Johannesburg 1966.
4. J.C. (Kay) de Villiers *Healers, Helpers and Hospitals* Protea Book House, Pretoria 2008.
5. Apollon Davidson, Irina Filatova *The Russians and the Anglo-Boer War* Human & Rousseau, Cape Town Pretoria Johannesburg 1998.
6. Gert van den Bergh *24 Battles and Battle fields of the North-West Province* The North West Tourism Association 1996.
7. Jacques Malan *Die Boere Offisiere* J.P. van der Walt, Pretoria 1990.
8. General J.C.G. Kemp *Vir Vryheid en vir Reg* Nasionale Pers Beperk, Cape Town, Bloemfontein and Port Elizabeth 1942.
9. J.F. Naudé *Veg en Vlug van Beyers en Kemp* Nijgh en van Ditmar, Rotterdam, Netherlands 1903 (reprint in Afrikaans Bienedell Uitgewers, Pretoria 1998).
10. Michael Davitt *The Boer Fight for Freedom* Funk & Wagnalls Company, New York and London 1902
11. Thomas Pakenham *The Boer War* Weidenfeld and Nicholson Limited, London 1979.
12. André Wessels (editor) *Lord Kitchener and the War in South Africa* Army Records Society 2006.
13. Mildred G. Dooner *The "Last Post"* J.B. Hayward & Son, Polstead, Suffolk 1980 (reprint of original, privately published in August 1903).
14. George Fleming Gibson *The Story of the Imperial Light Horse in the South African War 1899–1902* G.D. & Co. 1937.
15. Albert Blake *Boereverraaier* Tafelberg, Cape Town 2010.
16. Rob Milne *Anecdotes of the Anglo-Boer War* Covos Day Books, Weltevredenpark, Randburg 2000.

Yzerspruit

Tweebosch

Roodewal

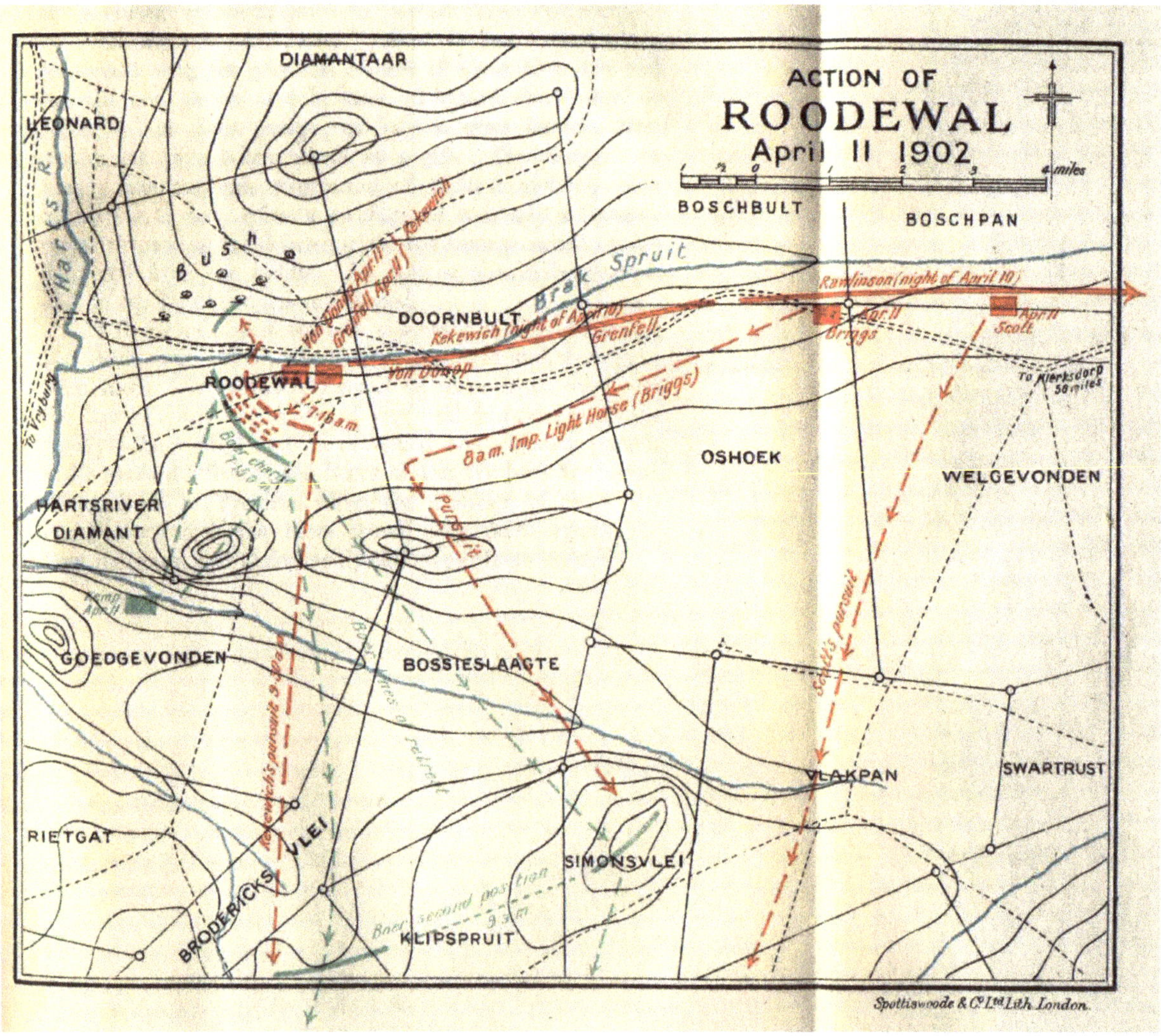

Survey maps key – Orange Free State
and western Transvaal.

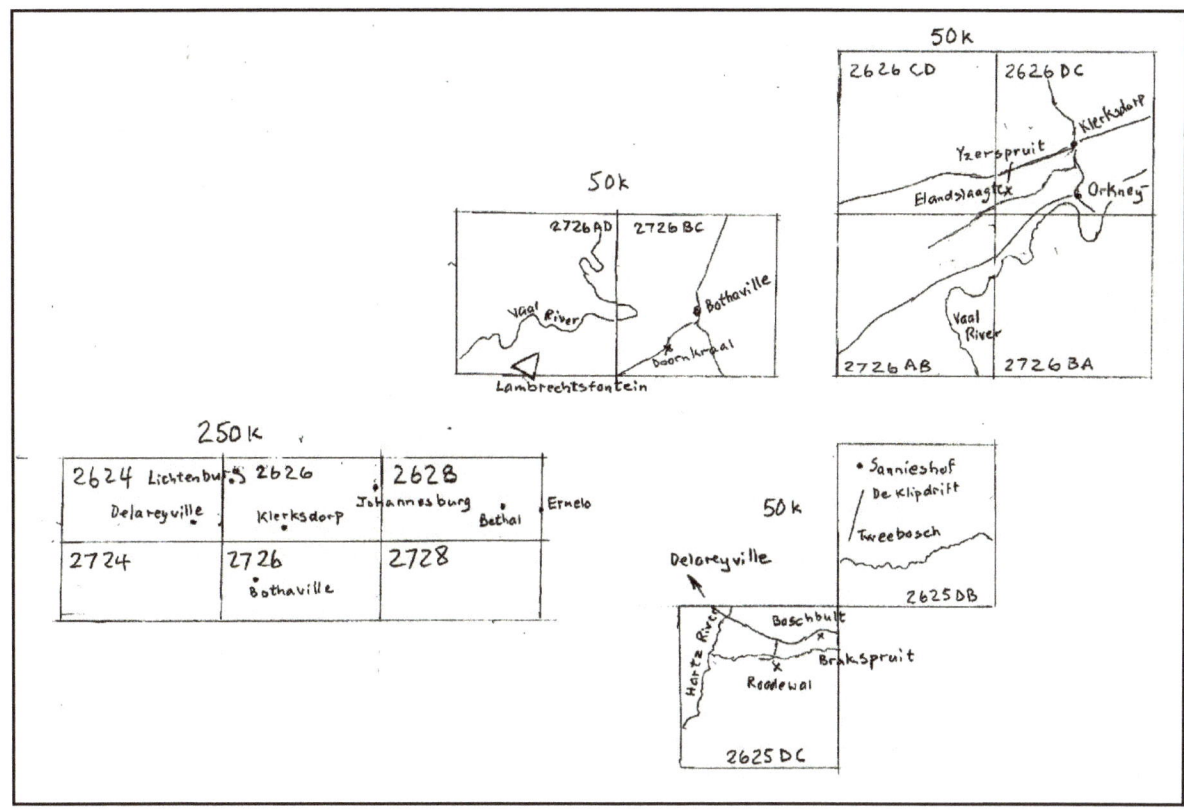

South Western Transvaal
50k survey maps.

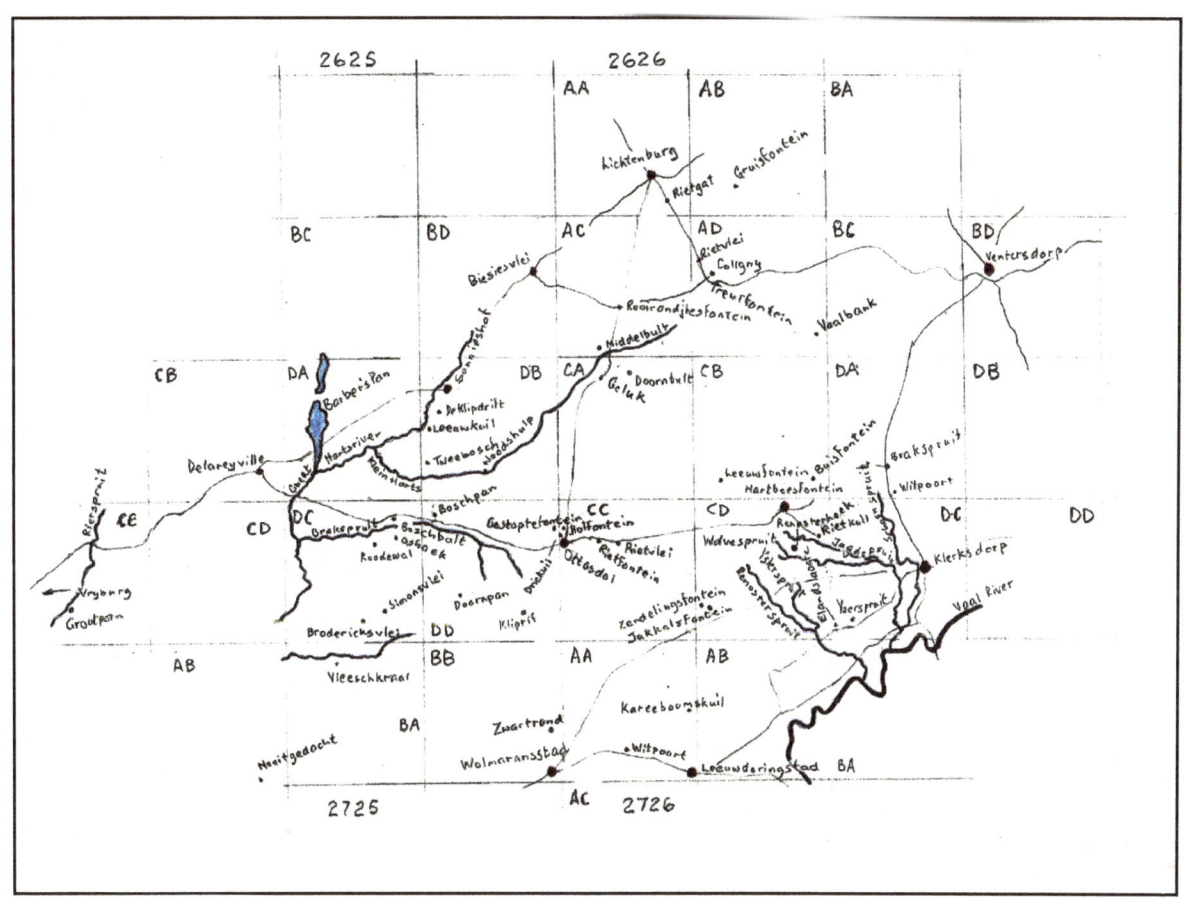

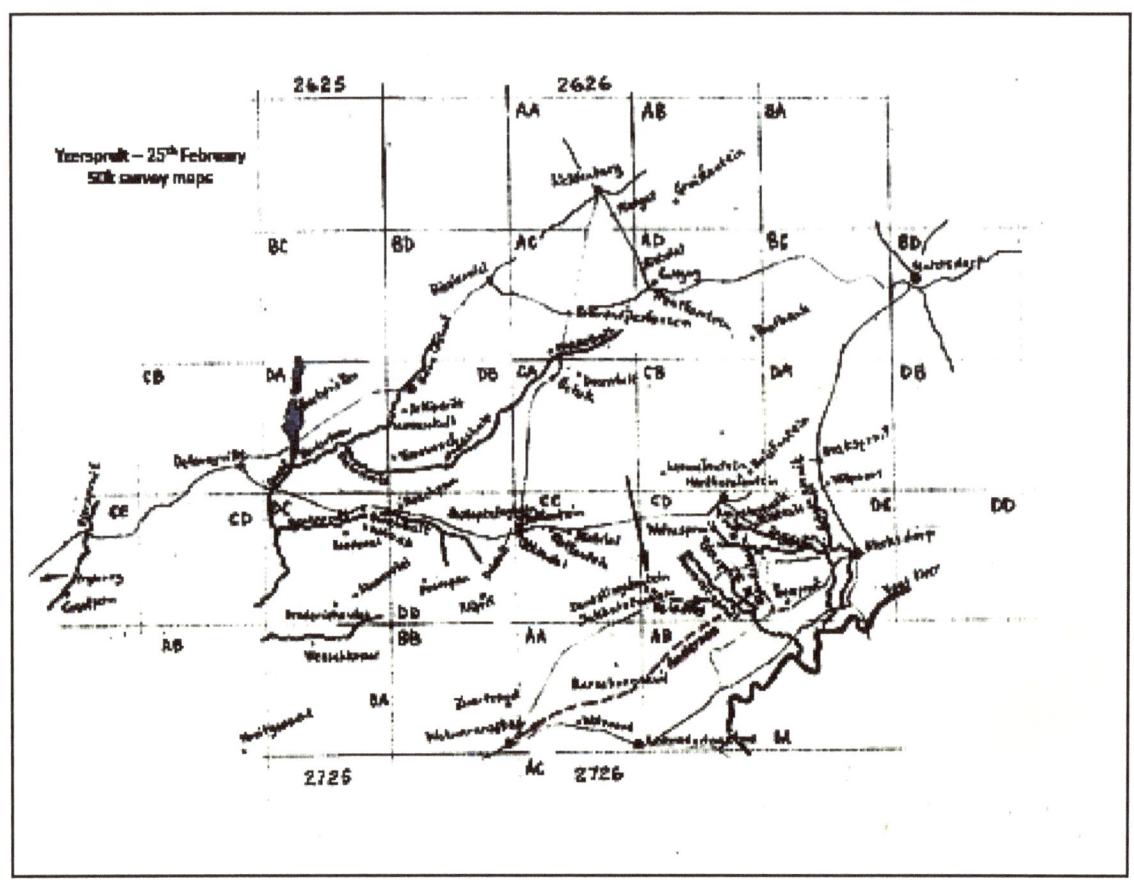

Yzerspruit – 25th February
50k survey maps

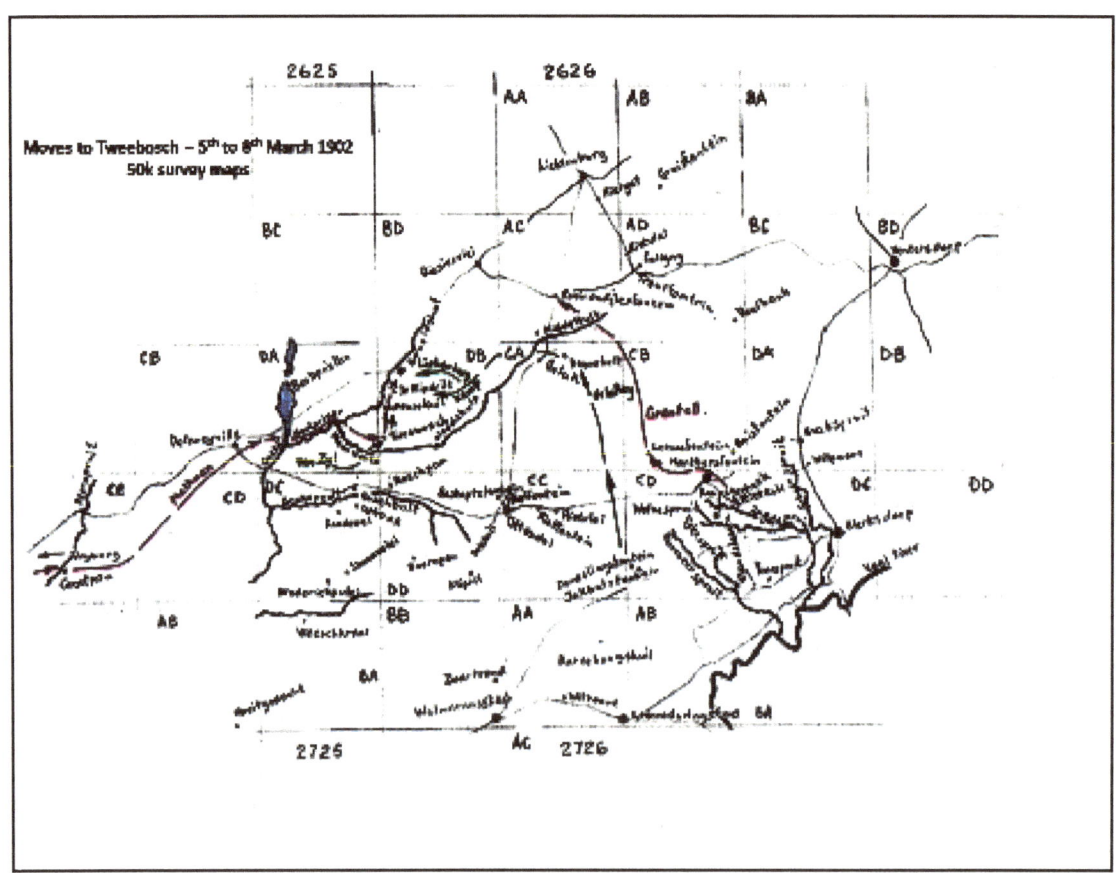

Moves to Tweebosch – 5th to 8th March 1902
50k survey maps